RAIDING THE LAND OF THE FOREIGNERS

RAIDING THE LAND OF
THE FOREIGNERS

Danilyn Rutherford

PRINCETON UNIVERSITY PRESS · PRINCETON AND OXFORD

Library of Congress Cataloging-in-Publication Data

Rutherford, Danilyn.
Raiding the land of the foreigners: the limits of the nation on an Indonesian frontier /
Danilyn Rutherford.
p. cm.
Includes bibliographical references.
ISBN 0-691-09590-6 (cloth : alk. paper) — ISBN 0-691-09591-4 (pbk. : alk. paper)
1. Ethnology—Indonesia—Biak Numfor. 2. Nationalism—Indonesia—Biak Numfor.
3. Biak Numfor (Indonesia)—History. 4. Biak Numfor (Indonesia)—Social life and
customs. 5. Indonesia—Foreign relations—Netherlands. 6. Indonesia—Colonization.
7. Netherlands—Colonies—Asia. I. Title.

GN635.I65 R88 2003
305.8′009—dc21   2002020132

British Library Cataloging-in-Publication Data is available

Frontispiece: Papuan and Chinese children gather around "The Hope of the World"

To Craig

Contents

Illustrations

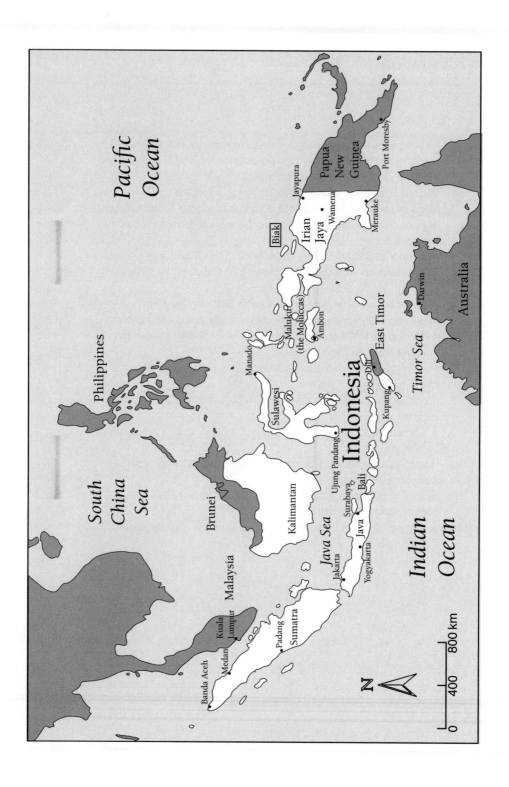

A Note on Languages and Locations

THE SETTING of this study is a multilingual place, and not simply by virtue of the large number of migrants who live within its borders. Biak-Numfor is an island regency, a subdivision of the Indonesian province of Irian Jaya, which lies just east of the Papua New Guinea border, a line that slices New Guinea in half. The islands' history of primary education dates back to the beginning of the twentieth century, so even older villagers tend to be conversant in Indonesian, the national language that grew out of Malay, the administrative lingua franca spoken in western New Guinea and throughout the Indies in colonial times. Biak, like Indonesian, is an Austronesian language. Linguists have placed it in the Eastern Malayo-Polynesian branch of the family, which includes the South Halmahera-West New Guinea group and the Oceanic group, which includes the Austronesian languages of Melanesia, Micronesia, and Polynesia (see Blust 1984: 29; Pawley and Ross 1995; Tryon 1995). Biak speakers (and linguists) describe the language as consisting of scores of different dialects (see Fautngil et al. 1994; van Hasselt and van Hasselt 1947). The Numfor version (sometimes called "Mefoorsche" or "Mafoorsche" by Dutch writers) once served as a lingua franca in Cendrawasih Bay and along the northern shores of the Bird's Head Peninsula, as well as in the Raja Ampat Islands to New Guinea's west.

Indonesian is very much a written language. Biak is not. Although the Protestant missionaries who settled among "Mefoorsche" speakers produced translations and original works in that dialect, there was little consensus in the early 1990s among my consultants as to how Biak words should be divided and/or spelled. My transcriptions of Biak texts are, as a result, idiosyncratic, although I have tried wherever possible to follow the lead of recent students of the language. I have used the symbol /b/ for what my consultants called a "soft /b/," a phoneme whose pronunciation lies between an English /b/ and /w/. Aside from this, my spelling of words is generally consistent with that found in Soeparno's (1977) dictionary (see Fautngil et al. 1994). I have identified terms and phrases as Indonesian (I) or Biak (B); the identity of other foreign terms (generally English or Dutch) should be clear from the text. I have taken the liberty of marking plural forms of Biak and Indonesian words by adding–s. Unless otherwise indicated, all translations are my own, as are the betrayals that this task always entails. A brief glossary of frequently used terms appears at the end of the book.

The western half of New Guinea has gone by many different names: Nederlands-Nieuw-Guinea and Tanah Papoea, in the writings of Dutch officials and missionaries; Irian Barat and Irian Jaya, in the speeches of Indonesian politicians; West Papua and West Melanesia, in the proclamations of exiled Papuan separatists. The islands that make up Biak-Numfor have gone by different toponyms, as well: Mafor, Mefor, Wiak, and the Schouten Islands, to name a few. In this book, I have used terms consistent with public usage in the context I am describing; thus the province now sometimes called Papua, in a concession to popular sentiment, appears as it was known at the time of my fieldwork, as Irian Jaya. I follow local practice in referring to Biak-Numfor as Biak, after its most populous island. The villages and cities I mention really exist, but I have changed the names of some of their inhabitants.

Preface

Becoming a Foreigner

ON SEPTEMBER 12, 1992, shortly after I arrived in Biak, Sally Bidwam, the nursing instructor who had just given me a place in her home, told me that she had once been the pen pal of Queen Juliana of the Netherlands. By that time I had already collected some strange and wonderful tales: from Mr. Mambur, a Biak official, who recounted the version of Biak's history he had learned in boarding school when Irian Jaya was Netherlands New Guinea and its inhabitants were known as Papuans, in a conversation punctuated with Dutch words and the names of Dutch texts; from Seth Warba, who regaled me with the story of his friendship with an American researcher, Mr. Jim, who had just returned from a trip to the highlands, where he had seen enormous lizards and all manner of extraordinary things; from Sally herself, who chimed in with her own account of remarkable research, by a scientist in search of the lost tribe of Israel, who came to Biak to measure the natives' noses.

Sally had welcomed me solemnly two days earlier, when I had appeared at the hospital with a letter of introduction from her niece, an anthropologist at the provincial university. She had slowly read the letter before leading me across the street to her sturdy, cinderblock house, where she had shown me a room and prepared me a snack of coffee and white bread with margarine and chocolate sprinkles. It was only after sitting in on my meeting with Mr. Mambur, a local notable whom Sally's niece had advised me to contact, and the bull session with Seth Warba, her voluble neighbor, that Sally was ready to make her own contribution to my research. Like Mr. Mambur, she retained the lessons of her colonial-era education. Like Seth Warba, she could still tell jokes in Dutch. But she had exchanged letters with the queen.

The following is an excerpt from my fieldnotes:

Over dinner, Sister Sally told me stories from her childhood during Dutch times (I: *jaman Belanda*). It began when I asked her about Biaks' aversion to Ambonese teachers after the war [something I had read about before coming to Biak]. She herself had had an Ambonese teacher when she was in elementary school. He was very strict. Children who did not speak clearly had to stand with their mouths propped open with sticks until they felt like their jaws were about to come loose. If a pupil made ten mistakes, the teacher would hit him or her ten times, sometimes so hard that the metal ruler would break. I asked Sally if she had told her parents about this teacher. She had—and her father had just laughed. He himself was a teacher; he had sent his daughter to live with his sister, who was married to a native administrator, when Sally was very young because she refused to go to school. It was not until she was with her father's sister in Korem that she first set foot in the classroom. Then she had this mean (I: *galak*) teacher, who scared her into studying.

The aunt's husband was transferred to North Supiori at the time Sally finished elementary school. She then took part in a test to get into the girls' middle school in Korido [see Figure 2], and passed. I asked if she had had any ambitions at this point; no, she had just taken the test as a matter of course. It was not until her third year at Korido that Sally decided that she wanted to be a teacher. But, unfortunately, only one space was offered for girls in the training school. Sally did not get it, so she was sent home to her mother and father, who were then in Bosnik.

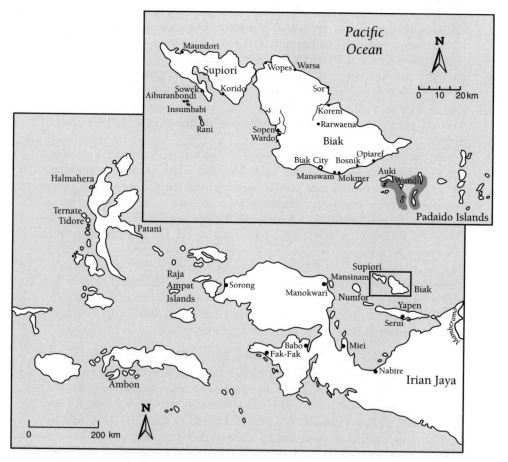

Figure 2. Maps of western New Guinea and the northern Moluccas, and of Biak, Supiori, and the Padaido Islands.

One day, this crazy (I: *sinting*) Dutch doctor came to visit Sally's father. He asked the teacher if the young girl who had served them was his maid. "No, that was my daughter." The crazy Dutch doctor then and there asked Sally's father if he could take Sally to work at the hospital. "Sure, why not?" Sally's father replied. Sally, meanwhile, was in back crying in her mother's arms. The doctor left at twelve noon, and Sally left with him, carrying only the clothes on her back. Her father promised to bring whatever stuff she might need later.

So Sally arrived at the Biak hospital. Only four other Biak girls were being trained. At that time, parents refused to send their daughters to work in the hospital, because it was considered a place of ill repute. Girls and paramedics, guards, doctors, and other men would interact with each other, night and day. Only people with important positions (I: *orang berpangkat*), men with careers like Sally's father, understood the hospital and allowed their daughters to work there. All the girls at the hospital in Biak were from prominent families.

While at the Biak hospital, Sally got her current name. It seems that there were too many Nelly's when she entered. The wife of the crazy Dutch doctor was an Irish woman named Sally. Little Nelly was renamed. She has kept the name Sister Sally ever since.

Also while at the Biak hospital, Sally began corresponding with Queen Juliana. She still remembers one of the Dutch nurses, a big, strong woman who smoked two packs of cigarettes in a night shift and tried to get the Papuan girls to smoke with her. She gave the girls some *Spiegel* magazines in which Sally and her friends found pictures and the address of Queen Juliana. She and her friends talked about writing to her—but Sally was the only one who followed through. She wrote Queen Juliana a letter, telling her how in Biak, children had no snow to play in because it only rained. The queen responded. One day, while Sally was sleeping off her night shift, she awoke in her bunk to find the room filled with doctors. She searched her mind—what did I do wrong?—sure that she was about to be sent home. (Not an uncommon occurrence; a girl who made one mistake was dismissed.) The crazy doctor told Sally to read the letter in his hand, first to herself, then to the others out loud. Queen Juliana had written back, telling Sally that yes, indeed, there was a lot of snow in Holland, but with all her responsibilities, she had little time to enjoy it. "A little girl like you should correspond with other little girls—but with big people (I: *orang besar*) like this?" the doctor teased her. But Sally kept writing—in Dutch; she immediately sent a response to the queen's response.

After working in Biak for a few years, Sally had an opportunity to study at the hospital in Hollandia [the capital of Netherlands New Guinea, later renamed Jayapura]. She tricked the doctor in charge, telling him that her parents had agreed to the plan. It wasn't until she arrived in Hollandia that she wrote to tell her parents where she was. Before she left for Hollandia, she did write to tell the queen that she was moving. Sure enough, in Hollandia, Sally was called to the director's office. Convinced that this meant that she was about to be dismissed, she had already wept with all her closest friends. Like the other doctor, the director said, "How can it be that such a small girl (Sally was the youngest) can write to such a big person!" But Sally kept it up, throughout her time in Hollandia and after she returned to Biak. In one letter, she told the queen that she would like to visit Holland. The queen responded that she would be happy to see her. Sally's dreams almost came true when a Dutch sailor's family asked her to return with them to Holland. Unfortunately, Sally hadn't finished her degree and the head doctor would not let her go. The sailor's family was forced to leave early, when the dispute with Indonesia heated up in 1963. Sally was devastated not to have a chance to meet Queen Juliana. The transfer to Indonesia cut her off from her pen pal. After 1963, she was afraid to write any more.

I asked Sally if she had saved the letters. At one time, she had had a big stack of correspondence. Sally had sent the queen a picture of her family; the queen had reciprocated with pictures of hers. But then, after the transfer, an Indonesian soldier whom she had treated (and befriended) came to her house and found the letters and photographs. He told her to burn them, warning her that she could get into trouble for having letters from the Dutch head of state. She took his advice and seems sad about it.

Under Indonesia, however, Sally has finally been able to realize her ambition to become a teacher. In 1983, she was sent to Java for a short course. Her boss decided to send her back in 1987. Her training in Bandung in Java, where she was the only Irianese student, prepared her finally to be a teacher—a teacher of nurses.

Of course, there is much more to Sally's story than a simple assertion of closeness to the Dutch queen. Sally set this episode in the context of a long history of exposure to powerful figures: from her harsh Ambonese teacher, to her father's distinguished brother-in-law, to the crazy Dutch doctor, to the Indonesian soldiers and bureaucrats who later controlled her fate. This series parallels decisive changes in the political status of western New Guinea. Colonial officials included western New Guinea in the Netherlands Indies as early as 1828, basing their claims on the supposed sovereignty of the north Moluccan sultans of Tidore over the "Papuans" residing in the territory.[1] For most of the nineteenth century, New Guinea's northwestern shorelines and islands lay just beyond the limits of effective colonial rule, as did many parts of what is now Indonesia. When Indonesia gained independence in 1949, New Guinea became a separate Dutch colony. The Dutch promised to prepare the Papuans for independence, then withdrew this pledge under pressure from the United States. After a brief period of oversight by the United Nations, Indonesia took control of the territory in May 1963. The memory of this betrayal stands as a lasting legacy of this experience, as do memories of the coercion that accompanied the so-called Act of Free Choice that validated the transfer of western New Guinea to Indonesia in 1969 (Sharp 1977; Osborne 1985; Djopari 1993; Kaisiëpo 1994; Saltford 2000, see also Lijphart

1966; de Bruyn 1978). This was a time of much terror and repression, pivotal in the formation of Papuan nationalism.

Sally's narrative illuminates the development of a local elite under tumultuous conditions: from her father and his peers, who were recruited to spread the Gospel by Dutch Protestant missionaries in the 1920s and 1930s, to her uncle and his classmates from the native school for administrators, who staffed the lower rungs of the colonial bureaucracy after World War II, to Sally's own generation of Biak men and, increasingly, women, who were groomed to lead the independent Papuan state that the Dutch government claimed to be building in western New Guinea. Sally's story arguably unfolds against the backdrop of a history in which the indigenous inhabitants of western New Guinea almost became citizens of their own independent polity. The Netherlands' promises, along with the material evidence of other Papuans' exploits in *jaman Belanda*, went up in smoke during the same period when the queen's letters to Sally burned.

It is perhaps not surprising that memories of other foreigners came to my consultants' minds when they first met me. Confronted by an American with a keen interest in their past, their thoughts returned to that checkered period of their history in which my country played such a pivotal, even shameful role. Still, stories like Sister Sally's cannot simply be reduced to an expression of the sufferings of an aborted Papuan nation. In Sally's story, the others who promise and the others who oppress bear a closer relationship to one another than one would expect, given the starker distinctions that my consultants drew when they spoke something resembling a language of Papuan nationalism. The Ambonese are "mean," with their sudden blows, but so is the "crazy" Dutch doctor, who wrenches Sally from her family, and threatens to send her back to them, in both cases without any warning. Strangely, given the Indonesian military's well-deserved reputation for brutality, the Indonesian soldier is the one who treats her the most gently; and it is under Indonesian rule that she finally is trained to become a teacher, having been denied this honor by the Dutch. This is not to say that Sally was an admirer of the New Order, the authoritarian regime that ruled Indonesia from the mid-1960s to the late 1990s. This formidable woman—clearly no longer a "little girl"—pulled no punches in this regard. Rather, it is to point to the ambivalence of Sally's relationship to the foreign figures in her story. They startle her by recognizing a future—and even a name—that she does not yet realize she has within her. But she also startles them, in this case with proof of her friendship with the most exalted of outsiders, the queen.

Sally's narrative is not simply the story of her loss of the queen's correspondence, a loss that could be read as a metaphor for the Papuans' exclusion from the discussions that sealed their political fate in the early 1960s. It is also the story of how Sally became a foreigner, a word expressed in Biak by the term *amber. Amber* is a Biak-language word with multiple meanings, which this book will explore from various angles, including that presented by Biak notions of gender. At the time of my fieldwork, Euro-Americans and non-Irian Jayan Indonesians were known as *amber*, but so were civil servants, soldiers, pastors, and village chiefs, all of them members of the Biak elite. In the logic of Sally's story, it is not simply hard work, cultural capital, and the concern of her parents that enable Sally to become an *amber*, that is, a prominent person. It is also her encounters with powerful outsiders, also known as *amber*. My Biak consultants sometimes played with this ambiguity. During a trip to a remote stretch of Biak's north coast, a man who had been drinking started following me and my friends, Jane and Edith. The young women persuaded him to turn back by saying that we were traveling with some other *amber*, a term he interpreted as referring to Indonesian soldiers. In fact, our companions were a local teacher and village chief who had taken a detour to do some hunting. It was absolutely true, Jane giggled; our guides were *amber*, and ones with guns.

Other Irianese have made fun of Biaks' thirst for this particular brand of status, in a way that highlights divisions within the Papuan nationalist movement. A joke has one highlander telling another about what will happen after West Papua gains independence. "All the Biaks will become foreigners" (I: *Orang Biak menjadi amber*). "And us?" "We'll all become Biaks!" (I: *Kitorong menjadi Biak!*) was the reply. But this usage can also have serious ramifications. The peculiar relationship to the foreign described in this book had implications for the way Biaks dealt with the demands of the New Order. It surely has implications for the current separatist movement, for which many Biaks have openly expressed their support.

During eighteen months of fieldwork on the islands that make up Biak-Numfor, I had many conversations like those I had during my first forty-eight hours in Biak City. Mr. Mambur, Seth Warba, and Sally Bidwam were like many of the men and women I met on Biak: enthusiastic and not a little amused at the prospect of sharing with me what they knew about Biak history and culture. That they backed up their stories by citing Westerners and their writings no longer surprised me by the time I left. Many of my friends and colleagues, when they recounted their life histories, told narratives that highlighted their experiences with outsiders—from Abe Rumapura, the farmer who was my host in the North Biak village of Sor, who decided on my first night in his household that I needed to hear about his experiences in the Dutch colonial army after World War II, to Edith, my companion on many journeys across the islands, whose account of how she became a church social worker was filled with references to the foreign missionaries she met along the way. An anthropologist's job is to be interested in what the people around her are interested in. A corollary to this task is to take an interest in whatever her consultants think she should know about themselves. In Biak, my presence often seemed to spark a response in which, through their language, life histories, and generally warm reaction to my presence, my consultants claimed a certain intimacy with what they imagined to be my world. They presented themselves as the perfect guides to Biak—because they were in some sense foreign, too.

This study builds on my fascination by this interest in the foreign. My object of inquiry is not the "truth" behind the "appearance" of Biak's integration into a nation, be it Indonesian or Papuan. Rather, it is a field of practices, consisting of arenas of social action that are linked as part of a wider social context, and iconic of one another, in that they share certain orienting values. By focusing on a discursive logic that runs from exchanges within and between families, to the poetics of performances, to the rhetorical strategies of Biak leaders, I have approached this social field at a level of abstraction that allows for significant variation across contexts and changes over time. There is nothing inherently deeper or more authentic in those aspects of people's lives that I include within the purview of this study than in those I do not highlight. If I asked my Biak consultants to choose the identity that best expresses who they feel they are today, "Papuan" would no doubt be a common response. And yet, such a claim would need to be contextualized carefully. Brubaker (1996) is correct in suggesting that "nationness" is less a state of being than an event—a mode of consciousness that crystallizes under particular historical conditions. Such an insight opens the way to an analysis of those practices through which a sense of nationality is generated. It also opens the way to an analysis of practices that posit what I will call "antinational" understandings of space, time, and self.

This book is based on a year of archival research and interviews in the Netherlands, and eighteen months of fieldwork on Biak, building on a familiarity with Indonesia that dates back to the early 1980s. On Biak, I became a member of two households: Sister Sally's in Biak City and Abe Rumapura's in the North Biak village of Sor. From these home bases, I traveled widely in the regency, accepting invitations to come to weddings and other ceremonies, and to hear songs and stories from those who were said to know them best. I conducted interviews in Indonesian, a language in which Biaks, young and old, have long been surprisingly fluent, and used more Biak as my familiarity with the vernacular grew. I enjoyed a great deal of expert assistance, from friends, performers, and adoptive relatives, in transcribing and interpreting Biak texts.

Like all research, mine has produced insights that are of necessity partial; they are based on an engagement with particular places, times, texts, and, above all, people. To register this particularity, I have written this study in what might be called the "ethnographic past." I do not mean to imply that the dynamics described here are no longer evident in Biak; my aim is merely to underscore their implications for Indonesian national integration at a particular moment in time. Although some of my consultants belonged to an elite whose members ranged from village teachers to the regency's head of government, or regent (I: *bupati*), others did not. The disparities of wealth and privilege associated with social class were a fact of life in Biak, but they were not experienced as immutable. One young farmer I knew loved to tell the story of how a guard at the hospital mistook him for an elementary school teacher. "I'm sorry, that's not me," Gabriel Bidwam responded. "I'm the high school teacher!" he gleefully went on. The multiple meanings embedded in the word *amber* enabled Biaks to downplay the differences that divided, say, a candidate for governor from a village deacon or clerk. In the chapters that follow, I have not privileged the insights of educated Biaks, but neither have I ignored them. I present my findings as applying to Biaks of different regions, classes, and genders. At the same time, I have tried not to underplay the differences that divide and crosscut these groups.

It comes as no news to anthropologists that fieldwork entails the forging of politically, ethically, and emotionally fraught relationships. In the case of this research, which focused on the negotiation of cultural difference, the ambiguities of the enterprise came into particularly sharp relief. Two aspects of my experience on Biak proved particularly unsettling. On the one hand, I kept finding continuity where I had expected to find rupture, a strange sensation at a time when it seems reasonable to presume that all ethnography is in some sense the ethnography of modernity. On the other, I kept meeting people who acted as if they already knew me and were pleased to see me back. As Mordden writes of Judy Garland, in her role as Dorothy in *The Wizard of Oz*, I was made to feel "extraordinarily welcome" in Biak, albeit in a different guise than my "Kansas" self (1990: 125 in Boon 2000: 445). Much has been written about the alienation anthropologists initially suffer in the field, be this in a strange country, region, or social network, or in a familiar community that they are approaching from a new angle. It can take many uncomfortable months for a researcher to feel accepted by the people among whom he or she works (see, for example, Geertz 1973: 412–417). Still, the experience of being immediately recognized as a fond friend, whose purposes are clear, can be equally disconcerting. Needless to say, in such circumstances, anthropologists have benefited from—and been deeply touched by—unexpected intimacies and the shared predicaments they bring to light (see, for example, Tsing 1993). Yet in Biak I found it important not to suppress the strangeness of this situation, as heartfelt as my friendships became, nor to forget that affection is always to some degree transferential: one is always accepted in another's place. Ethnography, as the truism goes, requires a capacity for rapport; but it also requires a capacity for reflection—a sense of respect for encounters that do not make sense in the terms one has prepared, for projects and lives that do not mirror one's own. During my fieldwork, I was forced to be engaged and analytic, self-aware without being self-indulgent, conscious that I too had become a foreigner, in ways I may never fully understand.

And yet, by virtue of these very complications, I am and will remain deeply indebted—and bound—to many more men and women than I can name. I have chosen to use pseudonyms for most of my Biak consultants, a decision that was difficult, given how many friends told me that they were looking forward to appearing in my study. But I hope that all those who shared their insights with me will find, if not their names, something of themselves in the chapters that follow.

I would like to single out the following individuals and organizations, whose generosity made this book possible. My research in the Netherlands and Biak was supported by a U.S. Department of Education Fulbright-Hays Doctoral Dissertation Research Abroad Fellowship, a Predoctoral Grant from the Wenner-Gren Foundation for Anthropological Research, a grant from the Joint Committee on Southeast Asia of the Social Science Research Council and the American Council of Learned Societies with funds provided by the Andrew W. Mellon Foundation, the Ford Foundation, and the Henry Luce Foundation, and a grant from the University of Chicago Social Sciences Divisional Research Committee's J. David Greenstone Memorial Fund. I never would have considered undertaking research in Biak if it had not been for a summer I spent with the Ford Foundation in Jakarta. In the Netherlands, I enjoyed the support of Cory Ap, Oppie and Theo Bekker-Kapissa, Dieter Bartels, Benny Giay, Fred and Corey Ireeuw, Betty Kaisiëpo, Victor Kaisiëpo, Ien de Vries, Dr. J. V. Kabel, Nel Lamme, Elsbeth Locher-Scholten, Eef Mamoribo, Nelly Mampioper, Jos Mansoben, Piet J. Merklijn, Jelle Miedema, Hengky and Glenda Padwa, Lea Padwa, Anton Ploeg, J. J. Reynders, Nico Schulte-Noordholt, Hein Steinhauer, Anne Marie von Dongen, C. L. Voorhoeve, Herman Wambrauw, the late Dr. J. V. van Baal, and Markus Kaisiëpo, and the staff of the Hendrik Kraemer Institute, the Algemeene Rijksarchief, and the Koninklijke Instituut voor Taal-, Land- en Volkenkunde. In Jakarta, Jayapura, and Biak, my research was facilitated by Helena Burdam, Salomina Burdam, Sary Burdam, Alan Feinstein, Paul Haenen, Hendrik Inekeb, Andris Kafiar, August Kafiar, Dolly Kaisiëpo, Yustina Kapitarau, Beatrix Koibur, Sam Koibur, Mecky Mambraser, Arnoldus Mampioper, Amandeus Mansnembra, John McGlynn, Fransina Noriwari, Sary Noriwari, Chris Padwa, Nelly Polhaupessy, Decky Rumaropen, Mientje Rumbiak, Marice Rumere, George Sabarofek, Frances Seymour, Suzanne Siskel, Koos Urbinas, Marinus Workrar, Albert Yafdas, Demitianus Yensenem, the late Ben Rumaropen, Sam Kapissa, Utrecht Wompere, and Dina Womsiwor, and by the singers and magicians of Ambroben, Dwar, Insrom, Korem, Mara, Mandenderi, Opiaref, Sor, Sunyar, Rarwaena, Warkimbon, and Wundi. To these men and women and their families, *Kasumasa nabor naba be au kam*.

The bulk of this manuscript was written at the Institute for Advanced

Study, where I enjoyed the encouragement of Joan Scott and Cliff Geertz and the cheerful assistance of Deborah Koehler, not to mention the friendship of an exceptional cohort of colleagues, including Gil Chaitin, Deborah Keates, Xiaorong Li, Mary Louise Roberts, and Eve Troutt-Powell, to name just a few. While formulating this project, I spent a semester at New York University, where Fred Myers, Bambi Schieffelin, Mick Taussig, and the late Annette Weiner contributed importantly to my thinking. At Cornell University, I am beholden to my advisors, Steve Sangren and Takashi Shiraishi, and to Benedict Anderson. My dissertation committee chair, James T. Siegel, who is no less kind than he is insightful, taught me more about cultural analysis than I can begin to describe.

I am fortunate to have wonderful colleagues at the University of Chicago, who, wittingly or unwittingly, have contributed to this book in countless ways. I have benefited from conversations with Jacqueline Goldsby, David Levin, Sandra Macpherson, Deborah Nelson, and the rest of our work-in-progress group, as well as with Andrew Apter, Nadia Abu-El Haj, John Comaroff, Lauren Derby, Rachel Fulton, Susan Gal, John Kelly, Nancy Munn, Elizabeth Povinelli, Marshall Sahlins, Michael Silverstein, Rupert Stasch, Michel-Rolph Trouillot, and Benjamin Zimmer. Others who have commented on evolving versions of this study include Suzanne Brenner, Fenella Cannell, Joan Fujimora, Ken George, Frances Gouda, Carol Greenhouse, Eva-Lotta Hedman, Simon Jarvis, Michael Herzfeld, John Norvell, John Pemberton, Anne Russ, Suzanne Rutherford, Richard Scaglion, Dan Segal, John Sidel, Patsy Spyer, Mary Steedly, G. G. Weix, Haru Yamada, and Philip Yampolsky. At Princeton University Press, Mary Murrell expertly shepherded me through the publication process, and Margaret Case provided careful and intelligent copyediting. Webb Keane and an anonymous reader reviewed the manuscript quickly and astutely; I am grateful to both for the time and thought they devoted to this task.

Last but not least, I would like to thank Donald and Marilyn Rutherford, and Craig Best, Ralph Rutherford Best, and Melitta Alta Rutherford Best for providing equal measures of inspiration and comic relief.

Parts of this book have been published in other venues. A version of chapter 2 may be found in "Love, Violence, and Foreign Wealth: Kinship and History in Biak, Irian Jaya," *Journal of the Royal Anthropological Institute* 4 (2) (1998): 257–281, and a version of chapter 4 is in "The White Edge of the Margin: Textuality and Authority in Biak, Irian Jaya, Indonesia," *American Ethnologist* 27 (2) (2000): 312–339. Sections of chapter 2 appear in "Of Birds and Gifts: Reviving Tradition on an Indonesian Frontier," *Cultural Anthropology* 11 (4) (1996): 577–616. All three articles are used with permission.

RAIDING THE LAND OF THE FOREIGNERS

CHAPTER ONE

On the Limits of Indonesia

O N July 2, 1998, a little over a month after the resignation of Indonesia's President Suharto, two young men climbed to the top of a water tower in the heart of Biak City and raised the Morning Star flag. Along with similar flags flown in municipalities throughout the Indonesian province of Irian Jaya, the flag raised in the capital of Biak-Numfor signaled a demand for the political independence of West Papua, an imagined nation comprising the western half of New Guinea, a resource-rich territory just short of Indonesia's easternmost frontier. During the thirty-two years that Suharto held office, ruling through a combination of patronage, terror, and manufactured consent, the military had little patience for such demonstrations. The flags raised by Papuan separatists never flew for long; they were lowered by soldiers who shot "security disrupters" on sight.[1] Undertaken at the dawn of Indonesia's new era reformasi (era of reform), the Biak flag raising lasted for four days. By noon of the first day, a large crowd of supporters had gathered under the water tower, where they listened to speeches and prayers, and sang and danced to Papuan nationalist songs. By afternoon, their numbers had grown to the point where they were able to repulse an attack by the regency police, who stormed the site in an effort to take down the flag. Over the next three days, the protesters managed to seal off a dozen square blocks of the city, creating a small zone of West Papuan sovereignty adjoining the regency's main market and port. The demonstration only ended after local military units, reinforced with additional troops, staged a predawn raid on the encampment. Some two hundred men, women, and children were guarding the flag when the soldiers opened fire. Philip Karma, the young civil servant who led the demonstration, was shot in both his legs before he was arrested. It is still not clear how many of his followers were wounded, raped, or killed.[2]

Indonesia is in trouble, the American media has told us on the basis of events like the Biak flag raising. Riots in Jakarta, ethnic clashes in Kalimantan and the Moluccas, separatism in East Timor, Aceh, and Irian Jaya—journalists have taken all this as evidence that Indonesian national unity was never anything but "enforced." "One country, one people, one language," begins a feature published shortly after the destruction that followed East Timor's vote for independence (Mydans 1999: 1). "As a national credo, displayed on banners and placards, it sounds simple enough. But in this scattered archipelago of 13,000 islands, roiling with an untamed mix of cultures, ethnic groups, histories, rivalries, gods, and spoken tongues, it begins to seem almost impossible. Some people say it is" (see also Landler 1999: 1). "The forces that most overtly held Indonesia together—the grip of a dictator and the harshness of the military—have retreated," the article goes on, creating a "vacuum" that "has been quickly filled by all the repressed passions of political, religious, and ethnic difference" (Mydans 1999: 1). In the case of Irian Jaya, whose "primitive people" are "as strange and exotic to the residents of modern Jakarta as they are to New Yorkers," these differences are particularly stark (ibid.: 2). Unacknowledged in these assessments is not only the fact that the regime justified decades of repression and corruption by evoking and sometimes staging displays of "primordial" violence; also obscured is the fact that the same publications once portrayed Indonesia's diversity as a form of national wealth.[3] Prior to the Asian financial crisis, and the combination of international pressure and domestic unrest that brought Suharto's presidency to an end, few mainstream journalists expressed any doubts about the strength of Indonesian national unity. If anything seemed to threaten the stability of Suharto's so-called New Order regime, it was the globalizing effects of development, forces that were leading urban Indonesians to oppose authoritarian rule (see *New York Times* 1996a, b; Friedman 1997; Mydans 1997).

But mainstream American journalists are not the only ones who have found themselves confronting the limits of Indonesian nationalism in the face of events like the Biak flag raising. Clifford Geertz, writing in the *New York Review of Books*, ponders the fate of Indonesia's nationalist project. Against the image of a nation born of anticolonial revolution as a "triumphalist, insurgent, liberationist power," Geertz notes that "more reflective Indonesians" are coming to question "how far this master idea, with its slogans, stories and radiant moments, remains a living force among either the country's elite or its population, and how far it has become just so much willed nostalgia—declamatory, a pretense, worn and seen through, cherished if at all by Western romantics and political scientists" (Geertz 2000: 22). Whatever we make of Geertz's prognosis on the political future of what he calls "big ideas," his reflections do suggest how recent events might challenge truths that many Indonesianists have long held dear. Much as some journalists represent primordialism as the natural state of non-Western affairs, postwar scholars of Indonesia have often approached national consciousness as a reality that it would be heresy to doubt.

Consider, for example, the first three paragraphs of Ruth McVey's contribution to a 1996 volume entitled *Making Indonesia*. The "ideological odd couple" of the nation-state, McVey opens, "has made itself into a particularly powerful focus of organization and thought, the institution which much of mankind now considers to be its proper source of social identity and center of loyalty, the apex of nearly all hierarchies, the almost unquestioned locus of power." Nation building in Indonesia is particularly instructive. "The archipelago had no common identity prior to its incarnation as the Netherlands

East Indies," and the colonial experience pulled regions apart, as much as it united them. And yet, "something" engaged the imagination of "a significant portion of the population . . . making it willing to follow new leaders in the name of a quite new idea, that of a collective Indonesian personality." In the wake of the revolution, the country "remained remarkably resistant to separatist tendencies," McVey asserts, noting that the "regional rebellions" that broke out in Sumatra and Sulawesi in the 1950s were really a struggle over who should rule in Jakarta. "It is therefore worth contemplating the things that went to make up Indonesian nationalism and the ways in which Indonesian leaders used, reshaped, and suppressed these elements in an effort to transform a desire for the future into an instrument of rule" (McVey 1996: 11). For McVey, in the absence of Sumatran and Sulawesian nationalism, Indonesian nationalism is the phenomenon to be explained. Despite the exceptions alluded to in McVey's opening comments, national consciousness, of one kind or another, stands as the norm.

Yet there is another way of interpreting events like the Biak flag raising. It is not simply that nation-states like Indonesia have reached their limits; our models of contemporary consciousness have reached their limits, as well. *Raiding the Land of the Foreigners* suggests the shortcomings of analyses that presume a seamless fit between representations of the nation as a homogeneous, territorially bounded community and the understandings one finds among people who live within the borders of a particular polity. This book calls into question the view that takes self-conscious national identity as a default condition, the natural outcome of the fact that this is a world of nation-states. There are good reasons why some scholars have taken for granted national identity—and modernity, more generally—as an object of inquiry. It would be unsavory to invoke any of the conventional alternatives to the national—the archaic, the agrarian, the primitive, the remote—alternatives that make some people's pasts into other people's futures (see Osborne 1995: 16; Appadurai 1996: 31). But this allergy to the thought of the limits of national consciousness has its costs. It is not only in "out-of-the-way places" that national identity can be subverted (see Tsing 1993). It also subverts itself from within.

It will be crucial to my argument, and obvious from the evidence I present, that Biak-Numfor, the site of this study, was in the waning years of the New Order regime unusually well integrated into the Indonesian nation-state by many measures. The city where the flag raising occurred was the capital of an administrative unit consisting of the islands of Biak, Supiori, and Numfor, along with the surrounding atolls. In the early 1990s, the Biak-speaking inhabitants of these islands attended Indonesian schools and universities, participated in Indonesian institutions and organizations, were highly fluent in the Indonesian national language and Indonesian national rhetorics of rule. Unlike recent ethnographic studies of resistance to the Indonesian state, this book does not linger on practices and persons that the New Order pushed to the margins (cf. Steedly 1993; Tsing 1993). Rather, it focuses on the failure of hegemony among people who participated enthusiastically in the programs and projects of the regime. Instead of a description of marginality, this study offers a new way of reading the diagnostics of national belonging, an analytic that illuminates a sociocultural economy that stands cheek by jowl with the discourses of Papuan separatism and Indonesian nationalism, yet radically undercuts them both. I use the term "sociocultural economy" to refer to an interconnected series of spaces of representation, appropriation, and production, whose reproduction rests on a dialectic in which social action is both oriented by and recreates cultural values. My analysis of this economy will make sense of how people who acted as loyal Indonesians in the early 1990s could so abruptly switch allegiances. Not only in their secret practices but also in the very midst of their submission to the state, the individuals described in this study undermined the New Order's authority. Scarcely the outcome of primordial attachments, the imperatives that led them to do so were no less a product of history than those that led other Indonesians to internalize national ideologies of rule.

Key to the economy I describe in this study is a dynamic I call the fetishization of the foreign. Let me state the punch line of this study plainly: to the extent that Biaks pursued the foreign as a source of value, prestige, and authority, they managed to participate in national institutions without adopting national points of view. In New Order Biak, the fetishization of the foreign resided in a web of social practices, sacred and banal, in ways of talking about intimacy and history, of producing and transacting objects, of evaluating speeches, gifts, dances, and songs. Built on observations from a range of arenas and historical moments, my evidence is subtle but suggestive. If I draw on particular bodies of theory in the course of analyzing this evidence, it is to bring unexpected correspondences into view. This study's ambitions come into focus most clearly when placed in the context of four sites of inquiry: the nation, the foreign, fetishism, and utopia. Let us begin with the first, and the assumptions concerning identity and representation that have pervaded scholarly assessments of the forces that integrate the modern nation-state.

The Nation

"What is it that holds a nation-state together?" In her 1989 study, *National Integration in Indonesia: Patterns and Policies*, Christine Drake evaluates Indonesia's performance in terms of four "factors of integration" that could hold the answer to this deceptively simple question. First she considers the "historical and political dimension," which consists of "common integrative historical experiences," from "shared suffering," to "common achievements," to the events and epochs that make up "the common heritage of a country." Next, she addresses the "sociocultural dimension," which includes "shared cultural attributes . . . common language, common cultural features associated with religious practices as well as other cultural elements, and opportunities to belong to nationwide organizations and share in common nationwide activities." Third, she assesses the "interactive dimension," the level of contact "among the diverse peoples within a nation-state" through "movement and communication between provinces, including land, sea and air transportation links, radio, television and telephone communications, migration and trade." Finally, she considers the "economic dimension," which takes into account the importance of "regional economic interdependence" and "regional balance in economic development," as well as the need for citizens to perceive "that standards of living are improving and that there is some measure of equity in the location of new industrial growth and development schemes" (Drake 1989: 2–3). Basing her analysis on statistical data collated at the provincial level, Drake is well aware of the limitations of her method—how it conceals intraprovincial inequities and the effects of interplay between factors. "Interaction" in the absence of "equity," for instance, may prove a disintegrating force; in some situations, familiarity breeds contempt. But despite pointing to the grievances that pose a threat to Indonesian national unity, Drake ends on a cautiously optimistic note.

> Indonesia remains a diverse and fascinating country, one in which great progress has been made toward the fuller integration of its many islands and peoples, yet one where enormous problems, particularly demographic, economic and political, remain. As the Indonesian government is aware, integration is a dynamic concept, a condition that has to be constantly nurtured, one where peoples of different social and cultural backgrounds and economic levels have to be bonded continually into a better functioning and more mutually interdependent whole. In this process, much has been accomplished, but much yet remains to be done, as Indonesia pursues its goal of "Unity in Diversity." (Drake 1989: 270)

Let us leave aside for the moment the way that Drake assumes the very subject whose presence her study is designed to establish: a nation that pursues a common goal. My point for the moment is that if Indonesia seemed to be making progress toward national integration at the time of Drake's writing, Biak-Numfor was clearly doing its small part. In all of the dimensions Drake covers, the regency scored remarkably well, especially given Irian Jaya's reputation for isolation. Converted to Christianity in the early twentieth century, with a long history of wage labor and government service, and an even longer history of travel and trade, the indigenous inhabitants of Biak-Numfor—*orang Biak* (Biaks), as they call themselves—pride themselves on their cosmopolitan ways. Of the 92,570 people counted in the regency's

1991 census, an estimated 66 percent were members of a single ethno-linguistic group.[4] Speakers of an Austronesian language, Biaks make up one of the larger and more dominant "tribes" in Irian Jaya. In the early 1990s, one found Biak migrants of various vintages and socioeconomic backgrounds living in villages in the Raja Ampat Islands, in the towns of Sorong, Manok-wari, Nabire, Wamena, Fak-Fak, and Merauke, in the provincial capital, Jay-apura, in the national capital, Jakarta, and in distant cities that included Cardiff, The Hague, and Delft. Worldwide, at the time, there were probably around 100,000 self-identified Biaks in all.

Biaks living in Biak-Numfor clearly shared sociocultural attributes with other citizens of Indonesia, including a "common language," Indonesian, in which rates of fluency and literacy long have been high, as I have noted, and "common cultural features associated with religious practice."[5] The vast majority of indigenous islanders belonged to Gereja Kristen Injili Irian Jaya (the Irian Jaya Evangelical Church, henceforth GKI), an active member of the national association of Protestant churches. As far as "membership in national organizations" goes, one simply had to note the number of adults and children wearing scouting, military, and government party uniforms to gauge the frequency with which Biaks joined such groups. On the "interactive dimension," Biak-Numfor was home to a growing population of migrants from across Indonesia: traders and cash croppers from South Sulawesi, Sino-Indonesian merchants from Java and Bali, Ambonese schoolteachers and doctors, Sumatran military commanders, Jakarta businessmen, and Men-adonese pastors, to name a few. Making their homes within the expanding boundaries of Biak City, new migrants found it easy to settle in the regency, which boasted a busy harbor and Frans Kaisiëpo Airport, the province's first port of call for domestic flights originating in Jakarta. A crucial factor for officials planning the development of tourism in the regency, the airport was also at the time Indonesia's first port of call for international flights originat-ing in Los Angeles, which stopped in Biak to refuel before continuing to Bali and other popular destinations farther west.[6]

Scattered along the coastlines of Biak, Supiori, and Numfor, the majority of the regency's villages lacked electricity and running water. But rural Biaks listened to battery-powered radios at home and watched television with urban relatives during their frequent trips to town. Although in 1992, at the beginning of my fieldwork, the eighty-mile trip from Biak's north coast to Biak City could take as long as the flight to the United States, by 1994, when I left, a new network of roads and bridges had dramatically shortened local voyages. For those who lived in Biak City, a new satellite system was making it easier to place long-distance calls. All of these initiatives belonged to a national "Go East" campaign designed to accelerate the economic develop-ment of "neglected" provinces, such as Irian Jaya. Although many villagers still relied on subsistence fishing and farming in locally controlled waters and on clan-owned land, growing numbers augmented their income through wage labor at the regency's cannery and plymill, or in various construction projects sponsored by the government. The master plan for Biak-Numfor projected the opening of luxury resorts and a tax-free processing zone, and officials promised that employment opportunities would only widen. Although some of my acquaintances had their doubts as to who really benefited from development, the general impression was that living standards were on the rise.

As for the first dimension in Drake's inventory—"common, integrative, historical experiences"—the situation in Biak-Numfor was complicated. The arrival of the first European missionaries in the territory (1855) and the opening of the first permanent administrative posts (1898) occurred at roughly the same time as similar events in what are now securely "Indonesian" provinces.[7] Thanks in part to an expansion in shipping and telegraph services, in part to the intervention of a colonial army no longer encumbered by a costly war in Aceh, a devoutly Muslim polity on the western tip of Sumatra whose inhabitants fought off the Dutch for nearly thirty years, north coastal New Guinea became an effective part of the Netherlands Indies during the early twentieth century, as did Bali, Lombok, Flores, Ceram, and the Sumatran and Sulawesian highlands (Locher-Scholten 1994; see also van Goor 1986). By virtue of their ancestors' involvement in regional networks centered in the Moluccas, long the world's foremost supplier of cloves, contemporary Biaks could point to an even longer history of "shared experience" with distant peoples than could many western Indonesian groups. Needless to say, the conditions that prevailed in western New Guinea's interior differed dramatically; yet the inhabitants of more accessible areas, including today's Biak-Numfor, participated, administratively and economically, in a wider colonial world. It was not until the early 1930s that some Europeans began to imagine western New Guinea as a region that was racially and culturally distinct from the rest of the Indies; not until the late 1940s that the Dutch government enforced a divorce (see Rutherford 1998).

As I suggested in the preface, the critical historical experience for today's Papuan nationalists dates to the period between 1949 and 1963, when the Netherlands ruled western New Guinea as a separate colony, thus retaining a fragment of the Indies after Indonesia gained independence. By the time of my fieldwork, there were no longer armed separatists on the island, and the military atrocities of the 1960s, 1970s, and early 1980s, if not forgotten, could be spoken of as a thing of the past. Biak officials I met were beginning to indulge in references to "the Papuan people" and "Melanesian culture"; they took it as a sign of the progress of national integration in Biak-Numfor that these once subversive expressions no longer marked their users as supporters of the separatist cause. In 1992, the coordinators of military intelligence in Jakarta felt optimistic enough about the situation in Irian Jaya to

allow the national research institute to issue permits to foreign scholars un-
affiliated with church or government projects who wished to conduct fieldwork in the province. To my knowledge, I was the second anthropologist
since the 1960s to receive a visa for this purpose. In the context of the
diagnostics Drake proposes, perhaps the best indication of the authorities'
confidence in Biaks' membership in the Indonesian nation is the research I
conducted for this book.

And yet, this study calls into question the view that would take national
belonging as the automatic outcome of the factors Drake describes. In doing
so, it challenges assumptions that lie at the heart of dominant theories concerning the emergence of modern nationalism. Writers who sharply disagree
on the nature of the phenomenon would recognize the imprint of their
thinking in various entries in Drake's list. In Drake's description of the historical dimension, one finds echoes of Smith's (1986) argument regarding the
important role preexisting "ethnie" can play in providing a basis for the modern nation; Hobsbawm's (1990) discussion of the contribution of various
forms of "protonationalism," based on long-standing religious and political
ties, would support Drake's reasoning here, as well. Drake's emphasis on the
importance of state-sponsored education and economic development in integrating the nation has affinities with Gellner's (1983) argument on the function of modern nationalism in meeting the "structural demands of industrial
society." Anderson's ([1983] 1991) characterization of the mechanisms that
lead to the imagining of a nation echo throughout Drake's statistics on the
prevalence of telephones, televisions, radios, and newspapers: the vehicles
that extend the "imagined community" to far-flung villages and towns.

This is not to say that these thinkers all conceive of their theories as
equally applicable to a nation-state like Indonesia. Smith and Hobsbawm,
despite their myriad differences, concur in the opinion that Indonesia is not
really a nation at all. Citing the strains caused by ethnic, religious, and linguistic heterogeneity, both scholars place Indonesia in the company of
"newly emerged states claiming a national homogeneity they do not possess"
(Hobsbawm 1990: 153).[8] Anderson and Gellner, more usefully, describe the
emergence of national identity in terms that do not automatically exclude
postcolonial polities; indeed, for Anderson, Indonesia serves as an exemplary
case. Far from posing an intractable obstacle to the formation of an authentic
nation, ethnic identities in Indonesia are the product of the same forces that
gave rise to nationalism, in a world where colonial scholars and officials
defined the subject of the nation before its members defined themselves (see
Anderson [1983] 1991: 163–184). In his focus on the impact of colonial
institutions and the categories they fostered, Anderson provides fodder for
the argument that ethnicity is the product of nation formation, not the substance from which nations are formed (see Williams 1989). Such an approach provides the basis for a clearer understanding of the political implica-

tions of Indonesia's "remarkable" cultural diversity than Smith or Hobsbawm can offer. Through the sponsoring of institutions that articulated selected forms of difference, the New Order regime defused social tensions and promoted crosscutting allegiances of ethnicity and religion while suppressing forms of consciousness based on class (see Kipp 1996).

Gellner shares with Anderson the virtue of taking neither ethnicity nor nationality for granted as a natural object of human thought. Although Anderson places more stress on the affective dimensions of national belonging, and its resemblance to older affinities of kinship and faith, both theorists describe national identity as a distinctly modern phenomenon. Nations conceive of themselves as homogenous and bounded, constituted of a population of logically equivalent, if anonymous, individuals, who participate as a unit in the series of equivalent polities that make up the global order of nation-states. National identity is intimately associated with modern notions of equality and progress; Anderson's "horizontal fraternity" is envisioned as moving forward through "homogeneous, empty time." Gellner explicitly relates this new mode of envisioning identity to broader processes of rationalization. What Kant and Hume saw as universal characteristics of human thought are the historical product of social and economic forces that broke down the hierarchies and overcame the cognitive discontinuities that characterized the agrarian world. To continue to prosper—and, indeed, to exist at all—industrial society requires both specialization and equality; functions must be distinguished, but individuals, in principle, should be capable of filling multiple roles. Hence, the age of industrialization is also the age of the emergence of standardized national languages, capable of communicating context-free information between strangers. Hence, it is also the age of mass education, through which citizens come to master this new code. Only the modern state is capable of funding and coordinating an educational system that enables a rationalized society to flourish. This is why ethnic minorities, who are at a disadvantage since their language does not provide the basis for the national standard, cherish dreams of having a state of their own.

But this account of nationalism as the correlate of economic modernization suffers its own limitations, not least of which is the evolutionary trajectory it follows.[9] It is possible to see how Gellner's model might apply to Papuan nationalism. Although their lingua franca is a dialect of Indonesian, not a separate vernacular, Irian Jayans long have faced the sort of discrimination that Gellner suggests leads to nationalism in unevenly industrializing countries. What is harder to see is what Gellner would make, for instance, not of Biaks' attendance at state-sponsored schools but of the terms in which they speak of success. Biaks are disproportionately represented in what Anderson might call the province's creole elite, a small, multilingual class of well-educated, well-connected men and women (see [1983] 1991: 52). This elite is the product of modern education, which is supposed to nurture forms of equality that render irrelevant ties of affinity and descent. Yet, as we will see, Biaks often explain the success of individuals in terms of kinship; as Biak mothers, in particular, often told me, it is not individual merit but gifts from intimate others that enable teachers and officials to rise in the ranks. In this regard, by Gellner's measure, Indonesia might qualify as a nation, but Biaks themselves would be held back from full participation by their "traditional" perspectives. Somehow Gellner would need to explain the persistence of attributes antithetical to national integration among people who are clearly entering the industrialized world.

This study documents the reproduction of antinational apprehensions of authority, space, time, and self under conditions that theorists have assumed would lead to the formation of a homogeneous nation. But its purpose is not simply to identify the limits of the nation in a particular corner of Indonesia; it is to identify the limits of the models through which the emergence of national consciousness has been conceived. Gellner, Anderson, Hobsbawm, and Smith, despite their differences, leave equally unexamined the sociocultural dynamics that mediate the impact of such forces as literacy, bureaucracy, transportation, and trade. In assuming that railroads, schools and markets automatically and irreversibly turn "peasants into Frenchmen," to borrow the title of Eugen Weber's famous (1976) study, adherents to this model of the modernization of identity posit a direct, causal relationship between exposure to shared technologies of representation and exchange, and the emergence of shared conceptions of self.[10] This model is grounded in dichotomies, the most problematic of which is its sheer opposition between the long-distance and the face-to-face. This study, by contrast, is premised on an approach to sociality that no more presumes the intimacy of supposedly traditional relationships than it does the alienation associated with modern life. I begin with the assumption that all identities are the outcome of semiotically mediated processes of recognition (see Siegel 1997; Keane 1997a). Entailing the objectification of a self for another, these processes have effects that are neither permanent nor assured. I approach the nation in the following chapters less as an achievement than as a limit, posited through a range of scholarly and political discourses and institutions, but never unequivocally achieved.

The discussions of the nation that have the most to contribute to my analysis are those that have examined how the production of national identity is both threatened and fueled by contradictions, which are locally distinct but spring from the vicissitudes of representation, broadly conceived. Thus Handler describes how French Canadian nationalism gives rise to "perpetual motions" in the form of "the constant doubts about national existence, the ongoing search for authentic culture, or the endless fragmentation of bureaucracies created to administer national existence and culture" (1988: 191). Handler's point is not that the Quebec nation in some sense falls short of actualization. Rather, he argues that the very processes that produce an image of national culture as an object of desire—the "stacks of loudspeakers and paying spectators" at a staged performance of folk dancing, for example—constitute an aspect of the "culture of the situation" that eludes the totalizing effort to produce the nation as a bounded whole (ibid.: 195).

For Berlant, the limit that nationalist discourse engages pertains to the abstract identities posited by the nation form. In the United States, what Berlant calls the "National Symbolic" projects a utopia that would bridge the local and the national, an impossible site where there is no longer a gap between one's "body and everyday life experience" and the national ideal (1991: 5, 12; see also 1997: 6). Turning to Indonesia, Pemberton's (1994) analysis of the New Order's cultural politics likewise foregrounds the inherently unattainable nature of the identities promoted by the state. In New Order Java, traditional culture (I: *budaya tradisionil*) acted as a "metaspook" that demanded obeisance to the generalized obligations of custom. But by virtue of its abstract character, those who submitted to the authority of custom could never fully meet its demands. An essence located at the heart of the national cultural subject, tradition was both a focus of desire and a source of anxiety. The compulsion to fulfill its imperatives fueled an unending series of rituals; one always feared falling short.

In this study, I follow scholars like Handler, Berlant, and Pemberton in stressing the limits of national identity. I assume that this identity, like any other, is only ever the product of historically specific and inherently contingent moments of representation, performances that evoke emergent abstractions, yet unfold in particular times and places, through the mediation of particular words and things. The problematic concreteness of social interaction, the underdetermined character of the "material" that mediates discourse—these aspects of representation expose national texts to multiple interpretations. But where in other studies these threats to the integrity of national identity prove crucial to its reproduction, in *Raiding the Land of the Foreigners* they serve in the perpetuation of a very different focus of interest and desire. The practices described in this study do not represent a symptom of their participants' illiteracy in the codes of nationality. In accentuating different functions of discourse from those emphasized in nationalist ideologies and the theories they inform, these practices illuminate, if anything, a fuller sense of what it could mean to read.[11]

The nation is a symbol, not an entity, Verdery (1993) has argued, mobilized in different ways to legitimate different regimes, which have different degrees of power to achieve homogeneity within their borders. Defined either as a correlate of citizenship or as the effect of ethnicity, history, and culture, national identities emerge as an effect of action on two levels: that of explicitly nationalist discourse and that of everyday practice, the "microphysics of power," à la Foucault. To appreciate how the discourses and practices described in this study could have antinational effects, one must begin with something like Verdery's formulations. But one must also delve deeper into the processes of identification on which this model of the nation as symbol rests. Žižek (1989) has criticized Althusser's (1971) account of interpellation, the process that leads individuals to recognize themselves from the perspective of the state and its apparatuses, which include, for Althusser, the mass media and such institutions as the church, family, and school. According to Žižek, Althusser obscures a critical stage in the recruitment of subjects in his description of how people respond to the ideological Other, which in Althusser's "little theoretical theater" assumes the guise of a policeman yelling "Hey you there!" This stage consists of a moment of hailing prior to identification, a moment when the subject is "desperately seeking a trace with which to identify," "for he [sic] does not understand the meaning of the call of the other" (1989: 43). Informed by a particular reading of Lacanian theory, Žižek views this "non-integrated surplus of senseless traumatism" as that which "confers on the law its unconditional authority: in other words, which—in so far as it escapes ideological sense—sustains what we might call the ideological jouis-sence—enjoyment-in-sense (enjoy-meant), proper to ideology" (ibid.: 43–44). Yet what Žižek describes as the "gap between the machine and its internalization" is open to other articulations. The very processes that would seem to lead to identification with the nation facilitate the nation's subversion. It is in these processes that one might look for an antinational impulse—a resistance akin to that depicted in Sakai's reflections on the difficulty of "overcoming the modern": a gesture that "disturbs the possible representational relationship between the self and the image." This resistance is not "negation, by which a subject is posited in opposition to that which it negates," but a movement to be likened to the "negativity . . . which continues to disturb a putative stasis in which the subject is made to be adequate to itself" (ibid.: 118–119).

In examining practices that play on the limits of the nation, it is not the goal of this study to excavate a perspective that would be self-consciously oppositional. Rather, what one finds described in the following chapters are genres of practice that only serve to marginalize national identity to the extent that they posit alternative sources of value, identity, pleasure, and power. These genres are performative, in the sense that they both presume an audience and wield the power to create the very realities to which they refer (see Austin 1976; Derrida 1982: 307–330; 1988; Parker and Sedgwick 1995). The category of the foreign, which gives coherence to these genres, is no more to be taken for granted than that of the nation. What Žižek and Sakai present as a theoretical possibility emerges in this study as a sociocultural construct, no less the product of a particular history than was the New Order national ideal. To understand the foreign, as I use the term in this study, one must consider the wider political settings in dialogue with which it emerged.

The Foreign

In the depositions taken by the Biak police during the weeks following the flag raising, one finds no indication of the brutality with which the army cut short the demonstration.[12] Military witnesses describe the end of the protest in antiseptic terms: troops finally moved in to "clean" the site. But one does get a sense of the attributes of Philip Karma, the leader who persuaded people to join the gathering at grave risk to their lives. Karma, who was thirty-eight years old at the time, was born of elite Biak parents and raised in Jayapura, the provincial capital. He went to college in Solo, a Central Javanese city, then completed a management course in Manila, before returning to Jayapura to work at the governor's office in the Department of Training and Development. Karma told his interrogators that he got the idea for the July 1 protest from reading a study published in Indonesia, *Pemberontakan Organisasi Papua Merdeka* (*The Free Papua Organization Rebellion*) (Djopari 1993). When he learned that the twenty-seventh anniversary of the Free Papua Organization's Declaration of West Papuan Independence would fall on July 1, the idea of leading a flag raising simply popped into his mind. Karma just happened to be on Biak in late June, having stopped on his way back from a business trip to visit his ailing father, a former regent who had retired to his natal village. But when he heard that they had raised the Morning Star flag in Jayapura, he recruited his siblings to help him find leaders in Biak City who were willing to do the same.

Once a crowd had gathered under the water tower, Karma read a declaration, written in Indonesian. Those present pledged not to lower the flag until UN Secretary General Kofi Annan arrived to hear the Papuans' demands. Rumors that powerful foreigners were on their way to the site reportedly swept Biak City, as did stories that the flag raising had been broadcast on CNN. But Karma appealed not only to international agencies in his speeches; he also claimed privileged knowledge of the national scene. He presented an analysis of Indonesia's economic woes and the corruption of its leaders, representing the nation-state as a sinking ship and the province as a lifeboat. Karma told his followers not to fear military reprisal; the government would not dare to violate their human rights for fear of losing sorely needed foreign aid. Echoing official speeches on Irian Jaya's development, Karma declared that the Indonesian government had failed to develop the province's "human resources" (I: *sumber daya manusia*); independent West Papua would educate its citizens for free. Karma explained to his followers that the independence movement was in accordance with the Indonesian Constitution of 1945, which proclaimed that all people had the right to self-determination. He also told them that the movement was not in violation of Pancasila, the official ideology that the New Order required all Indonesian organizations to adopt (see Kipp 1996: 107–108). After Karma's release from prison and dismissal from the provincial bureaucracy, he repeatedly appeared at political gatherings wearing his Indonesian civil service uniform, albeit with a Papuan flag affixed to his lapel.

One must appreciate the circumstances under which the depositions regarding the flag raising were taken—in all probability, under duress. Yet Karma's testimony, along with that of other witnesses, emphasized themes I often heard when Biaks discussed individuals with authority and power. On the day of the flag raising, Karma told his interrogators that he had "freed West Papua," with the help of people whose names he did not know. Although it is likely that Karma was protecting his supporters, his statement calls to mind the comments of elite Biaks I met during fieldwork when they returned to the island to intervene in local affairs. The fact that Karma knew few people in the regency confirmed his status as someone who had spent much of his time in distant places. He might not have known his supporters, but they knew him—as the successful son of a regent who had served in the highlands, as someone with access to resources from abroad. As I noted in the preface, in New Order Biak there was a word for such leaders, a term that gathered into one category western Indonesian migrants and civil servants, the citizens of distant nations, and indigenous teachers, scholars, and officials. They were all known as "foreigners" (B: *amber*)—and some were "big foreigners" (B: *amber beba*)—these men and women who had either originated from or sojourned in the Land of the Foreigners (B: *Sup Amber*). This foreign land could be the provincial university, it could be the regency bureaucracy, or it could be a place like England or Japan. A trader from Java, a social worker born on Biak, and I, the resident American anthropologist— we were all "female foreigners" (B: *bin amber*).

In a postcolonial setting like Biak, it is in some respects unsurprising to find a heightened concern with persons and objects defined as foreign. For some analysts, the effort to negotiate a relationship between the local and the foreign reflects the dilemmas of colonized and formerly colonized communities as they attempt to create a space for new nations in a global order where wealth, power, and influence are unevenly distributed. Partha Chatterjee has attacked on various fronts models of nationalism that take third-world movements as merely derivative of a universal process initiated in the West. In his analyses, the alien origins of the dominant models of the state and civil society become a factor with which nationalist thinkers must contend (1986; see also 1993). Similarly, Orlove and Bauer (1997a, b) have argued for an analytic approach to imports in Latin America that reads into the demand for foreign commodities the predicament of members of postcolonial nations, who strive to be indigenous and cosmopolitan, all at once. By obtaining goods defined as European or American, Latin American elites have long signaled their membership in a global community of nations; at the same time, these societies set limits on how much foreignness one may acquire without losing one's national sense of self. Through the consumption of commodities, postcolonial elites contend with the problem that national self-consciousness rests on an ability to see one's culture and society from the perspective of an outsider. The need to prove oneself in the eyes of powerful foreigners translates into a desire to prove one's capacity to acquire foreign things.

Refracted through Orlove and Bauer's model, the valorization of the foreign one finds in Biak looks like a member of a larger species of postcolonial phenomena. But a closer acquaintance with the history of Indonesian nationalism places the dynamic in a different light. Nationalism in the Indies arose in response to a new alignment between the foreign and the local, well after the "natives" succumbed to the allure of European goods. Scholars have dated the birth of Indonesian nationalism to a period that saw the displacement on Java of the "mestizo" world that characterized the earlier colonial period (Onghokham 1978; Rush 1983; Taylor 1983; Tsuchiya 1986, 1990; Shiraishi 1990; see also Stoler 1989a, b). As an effect of policies that limited the immigration of European women to the Indies, the colony's nineteenth-century ruling class consisted of a mixed-race population of Indo-European planters and officers, Chinese merchants, and the native nobles through whom the Dutch nominally governed Java and the Outer Islands. This elite combined a taste for the fashions of Europe with "native" household arrangements and a predilection for indigenous displays of respect. In certain respects, this society reproduced an older tendency to domesticate foreign elements, which Wolters (1982, 1994) attributes to early Southeast Asian polities and associates with the region's flexible methods of reckoning kinship and substantive conceptions of power (see also Reid 1988). But at the turn of the nineteenth to the twentieth century, when new laws, policies, and technologies initiated fresh waves of migration from the metropole, a growing community of pure-blooded European planters, officials, and their families oversaw the "modernization" of the Indies. The tiny class of Dutch-speaking natives that was cultivated to serve in the expanding administration was confronted with novel communications from Europe and beyond.

Anderson ([1979] 1990) captures the complexity of this class's experience of modernity in his oft-cited discussion of Soetomo, an early nationalist, who copied his European teachers by learning not to copy. Forsaking the principles of Javanese pedagogy, which privileged imitation, Soetomo became a good Indonesian, acceding to a novel position that was neither European nor Javanese. In Siegel's (1997) treatment of the birth of Indonesian national consciousness, the interaction between the foreign and the national proves even more convoluted. In Malay-language novels published in the vernacular press, the emergence of a national subject involved the domestication of wider possibilities for identification. At the beginning of the period, native authors were translators, who created original works at the same time that they reacted to messages from abroad. According to Siegel, the heady sense that they were being addressed as foreigners led these authors to insert commentary into their translations, assuming a new voice as one might don another's dress. These works were followed by novels that depicted the birth of a new form of hierarchy, in which nationalist leaders guaranteed the authenticity of one's newfound identity. The thrill of finding that one could pass as someone different gave way to the assurance that such an experience could only signal recognition of Indonesian-ness within oneself.

According to these analyses, the emergence of national consciousness in Indonesia entailed the end of a dynamic in which an elite gained prestige by incorporating alien attributes. To understand how the relationship to the outside world one finds on Biak diverges from this plot, one must consider more closely the New Order concept of *amber*. I first encountered the word *amber* in a nineteenth-century grammar written to acquaint missionaries with Mefoorsche, the name initially given to the dialect of Biak spoken by the natives among whom the first evangelists settled (see van Hasselt 1868: 35). Like "Wonggori!" (Crocodile!), "Amberi!" (Foreigner!) was used as an expletive, as something someone might shout in anger, fear, or surprise. No doubt this usage referred back to an era when the sultans of Tidore, who nominally governed the region, sent war fleets to attack recalcitrant villages (see Kamma 1947–49). By 1855, when the Dutch and German Protestants who founded New Guinea's first mission post first arrived in the region, the foreigners whom coastal groups encountered included Malay traders and the occasional European officer, conducting a tour of New Guinea's "unpacified" northern coastline. In their conversations with the missionaries and, presumably, among themselves, Biak speakers called these individuals *amber*. Later on, the category expanded to include not only the European evangelists but also the Ambonese Christians whom they imported to preach the Word. It was only after the mass conversions that swept the region in the early twentieth century that Biak teachers and evangelists became foreigners themselves.

But the idea that outsiders and their objects possessed a special potency that could be transmitted to others predates this shift in the field of reference of *amber*. Early reports describe how Papuan mothers would hold up small children in front of the missionaries' houses so they could absorb the power that supposedly emanated from their walls (Kamma 1972: 270). This practice finds an echo in Kamma's (1982) description of the voyages that Biak seafarers took to Tidore. Adventurers from the Raja Ampat Islands, the Bird's Head Peninsula, and what is now Biak-Numfor undertook long journeys in enormous canoes to deliver tribute to the sultan. Trading and raiding along the way, forging metal weapons to sell to or use on populations lacking this skill, they arrived in the Moluccas with a cargo of massoi bark, bird skins, and slaves, which they traded for beads, iron, porcelain, and cloth (see also

Kamma and Kooijman 1973). The travelers turned over their tribute to the sultan's vassals on the island of Halmahera. But they always proceeded the rest of the way to Tidore to pay homage at the sultan's court. Prostrating themselves before the throne, the Papuans claimed that they were absorbing *barak*, the Biak version of the Arabic word for the magical power that pervaded the sultan's person and surroundings. Along with imported objects, which the Papuans used as ceremonial wealth, and Tidoran titles, which they passed down to their descendants, the voyagers carried *barak* back to their communities. Upon disembarking, the travelers shook hands with their relatives, who then rubbed their own faces with the *barak* they had received.

The travelers stored the foreign goods they had acquired in their homes, to be used as bridewealth and on other ceremonial occasions. Like the *barak* they absorbed on their faces, the gifts given in life-cycle feasts were seen as protecting their recipients and endowing them with exceptional powers (see Kamma 1972: 270; 1976: 235; 1982: 62; compare Munn 1986: 105–128; Keane 1997a: 76). Tidore thus appeared to the Papuans as the source of valuables that served as evidence of a voyager's prowess, and of a potency that provided others with the ability to travel. This distant place provided the currency of value, in both of its functions: in the form of objects that reflected a person's past achievements, and in the form of an invisible substance that conveyed the capacity to act (compare Graeber 1996). In their talk about how children could be made into foreigners, New Order Biaks, as we will see, articulated assumptions about value and embodiment that bore the traces of this long history of commerce with distant centers of wealth and coercion. They still saw foreignness as an attribute of distant polities that individuals could incorporate by way of their exchanges with intimate others. Individuals like Philip Karma still seemed capable of absorbing the status, authority, and potential for violence associated with an alien state. Future leaders did this during the period of my fieldwork, not by identifying with foreign perspectives but by wearing foreign potency upon their skin.

The Biak-speaking Papuans, like their New Order descendants, were not up to something entirely unique in their treatment of foreign lands as a source of value and authority. As I mentioned above, historians have described a similar tendency to incorporate the foreign as a distinctive trait of precolonial Southeast Asia. The lowland polities of Java and mainland Southeast Asia had a long history of adopting outsiders' symbols, narratives, and objects; closer to Biak, Tidore's sister polity Ternate featured a ruler in the seventeenth century who called himself "Sultan Amsterdam" (Andaya 1993: 177). Smaller groups in the region's remote islands and highlands developed their own methods for appropriating foreign elements, often through shamanism and ceremonial exchange (see, for example, Atkinson 1989; Tsing 1993; McKinnon 1991; Hoskins 1993). Finding similar practices in Biak is somewhat ironic, given that western New Guinea is generally depicted as not belonging to Southeast Asia (see, for example, Defert 1996: 22). But Southeast Asia is not the only place where such practices are evident; according to Helms (1988, 1993), "traditional" societies throughout the world have turned resources from afar into a pillar of local rule (see also Orlove and Bauer 1997a: 18).[13] For analysts who emphasize the ideological underpinnings of all systems of sociality, it is only to be expected that people will represent the origins of value in an alienated form (Sangren 1993; see also Turner 1977). In a crude sense, such formulations are as old as *The Elementary Forms of the Religious Life*, where Durkheim describes how what seems "alien" to "human social relationships" comes to stand for their source ([1912] 1965: 245–255). For the purposes of this study, however, it is not enough simply to note these ethnographic continuities. The valorization of the foreign is not simply a trait of Biak culture; it holds clues as to the historical processes by which what appears as culture is produced.

For it is critical to place depictions of Biak encounters with Tidore in their proper historical context. That entails considering two distinct settings: one in which Biak-speaking seafarers delivered tribute to Tidore, and another in which Biak speakers recounted narratives describing these trips. In both cases, one finds treatments of authority that stand in tension with the forms of hegemony held to prevail in the region at the time. Andaya describes the precolonial sultanates of Tidore and Ternate as forming a kind of family: an order whose members' common interests and perceptions were expressed in shared myth (1993: 82). Yet the seafarers who delivered tribute to Tidore clearly diverged in their understandings of the gesture from the sultan, who interpreted their prostrated bodies as a sign of submission to his will. The sultan rewarded at least one group of Papuan visitors with permission to plunder his territories on their way home (Kamma 1982: 73). Arguably, for these "notorious pirates," the seizing of foreign value began at the sultan's court. If the travelers' performances, from a local perspective, turned obeisance into theft, a similar mismatch in perspectives comes into view when one considers where Kamma (1982), on whom Andaya draws, received his information on the voyages. Recorded by missionaries at the end of the 1880s, the eyewitness reports Kamma cites depicted events that could have occurred no earlier than the start of the nineteenth century. Andaya used Kamma's article as evidence of the nature of the precolonial order; yet it seems likely that Kamma's account of the delivery of tribute refers to events that occurred well after the seventeenth century, when Tidore lost much of its autonomy to the Dutch.[14] Where Andaya attributes reports of Tidoran aggression to the rapacious demands of the Moluccas' new European rulers, Biak memories do not draw a sharp distinction between the violence and the value associated with Tidore. They date the delivery of tribute to the same period that featured attacks by the Tidoran war fleet, which increasingly sailed in the company of Dutch ships. Even in a period when regional politics were already adulterated by European forces, a period that saw the gradual emergence of "rationalized" forms of rule, some Biak speakers continued to turn what looked like an act of submission into a raid.

The foreign in Biak is a historical category. I mean this not merely in the sense that it is the product of these islands' history on the frontier of powerful polities. Nor do I mean this merely in the sense that what is defined as foreign has expanded and shifted as Biaks' relationships with outsiders have evolved. If the foreign has a history, it is because it is a category with historicity; it can only be grasped as the outcome and precondition of processes that unfold in time. No less than the nation, the foreign as it appears in this study is an object of indestructible longings, which aim at a goal that can never fully be reached. It is only by grasping the fetishistic character of this protean notion that we can understand how a dynamic with roots in a supposedly precolonial past could prove so central in relations with a postcolonial state.

Fetishism

Philip Karma's vocabulary, his privileged knowledge, his position in the government—all could be read as proof of encounters in the Land of the Foreigners. Recalling Karma's experiences in distant, possibly dangerous lands, these attributes pointed to the leader's special capacities, the unusual powers that drew a crowd to hear his words. Even a pastor sent by the authorities to persuade Karma to call off the demonstration was struck by what one might call his charisma. Reportedly, the pastor returned from the meeting to tell friends and neighbors about the heavenly light that shone in Karma's eyes. But Karma's authority was not simply an effect of his personal talents. The appearance of charisma depends on what one might call protocols of visibility, paradigms invoked and reproduced in real-time events that define what is happening as the token of a type (Anderson [1985] 1990). Nor was his authority simply the outcome of objective conditions, such as the strength of the institutions he mentioned. The United Nations could only lend its force to Karma's cause by virtue of a presumption that the orator and his followers shared—their expectation that words could serve not only as a vehicle of referential meaning but also as evidence of their speaker's experiences in an absent scene. This presumption, and others, coalesced in an ideology of a sort analogous to that described by recent analysts of language ideologies, who have examined how particular, necessarily partial, understandings of the functions and capacities of language both shape and are shaped by linguistic interactions (Woolard and Schieffelin 1994; Kroskrity 2000; see also Silverstein 1976). Karma's audience, like the audiences of the seafarers of old, partook of an ideology that, in an explicit and implicit fashion, turned what is foreign into a source of agency and an object of desire.

No less than the allure of imported porcelain, or the transmissible potency available in Tidore, Karma's authority depended on his followers' recognition. And this recognition, in turn, rested on his audience's participation in what I referred to above as a sociocultural economy—a system of production, representation, and exchange, encompassing an interconnected series of sites, locations in a geography at once imagined and concrete (Soja 1989). From distant courts and capitals to the intimate interior of a Biak home, value circulated through this geography in a particular form. The historical settings of the flag raising and the voyages to Tidore are not to be conflated. But both illustrate how one might apply an analytic concept that proves critical for exploring the economy that fostered the subversion of New Order nationality in Biak: that is, the fetishization of the foreign. The term "fetishism," as opposed to "valorization," or simply "belief," allows me to capture a dynamic encountered on multiple levels: in the content of narratives, in formal patterns of narration, in institutions that materialize values, and in values that mediate appropriations of the material world. The concept proves useful in illuminating the workings of ideology, for it takes us beyond a perspective that approaches beliefs as misrepresentations of social reality to one that attends to how social reality is generated (see Marx [1867] 1967; see also Žižek 1994). In the same way that Marx argued that the fetishism of commodities was not simply a mystification but a constitutive element of the capitalist economy, I show in this work how the fetishization of the foreign was, in the early 1990s, constitutive of a particular sociocultural order. This order's "secret" resided less in the webs of meaning that mediated a cultural experience of the world than in the reproduction of the values people pursued.

The word "fetishism" has negative connotations, no doubt related to its long-standing deployment as an accusation leveled against "irrational" others. But there are historical reasons why the concept is suited to the analysis of cultural boundaries, as recent studies suggest (see Spyer 1998). These works draw inspiration from Pietz's (1985, 1987, 1988) genealogy of the fetish, which reveals how the concept, developed under the influence of Hegel ([1822] 1991), Marx ([1867] 1967) and Freud ([1922] 1963, [1927] 1963, [1938] 1963), originated in the sixteenth century. The word *fetisso* was first used in the settlements that sprang up along the coast of African Guinea as part of a new commerce in gold and slaves. The birthplace of the fetish, as Pietz describes it, has much in common with what might be called the birthplace of Biak's fetishization of the foreign. The trading zones of coastal Guinea and coastal New Guinea were both frontiers, properly belonging neither to the natives nor to those who confronted them from the West. But when I deploy the term "fetishism" to describe Biak modes of appropriation, it is with the goal of tracking a particular dynamic, not simply noting shared traits, however significant they might be for an understanding of the genealogy of my analytic tools.

My analysis brings together divergent traditions of thought on the fetish. Like Pietz and Spyer, I am interested in a historically specific border phenomenon. Like Turner (1991) and Sangren (1991, 1993, 1995), who have worked from a particular reading of Marx, I am concerned with the ideological status of representations of the foreign as the outcome and precondition of the production of Biak "selves." But my understanding of fetishism goes further than a sociological reading that finds the value of the fetish in a society's productive power, in that I focus on the way in which the fetish's paradoxical nature relates to its ideological-cum-historical role. Freud ([1922] 1963, [1927] 1963, [1938] 1963) presents the fetish as an ambivalent site of uncertain knowledge and incommensurate value (see also Derrida 1986: 211). One will recall that Freud interpreted the fetish as a substitute for the mother's missing penis, embraced as a "compromise formation" that enabled the child simultaneously to acknowledge and deny the possibility of castration. The fetish reassures its adherents that nothing is missing, but it also reminds them that something might be, which means they need the fetish all the more. This inescapable cycle of desire and disavowal is what accounts for the border-straddling character of the fetish: the utopian dreams it incessantly rekindles, the way it works all the better because it fails.

For my purposes in this study, the structure of consciousness associated with the Freudian fetish is more relevant than its narrowly sexual content. In anthropological analyses, as in psychoanalysis, the fetish has functioned as the site of stubborn desires, which are reproduced through the very actions through which their bearers struggle to satisfy them. Consider Spyer's (1997) discussion of the ideas and practices associated with sea wives, underwater spirits seen as crucial to the livelihood of pearl-diving villagers on the Indonesian island of Aru. Spyer depicts the sea wives as a fetish that mediates between local society and the global economy that encompasses it. The sea wives offer pearls that could liberate Aruese divers from debt, but they also demand repayment in store-bought plates and jewelry. Through these gifts, the divers reproduce their obligations to Sino-Indonesian shopkeepers and the allure of the watery women who perpetually promise to release them from their economic plight. In Sangren's (1991) analysis of Chinese religion in Taiwan, Ma Tsu statues, covered with incense, appear to worshipers as an embodiment of magical power. But the residue is the trace not only of gifts of gratitude from those whom the goddess has helped but also of offerings burnt by others who seek her aid. Like the divers described by Spyer, these worshipers reproduce the very values that orient their practices through their recourse to a fetishized figure of power.

Taken as a moment in the reproduction of social relations and as a focus of disavowal, the concept of fetishism encourages these analysts to attend to constitutive contradictions, rather than reducing social phenomena to some preexisting force. On an elementary level, the fetishistic quality of the foreign, as it orients Biak practice, becomes clear when one considers the ambivalent nature of the category *amber*. Recall the early appearance of the word in mission grammars as an expletive, "an exclamation or oath, esp. one that is obscene" (*American Heritage Dictionary* 1982: 477). As I noted, the word might have evoked the sporadic attacks Papuan communities suffered at the hands of powerful outsiders. Yet the referent for such an expletive is not a particular entity; it is a particular frame of mind: the wonder, shock, fear, or anger that led Biak speakers to shout "Amberi!" What is fetishized in the economy this study examines is not what Pietz (1985: 7) describes as an irreducibly material object, but an irreducibly inexpressible experience. But while it denotes the unfamiliar, unprecedented, startling, and excessive, *amber* is nonetheless a Biak word. Through this paradox, in which an utterance tames the very strangeness it seeks to name, *amber* participates in the undecidable structure of the fetish. The truly foreign would be unthinkable, utterly resistant to categorization. The foreign, in whatever language, is already domesticated, from the moment it enters discourse in local terms.

Far from residing only on this level of abstraction, this fetishistic structure is discernible in the concrete settings in which Biaks living under the New Order dealt with this regime that in so many ways impinged upon their lives. In the first half of this study, I examine different arenas in which the Land of the Foreigners, a category that includes spaces associated with the Indonesian nation-state, was reproduced as a fetishized source of value, pleasure, and authority. In chapter 2, I consider the production of intimacy and social identity in the context of Biak families. I show how marriage, in particular, provided a setting in which social action reproduced the foreignness that oriented desire. Through an exploration of the relations of debt and displacement that define the intimate core of Biak kinship, I examine how my consultants constituted alien realms as a reservoir of inexhaustible wealth, which they used to recall, if not resolve, the loss of sisters and daughters to other groups. In chapter 3, which covers magic, music, and dance, I show how these genres of performance represent alien persons, objects, and places as a source of startling yet pleasurable experiences. The most striking example is Biak *wor*, a song form whose poetic structure reproduces the surprise said to inspire every song. At the same time that wor offered its New Order-era composers a way of responding to strange and shocking events, it ensured that encounters that might otherwise have seemed banal were recurrently coded as new. Chapter 3 shows how the pursuit of pleasure fueled an aesthetic that stressed the foreignness of national settings and institutions. It sets the stage for chapter 4, which examines how the pursuit of authority fueled interpretive practices that recreated the untranslatability of Christian and national texts. Comparing the performances of three big foreigners, I show how their translations of the Bible and New Order government rhetoric created an image of the Land of the Foreigners as the origin of communications whose full significance remained forever opaque.

In all of these chapters, one finds men and women emphasizing characteristics of words and things that other actors have downplayed in order to convey the impression of commensurate values, orderly routines, and transparent, transmissible meanings. Their practices mobilized, in a fetishistic fashion, the potential for alienation inherent in every social gesture, every instance of exchange, thought, or speech. This is not to say that these practices somehow reflected a more truthful understanding of the nature of representation and the wider geographies in which my consultants lived. Under New Order conditions, the more Biaks pursued the powers of outsiders, the more outsiders' viewpoints eluded them. In their quest for recognition from a local audience, they obscured a force that was omnipresent in the regency, in the form of national institutions and apparatuses that encouraged them to see themselves through very different eyes.

Thus one finds in the social arenas depicted in these three chapters a dynamic not unlike that evident in nationalist discourse: one in which the pursuit of an object proves incessant, for the quest reproduces the very conditions that prevent satisfaction. But this fetishism is associated with different visions of agency and personhood than those associated with membership in a modern nation-state. Unlike New Order nationality, as Pemberton and others have described it, foreignness was envisioned as occupying not the soul of a person, but rather the surface. Those who sought authority by virtue of their access to the Land of the Foreigners faced a different contradiction from that faced by those who claimed to express their innermost cultural selves. In their pursuit of recognition, the actors I consider in this study faced what Stewart describes as "the paradox of willed possession" (1995: 36; see also Keane 1997b; Du Bois 1993). They had to present their words, gestures, and objects as evidence of something other than their own intentions, and yet they had to be able to take credit for conveying them. They had to adhere to expectations regarding authoritative action that required the seat of agency to appear as displaced. In light of this dilemma, it is no accident that Biaks saw the skin as the surface that absorbed the invisible potency of foreign objects and places, as we shall see. As an intimate interface between the locality of an interior and an alien, outside world, this hybrid surface allowed Biaks to make absence present, as it were—to lay claim to the potency of arenas like the bureaucracy, while maintaining the alien character of such sources of power.

One can do more than just infer this conception of agency as a form of "practical consciousness" evident in quotidian interactions (Kroskrity 2000: 19). One finds a vivid figure of Biak fetishism and its contradictions in narratives and practices associated with Koreri, the name given to the messianic movement that has recurred throughout the region's colonial and postcolonial history. Kamma (1972) includes incidents from migrant communities in the Bird's Head and the Raja Ampat Islands, as well as the islands now included in Biak-Numfor and nearby Yapen-Waropen, when he documents 45 outbreaks of Koreri occurring over 112 years. In each case, followers gathered to welcome Manarmakeri, literally "The Itchy Old Man," the Biak ancestor believed to be the secret origin of foreign wealth and power. The Itchy Old Man embodies the disavowal at the heart of Biak sociality—the simultaneous recognition and denial that the foreign is a local creation. Yet this Old Man is by no means unambiguously local. The source of Manarmakeri's power is his itching skin, a repugnant substance that is the effect of an action—scratching—that literally reproduces its own cause. But the myth does more than just epitomize the logic of a sociocultural economy based on the fetishization of the foreign; it also marks the limits of this economy. Which takes us to a final site of inquiry, the utopian moment when the foreign, the local, and the national coincide.

Utopia

As most Papuan nationalists can tell you, the Morning Star depicted on the flag that flew over Biak City and other towns in the province refers to a central episode in the myth of Manarmakeri. The Itchy Old Man, it is said, gained the secret to creating foreign wealth and potency from this celestial body, whom he caught stealing palm wine from his tree. During my fieldwork in the early 1990s, older people hesitated to sing songs or tell stories associated with Manarmakeri, for fear of being labeled separatists by the Indonesian military. Even though the commanding officers I met seemed far less versed in local prophecy than some Biaks imagined they were, my friends' anxieties were not utterly unfounded. The Koreri movement of 1939–43, which was the most violent and tenacious in the long series of colonial-era uprisings, featured leaders who turned the messianic expectations associated with the myth in an explicitly political direction. The woman who started the outbreak, a healer named Angganeta Menufandu, appeared to her supporters as New Guinea's new queen. During the period of extended colonial rule that followed World War II, Biaks caught with Koreri paraphernalia such as loin clothes, flags, and magic sticks sometimes landed in jail (Galis 1946; de Bruyn 1948). Whereas under Dutch rule officials associated Koreri with the specter of Indonesian nationalism, under Indonesian rule, they associated the movement with the Free Papua Organization (I: Organisasi Papua Merdeka, or OPM). And, indeed, some of the guerrillas who hid in Biak's forested interior during the 1970s reportedly gained strength and courage by singing and dancing to Koreri songs (Kapissa 1980). Papuan nationalists claim Koreri as part of a broadly shared Papuan heritage of resistance (Sharp with Kaisiëpo 1994). Analysts have noted that, in the 1980s, nationalist intellectuals made a special effort to revive interest in the myth (Osborne 1985: 99; see also Defert 1996: 361).

In his speeches at the flag raising, Philip Karma never mentioned Koreri, although listeners accustomed to contemporary prophets' tendency to employ Christian terms may well have read millennial references into his messages. Still, it is possible to identify loose parallels between the demonstration and the World War II-era uprising. Both movements began through the initiative of leaders with experience outside the islands. Both movements occurred following the collapse of seemingly permanent regimes—the New Order, following the Asian financial crisis, and the Dutch colonial state, following the Indies' invasion by Japan. Both movements engaged followers in long bouts of singing, dancing, and praying, in growing encampments that leaders swore not to disband until the longed-for transformation occurred. The followers of both movements saw this transformation as foreshadowed by the arrival of messages and persons from abroad. Both movements began peacefully and grew increasingly more aggressive. In both cases, followers went on a violent rampage after the massacres that brought each uprising to an end. This is not to say that the flag raising failed to express recognizably nationalist aspirations. It is simply to point out what may have lain behind the protesters' remarkable courage: the fact that many envisioned international acknowledgement of the Papuan nation as leading to an eschatological transformation. The raising of the flag was supposed to elicit the arrival of powerful outsiders and engage the force of the divine.

Scholars of millenarianism have tended to classify Koreri as a "cargo cult": an organized effort to obtain, through ritualized methods, the commodities and authority possessed by outsiders (Lanternari 1963; Worsley 1968; Burridge 1960, 1969). As recent studies have suggested, however, the various movements that have classically fallen under this rubric are considerably more complicated in their origins and aspirations than the label would lead one to expect (Lindstrom 1990, 1993; Kaplan 1995; Tuzin 1997; Lattas 1998; see also Clastres [1975] 1995).[15] In lay person's terms, one can describe Koreri as a utopia: an imagined state of pleasure and perfection. Biaks past and present have captured the essence of Koreri, a Biak word that means "We Shed Our Skin," with the Biak phrase "K'an do mob oser," "We eat in one place." "Eating in one place. Everything we ask for will happen," explained Domingus Warseren, a descendant of Biromor, one of the Koreri prophets discussed in chapter 6. He described how Biromor provided a sign of the coming transformation by standing on the shore and summoning a fish for his astonished followers to eat. The author of a long manuscript on the World War II uprising elaborated on Domingus's observation that the phrase also meant, "We will become a nation." The participants wanted to "hold the power themselves. Sort of like nationalism. They didn't have any education; they didn't have any bureaucratic skills. But with the messiah, all that would change." Justina Wakwar, who was present at Angganeta's encampment, stressed another component of the dream. The dancers were after "Koreri, which is promised in the Bible. The living and the dead will be as one." Transforming a local topography and redrawing a global geography of power, the return of Manarmakeri was seen as obviating the need to toil or travel; no longer would Biaks have to raid distant places to earn recognition or simply to survive. But to speak of the earning of recognition in the context of Koreri is somewhat misleading, for with the return of Manarmakeri, there would no longer be any differences between Biaks and foreigners or among Biaks themselves. With the "opening" of Koreri, believers would participate in the recursive impulse epitomized in the Itchy Old Man's condition, with Manarmakeri's interminable cycle of suffering transformed into his followers' interminable cycle of pleasure. The distinctions generated by the fetishistic pursuit of the foreign would collapse as the faithful entered the unending state of "eating in one place."

It is not only in lay persons' terms that one can call Koreri a utopia. Louis Marin (1992) has described the emergence of the notion of utopia at the dawn of European modernity (see also 1984). Finding its paradigm as a fictive geography in More's book by the name, this new notion of utopia arose in conjunction with a new configuration of concepts, engaging such terms as "horizon," "limit," and "frontier." In such phrases as the "limitless horizon," words that once designated the boundaries of vision and power came to express dreams of infinity. Evoking both "no place" and "the happy place," utopia, in Marin's words, "names the limit, the gap between two frontiers or two continents, the old and the new worlds." Koreri, as an imagined space and state, diverges in important respects from the phenomenon analyzed by Marin. Koreri is not located in a fictive site beyond the horizon; it is anticipated as arising on Biak when the foreign and the local converge. Nevertheless, borrowing from Marin's description of utopia, Koreri could be described as deploying "a strange nominal figure of the frontier (horizon, limit), that is to say, a name that would constitute a distance, a gap neither before nor after affirmation, but 'in between' them" (1992: 411).[16] Evoking frontiers that are not only spatial but also conceptual, Koreri arises in between the two scales of sociality, Biak and Indonesian, that intersect in this study, each oriented to an object that can only be approached after the fashion of a mathematical limit: the foreign or the national as such. Moreover, to borrow from Marin yet again, Koreri "is not an image or a representation . . . it is the monogram of the art of pure fiction on all these boundaries and frontiers that human thought sketches out so as to achieve a knowledge shared by several human beings, that human will marks and displaces to become a collective power and to accomplish itself in common action" (ibid.: 412–13). Marin draws on Kant for the opposition between the image and the monogram, the former being the "product of the empirical faculty of reproductive imagination," the latter "a product of pure a priori imagination, through which, and in accordance with which, images themselves first become possible" (ibid.: 412). Marin's definition is useful in evoking the way Koreri figuratively articulates the logic of social action in Biak, along with a particular way of envisioning the wider world.

To the degree that Koreri does not simply figure the fictive origin of social differences but also promises an eschatological transformation that will collapse the social world, this Biak utopia is also an apocalypse, in Bull's (1999) sense of the term. Bull argues that all societies, in setting up the dichotomies that define social life and human thought, must contend with the contradiction presented by the indeterminate, those forms of impurity that both mediate and undermine conceptual distinctions. Unlike sacrifice, which commemorates the destruction of the indeterminate, or taboo, which regulates its presence, apocalyptic practice projects into the future an eschatological moment in which indeterminacy is reincorporated into everyday life. Bull's model accounts for many characteristics of Biak prophecy, above all the way that the "scapegoat," an old man excluded from his community, becomes the "apocalyptic hero" who will someday return (1999: 76).[17] But Koreri, as we will see, is not simply the byproduct of a universal predilection for dualism; one must approach the movement by way of the pragmatics of discourse, and not simply the universal structures of the mind. In this study, as the previous sections would suggest, I set Koreri in the context of what Keane (1997a) refers to as the "risks of representation"—those vicissitudes that stem from the fact that all identities are the product of recognition, a process dependent on media whose qualities render them vulnerable to subversion and loss. As Marin's formulations suggest, and the relationship between prophecy and day-to-day practice in Biak makes clear, these risks never appear transparently to social actors; the limits of representation are only discernible in figural form.

What concerns me in the second half of this book, where I take up the problem of Koreri, is not merely the apocalyptic, utopian character of the movement but also its recurrence under particular historical conditions. The challenge is not simply to draw connections between myth and prophecy, and the dilemmas of Biak sociality; it is to chart the conditions that have led Biaks to anticipate Manarmakeri's return. Given that Koreri promises reunion with the origin of foreignness, it should not be surprising to find that the apocalyptic longings associated with Manarmakeri have arisen at times when colonial and postcolonial authorities have pressured Biaks to see themselves through outsiders' eyes. Koreri is not simply a particular solution to a universal problem; it has provided, more importantly, a figure of the limit associated with a particular form of fetishistic desire. One finds a dynamic in Biak that is akin to that depicted by Abraham and Torok (1986, 1994), who account for the resilience of a historically specific form of fetishism, in which the other whom one might otherwise "introject"—that is, internalize as a point of reference for viewing one's identity—becomes "incorporated" as an alien body within the self. Rather than consciously perceiving themselves as they would appear to a beloved parent or sibling, Abraham and Torok's patients became their loved ones, possessed by thoughts and impulses that were not their own. To borrow Abraham and Torok's terms for a purpose unlike that for which they were coined, one could say that through Biaks' collective social practices, the foreign has been incorporated; it has not been introjected. The foreign has remained the object of a "contradictory and therefore utopian hope" that one will gain access to pleasures that others have promised, yet never fully allowed one to enjoy (1994: 116). At moments when Biaks have suddenly seen themselves from the perspective of outsiders, and thus discovered something new within their own society and culture, the startling closure of the gap between self and other has elicited a utopian reaction. In the place of the emergence of new conceptions of identity, believers have awaited the miracle of eating in one place.

Through Koreri, the force of national institutions and economies has been acknowledged, but only through narratives and practices that have projected their effects across an eschatological horizon. In chapter 5, I begin my exploration of how Biaks' conversion to national-cultural forms of subjectivity is both figured and deferred with a close reading of the myth of Manarmakeri. My analysis, which sets the myth in the context of narratives recounting the emergence of a modern Christian subject, reveals how the narrative provides an origin and endpoint for the fetishistic practices described in chapters 2, 3, and 4. I show how the conditions allowing for the adoption of new identities are registered within the myth, at the same time that their realization is postponed. In chapter 6, I consider the history of Koreri uprisings in the context of the forces of modernization that worked to integrate north-coastal New Guinea more fully into the Indies. At the same time that I place these uprisings in a broader historical context, I show why it makes sense to think of Koreri as more than merely a colonial invention (cf. Lindstrom 1993; Kaplan 1995). I focus on the changes that led up to the 1939–43 movement, exploring how missionary and government attempts to produce a docile Papuan subject set the stage for Manarmakeri's return. In chapter 7, I return to the recent New Order past to examine how men and women of different classes and generations responded to official efforts to revive Biak tradition. Here, I show how the recognition of outsiders, under conditions that seemed to herald Biaks' integration into the nation, had mildly millennial effects.

In each of these failed apocalypses, these evocations of utopia, one sees an acknowledgment of what Biak "foreigners" had to deny in order to sustain the alien basis of their authority—the degree to which national and global institutions and economies thoroughly penetrated local lives. But one also sees a figure—a monogram, in Marin's sense—of the dilemmas of sociality in Biak. Not just an effect of physical distances, the foreignness described in this study at once conjures and obscures what would be truly alien: the presence of a difference that could never be anticipated, never named. Refracted through these forms of domestication, one can discern something like that which "bears and haunts" discourse in every historical and ethnographic setting (Derrida 1976). But that does not mean that the dynamics I depict are any less the product of contingencies born of a particular era, of particular places and times.

Envoi: Between Awakenings

Beginning with an ethnographic analysis of practices observed in the early 1990s, ending with an investigation of the utopian crossings of Koreri that runs from the nineteenth century back to the recent past, *Raiding the Land of the Foreigners* explores the limits of the nation by way of what one might call the history of a particular New Order present. In Pemberton's study of the politics of culture at the height of the New Order's hegemony, he confronts the impossibility of fixing a definitive origin for the culturalist discourses and practices that lent legitimacy to the regime. He selects the relocation of the palace of the sultan of Surakarta, through Dutch East India Company intervention, as exemplary of the "seminal contradiction" that sustained New Order national-cultural longings. This choice, he admits, finds its rationale in "the conditions of New Order cultural discourse, conditions demanding that origins be repeatedly recovered" (1994: 25). The event is critical due to its elaboration in subsequent historical moments, and not because of its status as the intrinsic beginning of colonial hegemony, as such. Although the focus of this study differs in significant ways—not least in its relation to the New Order regime—any attempt to fix an origin for the fetishization of the foreign runs up against a similar historiographical dilemma. As Freud concluded, not only is it impossible to ascertain the reality of the trauma that gives rise to the fetish; reality is in some sense beside the point, given a dynamic that produces its own phantasmatic origin ([1918] 1963). In the case of Biak, this phantasmatic origin might be imagined as the trauma of first contact across a cultural boundary. Yet, as this study shows, such a boundary is only conceivable as the product of the very practices in which the fetishization of the foreign can be discerned.

This is not to argue that the fetishistic logic depicted in this study is in some sense eternal. It clearly reflects Biak's position in a regional and global geography that has taken on new configurations over time. It emerged in dialogue with colonial and postcolonial policies and practices, reflecting the problematic position of New Guinea in the Indies and the Indonesian nation-state. Although there is no way to fix an origin for the dynamic that informs them, one can, with some imaginative effort, date the emergence of the general configuration of practices this study describes. In New Order Biak, people not only valorized unprecedented experiences and alien things, turning signs of disruption into signifiers of identity; they also valorized alien narratives. The most celebrated of these narratives was that contained in Christian texts. If one were asked to name the year when the Christian Bible began to appear as a translation of local myth, a logical candidate would be 1908, when communities on the islands that make up today's Biak-Numfor began to embrace Christianity. This evangelical victory occurred during the mass conversions that swept northwestern New Guinea in the years following the establishment of a permanent government presence in the region. The Dutch Protestant missionaries who officiated over this "awakening," after fifty years of preaching to the Papuans more or less in vain, were quite aware of the risk that the Biaks who converted saw their action as inaugurating a messianic transformation. And yet, during this period when colonial steamships and soldiers finally reached the region, they welcomed any indication of the breaking of a Christian dawn.

Like the awakening of Papuan Biak that has followed the fall of the New Order, the awakening of Christian Biak involved the efforts of an individual who mediated between local society and a wider arena. Philip Karma's predecessor, in this regard, was a native evangelist named Petrus Kafiar, a former slave who became a Christian after mission leaders bought his freedom from some local warriors who had captured him in a raid. Raised in an Ambonese family, educated on Java, versed in the niceties of Scripture and fluent in Dutch and Malay, Petrus Kafiar appeared in mission publications as a model for the "saved" Papuan to come. But Petrus Kafiar was also a foreigner *avant la lettre*. His ability to persuade so many Biaks to convert to Christianity rested in part on the efforts of individuals on the islands who lured him home in order to claim him as their kin.

The story told in this book unfolds in the interval between the awakenings led by Petrus Kafiar and Philip Karma. Although I argue that the fetishistic dynamic on which I focus has proven remarkably resilient, that does not mean that I take it as a permanent fixture of social life on Biak; its fate in post-New Order Indonesia remains to be seen. Yet the particular ways in which New Order Biaks played upon the limits of national identity bear witness to a dynamic that has persisted across major periods of transformation. To catch a first glimpse of the basis of this persistence, let us begin at the dawn of an era, with the rivalry and longing that led to Petrus Kafiar's return.

CHAPTER TWO

Frontier Families

IN 1908, in a settlement on the eastern edge of the Netherlands Indies, the Johannes van Hasselt Society for Bible Study and Prayer lost a founding member when Petrus Kafiar's mother finally succeeded in her quest to bring him home. From Supiori, one of the islands that make up today's Biak-Numfor, she had frequently visited Mansinam, a popular trading stop on the Bird's Head Peninsula at Doreh Bay, where two Germans established a mission post in 1855. There, her son was one of Johannes van Hasselt's Papuan assistants, who started an organization named in the senior evangelist's honor in an effort to further New Guinea's Christian "awakening."[1] Like the other Papuans who belonged to the society, the young Kafiar clansman was a "redeemed" or "free-bought" (*vrijgekocht*) slave, as the Dutch Protestants who took over operations along the Bird's Head called the women and children whose freedom they purchased in an effort to expand their tiny native flock (see Figure 3). Much to the consternation of the Utrecht Mission Society (Utrechtsche Zendingsvereeniging), which funded the field, former captives made up the vast majority of the small number of "heathens" who converted to Christianity in northwestern New Guinea during the nineteenth century (see Adriani et al. 1896; Kamma 1976, 1977). These captives had been abducted by Papuan seafarers, who had long included slaves as part of the tribute they delivered to Tidore. Some of these seafarers, like the migrants from Numfor who lived near the mission post, also kept servants from the interior to do their gardening. Others, like the Biaks, integrated many of the Moluccans and Papuans they captured into their clans or *keret*; a slave would drink, then bathe with water in which an ornament was immersed to change his or her "lead" blood into the gold or silver blood of the free (Kamma 1976: 58, 227). Even in the late nineteenth century, warfare was common among the coastal Papuans, who launched surprise raids in their enormous canoes, taking heads, booty, and, increasingly, captives to sell in distant ports. The missionaries' practice of buying and manumitting enslaved women and children arguably added to the unrest in this long unpacified region.

Petrus Kafiar was a typical victim. Raiders from a neighboring village abducted the young Biak when he was seven years old and delivered him to Mansinam, where a Moluccan carpenter paid fifty florins for the boy. A Christian convert who was himself married to a "free-bought" slave, the Moluccan "foster father" raised young Petrus according to the strictures set by

Figure 3. Johannes van Hasselt and his wife, daughter, and many Papuan foster children

the Dutch pastor and his wife. Baptised, given a new name, and educated in the mission school, Petrus and the other "foster children" enjoyed an odd sort of freedom. Although in theory they were at liberty to leave the compound, in practice they remained utterly dependent on their foster parents for food, clothing, and, above all, security. Cut off from their natal kin and forbidden to take part in "heathen" celebrations, the "free-bought" Christians remained slaves in the eyes of their "free-born" neighbors, who felt little compunction at recapturing those who strayed too far from their masters. And yet, despite Petrus's apparent alienation from local society, the bonds of Biak kinship still were strong.

In the wake of an attack, when Biak families located captured relatives they usually tried to buy them back (Feuilletau de Bruyn 1920: 26–27; see also Held 1957: 228). In the case of Petrus Kafiar, the young man's relatives tracked him down in 1898, not long after his return from the Protestant seminary for native evangelists in Depok, Java, when a trading expedition returned from the mission post to Maundori, Petrus's natal village, and informed his mother that her son was still alive.[2] Petrus's brother, an infamous warrior, was the first to venture to Mansinam; his mother followed on later trips. Petrus treated the "heathen" woman "tactfully," the Dutch missionaries noted (Kamma 1977: 619). Dressed in a loincloth, she squatted in his room, chewing betel nut and smoking, and Petrus never acted ashamed. She finally succeeded in recovering her son with the family's promise to embrace Christian ways. At his family's urging, Petrus visited Biak, where he found the locals remarkably attentive to his message.[3] Although the islands were only a two-day paddle from the mission post, this tour was the first of its kind. In the almost fifty years since the first European "brothers" had settled in Mansinam, the missionaries had only encountered Biak's so-called "pirates" when they raided and traded along the mainland. Initially, the Dutch missionaries refused to grant Petrus's request to settle in the islands, whose inhabitants were notorious for their *raakzucht* (lust for plunder, a Dutch neologism from the Biak word for "raid"). It was not until 1908, after other coastal groups began to convert, that F.J.F. van Hasselt, Johannes's son and successor, escorted Petrus Kafiar to Maundori and installed him as Biak's first teacher and evangelist. Biak's Christian awakening had finally begun.

The tale of Petrus Kafiar's capture and return to Biak was the stuff of stirring mission propaganda. Protestant publishers in the Netherlands produced versions of the story that had the Lord's fingerprints on every page.[4] Yet even in the absence of divine intervention, the saga remains remarkable. At a time when global transformations were setting the stage for coastal New Guinea's Christian conversion, the Biak evangelist's return to his village bore witness to a set of local forces. At a critical juncture, when colonial steamships and soldiers crossed the reefs that sheltered Biak, some of its "heathens" reclaimed a relative with powerful friends. In a certain sense, Petrus Kafiar was the islands' first local foreigner—in contemporary Biak parlance, an *amber*.

It is fitting that Petrus Kafiar's mother was the one to bring him home. The path from the foreign to the local followed the field of debt and desire that connected male and female kin. In the early 1990s, under very different conditions, sexual difference mediated between Biak and the Land of the Foreigners, *Sup Biaki* and *Sup Amber*. In public ceremonies and the intimate gestures of everyday life, foreign wealth became "proper" to local selves by passing across a gendered divide. Objects that recalled distant encounters entered circulation as gifts from brothers to sisters. Mothers conserved what their brothers expended, turning "booty" into the media of identity. Porcelain bowls, silver bracelets, imported clothing and cash, and other ceremonial valuables were treasured for their exoticness, as were the Tidoran honorary titles that long had circulated on the islands. Foreign wealth was seen as conveying the extraordinary qualities a person needed to succeed in foreign worlds. By encouraging her brothers to give her resources that enhanced her children's prospects, a woman demonstrated her worth. This aspect of the fetishization of the foreign depended on mothers who presented themselves as the source of personhood, and on sisters who engaged their brothers in extravagant exchanges that benefited the women's daughters and sons.

From the perspective of Biak kinship, the Land of the Foreigners appeared as a source of both violence and value, as the home of dangerous strangers and long-lost kin. In this chapter, I show how this representation was at once a product and precondition of the forms of social action through which persons and their reputations were produced. Beginning with a household map, I move through the relationships that defined family life in Biak under the New Order: mothers and children, brothers and sisters, and brothers and brothers. My goal is to link the figure of the foreign to the tensions that arose as Biaks pursued recognition—in their words, a "name"—by exchanging objects and words. The practices I describe fueled a dialectic that was as important in contemporary Biak as it had been in the past. However integrated into the Indonesian nation Biak households may have sometimes seemed, they remained the home of frontier families, groups created through their members' dealings with a wealthy and threatening outside world. In the sphere of kinship, as in the other arenas described in this book, the prevailing dynamic was fetishistic. Biaks reproduced an endlessly alien Land of the Foreigners in the very act of raiding it for value and power.

The Dislocation of Kinship

We begin our exploration of the fetishization of the foreign at an obvious starting point. Domestication, one might say, begins at home. Still, this strategy is problematic in some respects. Readers familiar with the New Order's cultural politics will find the formal ceremonies described in this chapter an unlikely place to look for the roots of subversion. The integration of Irian Jayans into the ranks of orderly Indonesian subjects rested on the production of tokens of local culture, of which weddings proved the paradigmatic type. I attended several elite weddings in Biak in the early 1990s that took place in a large reception hall, equipped with neat rows of chairs and a decorated stage on which the bride and groom sat in state. Although the couples were dressed in "traditional" Biak costumes—from the groom's loincloth to the bird of paradise perched in the bride's hair—their model was clearly a "traditional" Javanese wedding. It was not only in these obviously novel performances of local culture that the influence of New Order ideology was felt. Adding to the impact of earlier episodes of colonial repression, the New Order's promotion of the nuclear family was no doubt responsible for the vitality of Biak weddings and the languishing of other kinds of "rites" (compare Brenner 1998: 237). It was easy to conduct research on marriage in New Order Biak; this was where Biak's official culture lived.

Still, something else resided in the Biak wedding feasts I attended, as well:

other sets of assumptions about difference and intimacy, other horizons in space and time. To get a sense of these horizons, one must turn to different accounts of regional culture—accounts potentially supportive of New Order representations, but more complicated in their implications for the modern nation-state. Over the years, kinship has played a critical role in colonial and postcolonial efforts to define a regional "field of study" in Southeast Asia. J.P.B. de Josselin de Jong, the so-called Father of Dutch Structuralism, identi-fied four features of the structural core of Indonesian cultures, old and new: circulating connubium (mother's brother's daughter marriage), double uni-lineal descent, cosmological dualism, and—almost as an afterthought—"the reaction of indigenous cultures to certain powerful cultural influences from without" (de Josselin de Jong [1935] 1977: 174). Oliver Wolters, who fore-grounds the reaction to outside influences in his (1982) model of early Southeast Asian polities, took a more integrated approach. To account for the capacity of these polities to "localize" the foreign, Wolters stressed the quali-ties of their "prehistoric" predecessors. These were small, localized societies, composed of cognatic kin groups, that is, groups whose members reckoned descent by way of both male and female forebears. "Prehistoric" leaders were not hereditary chiefs but "men of prowess," individuals whose authority rested on their deeds and not just on their birth. These tendencies persisted into the historical period, Wolters insisted, even as the region's polities grew in scale and complexity.

> What gave distinctive shape to public life in Southeast Asia itself was a cultural emphasis on "person" and "achievement" rather than on "group" and "hereditary status." At the same time—and in contrast with South and East Asia, with their emphasis on ascribed status and collective unities such as family, lineage, and caste—there was a downgrading in the importance of lineage based on claims to status through descent. Society had to be continuously monitored to spot potential leaders in a particular generation, and this outlook encouraged the habit of "pres-entmindedness." "Government" was not a matter of elaborate institutions but of a relaxed unbureaucratic style of public life, where importance was attached to man-management and ceremony and where personal qualities of leadership and example played the major role. (Wolters 1994: 6 in Day 1996: 392–393)

Wolters's portrait finds support in Anderson's ([1972] 1990) depiction of the Javanese notion of power—as a substance, not a relation, dispersed through-out the polity and concentrated at the center like the light from a lamp. More recent writers have complicated both of these models in ways highly relevant to kinship in Biak, given its history of relations with Southeast Asian polities. Some have turned their attention to the ideologies of the periphery and how they draw upon and recast the ideologies of the center (Atkinson 1989; Tsing 1993; Spyer 1996; Tooker 1996). Others have redressed a misplaced stress on "male achievement" by relating regional notions of "power" to regional concepts of gender and siblingship (Errington 1989, 1990; Day 1996; Carsten 1995a, 1995b; Cannell 1996, 1999). Still others have broken the boundaries of colonial ethnology by extending the field of comparison to encompass a wider Austronesian-speaking world (Bellwood et al. 1995; Fox 1995; see also Blust 1984: 32). Their work has shown how "cognatic kinship" and the "downgrading of lineages" find expression in social systems of varied forms.

In a sweeping treatment of the dynamics of Southeast Asian kinship, Errington (1989, 1990) proposes a model that divides the societies of the region into two distinct categories. Errington's "centrist archipelago," where people practice endogamous marriage, includes both hierarchical polities and the "level" societies in their periphery. The first locates power in a still and silent center, the second in a dangerous "outside." The "exchange archipelago," found in places inhabited by exogamous kin groups, includes societies in eastern Indonesia and Sumatra that are divided into named patrilineal "houses." Here, power derives from a lost unity. Forever attempting to heal the divide, these societies practice mother's brother's daughter's marriage, which ranks groups in terms of their status as wife-givers and wife-takers, that is, according to their place in the so-called "flow of life" (see also van Wouden 1968; Fox 1980; Traube 1986).[5]

For Errington (1990: 48–51), the importance of siblingship in orienting diverse forms of social order lies in its ability to mediate between similarity and two kinds of difference: birth order, which provides a basis for hierarchy on the "centrist" model, in which all society is fictively encompassed in one all-embracing "house," and gender, which, in the model of "exchange," mediates between ranked exogamous groups (see also Boon 1990: 222–223; Barraud 1994). Studies that draw most suggestively on Errington's framework have revealed the ambiguities at work in relationships, which, to begin with, hold the potential for bearing contradictory meanings. Building on the insight that Errington's categories can be seen as transformations of one another, with "centrist societies haunted by the principle of dualism and the dualistic ones haunted by the principle of centrism" (Carsten 1997: 26), both Cannell (1999) and Carsten (1995a, 1997) have described, in contrasting ethnographic and historical situations, how an interplay between countervailing tendencies might turn on the transformative character of cognatic siblingship, with its capacity to move between "sharing" and inequality and to turn affines and spouses into kin.

Although these studies point to the polyvalent meanings of kinship as "process" in "centrist" settings outside the context of a fixed hierarchy determined by birth, my findings from Biak offer a complication in the relation between siblingship and affinity said to prevail where marriage exchange is the norm. I have mentioned the keret, Biak's named, patrilineal, patrilocal descent group. According to some sources, the word derives from the term for the small cabins that stood in the middle of the enormous, seafaring canoes once used in the region (Adatrechtbundels 1955a: 150). But there is evidence that the keret also has been imagined as a "house": from the large clan dwellings where my older consultants remembered living to the fact that many keret surnames begin with the Biak word for "house" (rum).[6] The contemporary kerets I encountered in the early 1990s varied in size and complexity, from a few households in a single village to dozens of families living in different parts of Biak, Numfor, and the Raja Ampat Islands. Larger kerets were divided into "rooms" (B: sim), which consisted of the descendants of a particular ancestral brother who was remembered in more or less personalized terms. My consultants often spoke of members of a keret as having interests in common, as when the musician and scholar Sam Kapissa explained why Biaks were more "open" with foreign ethnographers than with their fellow Biaks. "They think, 'Why should I give a college degree to a kid from another clan? His clan will be great (I: hebat), and mine will be just like this!'" People described weddings and other feasts as entailing a similar struggle for "greatness," even though the individuals who participated on either "side" never coincided with the full membership of a clan. In practical terms, keret membership had two significant consequences: kerets provided people with surnames and rights to land. My consultants divided Biak and Supiori into keret domains, most extending in parallel columns from the coast into the interior. These domains' boundaries were marked by natural features of the landscape and were validated by narratives that described the travels of keret ancestors. Within these domains, male members of a keret had the right to open taro gardens on uncultivated land.[7] Sons and, less frequently, daughters inherited use rights to the plots their parents had farmed, along with any trees they had planted to mark their claim. Kerets allocated resources with varying degrees of formality; in some West Biak clans, a keret head (I: kepala keret, B: mananwir) supposedly oversaw the division of house plots and gardening land. Yet even members of more loosely organized kerets united during the disputes that erupted when outsiders tried to purchase land.

Significant for my argument in this chapter is the fact that not only men but also women were regarded as permanent members of the keret into which they were born. Boys and girls automatically inherited their keret identity from their fathers. Women retained their keret names after they married, although for official purposes they sometimes used the hyphenated form common in Germany and the Netherlands. Depending on the context, someone might refer to a bureaucrat's wife by her husband's position ("Mrs. District Chief"), but her keret identity remained common knowledge. Women contributed and received bridewealth for their siblings as members of their natal keret, and if their kerets had special taboos or powers, they inherited them. A female member of the district parliament told me why this was the case: "You can't change your blood (I: *darah*); it always stays the same."

This stress on a married woman's ongoing membership in her natal keret had far-reaching implications during the period of my fieldwork. With a few exceptions discussed below, the Biak kerets I encountered were exogamous. Villagers tended to marry spouses from their own or neighboring communities, but sometimes went further afield. Although "credit marriages" (I: *kawin kredit*) were quite common, young and old concurred in the belief that the groom's family should eventually pay bridewealth to the bride's, and that the bride's relatives should reciprocate with ongoing gifts to the couple and their children. Certain kerets in the North Biak villages where I collected detailed marriage histories made a habit of frequent intermarriage: a de facto sort of sister exchange, my consultants noted. An outmarried woman's special claim to the affections of her natal relatives motivated repeated exchanges between bride-givers and bride-takers, and repeated unions over the longer term. When I asked Niko Mambos, a young village chief, to describe the bond between brothers and sisters, he spoke of love and attenuated loss. "Brothers, sisters, they're all siblings. But people value their sisters more. Women are given to other people to marry. We go along (I: *kami ikut*)." Indeed, in my experience, brothers did follow after their out-married sisters, ideally bringing with them the lion's share of the bridewealth they had received in the form of gifts for these women's daughters and sons.

Where, as Boon (1990: 219) puts it, "the ideal of mother's brother's daughter marriage simultaneously divides and repairs society; that is, the values constitute 'society' as reparably divided," Biak ideology, as I knew it in the early 1990s, took the irreducibility of divisions to an extreme. My consultants described their society as consisting of named "houses" among which bride-givers were superior to bride-takers. But, like members of the "level" societies of the uplands, the men and women who made up these groups prevented the emergence of a stable hierarchy. Biaks have never practiced cross-cousin marriage (cf. Platenkamp 1984: 176 ; Visser 1984: 199; Barraud 1994: 99; Teljeur 1994: 184–85).[8] Women and wealth have never traveled in a unidirectional fashion, but have continually doubled back to each group. The "reparation" described by Boon would come with the assurance that one's spouse belonged to the same "flow" as one's mother and sister. But the Biaks I knew were not satisfied with the replacement of siblings by spouses; nor, as I explain in chapter 5, which discusses the apocalyptic myth of Manarmakeri, were they content to relegate the prospect of "unity" to the past. Forever projected onto a dangerous "outside," power remained mobile and unpredictable. No one could monopolize its "source."

Scholars of Southeast Asia have invited us to consider the role of kinship in shaping the region's early history. The data from Biak invite us to complicate the puzzle by viewing matters dialectically. One way to account for the features taken as distinctive to Southeast Asia may be to consider the nature of historical relations between societies and the way they interact with the tensions at work in each group. In New Order Biak, as I hope to show, there were clear connections between a "downgrading" in the importance of descent and the ongoing adoption of foreign elements. But this society's capacity and tendency to "localize" the foreign was not merely the effect of a stress on male achievement. It had to do with the way in which mothers presented themselves as a channel for extraordinary forms of value. Those "alien" to the patriline were key to its reproduction—and key to the reproduction of a fetishized outside world.

This comparative project is, of course, complicated by Biak's colonial history, as well as by the fact that the localization of foreign elements is scarcely limited to "early Southeast Asia." Some forty years ago, writing of the neighboring Waropen, the Dutch anthropologist G. J. Held described a society with many features in common with Biak: a tradition of trading and raiding, the stress placed on relations between brothers and sisters, the importance of foreign valuables in ceremonial exchange (1957).[9] At the time when Held's study was published, according to many of his Dutch readers, none of western New Guinea's native societies had anything in common with their Indonesian counterparts at all. In line with recent scholarship on South Moluccan societies, this chapter stresses the importance of the brother-sister relationship to the constitution of stable social entities and the temporal dynamics that connect discrete groups (see McKinnon 1991; Pauwels 1994; Barraud 1994). But it follows the lead of Weiner (1985, 1992) and Munn (1986) in linking structural outcomes to the phenomenological perspectives of social actors who pursue recognition through exchange. The relationship between men's pursuit of "fame" and women's production of "value" has proven as important in Biak as it is in the Massim, that well-studied corner of today's Papua New Guinea (see Weiner 1976). The force of circumstances, as well as the character of Biak society, forces one to look east as well as west for analogies. But Biak's marginal position also forces one to confront the limits of regional models, which always reflect specific histories of rule.

The dynamics described in this chapter should lead us to ponder what lay behind the complicity of elite Biaks who staged "traditional" New Order weddings. The irony of New Order efforts to revive and reform "Papuan" culture was not lost on many of my Biak friends. But on another level, they viewed the luminaries who spearheaded such initiatives as providing evidence of their mastery of alien worlds. To capture this level, where weddings participated in the production of "foreigners," requires an analysis that links formal performances to quotidian encounters as subtle as a brother's glare or a cousin's caress (cf. Cannell 1999). In raiding the Land of the Foreigners for its violence and value, the people I describe in this chapter responded to a sense of loss and indebtedness whose ultimate origins were impossible to place. Those who tried to turn Biak weddings into emblems of Indonesian national culture always ran up against a stubborn remainder. In New Order Biak, domestication was never more than temporary: the beast that slept by the hearth began and ended as something wild.

Front Doors, Back Doors

The raiders came from the sea, the teacher Petrus Kafiar's biographers reported in their accounts of his enslavement.[10] Petrus's family lost their young son in an instant of terror and mayhem. They recovered him decades later after painstaking negotiations. Petrus's story tells us something about the very different passages leading between Biak and the Land of the Foreigners. Swept away in an explosion of unpredictable potency, he was recovered at the gentle urging of female kin. Petrus Kafiar's movement between the foreign and the local took place in the context of a broader mapping of trajectories: through domesticated space, through the life cycle, through generational time. In New Order Biak, this mapping remained legible in the lived geography of rural and urban homes.

In the nineteenth and early twentieth centuries, European explorers described the layout of the area's coastal houses (Forrest [1780] 1969: 103– 104; de Bruyn Kops 1850: 174, 202; Wallace [1896] 1986: 499–500, 511– 512; Robide van der Aa 1879: 77, 197; von Rosenberg 1875: 77, 197; van Eck 1881: 387– 88; Lorentz n.d.: 195–96; see also Goudswaard 1863: 29– 30; Geissler 1857; Feuilletau de Bruyn 1920: 30–34). Raised on poles over the tidal flats, the collective house, or *rumsom*, inhabited by members of Biak's named patrilineal clans, or keret, was split down the center by a hallway over which hung an enormous canoe (see Figure 4). The hall opened on both sides onto five or more small apartments, where each married couple had a hearth, a sleeping mat, and a trunk or basket for valued possessions. During the day, men sat on the protected front porch, smoking as they repaired their spears and harpoons. Women sat on an open rear veranda, pounding bark cloth and weaving baskets as they chatted with relatives and friends. Visitors who approached the front of the house came over a horizon where a raiding party just as easily might appear. Visitors who approached the back made their way from the forest across a rickety walkway of planks. A European helped into the house from shore could expect a far warmer reception than one who approached it by boat (Forrest [1780] 1969: 103– 104; de Bruyn Kops 1850: 202). Canoe-shaped, with a canoe stored along its backbone, the house was bounded by a masculine landing and a feminine bridge. Petrus Kafiar, one might surmise from this floor plan, left by the front door and returned by the back.

Over a century later, the contemporary Biak household seemed to have

Figure 4. An illustration of a *rumsom* in Doreh Bay, not far from Mansinam, 1839

little in common with its predecessor. In a campaign continued under Indonesian rule, the colonial government split up the "unhygienic" group dwellings and moved their residents onto dry land.[11] Yet the logic of the *rumsom* still infused the most "modern" Biak homes. In the early 1990s, the children and grandchildren of early teachers, like Petrus Kafiar, filled the ranks of Biak's urban elite. Many of them lived in houses built for Dutch soldiers on the windswept heights above the airport. On the "Ridge," Biak dwellings displayed the same watchful face as those in the villages. A visitor who approached someone's residence from the front found it locked, curtained, and dark. A tap on the glass met with silence, then a muffled whisper as a child was sent to peak through the curtain. "Guest!" he or she hissed, and scuffling ensued, as the head of the household made him or herself presentable. Just as a good Biak guest approached a front door cautiously, a good host received a visitor slowly and deliberately, as if a sudden motion might cause the stranger to bolt. Many moments often had to pass before a caller actually made it through the door. Having endured this strained welcome, a guest would have detected little to distinguish a middle-class Biak household from its counterparts elsewhere in Indonesia (see Shiraishi 1986). Male visitors—and female researchers or civil servants—sat in the guestroom with its upholstered furniture, plastic flowers, television, and decorative plates. A visitor who ventured beyond it onto the open back porch found a relaxed domestic scene. Scattered fibers and rinds bore witness to the family's passion for betel nut. At a wobbly wooden table, women in housedresses gossiped and gulped tea. On a stool nearby, a young girl squatted over a bucket of laundry. Seated on the cool concrete floor, an old woman wove a basket and rocked a grand-child, pausing occasionally to correct her children on some aspect of family lore. The house seemed to divide into a public, predominately male façade and a private, predominately female core.

Yet a closer examination of Biak homes complicates this predictable map-ping of gender and space. A comparison proves revealing. Middle-class Java-nese households in the mid-1980s were divided into increasingly intimate zones. Visitors sat in the front room; family members watched television in the next room back; in an interior courtyard behind the dining room one found the domestic "help" (Shiraishi 1986: 94–100).[12] The Biak households I visited had a front, for strangers, and a back, for everyone else, including the nieces and daughters who took the place of servants. As important as the home's depth was what one found at its heart. One penetrated the layers of a Javanese household to find a center that was feminine and contained (Geertz 1961: 46). One pierced the layers of a Biak household to find oneself back in the street. Biak's domestic center stood open to the neighborhood. The inti-mate core of a Biak home was not really a core at all; it was a gate.

One might be tempted to explain the *rumsom* and its successors as prod-ucts of a regional pattern in which women stand for the autochthonous and men for foreign worlds (see Sahlins 1981; 1985: esp. 73–103; McKinnon 1991: 79–82, 95–97). But the feminine portals at the rear of the Biak homes I knew best connected their households to more than the families' land. Sitting in the shade of the porch or under a tree, the members of Sister Sally Bidwam's urban household kept tabs on who was loitering at a nearby shop or getting out of a taxi in the midday sun. Neighbors cut through the yard and stopped to chat. Conversations on the porch even seemed to open out-ward. Sally's guestroom was the sphere of formal Indonesian; her back porch echoed with tall tales, loud laughter, and rapid talk in a mixture of tongues. A young woman got a scolding in Indonesian and Biak. An old man slipped in some Dutch or English to punctuate a story or joke. Newcomers joined the discussion. No walls or passageways separated the yard from the town. At any time, night or day, relatives of all degrees and walks of life took the well-worn path to the porch from the road.

In Biak City, as in the villages, people did their best to transform front-door guests into back-porch kin. When I first arrived in Biak, my friend Ricky often came to Sally's house to visit. An activist raised in a distant city, Ricky was a rare figure among my Biak acquaintances: someone whom my family did not already know. At first, Sally froze whenever she heard Ricky's motorcycle. After letting him in the front door, she would retreat to a safe distance as we conversed. A stiff formality pervaded her encounters with my friend—until Ricky found a place on Sally's social map, thanks to the discovery of a shared relative in his grandparents' generation. After that, Ricky started calling at the rear of the house. Boisterous greetings took the place of suspicious stares; the happy discovery of a genealogical connection made my friend the butt of good-natured jokes. By using the back door, Ricky established himself as family. Classificatory or close, kinship formed the route from the dangerous world of strangers into the affectionate core of a Biak home.

It was a special kind of kinship that marked the way into a Biak household. If the back porch was a household's core and/or gate, outsiders passed into and/or through it most readily by virtue of a shared female relative. The descendants of brothers and sisters called each other *famili*, an Indonesian word derived from the Dutch, which is used for the Biak terms *napirem* (cross-cousin), *mebin* (father's sister or mother's brother's wife), *imem* (mother's brother or father's sister's husband), and *fno* (brother or sister's child). The affection that prevailed among these relatives was said to recall the love of siblings separated by marriage. One gets a sense of the contrast between such relatives and strangers by considering the gingerly way people approached new acquaintances. A good hostess, I was told, should never bring her guests tea and biscuits too quickly. Instead, it was better to postpone these little prestations, so that her callers would not think they were being paid to leave. The fragile bonds created in the front of the house differed dramatically from the durable debts that linked those in back. Bound by "ties that never release," as my consultants put it, the denizens of the porch were joined in the memory of an out-married sister and a dead mother, whose gifts could never be forgotten or repaid.

As I hope to show in what follows, the way into the heart of a Biak household was through its inhabitants' stomachs. In the next section, I examine how the mothers I met used food and the idiom of feeding to create indebtedness. When someone ate a woman's cooking, he or she entered a lasting relationship. A mother's status depended on her power to restrain her appetites so that others could "eat first." By deferring their own consumption, these mothers were able to make gifts that controlled others' memories and minds.

Mothers and Children

On a dark night in Sopen, West Biak, Laurensina Wanma told her relatives and me an old story. One day, two brothers ventured deep into the forest and killed a gigantic boar. Before returning to the coast, the brothers decided to roast the meat. To find a flame to light the fire, the younger brother followed a curl of smoke to an apparently empty little house. Reaching out to take a brand from the hearth, the boy was shocked to discover that he was in the home of a talking skull. When Doberok (the Noisy Thing) asked the younger brother why he needed a light, he lied about the menu, sure that the skull would demand a share of the pork. But Doberok was not so easily deceived. Speaking in verse, the skull retorted, "You can't be eating shrimp; I own all the shrimp. You can't be eating mushrooms; I own all the mushrooms." Finally, the younger brother told the skull the truth, and Doberok fulfilled his request. After accepting some cooked taro, the boy rushed away, hoping to elude his grisly host. But Doberok's gift of food prevented the skull's guest from escaping. The skull propelled itself along on two sticks, calling the boy, who had no choice but to reply. The bits of taro in his mouth and stomach cried out, "Over here!"[13]

When the old woman reached this part of the legend, many of us laughed. Anyone who had ever enjoyed a Biak mother's hospitality could appreciate the boy's predicament. Woe to the guest who attempted to escape a Biak household without a meal and some provisions for the road. My visit to Sopen was to be no exception: I set off the next day, bloated on sago pudding and burdened with a squawking chicken, a bag of taro, some betel nut, and some fruit. My "mother" in North Biak never let me through her door without feeding me—even if I was on my way to a feast. Like the Noisy Thing that claimed to "own" all nourishment, these Biak mothers knew the power of food.

As the story of Doberok makes clear, gifts of food in Biak have always insisted on a reply. During my fieldwork, the most immediate return to a generous hostess was her family's reputation. To call someone "starving" was a terrible insult. The plentiful provisions assembled for the smallest social gathering reflected how hard people worked to avoid falling short. A rural feast was considered successful if there were lots of leftover refreshments. Prayer meetings in town always featured more pastries than the faithful possibly could consume. Even a friend who professed a hatred for what she saw as "heathen" bouts of gluttony never hosted her Protestant brethren without investing in dozens of cream puffs. Abundant food was supposed to draw abundant guests, the counters in a neighborhood contest for what my consultants called "respect" (I: penghargaan).

For the women who controlled their households' larders, gifts of food also yielded personal status. As Biaks often told me, a "good woman" (B: bin syowe) would call birds from the sky and paddlers from the sea to invite them to eat. If a reputation for virtue was the reward for service to strangers, women received tangible returns when they fed particular people. At the time of my fieldwork, Sally Bidwam began a feud with her classificatory brother's widowed mother when she starting serving lunch to the young man, who drove a taxi in Biak City. Another friend told me about a man who had taken a second wife: he had to dine each night at two separate tables in order to keep his household at peace. Sooner or later, the woman who served someone a meal might find herself in a position to influence his or her decisions. Whether the reward was transportation or a husband's salary, gifts of food created a commitment that enabled the "feeder" to make demands of the "fed."

The most important bond created by feeding connected mothers and their children. A woman could not assert herself through the medium of food until she had a family of her own. The humblest members of most of the households I visited were the unmarried daughters and nieces who performed the heavy domestic work. Likewise, young wives remained under their mother-in-laws' thumbs until they had their own children to nurture and command. But motherhood was not simply a biological function. Female civil servants sometimes refused to marry, but they rarely gave up having a family. They borrowed or adopted their relatives' offspring, as did widows and divorced or married women who wanted to add to their brood.

What these women sought by becoming mothers was recognition as the creators of recognized persons: individuals who were not "just anyone" (I: *sembarang orang*). The prototype for such a person was the civil servant, someone whom everyone in the neighborhood (including his or her parents) identified with his or her role: Mr. Teacher (I: *Pak Guru*), Mrs. Local Soldier (I: *Ibu Babinsa*), and my favorite, Mrs. Animal (I: *Ibu Binatang*, whose husband was a livestock extension officer). Other examples included people whose travels outside of Biak or unusual life experiences lent them status: Mr. Tobelo (who had worked in this area of Halmahera), Mr. KNIL (formerly a corporal in the Dutch colonial army, the Koninklijk Nederlands Indonesisch Leger). Successful men sometimes mused on their similarities with famous Biak warriors, like Inbayau, an older evangelist's pirate uncle, whose name referred both to a dangerous fish and a man of extraordinary wealth. People who did not merit this respect were identified with a dismissive mention of their keret—"this Rumaropen" (B: Rumaropen *ine*)—or simply called by their first name. When acquaintances gossiped in Indonesian, I heard references to broader categories. In this or that family, there were "lots of college graduates" (I: *banyak sarjana*), "lots of people with rank" (I: *banyak orang berpangkat*), or more disparagingly, "no one who had turned out" (I: *tidak ada yang jadi*). Although my consultants would sometimes use neologisms (B: *sibejadi ba*: "they didn't turn out"), the Biak-language term that most effectively captured the most valued category of personhood was, as I have noted, *amber*. People used the word to speak of "foreign" objects, as one old man did when he told me he was too old to have his voice recorded on that "foreign instrument" (B: *alat amber*). As a noun, it provided a way of designating noteworthy persons, as when my consultants divided the participants in a bridewealth exchange into "big foreigners" (B: *amber beba*) and "small foreigners" (B: *amber kasun*).

Mothers took credit when their children became *amber*, and accepted the blame when they didn't "turn out." When I visited middle-aged women in town, they usually began our conversation by listing their children and their whereabouts, focusing on those furthest away. "Teacher, soldier, college student," my new acquaintance would say, pointing to the pictures on her wall. "I helped all these people come into this world," a midwife sighed, describing how she was always running into college graduates who were born with her help. "But my own child can't seem to become a human being" (I: *menjadi manusia*). "I'm the one who made them into people" (B: *snon kaku*), older village women often bragged, naming the high-ranking officials they had helped to raise.[14] One of them taught me a song in which an official reminisces about the roasted tubers his grandmother fed him each morning so he could grow up and become a success. Attributing a local source to a person's "foreignness," this maternal discourse condensed a range of contingencies into a nurturing gift. Much more than luck, paternity, or help from the government, the local foreigner had his mother's taro root to thank.

The division of labor in Biak villages supported these women's claim that they had created valued persons. When mothers described the household economy, they stressed their control over the production and distribution of resources. Although a young, unmarried daughter might cook a meal, it was still considered her mother's offering. Although men did the backbreaking work of opening new swiddens, women referred to their families' plots as "my gardens."[15] Although land, sago groves, and fruit trees technically belonged to a woman's husband and his clan, she set the work schedule and took charge of the harvest. Women sold a portion of their family's crops in local markets or Biak City, where they transformed their earnings into rice, kerosene, clothing, school fees, utensils, and treats for their children. They kept the family's ceremonial valuables hidden in the rafters of their homes and vetted prospective wives for their sons. Fathers claimed to be the heads of their households, but mothers transacted the media through which adults were produced.

In Biak, wives appropriated their husband's capital and labor by bringing jointly produced objects into circulation (cf. Strathern 1988: 165, 309–339). What was true for village women was also true for the spouses of civil servants, who used their husbands' salaries to purchase maternal gifts. The association of women with the garden and men with the sea coincided with Biak assumptions about contrasting traits of each gender. Mothers took credit for farming's stable fortunes, while deriding fishing's unstable yields. Village children could eat taro from a single garden for weeks on end; given Biak's dangerous waters and simple technologies, fish were always a special treat. As in many parts of Southeast Asia, men in Biak did not sell their family's produce—or let others eat first—because it was assumed that they could not restrain their appetites (Brenner 1995, 1998). In the market, they would quickly accept a reduced price for their goods, then spend their earnings on cigarettes, prostitutes, and drink. "Women are thriftier," one of my neighbors in Sor told me. "A mother is always calculating, 'What will we eat?'" "Mother saves," added another, repeating the Biak saying, "Awin ikram." When I asked these villagers what made a good woman and what made a good man, I received different lists of tools—baskets for women, harpoons for men— and almost identical lists of qualities. Both men and women were supposed to be energetic and brave. But women had to be able to conserve.

When the flight from Jakarta to Jayapura touched down at Biak's airport, well-dressed women were always waiting in the lounge with boxes of taro for traveling relatives. This association of food and mobility calls to mind Munn's (1986) account of practices on Gawa, an island in the Massim that is part of the kula, the regional exchange system made famous by Malinowski ([1922] 1961) and Mauss ([1925] 1967), where men deferred consumption in order to create "space time" through transactions that made them the object of the regard of distant others. As resources ideally exchanged for more durable goods, garden products remained at the inferior pole in Gawan "qualisigns" of value. Gawan men who ate from their own gardens, instead of reserving food for guests, grew heavy and listless; because their names did not circulate, they were unable to attract valuables from distant partners. In contrast, among Biaks, consumption was seen as enhancing mobility; to gain strength for a journey, a person had to eat. By exchanging food for kula goods, Gawan men "mastered the paths" of traveling objects; Biak men dispensed objects as "proof" that they had traveled themselves. Biak mothers deferred for the sake of moving persons, not things. By constantly reminding others of their privileged relationship to, say, "Mr. Subdistrict Chief," they ensured that their neighbors—and visiting researchers—would know about this individual. Presenting food as a gift that was impossible to repay, they circulated the stories that spread their children's fame.

Given their expectations, Biak mothers could never be satisfied by their children's expressions of gratitude. "Look at all the foreigners I've fed," eighty-year-old Nina Siworwom often sighed. "What have they done for me?"[16] Only by dying could a mother confront those she had "created" with the magnitude of what they owed her. If a mother's boasting built an audience for her children, her children formed the audience at her demise. "When someone has given a great deal, lots of people come when they die," Lukas Burmambo, an official on home leave in Sor, explained to me. "It is as if people don't want them to go." Aging mothers often expressed displeasure by refusing to eat. When an older woman passed away, people sometimes assumed that she had taken this gesture to an extreme. Nina's death set off rumors and recriminations as her descendants confronted what they viewed as her self-starvation. The seven daughters who watched over the dying woman told me seven different stories of her final days. After blaming her siblings for Nina's unhappiness, each daughter described how she had fed her mother shortly before she passed away. Through their accounts of nurturing the dying woman, the daughters imagined the easing of an unbalanced relationship. The many foster children who learned of Nina's illness too late were furious that they were absent during her final hours. No narrative of giving could cushion their debt to the dead.

After a mother's death, the anguish felt by her children did not abate quickly. The refusal of reciprocity sometimes seemed to raise the possibility that the dead mother might retract her gifts. An activist told me how he constantly saw his dead mother's face in crowds in distant cities. His mother's brother finally convinced him to hold a special ceremony so that this haunting would cease. Likewise, when a child fell ill, her family's first impulse was often to weed her grandmother's plot. After Sophia died of a stomach ailment that made it impossible to hold down food, her children spent every spare moment by her grave, which was nestled against the family house. From the tin roof they erected to protect "Mama" from the rain, the children hung a lantern that illuminated the plastic flowers, porcelain plates, and colorful banners that decorated the smooth rectangle of sand. As soon as the ground settled, Sophia's husband planned to pave it with cement. The widower gently laughed at Mama's "unreasonable" demands. "Mama cared for us when she was alive. Now we have to care for her forever." Village cemeteries were filled with ramshackle graves, which offered a roost for goats and chickens. But as long as those Sophia nurtured remained in the vicinity of her grave, they would maintain a monument to their debt.

This notion of a debt one can acknowledge, but never fully efface, takes us back to Laurensina's legend about the talking skull. Doberok's gift of taro also elicited a response to the dead. After our laughter died down, Laurensina continued the story. Following the younger brother back to the boar, Doberok demanded the pig's stomach to use as a cap. The skull then fitted the remainder of the pork into a magical purse for the boys to carry home. If they only took small amounts from the top, the skull told them, the meat would never spoil or run out. Doberok's offering of food was followed by a promise of wealth. Three days later, the skull hopped toward Sopen with a marching forest of trees that were hung with food and porcelain plates. Unfortunately, the villagers failed to obey Doberok's command not to watch the procession. When a little boy peeked outside and shouted in amazement, the skull turned to stone and the community lost the gifts.

Doberok may be an ancestral figure, as Kamma (1972: 75) suggests, but he is not a member of any particular lineage. Moreover, for the villagers to receive his marvelous gifts, they must not look for his arrival. The skull must remain hidden from view until the astonishing moment when the villagers make his bounty their own. Once located by the little boy, whose shouting freezes the spectacle, Doberok's power is lost. This notion of ancestral power as a potency whose origin can never be definitively fixed will prove crucial in later chapters. For now, what matters are the parallels one can draw with the materials at hand. Members of their natal lineages in life as in death, the Biak mothers I knew remained outsiders to their children, who automatically belonged to their fathers' clans. The mothers' goal was not only to produce "human beings"; it was also to enable their children to stand out among their peers. As the alien source of social differences, mothers both demanded and deflected a return for their gifts. To understand why, one must examine how mothers were able to become a source of foreign capacities and possessions. In New Order Biak, it was not only mothers but also brothers who deferred their desires. Their prestige depended on the sisters they had given up— their out-married bingon.

Brothers and Sisters

During my research in Sor, the household I joined included a two-year-old who was learning to talk. The little girl engaged in two interesting routines. Whenever Nesi took a tumble, her mother would interrupt her wailing with a furious question. "Who hit Nesi? Was it Dina?" She would then turn to her teenage daughter and give her a playful whack, before comforting the sniffling little girl. Soon enough, Nesi learned to strike a nearby family member whenever she hurt herself. Nesi's other routine began whenever a distant rumbling signaled the approach of "Safety Two," the broken-down truck that sporadically carried passengers to and from the coastal villages. As the vehicle passed, the other children taught Nesi to shout, "Safety Two! Town! Mama!" Like her older friends, Nesi rejoiced at the truck's arrival, which often meant her mother's return from the market. By the end of my stay, Nesi's sister and mother had her greeting the truck by calling out the name of a brother who had just entered high school in town (cf. Schieffelin 1990: 82–86). One day, I came upon Nesi playing this game in the absence of the truck. "Tom! Town!" she chirped, pointing through the trees, then turned to me beaming. Nesi learned two lessons as she was learning to talk. The first established those in her immediate proximity as the source of injury or aggression, an assumption considered at the end of this chapter. The second made her absent brother an object of interest on the horizon of her world.

The affection cultivated in young brothers and sisters was said to last until the end of their days. The little girl awaiting her "treat" would someday be an old woman longing for her dead or distant brother. Whether they lived at opposite ends of the village or the nation, brothers and sisters and their descendants greeted each other with such tenderness that I often mistook them for lovers. Staring wordlessly into her eyes, Abe Rumapura gently caressed his cross-cousin's cheek, as if to persuade himself that she was really there. His visits with his widowed sister lapsed into a similar reverie. One day, as we carried home a bag of his sister's taro, the older man told me how in the past he would end his trips to sea at her door, so he could nap peacefully as she fried up his catch. Abe's unblinking attention to his sister and his long-lost mother's brother's daughter differed dramatically from his dealings with his wife. Spouses bickered or treated each other with cool indifference; their relationship seemed ephemeral no matter how many children they had. An apparently happily married man once told me who would be with him at the end. His smiling wife would have replaced him with another husband before his sister had stopped weeping over his corpse.

Nothing seemed more natural to the Biaks I knew than the undying devotion of brothers and sisters. The brother-sister pair provides what might be called the "elementary principle" of Biak kinship (Weiner 1992: 81; see also Held 1957: 116). Like others who follow the so-called "Iroquois" system, my consultants distinguished between two sets of relatives, one consisting of relatives related through cross-sex siblings or *srar*, the other including those related through same-sex siblings or *naek*.[17] As will become clear below, uncles and aunts, as we might gloss *imem* (mother's brother or father's sister's husband) and *mebin* (father's sister or mother's brother's wife), had special relationships with their nephews and nieces, or *fno*, which differed from those that prevailed between elder or younger mothers and fathers and their extended set of children. Cross-cousins (B: *napirem*) were expected to accord each other the deepest loyalty and respect.

As I have noted, Biaks prohibited cross-cousins from marrying.[18] I was told that if a sister's son married a brother's daughter, he would be "taking a woman from the source where he had eaten," consuming not only gifts but also a woman from his mother's brother (cf. Carsten 1995b: 227; Platenkamp 1984: 179). If a mother's brother took his sister's daughter for his son, he would be "eating" a woman he had "fed." The descendants of cross-sex siblings had to "travel far" to find marriage partners before their children could reunite. In the fourth generation, the term *napirem* no longer applied, and a marriage between the descendants of a brother and a sister became both possible and highly desirable. A typical depiction of marriage negotiations in the past had a pair of distant cross-cousins agreeing to join their son and daughter in wedlock. When discussing the less formal unions of the early 1990s, relatives still expressed great joy when the descendant of an outmarried woman happened to "come back." Ideally, marital relations in Biak were characterized by a deferred oscillation, as the sister relinquished in one generation was recovered in another. The ties between brothers and sisters and cross-cousins were infused with an intimacy that evoked at the same time that it precluded sexual relations (cf. Weiner 1992: 75; Bataille [1957] 1987: 63–70). The memory of the forbidden sibling was kept alive through the enduring prohibition. Emotionally charged, their relationship remained salient until a new marriage in another generation could recreate the original pair.

In such a system, a brother "loves" his sister partly because her bride-wealth enables him to marry. Contemporary parents often paired off their sons and daughters in anticipation of their marriages. Those who received a portion of a given daughter's bridewealth were expected to help pay for one of her brothers' wives. At the same time, a brother's expressions of affection inflated his sister's worth by demonstrating how reluctant he was to give her up. Certain clans made a virtue of what others regarded as a vice; they claimed that their women were so valuable that they could not bear to let them go. When a Noripuri woman married a Noripuri man of a differently named subclan or "room" (B: *sim*), others shook their heads, but accepted the familiar explanation: "Never sell warriors!" Although my consultants differed in their definitions of permissible marriage, they agreed with the adage that beautiful women produced illustrious sons. By marrying in, a clan asserted its potency and raised the stakes on the women it married out.

Although a few famous warriors included birth sisters among their many wives, contemporary Biaks regarded the extreme of in-marriage as a heinous sin.[19] They said that men who had sex with their own sisters, daughters, or mothers "ate their own placenta" (B: *san snekau*), an expression taken as a vile curse. This form of incest was seen as leading to infertility, death, and the birth of crippled or over-sexed offspring. Nevertheless, a bit of the warrior entered the picture when Biaks gossiped about those guilty of the transgression, usually inspired by stories someone had read in the provincial paper. A woman described a man who had married his own daughter as "evil" (I: *jahat*). But the same woman also described her husband as *jahat*, explaining that he was quiet but quick to anger and dangerous to those who offended him—qualities considered virtues in a Biak man.

Childhood love and the forbidden dream of incest arose after the fact, as it were, in anticipation of the sibling's loss. The intimacy between brothers and sisters took on its full significance when a sister became an out-married kinswoman (B: b*ingon*). One of my consultants traced the now defunct practice of sister exchange to the longing of out-married women. These sisters found brides for their brothers from among their husbands' relatives so that the siblings could remain close. A b*ingon* quite literally made her brothers mobile. In the distant past, a b*in babiak* was a woman whose marriage reconciled previously warring groups. The children she bore replaced the victims lost in battle. They would be the cross-cousins of her brother's children, who would enjoy safe passage through previously hostile terrain. In times of peace, a distant b*ingon* offered security to her siblings, who could flee to her during famines or epidemics. During my fieldwork, brothers counted on out-married sisters more than any other relatives for shelter when they ventured to Jayapura, Jakarta, or The Hague.[20] A good brother had to stay with his sister whenever he came to town and tuck some money in her palm when he left.

Some siblings went to great lengths to live up to this ideal.

Until past midnight, Oktofina, Nelly, Yulia, and Sally were busy bundling up three huge boxes of taro for Andris [their mother's sister's son, a subdistrict chief on the island of Waigeo] to take home. I tagged along with Yulia, Oktofina, and her son and daughter when they escorted him to the port. A sunny Sunday morning, made brighter by the colorfully dressed crowd of traders, students, matrons, and civil servants gathered on the bridge in front of the huge white ship. Boarding took forever. We found shelter in the shade, while the other passengers milled about on the pavement, before packing themselves into a tiny waiting room, from which they were led to the ship. Mr. Subdistrict Chief, as the sisters called him, held back until the last moment. He was traveling first class, and had a cabin guaranteed. Besides, he had a military sticker on his brief case and a Westerner by his side; no one would mess with him. . . . Oktofina and Yulia agreed that we would not stay until the ship set sail. The second whistle blew, and we turned to leave. But then Yulia caught sight of Andris and his teenage daughter waving from the top deck. "He's seen us. Now we can't go," she sighed. Oktofina, however, signaled to Andris that we were leaving. "Wait!!" he signaled back. Yulia groaned as Andris scurried down the stairs onto the empty dock. What was he doing? While his daughter watched nervously, Andris jogged to the fence and reached through the gate to deposit a neatly folded 10,000 rupiah bill into Yulia's hand. "Taxi fare!" he smiled, then rushed back to the boat. We waved to the subdistrict chief and his daughter, then made our way to the public vans [which cost a small fraction of what he had given us] laughing.

As this very public display of sibling affection suggests, an out-married sister's duty was to feed her brother. Her brother's duty was to provide resources for his sister's descendants by replacing her perishable offerings with more durable forms of value. At the same time, a sister's alienation enhanced her brothers' mobility and enabled them to transform their travels into a source of prestige. As the incident at the port suggests, however obliquely, brothers got more than food and protection from their out-married sisters; they gained an arena for the social validation of their achievements. A civil servant's status was still at stake in the generosity he showed his sisters, even if his gifts sometimes paled in comparison with the dramatic expenditures that occurred during Biak's formerly frequent celebrations, known by the Biak word *wor*, which also designates the music associated with these feasts (see chapter 3). Pitting a sister's ability to amass food against her brothers' ability to amass foreign wealth, these dance feasts confirmed the connection between a mother's value and her brother's fame.

According to accounts from the early twentieth century, Biaks tightened the tie between a brother and a sister before either married. At a boy's initiation, his sisters consumed sago cakes mixed with blood from his foreskin (Jens 1916: esp. 407–410).[21] A girl's initiation entailed long months of motionless seclusion in a tent made of mats. Meanwhile, her parents arranged her marriage and oversaw the receipt and division of her bridewealth. At the marriage ceremony that followed this ordeal, the bride was draped in cloth and adorned with beads, flowers, and silver and shell bracelets for the procession to her new husband's home. Surrounded by women carrying stacks of porcelain plates, the bride paraded her family's prestige. Initiating the return of a major portion of the woman's bridewealth, this procession set the stage for an ongoing series of dance feasts hosted by the out-married kinswoman for her relatives. Although the number of feasts had shrunk from several dozen to an infrequent handful by the early 1990s, the logic of the transactions remained the same.[22] Whether a child was going to church for the first time or had just returned from a trip, his or her mother's siblings offered services, clothing, titles, and wealth believed to protect their sister's progeny and fill them with vitality and power.[23]

The feasts my consultants mentioned most often included haircutting feasts (B: *wor kapnaknik*), clothing feasts (B: *wor famarmar*), and anointing feasts (B: *wor ramrem*), all of which required a woman's brothers to perform particular services for her children. They each repeated the pattern of exchanges established when a bride left her natal clan. Although many young Biaks insisted on choosing their own spouses, their parents recalled—and sometimes attempted to recreate—formal mechanisms for arranging marriages. Older people remembered how two families might agree to the engagement of their infant son and daughter.[24] During the following years, gifts of food called "nurture" (B: *fan-fan*) were sent from the boy's parents to the girl's relatives to confirm the relationship, which sometimes required the bride to join her future husband's household.[25] In contemporary times, a prospective mother-in-law would sometimes "test" her son's fiancée by putting her to work in the kitchen, but the engagement period was far shorter. It began when the groom's parents' spokesman, often a mother's brother, initiated informal discussions with the bride's family. If the response was positive, a group of the groom's relatives set out in the wee hours of the morning to "betel nut" (I: *minang*) the woman. Although the man's birth parents usually tagged along, they remained silent during the discussions, leaving others to present any opening gifts and receive the request for bridewealth (B: *ararem*). Arriving at the bride's doorstep before dawn, the groom's sister or father's sister was supposed to stamp on the house-ladder or scrape her feet on the front porch to warn the household of her family's intentions. I was told that this act confirmed that the two sides meant business. Later, if the spouses argued, their relatives could remind them of how dreadfully early they got up on the couple's behalf.

The prospective bride's representatives received the groom's party. These representatives generally included a descendant of the paternal kinsman who had procured the bride's mother's bridewealth. Claiming the bride as his b*inawe*, he had the right to dictate the quantity of cash and valuables included in her bridewealth, which ideally equaled what was paid for her mother.[26] The same man later divided the money and valuables among the bride's kin. If all went well at the meeting, shortly thereafter the bride's representatives sent the groom's family a written request. When the individual in charge of procuring the bridewealth was ready, he set a date for the bride's family to inspect the collected wealth. In addition to the dinner plates and serving bowls contributed by a broad network of relatives, the objects on display had to include a "head" (B: *bukor*) consisting of "big bowls" of heavy porcelain from China or Europe (B: *ben beba*); large "hanging plates" decorated with castles or waterfalls (B: *ben ahmer*); silver bracelets forged from Dutch coins (B: *sarak*); and anywhere from one to three of the "antique dishes" (B: *ben bepon*) that were the most highly valued element of bridewealth. Classified according to a baffling array of schemes based on size, shape, pattern, and provenance, these *ben bepon* might feature a vase decorated with a blue dragon (B: *more-more*); a Chinese "fish dish" (B: *ben in*); a bumpy white "leprosy" platter (B: *ben lepra*); or a covered "Batavia Petroleum Company bowl" (I: *piring BPM*) of the type sold in the oil fields on the south side of New Guinea's Bird's Head Peninsula during the 1930s and 1950s. Although some families cherished hopes of obtaining a particular piece of porcelain, what mattered most was an antique dish's authenticity, as judged by the imperfections in its base and its tone when tapped by the old women who took charge of such inspections.[27]

When the quantity and quality of the bridewealth met the bride's family's approval, the groom's relatives delivered it in a noisy parade (see Figure 5). In the processions I watched in Biak City and rural villages, female relatives trotted along, plates poised on their heads, singing in shrill harmony to the string band that took up the rear. Toward the middle of the group, the groom's father's sisters carried the "head" dishes in woven bags; nearby a kinsman hoisted an Indonesian flag. The parade's participants usually circled in the bride's courtyard before relinquishing their burden. Depending on local practice, those who delivered the bridewealth then received anything from some betel nut and tobacco to a meal.[28] With this stage in the arrangements completed, the two families set a date for the wedding and began preparing for the bridal feast, called the *umbanbin* in North Biak and the *yakyaker* elsewhere.

The wedding day almost always commenced in church with a Christian ceremony.[29] The couple's relatives somehow always managed to find a white gown for the bride and a black suit for the groom to wear on this solemn occasion. Solemn it was, in most cases, set to the plaintive sobs of the bride's mothers, sisters, and cousins, not to mention the bride herself.[30] After the

Figure 5. The "men's side" delivers bridewealth in Sor, North Biak

service, the bride retreated with her relatives to prepare for the evening's procession. Just as a groom's relatives delivered bridewealth in haughty triumph—making sure that everyone in the vicinity knew they had met the challenge—a bride's relatives delivered the newly outmarried woman and the wealth that accompanied her in a spirit of extravagant display. Everyone who had "eaten" the bride's bridewealth was supposed to contribute to the return gift offered on the day of the wedding, which consisted of dinner plates, serving bowls, money, silver bracelets, *ben beba* and, ideally, one or two *ben bepon*.[31] As the proud father of one bride told me, "We only asked for lots of bridewealth because we knew we would give back much more than we received."

In the beachfront village of Dwar, I watched a bride trade her wedding gown for a blouse and *sarong* (a textile worn around the waist in many parts of Indonesia). She then stood motionless as her aunts and sisters wrapped additional textiles around her waist, pinned gaily printed skirts and dresses to her chest and back, and filled her wrists with silver bracelets and her hair with flowers and ten-thousand-rupiah bills, each worth roughly five U.S. dollars. Meanwhile, an uncle made a list of everyone who had provided ornaments and porcelain; the names of contributors were also taped to some of the plates. Outside, the bride's brothers argued over who would get to carry the flag as the band members tuned their guitars and ukuleles. Finally, with a father's sister on each arm and clutching a *ben bepon* to her chest, the bride set out with her singing, shouting, and dancing relatives for her new home. As was the case in other wedding feasts I attended, the bride-givers descended on their hosts like a party of warriors returning from a raid. As the father of one groom told me, the bride's family tried to "startle" their hosts, so they would not have time to hide any food.

When the bride's entourage reached the groom's courtyard, a complicated series of exchanges began. The leaders turned into a circle, and the hubbub grew as the band switched from farewell anthems to ditties demanding betel nut and drink. A few of the groom's kinswomen made their way through the crowd, pressing refreshments into the dancers' palms. Meanwhile, other relatives doled out money and plates to "replace" the flag and the leafy twigs that some guests were defiantly waving. The procession included relatives carrying an odd assortment of objects: one woman had a taro plant on her head; another had a rice pot; a man hoisted a stick supporting a small cardboard canoe from which dangled a tiny cardboard fish. A flashlight bounced from the end of one branch; a condensed milk can from another.[32] A friend explained that these "props" referred to the debts incurred by the bride during her childhood. The boat stood for the fish her male relatives had caught for her; sticks represented the times she had struck her younger siblings; the taro plant recalled the gardens from which she had eaten and the crops she had learned to raise.[33] At the wedding feast, as at each of the *wor* the bride would someday host, the groom's family had to give money or porcelain to each person who carried such an item. Recalling the value embedded in the woman, the props made a claim that had to be acknowledged but could never entirely be redeemed.

Before the bride could enter the groom's household, other demands had to be met. After several turns around the yard, the bride's escorts steered their charge toward the ladder of her new husband's house, only to find their way blocked. One of the bride's father's sisters had planted herself on the threshold and refused to budge until the groom's relatives presented her with an adequate gift. I watched the frowning woman shove back a dinner plate, then wad up a bill and hurl it to the ground, stubbornly averting her face until someone brought her a *ben in*. Along with those bearing the signs of nurture, relatives like this woman, who claimed not to have received enough bridewealth, would give repeat performances at the new couple's future feasts.

When the path was cleared, the bride and her escorts poured into the groom's house. The groom's female relatives whisked away the stacks of plates, then led the bride to a room in the rear, where her mother-in-law took the *ben bepon*, and her sisters-in-law quickly divested her of bracelets, clothing, and money. Although the mechanics of their weddings varied, the men and women I spoke with agreed upon the importance of these valuables. The adornments and dishes both asserted the bride's family's status and strengthened her position within her husband's household. I was told that if the new wife got in a dispute with her in-laws, their anger would fade when they recalled the wealth she had brought on her wedding day. Her relatives gave the valuables "so she would have a voice" (I: *supaya dia punya suara*). The bride's husband would not be able to silence her by saying, "Shut up! You were sold!" In Dwar, the wife-takers had to replace the bride's decorations with fixed amounts of raw food. To keep a silver bracelet or an antique dish they had to come up with hundreds of kilograms of rice, if not an item of equal worth (cf. Weiner 1992: 89). Although other Biaks viewed this practice as unseemly, whether the bride's in-laws retained her gifts or not they were said to call to mind the value the new wife would attract from her brothers across the newly opened division between their homes.

Meanwhile, in the courtyard, silence briefly reigned as the guests tucked into huge vats of taro root, sago pudding, vegetables, and fish or meat. Wedding feasts, like all wor, lasted all night. A feast always began with *fandadiwer*, a lavish "free meal" served by the groom's female kin. After the meals they consumed later in the evening, the guests had to leave money in their empty plates. In the morning, those who had contributed to the return gift negotiated with the bride-takers for a share of raw food. Conducted by women, these *munsasu* exchanges gave the groom's relatives who had provided valuable pieces of porcelain a chance to "buy back" their dishes from the bride-givers. Loss was unavoidable, however; those who contributed to the bridewealth had to compete with distant relatives who came to wedding feasts to "shop" for porcelain and food. Unlike Biak's strangely tranquil markets, the *munsasu* was a scene of hard-nosed haggling (see also Rutherford 2001b). A woman who did not like what she was offered would gather her wares in a flash of anger and head for home.

At least one Dutch observer depicted the feasts held on the infertile islands as foolish orgies of expenditure (Feuilletau de Bruyn 1920: 40). The weddings I attended unfolded as a tournament of appetites, with each side competing to present more food or valuables than their counterparts could possibly "eat." Although individuals hoping to recover specific objects underwrote each transaction, what was at stake in the oscillating flow of wealth was the reputation of individuals and social groups. The groom's family paid bridewealth for a woman, I was repeatedly told, "because she will produce descendants" (I: *karena dia akan punya keturunan*). It was also a way of preventing polygamy, a rural deacon ventured; if marriage were not so expensive,

"Biak men would have a hundred wives each." Although some of my consultants described bridewealth as an expression of a woman's self-respect (I: *harga diri*), others spoke more bluntly. "Women are sold" (I: *dijual*), villagers told me in Indonesian, even though, when pressed, they admitted that the Biak terms for marriage transactions differed from those used for commodity exchange.[34] The return gift presented at the time of the wedding both confirmed and undid this interpretation. A bureaucrat in Jayapura summed up the dominant line of thinking on the question. When his daughter got married, his family would pay the groom's side double the amount of her bridewealth. That way they would demonstrate the "fortune" (I: *rejeki*) brought by their daughter and establish that she was "not a slave" (I: *bukan budak*).[35] When men spoke of giving away their sisters and following them in a single breath, the contradiction was only apparent.[36] Their refusal to resolve the losses associated with exogamy was central to their pursuit of status. In the life-cycle feasts that followed this focus sharpened, bringing into view the valor of a brother and the value of a *bingon*.

An out-married woman laid the groundwork for future feasts through ongoing gifts of food to her natal kin. Rural women presented their brothers with bags of taro root and sago every time the men came to visit. Like the generous "taxi fare" Andris gave his sisters, these gifts were given "for free," in contrast to the formal offerings (B: *fan-fan*) that out-married women sent their relatives in the months preceding a wor. Although there were events in children's lives that called for wor—their "first trip to church" (that is, baptism) being the paradigmatic example—brothers and sisters took into account the health and wealth of their respective social networks in planning a feast. "Clothing feasts" were particularly popular, because they could be held for offspring of any age. I was told that the preparations for such an event always began with a "signal" (B: *fasasnai*), in which the out-married woman prepared a batch of cooked food and set off with her husband to deliver it to her brother's home. The couple spent the night, and the next morning, the brother indicated that he would participate by presenting his sister with an antique dish and some dinner plates to take home. The *bingon* and her husband then planted a garden, using the harvest to supply the woman's brothers and sisters. The prospective guests kept track of the raw food they received so they could repay their hosts in excess on the day of the wor; the *bingon* "had to make a profit," as one consultant said. Their kinswoman and her husband planted another garden, and if the harvest looked good, they set a date for the event and warned the woman's siblings to get ready. The *bingon*'s husband organized fishing and hunting expeditions to add to the feast.

A clothing feast began, like a wedding feast, with a procession of guests bearing gifts. The *bingon*'s relatives loudly descended on their out-married kinswoman's home, bouncing stacks of porcelain and brandishing a flag and other props. The sister/hostess, called the "woman holding the party" (B: *bin* bena wor), had to serve her guests betel nut, cigarettes, and palm wine, then a generous meal, keeping plenty of refreshments in reserve for dancers who got hungry as the night wore on. Close to dawn, the wives of the bin bena wor's brothers took the hostess and her children to a separate hut. There, they dressed them in new clothes and decorated them with money and silver bracelets. After handing them valuable porcelain (either ben bepon or ben beba), these women, who were the children's maternal mebins (mother's brother's wives), escorted them and their mother back to their home, where their paternal mebins (father's sisters) stood blocking the doorway. Paid off by the hostess's brothers, the women retreated. The decorated children and their mother were then escorted into the house, where their father's relatives received them. Some of the wealth compensated for the fan-fan that led up to the ceremony. Like a wedding feast, the wor ended with munsasu exchanges of valuables for raw food.

Formerly, given the sheer volume of goods that changed hands, the extensive cycle of wor placed heavy demands on brothers and sisters.[37] My older informants scoffed when I tried to tease out the "ritual" aspects of the feasts. Wor served as Biak's marketplace, Utrecht Wompere explained to me. "There was no other way to trade!" (I: Cara berdagang lain tidak ada!). To accumulate enough valuables to pull off such a feast, a woman's brothers had to "look for valuables" (B: sewar robena), as people put it: to travel far and wide in search of wealth. Locally, a man and his wife might open a big garden and offer fan-fan to the woman's brothers in return for wealth. Or the couple might trade sago and taro directly for valuables at a fellow villager's feast. But the names assigned to the most valued types of porcelain emphasized the more distant locations where Biaks searched for valuables. If Dutch observers were correct, "looking for things" entailed both trading expeditions and raids, along with stints of wage labor in plantations and ports (see Feuilletau de Bruyn 1954). From the shell bracelets (B: samfar) travelers acquired in the Moluccas to the dishes coolies bought at the oil company store, Biaks used a changing array of objects as "proof" of their access to exogenous sources of wealth. Brothers who failed to attend their sister's wor faced the scorn of their female affines. How could they "have nothing" (B: nyaroba) after "selling" their sister at such a steep price? But the brother who answered his sister's challenge with an extravagant expenditure of wealth became a "big man" (B: snon beba) never forgotten by her children. For decades to come, his name was glorified in the stories told of the event.

An outmarried woman and her husband also shouldered a heavy burden when they held a wor. Hosts who ran out of food earned a reputation for poverty; word got around that they "had nothing at all." As at a wedding feast, a guest who felt slighted by the service was likely to hack down the cooking tent, then storm away. The bingon and her husband also had to be ready for guests who refused to leave—relatives who had missed out on the woman's bridewealth and demanded payment on the spot. Armed with a machete and emboldened by palm wine, anyone might make a sudden and extravagant demand. Events of this sort occurred whenever someone felt that their contribution to the *bingon's* upbringing had been belittled. The fury that resulted often proved so dangerous that the police were hesitant to issue permits for all-night feasts. The transactions between affines ensured that marriage generated an infinite debt; no one could adequately compensate the wife-givers for the trouble of raising a woman or the descendants she would produce. But the same transactions ensured that a woman's value rested on more than her ability to bear children; she created persons by enticing her brothers to give to her daughters and sons.

By setting the stage for the expenditures that differentiated men and social groups, what a sister attempted to get from her brothers and other natal relatives were the media that would distinguish her offspring from their peers. Out of love for his sister, a mother's brother gave his nieces and nephews porcelain plates and silver bracelets, clothing and courage, names and the honorary titles from Tidore mentioned in chapter 1. As the clothing feast suggests, the potency associated with these gifts seemed to envelop their receivers, who gained special capacities. The use of silver and gold ornaments in the slave adoption rites mentioned at the beginning of this chapter provides further evidence of the transformation believed to be effected when a person's body came into contact with a valued good. A sister's son who had won his mother's brother's affection might be fed magic leaves that made him a talented smith, fisherman, hunter, or singer, as well as an alluring lover. A beloved sister's daughter gained talents and possessions to pass down to her sons. A contemporary mother's brother could be a bureaucrat in Jayapura or Jakarta who blessed his sister's children with admission to college and a job. The connection between a brother's love and an aging sister's legacy was once made explicit in the "breaking-the-walking-stick feast" (B: *wor angyon*), in which a woman's brothers and their children commemorated a life's worth of "nurture" with a stack of antique porcelain for the hostess's descendants (see Figure 6). After this feast, the *bingon* would no longer work or send food to her relatives, having transformed her gifts into an inheritance for her daughters and sons.

With each feast recalling and anticipating a range of transactions from quotidian gestures of generosity to formal instances of exchange, Biak *wor* provided a privileged perspective on a complex system of social production. Through the symbols her relatives carried, the hostess explicitly appeared as the product of past acts of nurture. By contrast, her brothers left implicit what they owed to their own mothers and uncles, who may well have held *wor* for them when they were young. Depending on the context and one's position in the cycle, the origin of value shifted positions, with men sometimes taking full credit for their achievements and at other times recalling

Figure 6. Breaking the walking stick in West Biak. The hostess is draped in store-bought clothing and textiles, and surrounded by gifts of porcelain

maternal debts. Mediated by the bond between a brother and a sister, two mutually reinforcing yet contradictory sources of status commanded the gratitude of outstanding Biaks: the irredeemable offerings of an "alien" mother and the inexhaustible plenitude raided from distant worlds.

Wor thus played a direct role in the production of valued forms of personhood. Indirectly, the feasts produced continuity within the collectives defined in the cycle. The celebrations occasioned the reproduction of relations among lineages that had negotiated, provided, and divided each other's bridewealth. The circulation of unnamed and inconsistently ranked pieces of porcelain did not generate lasting hierarchies, but it did serve to reproduce stable ties among persons and groups that otherwise competed for land, leadership, and renown.[38] Between affines, as well, the exchanges mediated by a brother-sister pair inscribed relations that endured for generations. In marrying, the descendants of a brother and sister did more than reproduce certain structural patterns. Social reproduction rested on the recollection of the value, glory, and continuity yielded in transactions between divided kin.

During the period of my fieldwork, village families were sometimes forced to sell antique porcelain to cover the costs of their children's education. Although men and women often told me of their plans for future feasts, it was not easy to accumulate the resources needed to sponsor a successful wor. But the logic that governed the feasts remained salient. To secure their position within their husband's household, sisters found other ways to push their brothers outward for the valuables whose expenditure yielded men a name. A lasting effect of the importance of sisters in the lives of their brothers was the violence that erupted between husbands and wives (cf. Stølen 1991). The aunt who blocked the doorway at a feast remained the sister with whom a man's wife had to contend to preserve resources for the sake of her descendants. It is no accident that the most scandalous story of sibling incest I heard on Biak came from the wife of the accused.

If spouses could divorce, brothers and sisters could never give each other up. In an old story, a negligent sister allows her husband to serve her younger brothers dog faeces instead of food (Anonymous 1960). When the youths leave in disgust, their weeping sister follows them home in a canoe, calling "Come back so we can sleep together on mother's mat." When they reach their village, the brothers eat a poisonous coconut, so deep is their shame. Their sister prepares their corpses for burial, then commits suicide herself. In Biak, social vitality depended on a sister's alienation, as well as her kindness. If the distancing of a sister brought life and status, the bond's collapse could only bring death.

Interlude on Love, Violence, and Debt

By way of Biak dance feasts, and the intimate relationships they presumed and recreated, one gains a clear sense of one facet of the fetishization of the foreign. In taking the Land of the Foreigners as the source of a valued surplus—the "fortune" a beloved sister brought her husband's clan—the practices I have discussed served not simply to mask social reality, but to generate it as such. What I have just described is an economy in the broadest sense of the word: a system of transactions and transformations through which social distinctions and relationships are produced and reproduced. In using this word, I do not mean to leave an impression of closure. Under the New Order, Biak transactions were, of course, embedded in a national economy in which the government was the most reliable provider of salaries and hard cash. In this chapter, I have bracketed off this wider context in order to bring into focus a locally distinctive logic: the dynamic that emerges when we trace the path by which each gift results in a return. Dialectically engaged in the generation of value, Biak's extravagant feasts and quotidian kindnesses belonged to the same web of exchange.

Nevertheless, what Biaks had to say about their society leaves us with some interesting oddities. The economy discernible in their domestic interactions seemed to function through a desire to surpass it. Inflation was built into the system. The flow of marriage exchanges had a woman's bridewealth repaying debts among her kinsmen—and streaming back to her in-laws in an excessive return gift. Brothers "sold" their sisters—but they also ensured that the "ties of blood" between siblings "never released." The hosts repaid their guests for the ornaments and porcelain the bride brought to her new household—yet their delivery was said to give the new wife a "voice." The feast was a "market" for buying and selling—yet it was approached as a contest to out-expend the other side. However effectively I might trace an ongoing pattern, Biak voices would still ring in my ears. For reasons more complicated than those proposed by a long line of kinship theorists, the marriage of a sister, like the care of a mother, created a debt that was impossible to repay (see, for example, Lévi-Strauss [1949] 1969).

The ongoing emphasis that Biaks placed on the debt produced by mothers was crucial to the resilience of a local ideology—a "cosmography," as Helms (1993) puts it—that made the horizon a source of violence and value. In the context of kinship, we find what we will see in other spheres of social action: a fetishization of the foreign fueling the reproduction of inherently contradictory desires. In New Order Biak, the effort to give an unreciprocable gift reproduced social relations. Although their symbolic economy always yielded a return, Biaks insisted upon the possibility that it would not. The violence involved in such an insistence on giving becomes clear in Mauss's ([1925] 1967) depiction of the potlatch, that famous feast of expenditure that seemed to approach the ideal of an unreciprocated act. But even here, at the furthest limit of reciprocity, as Mauss describes it, destruction still evoked a response. Those who could not reply with objects had to pay with their persons: they became the winning chief's slaves.

Mauss's depiction of the relationship between violence and the goal of unreciprocated giving has been confirmed by a range of writers (Raheja 1988; Young 1971; Rafael [1988] 1993; see also Bataille [1967] 1991).[39] What ethnographers have viewed empirically, Derrida (1992) has approached conceptually, in an analysis that interprets Mauss's classic as a reflection on the impossibility of the pure gift. Derrida's analysis might seem to contradict Parry's important argument that Mauss's central aim was to expose the notion of disinterested giving as a modern capitalist fantasy (1986). Only with the rise of salvationist religion and the commodification of social relations, Parry argues, does it become possible to imagine a gift with no return. Still, it is arguably the structural impossibility of such a gesture that provides the grounds for Mauss's polemic. Before the countergift, before debt, before the conscious intention to give or receive, at the very instant the gift presents itself as such, it enters symbolization and conditions an exchange (Derrida 1992: 41). To be a pure gift, an offering would have to be utterly unanticipated and entirely forgotten—not only by its recipients but also by its bestowers, who would get no credit for the action, not even from themselves. The same would be true of a pure act of violence. Riches (1991: 287; see also 1986) has argued that the word "violence," by its very nature, implies a privileging of the perspectives of witnesses and victims. Only by disqualifying any possible justification could a perpetrator conceive of his or her violence as such. The pure act of violence, like the pure gift, would be an impossible gesture, if we accept that the anticipation of another's regard is a constitutive element of any social act. Given this connection between violence and giving, it is not surprising that Biaks performed the delivery of bridewealth as a raid. The dangerous outside was a resource for the reproduction of debt. It was a space where brothers could acquire the valuables that enabled them to give excessively. But debt was also a resource for the reproduction of Biak notions of the foreign. Through their insistence that they gave excessively, these same brothers inscribed a boundary between social settings, so that a distant oil field or local government office could appear as a place to capture extra wealth. In their effort to exceed local categories, Biaks continually recreated them, through practices that made their offerings come as a surprise.

In the logic of Biak kinship, the violence of the foreign and the value of brother-sister love are mutually constitutive. At the heart of society lies a sister whose capacity for giving derives not from violence but from her mediating position. In Lacan's terms, we might say that this is a sister who loves—she gives what she does not have to give (1982: 80). Where the brothers I witnessed symbolically resisted reciprocity by evoking violent acts, out-married sisters did the same by prompting exchanges that made their loss to another patriline forever unresolved. Linking the foreign and the local, her brothers and her children, what a sister gave was defined not as an attribute of her lineage but as value captured from alien realms. In this sense, the Biak mother could never be repaid, for she was not the source of her gifts.[40] The language for love that I recorded picks up on these connections between feminine giving and distance: saneraro, a sigh, is derived from the word for "stomach"; *yaswar* means "I love," "I long for," and "I miss." The Biak brother wanted his sister's love: his expenditure of goods in her honor yielded him prestige. His reward was not a specific object but the dissemination of his name. In turn, the sister wanted her brother's love, but through a complex doubling that transformed taking into giving. She received the valuables her brother gave in her honor, but only in order to pass them on. Her reward was the dissemination of "foreigners" who owed her their fame. This fame depended on a continual displacement of the signifiers of identity: a mother made her children different not only from their peers but also from their mother herself. The production of a person's prowess rested on public displays of expenditure, made possible by excursions into distant and dangerous lands.

The exchanges that produced Biak identities reproduced their own origin: "natural" sibling love across a "natural" divide. In turn, this intimacy reproduced an overarching source of value—the Land of the Foreigners, the realm of wealth and violence that offered the resources through which Biaks pursued power and renown. But to account for this dynamic, one must consider yet another aspect of the Biak family. If those who were different yet mediated offered one another social recognition, those who faced each other as equals posed the specter of replacement. As little Nesi learned as she was beginning to talk, those who were "closest" threatened the person with loss.

Brothers and Brothers

The Dutch wife of a Biak activist told me that after years of confusion she had discovered the best way to tell if two Biaks were not on intimate terms: if they shared the same surname it was unlikely that they were allies. The animosity between her husband's father, Markus Kaisiëpo, and his clan brother, Frans Kaisiëpo, illustrated her point. At the time of my fieldwork, the aging Markus was the president-in-exile of West Papua; the late Frans was a hero of the Indonesian state (*Cendrawasih Pos* 1993a, b, c; see also Osborne 1985). My acquaintance's rule of thumb confirmed what Biaks told me about siblings. "During battle, if a man is hit, his younger brother flees," Niko Mambos explained. "That way there will be a replacement. But if my *napirem* [cross-cousin] dies today, I die too." When a man spent the night at his sister's home, he knew he could sleep soundly; at his brother's he had to keep up his guard. Cross-cousins could not bring themselves to step over each other's feet, but brothers could fight to the death.

During my fieldwork, I saw these aphorisms dramatized in outbursts great and small. While I was helping myself to some taro at a feast celebrating the partial completion of Sor's new church, I found myself flung into the serving table as two young men hurled past. "Brothers," my companion whispered, as she reached to rescue a stack of plates. As the crowd pulled the combatants apart, I learned that the older man was angry with his younger brother, who had slapped his toddler several days before. Although spats between birth brothers rarely ended in bloodshed, those between their descendants often did. Where the links between a brother and a sister were commemorated in an ever more elaborated fashion, the descendants of brothers seemed to grow more hostile with each passing generation. With the pace of "development" quickening in the early 1990s, pressure on the regency's resources often led to violent eruptions within its patrilineal groups.

One must consider the relationship between Biak brothers to make sense of the Biak keret. Colonial observers who attempted to characterize Biak's patrilineal descent groups found themselves caught up in contradictions. One officer saw signs of primitive communism (Feuilletau de Bruyn 1920: 49–50); the missionaries saw markers of a fallen matriarchy (Jens 1916: 410). One scholar divided Biaks into nobles and commoners (Kamma 1972: 13); another stressed their refusal to run with the herd (van Gendt 1954: 34). Still another drew on Biak in his depiction of "the Papuan" as a "cultural improviser" (see Held 1951). Although the literature contains reports of primogeniture, with eldest sons inheriting their fathers' titles and a larger portion of their land, the same scholars also noted that an accomplished younger brother or the son of an eldest daughter could take the older sibling's place (Adatrechtbundels 1955b: 536). Biak, like other societies in Melanesia and Southeast Asia, was described by anthropologists as "loosely structured," in contrast to the clear-cut lineage systems then attributed to African tribes (Keesing 1987; see also McKinnon 2000). I too was confused by the apparent "looseness" of Biak's "structure" until I attended to the logic of my consultants' conflicting stories. I had to consider how Biaks could insist that all men were born equal and yet argue that inherited hierarchies should apply.

What Dutch scholars depict as a conflict between achievement and ascription was really the product of contrasting principles of inheritance. Out of love for his favorite sister, a brother gave distinguishing properties to her most promising children. As I have noted, a father automatically passed down his keret identity and divided his orchards and garden plots equally among his sons. With a lineage's patrimony diminishing in each generation, every man had to open new land and plant new trees for his descendants. The struggle to leave a legacy pitted brothers against each other at the same time that it erased their father's contribution. At once a medium of identity and a factor of production, communal land could be a source of endless tension.[41] If ties to territory and ancestors defined a Biak keret, neither could generate stable differences among the men who shared its name.

In the early 1990s, whereas claims to land were contested, claims to inherited authority proved so controversial that few people I knew would venture to make them publicly. My interest in village history yielded a surreptitious parade of visitors who were eager for me to document their versions of the past.[42] Yet within the genealogy one young man gave me on four enormous sheets of paper, prerogatives jumped from senior to junior lines with no apparent rhyme or reason. Nor could the man attach a function to the titles that his forebears had received so long ago. Travelers who delivered tribute to Tidore supposedly chose the name they fancied, and their heirs chose freely among their ancestors' appellations. Instead of establishing a chain of command, the Moluccan titles simply marked divisions within the clan (Ellen 1986: 57–63; cf. Baker 1994). My informant desperately wanted me to believe that as the eldest son of the last title-bearer's eldest son he was "*the* Sanadi of Sor." But the most other villagers would grant him was membership in his keret's Sanadi sublineage, a trait that carried no special privileges for those born in this "room."

It was not surprising that the young man's neighbors paid little heed to his stories. Most of the Biaks I knew viewed with distrust those who claimed to know their ancestors' names beyond the second ascending generation. People liked to tell me stories about their distant "grandfathers," but few could trace their descent from these figures.[43] The shallowness of Biak genealogies did not imply, however, that clan legends were unimportant. One will recall that stories of migrating ancestors were crucial for legitimating a keret's claim to land. Although younger keret members respected their elders' right to repeat the authorized versions of these tales, the narratives did not validate age-based hierarchies (cf. Myers 1986a: 240–243). Origin stories were not secret, and wives were often better versed in their husband's ancestral lore than the men were themselves.[44] In the absence of "proof" and a history of "experience outside," a man's pretences to knowledge failed to impress his peers. Whereas sisters often urged me to consult their brothers, men never did the same. My adoptive father in Sor discouraged me from going next door to interview his brother, a former evangelist and the oldest living member of his keret. Instead, Abe directed me to his cross-cousin, a less famous old man whom he could guarantee would tell me "the truth."

The telling of clan history taught me as much about the subversion of authority as its constitution within contemporary kerets. Men and women repeated narratives that resembled those complied by an energetic Dutch official who collected scores of "histories" (I: *asal usul*), the term Biaks used to refer to their legends. Dr. J. V. de Bruyn tabulated his results and reached the modest conclusion that fights over dogs and women were major factors in the formation of Biak's named groups (1948: 7–9). The typical keret history began with a bloody dispute among siblings. A dog defecated in someone's sleeping area, and no one would take the blame. A man caught a marsupial and let his brothers take it home, where they devoured it before he could get his share. A fierce battle broke out over the heart of a lizard, which four brothers each insisted they wanted to eat. In each case, the eruption of violence ended in the siblings' dispersal. Alone and in pairs, some-times with a sister, the brothers fanned out across Biak's interior, naming prominent features of the landscape as they descended toward the beach. The *usul* or "issue" of these stories was far more politically salient than the *asal* or "source," which was not a beginning but a disruption of descent.[45] The stories depicted a new keret as born of aggression among undifferenti-ated siblings in relation to shared objects of desire. In close proximity, a household's members could find no means of coordinating their wills. Only violence and a migration that literally set them apart could introduce the distinctions that allowed for exchange.

Outside the sphere of kinship, groups organized along egalitarian lines had to contend with the same forces that divided ancestral brothers. When I joined the South Biak Women's Union's expedition to Miei, a village on the mainland that was the site of a mission seminary, my "younger mother," Oktofina, made it her duty to protect my possessions from the other dele-gates.[46] I scoffed but soon saw her point. Theft was a constant preoccupation for the eighty Protestant women packed together in the village's junior high school. T-shirts, blouses, and hymnals could disappear at any moment, leav-ing their owners sputtering in fury. The fact that the participants wore identi-cal uniforms and used identical bags and books lent a tangible force to their fear that "someone" had taken their things. I learned quickly enough that I could expect no special treatment. I tried to remain objective, but by the time my sandals had vanished for the fourth time, I could scarcely contain my rage.

The delegates' contagious distrust was cast in sharp relief when the mem-bers met up with their trade friends (B: *manibobs*) in Miei. These women showered their Biak partners with hospitality in exchange for store-bought gifts. Pairs of *manibobs* walked arm in arm, exuding the intimacy of long-lost friends. The difference between our departure from Miei and our arrival back in Biak underlined the contrast between the two relationships. On the dock in Miei, in a scene of tearful parting, Biak women removed their silver brace-lets and forced them onto their trade friends' wrists, giving up valuable heir-looms to virtual strangers. In the chaos that accompanied the ship's unload-ing in Biak, more than one woman stormed around the jetty in search of a "stolen" bag of betel nuts or bananas. At Oktofina's advice, I had carefully labeled my *manibob's* gifts, and still I came up short. Oktofina whispered to me later that she had seen one of the delegation's leaders absconding with my things.

Differences in ethnicity or status had little bearing on the Miei trip's dy-namics. A victim was as quick to suspect a bureaucrat as a farmer; the women least trusted were those who had organized the trip. The fact that the participants were female did little to muffle their aggression; indeed, one could argue that by taking a sea voyage to visit trade friends, they assumed a position conventionally conceived as male.[47] If "sisterly love" often seemed more pronounced than "brotherly love," it was because in many contexts out-married sisters acted as exchange partners and not simply as doubles. Close kin of either sex were quick to suspect each other of thievery when a parent's death turned siblings into competing heirs. Taken to an extreme, the tensions among bereaved children sometimes gave rise to rumors that someone had been stealing from the coffin of the deceased. In the family, the clan, or the transient collective, the equivalent other was associated with loss.[48]

The linkage between death and the loss of possessions closely associated with a person suggests what was at stake in protecting one's distinct position in society. The most common way to bewitch someone was to steal an item of his or her wardrobe, cut it to pieces, and hide it someplace "haunted" (I: *angker*) like a waterfall or a cave. Older women scolded their daughters when they caught them wearing their husbands' jackets. By adopting a practice reserved for wives who were in mourning, these young women betrayed a desire for their spouse's demise. In former times, Biaks regarded the murder of a man caught in flagrante delicto with his killer's wife as justifiable homicide. Since the lover had replaced the husband in relation to the wife, his murder was approached as a form of self-defence. Since young widows often married their husbands' kinsmen to protect their children's rights, brothers appeared as threatening substitutes along multiple dimensions. The fear of replacement worked across generations, as well as within them. Expert singers and smiths referred to the magical leaves they ate to augment their talents as their "backbone." They told me they were sure they would perish soon after surrendering their secret to their heirs.

Given these anxieties, one can see why people tended to assume that the elderly would take most of their knowledge to the grave. A friend would tell me enthusiastically that his grandfather knew everything about a particular event, then sigh, "too bad he is dead." The valuable secrets kept by the dead kept them alive for their descendants, who might otherwise have exhaustively assumed their place (cf. Traube 1986: 31). For if replacement was the fear that infused Biak families, remembrance remained the ideal. The Biak men I knew said they wanted to live on in the lives of their descendants. Through their achievements, they hoped to leave a legacy for their grandchildren, whose prospects they often discussed. Yet behind the wish to be recognized by future generations stood the realization that most ancestors were not.

The practices associated with death fed the pathos of Biak dreams of survival. The dead were buried with their baptismal certificates, marriage licenses, diplomas, and badges of honor, along with bibles, eyeglasses, and most of their clothes. Distraught relatives used to smash a dead man's porcelain and hack up his tools and boats. These items—like the Miei trip delegates' uniforms and sandals—were closely associated with an embodied individual. In earlier times, the possessions of the deceased were called *romowi*, a word meaning "cursed thing" (Kamma 1981, vol. 1: 296). The *romowi's* destruction coincided with the corpse's decay, ensuring that the objects would accompany their owner to the land of the dead. My informants viewed the practice as protecting the living. If things associated with the deceased remained in use, his or her spirit would never leave the mourners alone.

Death and destruction were followed by the forgetting of names. After one warrior's death, his children kept his skull so that they would have "proof" when they told stories about their father. But the warrior's grandchildren soon lost respect for the relic. Taking the skull from the shelf, they "played" with it until it shattered. This anecdote confirms Dutch reports about the short "shelf life" of *korwars*, the wooden statues that once contained the skulls and spirits of recently deceased relatives. These small reliquaries were only kept as long as the spirits within them maintained a good connection to the spirits of the winds and seas.[49] When a *korwar* stopped working, its owner would discard it—or sell it to the members of a passing expedition. The traffic in abandoned "idols" enriched collectors and filled the missionaries with hope. But the destruction of the *korwars*, like the smashing of the skull, was less an effect of Christian conversion than of the impossibility of keeping the past "alive."

It was no coincidence that the man who related the story of the skull was born of the warrior's daughter. Forgotten by his paternal heirs, the ancestor remained an important figure to his daughter's sons. A man was more likely to generate a lasting impression through what he gave his sister's children than through what he gave his sons (cf. Pauwels 1994: 84). A brother, I was told, gave gifts to his sister's children so they would "always remember their uncle." Clan names and clan land descended from one generation to the next and generated no fame or notoriety for those who passed them on. Where identity was an effect of difference and all were "born equal," what was "proper" to a person had to flow from a space beyond the clan. And, indeed, my research profited from this assumption. My Biak consultants often spoke of the distant Dutch archives that held authentic versions of their clan histories. Comparing me to the missionaries and officials who collected their ancestors' stories, they seemed pleased that I would take their knowledge to America, where their descendants someday could go to discover the "truth." The passages of persons, porcelain, and memory retraced the same Odyssean plot. To save something of and for themselves, Biaks had to send it across the horizon into a realm of nostalgia and desire.

History Revisited

And so we return to Petrus Kafiar and his mother, the characters that opened this chapter. I am aware that my method opens me to the criticism that their

Biak had little to do with the Biak I knew in the early 1990s. A brief glance at the regency's capital city was sure to reveal that its "culture" was far from "pristine." In what one American called the "Gary, Indiana of Indonesia," with its rusting roofs and crumbling monuments, foreign influences confronted the tourist at every turn. But that is precisely the point of my analysis. It is a systematic relationship to these influences that this book is attempting to explain.

My analysis has stressed circularity. I have tried to map an economy in which the pursuit of prestige reproduced the forms of value of which it was a product. Attending to the circulation of food, wealth, and persons, I have linked the logic of relations within and across clan boundaries. What I have depicted is a tautology: because brothers "exported" the signs and sources of their potency, the keret remained a collection of competing equals. Because the keret was a collection of competing equals, children looked beyond it for what would set them apart. In the exchanges that generated the components and qualities of the group, sexual difference breached a path to the horizon. Biaks accounted for the contradictions latent in the "system" by combining a romanticized notion of brother-sister "love" with a fetishized notion of the foreign. The Land of the Foreigners, with its violence and excessive value, was what seemed to balance the books.

But the forms of intimacy I witnessed on Biak were not simply systematic; they were also intrinsically historical. They had important political implications in the early 1990s. In making an official's status the product of love and nurture, sisters and mothers obscured a competing source of identity: the government for which most "foreigners" worked. In the course of producing valued persons, New Order Biaks replaced the image of a rational bureaucracy with the figure of a dangerous and alluring outside world. Under the New Order, marriage was a crucial site for the improvement of Irian Jaya's "primitive" customs and their integration into the ranks of orderly regional traditions. Yet, even as they functioned as emblems of an official national culture, the practices of Biak families bore witness to a different relationship to the regime.

In the next chapter, I turn to genres of performance that open another vista on the allure of the foreign. Magic, music, and dance in Biak, equally emblematic of national culture, recaptured history through a poetics that allowed performers and their audiences to derive pleasure from surprise. Like the participants in a Biak wedding, the practitioners of these genres indexed moments of risk and exchange, chance conjunctures on a colonial frontier. The same "natives" who welcomed Dutch guests at the rear of their homes shrank in terror from the landing craft that approached from the front.[50] They used the same word, *hongi*, for the Dutch navy and its Moluccan supporters as they did for local attackers (Lorentz n.d.: 210–211). Manned by nameless captives, the Tidoran war fleet might be imagined as the most fearful specter of the unmediated equal. In this chapter, I have begun to explore the fetishization of the foreign by following a trail from exchange to history. But one should not be deceived by the coherence of the economy I have described. We can only grasp its significance by following another path of analysis: the one that leads through a legacy of colonial violence and takes us from history to exchange.

CHAPTER THREE

The Poetics of Surprise

AT THE END of my fieldwork, an explosion of violence violated much of what I thought I knew about Biak kinship. Late one night, in a West Biak village, Martin Bidwam broke into the newly built house of his father's sister, my friend Yulia, and gutted it with an axe. I gradually learned that Yulia had pushed for Martin's eviction from her late parents' home after learning of his rudeness to his elders. I made sense of this stupendous breach in Biak mores by considering Yulia's structural position. A government official with no apparent desire to marry, she was Martin's rival for space on the shrinking Bidwam land. Yulia reacted to the outrage by disowning her nephew. "I am no longer his father's sister (B: *mebin*)," she told the army officers from whom she had rescued Martin after similar scrapes.[1]

Colonial anthropologists, who were struck by the Papuans' "deeply rooted indiscipline" and "unreflective attitude toward life," would not have been surprised by Martin's dramatic transgression of social norms (van Baal 1954 in van der Leeden 1960: 120; see also Held 1951). For Dutch structuralists like van der Leeden, a mismatch between practice and prescription was an essential trait of western New Guinea's societies. Their "merciless and even hostile" surroundings had prevented the Papuans from fully expressing the principle latent within their kinship system: circulating connubiuum, the form of marriage that was for these scholars, as we have seen, the central cultural trait that united the Malay archipelago (van der Leeden 1956, cited in Pouwer 1960: 109; see also chapter 2). Under harsh conditions, the "loosening" of Papuan "structures" offered some security against loss. Lévi-Strauss had similar things to say when he explained father's sister's daughter's marriage as a means of shortening marriage cycles when "instability" militated against the "gamble" of a system in which groups received wealth, instead of women, for the sisters they gave up (Lévi-Strauss [1949] 1969: 442–55, esp. 448). Coming from someone whom a Dutch advocate of descent theory saw as "steeped in Lévi-Strauss" (Pouwer 1960: 110), van der Leeden's reasoning was as suspicious as his mentor's. Would his informants really have traded their forest home for North Sumatra's plantations or Timor's arid uplands, assuming that, like the ethnographer, they could have made such a comparison? It was not the Papuan but the Dutchman who would have found these other colonial sites more "hospitable" than the New Guinea bush.

In the shaping of societies like Biak's, what mattered was New Guinea's notorious "inhospitality" to interlopers from the West (see van Baal 1989, vol. 2: 139). In the preceding chapter, I drew connections between the dynamics of kinship in Biak and the islands' history on the frontier of larger, more powerful polities. I showed how the flow of foreign valuables, which I observed in the context of Biak families, generated a figure of the Land of the Foreigners as a source of surplus. Clearly, I could not account for this system of exchange without considering the influence of a regional economy in which distant centers have long monopolized the channels through which key commodities enter New Guinea. But to explain how my consultants were able to construe wage labor as a form of "raiding," I had to go further than the facts of regional history. I had to consider the fetishistic gesture through which the image of a surplus was not simply registered but also reproduced.

One way to fetishize the alien is to figure it as the origin of a valued surplus; another is to figure it as the origin of surprise. In my discussion of kinship, I alluded to the links Biaks have drawn between plenitude and shock. The Land of the Foreigners appeared, from the perspective of domestic exchanges, as the source of valued goods and the power to raid them. Violence and value came together in the aesthetics of the weddings I attended, which represented the delivery of the bride and the return of a portion of her bridewealth as a forceful, even predatory act. The domestic economy set up the love of mothers and outmarried sisters as the pivot that turned foreign wealth into locally acknowledged forms of distinction. At the same time, this economy relegated the dangerous face of the alien to relations between brothers, who were unmediated rivals rather than partners in exchange. But there were more explicit ways in which the Land of the Foreigners was reproduced during the period of my fieldwork as an object of both fear and desire. In this chapter, I home in on the unexpectedness of the foreign, as figured in the performances through which Biaks sought pleasure and prestige.

Faced with a kinswoman who refused to marry and, hence, denied him recognition, Martin did what other men did in a more conventional fashion when they hacked down the cooking tents of hostesses who refused to meet their demands. But Martin's deed not only reflected tensions at the heart of Biak kinship; it also enacted a poetics, a word I use loosely to refer to the generic structuring of social action to produce an aesthetic effect. I borrow the term from Jakobson (1987: 69), who analyzed the "poetic function" in a speech event as based on a focus on the "message" as such. In the case of Martin's outburst, such a focus would fix upon the sudden, exorbitant fashion in which he expressed his displeasure with the current state of family affairs. This is not to say that the "referential" and "emotive" functions attributed to Martin's performance were unimportant; rather, we must attend to a multiplication of senses and contexts (ibid.: 85). Although they differed in other dimensions, the genres discussed in this chapter shared formal traits that made them seem both indexical (causally linked, like a jet and a jet stream or a spill and a stain) and iconic (imitative) of a particular experience: the surprise of an encounter with the new.

In this chapter, I use the word "surprise" to cover certain stimuli with what Wittgenstein would call a family resemblance to one another (1958: 32). Sometimes I will be concerned with the shock of sudden violence, sometimes with the strange sound of foreign words, sometimes with the novelty of new experiences, sights, and gestures. The practices I consider present these stimuli as eliciting a range of emotional responses from terror to longing to delight. I do not know of a word in Indonesian or Biak that perfectly captures the incongruous character of these imagined experiences. The one that comes closest is a term repeatedly used to describe acts like Martin's: *sembarang*, an Indonesian term translated as "of any kind, no particular one" (Echols and Shadily 1989: 496).[2] Rendered as *nap-nap, fanfnom,* or *sekormbai* in Biak, the word refers to that which is dangerous and creative, undistinguished and awesome, an "anything" and "everything" that both stimulates and silences speech. I heard the term when Biaks talked about the least valued of activities: the drinking and fighting that sometimes occurred at the Biak City terminal. The anonymous youths that loitered there "walked at random" (B: *simbran nap-nap*), following their appetites with little regard for their reputations. But I also heard it when practitioners described expert performances of various sorts. As we will see, random acts were depicted as essential to the creation and restoration of social alliances. They also were central to the capture of flying fish and the enjoyment of Indonesian holidays and family feasts.

In this chapter, I compare the random acts of warriors and disputants with moments in the creation of magic, music, and dance. As such, I not only undermine analyses that have opposed violence to discourse; I link spheres of cultural production highly valued by the national government to arenas harshly suppressed by colonial and postcolonial regimes. What unites these highly disparate categories of social action is the way they rested upon and reproduced a conception of agency that displaced the origin of creativity away from self-conscious individuals. The actors I consider, to borrow a phrase from Keane (1997b: 688), acted "as if they sought agency, but not exactly to claim it for themselves." As such, they instantiated the contradiction inherent to the effort to become a foreigner, which I depicted in the preceding chapter. Those who excelled in these genres gained recognition precisely by not appearing as their (cultural) selves. In the case of wor and yospan, the song and dance forms I discuss later in this chapter, this conception of agency has important implications for how we understand the incorporation of these practices into a national politics of identity. Yospan was the official "welcome dance" of Irian Jaya during the period of my fieldwork. At the end of my research, as I discuss in chapter 7, wor was "revived" as an equally official emblem of Biakness. But neither genre was simply a medium of cultural self-expression. To serve as a source of prestige for performers and pleasure for their audiences, the performances I discuss had to appear as the product of encounters in alien worlds.

"Perfection of rhyme," Poe wrote, "is attainable only in the combination of two elements: Equality and Unexpectedness. But as evil cannot exist without good, so unexpectedness must arise from the expected" (1981: 96–97). Something like the paradox described by Poe was at work in the performances considered in this chapter, which created conventional frameworks in which the novel could erupt. In the context of New Order Biak, these performances subverted national understandings by defamiliarizing experiences that might otherwise have seemed banal. By drawing pleasure from all that was startling and new, Biaks tacitly commemorated the violence wrought by outsiders. This memory survived through the fetishistic recreation of the strange.

The Unpredictable Potency of Biak Warriors

On my first morning in Biak City, Sally Bidwam prevented me from taking my customary morning run until after daybreak. I had risen in the dark with the rest of her family in order to take a jog through the cool, dewy starlight that hung over the avenues of the Ridge. During a previous stint in Yogyakarta, I had grown fond of running before dawn. In that crowded Central Javanese city, I had learned that I was much less likely to be bothered if I could not be seen. It astounded me that Sally could find Biak's darkened streets so perilous. But Sally was adamant, and so I waited until sunrise to run with her niece, who was charged with bringing me back alive.

What Sally feared, her niece gasped as we trotted along, was "intoxicated people" (I: *orang mabuk*). Strange as I found her explanation then, I soon got used to people voicing this anxiety. Whenever someone warned me against venturing to a particular beach alone, they would refer to the intoxicated people known to frequent the place. In my North Biak neighborhood, the whispered warning that someone inebriated was coming up the path was enough to send families scurrying inside. I once waited behind a locked front door with a friend as her drunken younger brother ambled noisily past, singing a ditty and swinging a machete. Like a crashing wave or a rabid dog, intoxicated people were expected to unleash their aggression on anyone who crossed their path. Biak fears of random violence were not projected onto a ghetto or congealed into a thief—figures that can serve to localize "meaningless" loss (cf. Willis 1989; Siegel 1986: 34–58). Intoxicated action had an ambiguous function, as we will see; it both eradicated differences and produced prestige.

In the warnings that I received during my first month on the islands, the threat sometimes seemed without gender. However, as I learned more about the dangers lurking at dawn, it became clear that the person pictured was male. Feminine intoxication was said to lead to chatter. High on palm wine and good cheer, village women clowned as they carried out their duties at the church construction site in Sor. They told me that they always drank on workdays to spice up the drudgery of hauling all those baskets of sand. When women got angry, I seldom saw them express their wrath physically. Women tended to answer mockery with mockery, abuse with abuse, wounding their opponents with their words.[3] Enraged men, it was feared, would answer words with blows, starting a cycle that could escalate with lethal results.

The most lethal and celebrated of the men described by my informants were ancestors known as warriors, literally, "brave men" (B: *mambri*), who once hunted heads and plundered villages throughout the region. Stories about their exploits brought random violence from the margins to the center of social life. Raiding by land or by sea, these adventurers embodied a reservoir of volatile force. The names given to warriors reflected their attributes. Korwamba (Does Not Count the Waves) would plunge his canoe into the highest surf without waiting for a moment of calm. Simgakmonda (They Could Only Be Frightened) was a man whose very mention elicited terror. Marisan was a "Hot Pepper," Randip, a "Wild Boar," Biromor, a spookily "Impenetrable Grove." Although those who told me about their dangerous forebears usually recalled these warriors' clan names, they rarely mentioned them in their stories. Even in the mission documents that I read in Holland, warriors were identified with a single fearsome moniker.

Just as these warriors' names depicted their boldness and ferocity, stories of their deeds conveyed their capacity to surprise. My informants always used the term *sembarang* when they described how warriors used to kill. In the past, they told me, Biaks employed third parties to avenge offences. If someone in a person's group was injured or killed, he would summon a warrior from elsewhere to even the score. After promising the warrior a woman if he carried out the killing, the "client" would incite him with a stream of abuse. He might offer him an arrow with a feather attached to it, a codified affront to the recipient's virility. He might serve him sago pudding in a coconut shell instead of a bowl. He might spit into some palm wine, then dare the warrior to drink it. After working his guest into an intoxicated rage, the client would point the warrior's machete in the direction of the enemy, saying, "If you are a man, the *apiok* (a Biak curse word) is over there." Launched like a torpedo, the warrior immediately set out to kill the first person he met. That the detonated warrior often missed the target proved of little concern to the person who hired him. A single death satisfied both the warrior and his client, and anyone, *sembarang orang*, would do. And so the violence circulated, as the relatives of the victim recruited another warrior to attack the killer's clan.

When New Guinea's early missionaries surveyed the heathens' regional relations, they saw nothing but a series of bloody vendettas (Kamma 1976, 1977). But in Biak portrayals of the period before "pacification," the warriors' fury set more in motion than a cycle of fatal blows. The woman that a warrior received for his services became his wife, and the client became his children's affectionate mother's brother. Buffered by sibling love and maternal loyalty from the *mambri's* lethal wrath, former clients reciprocated by hiding the warrior from his enemies—even when these included government troops (Feuilletau de Bruyn 1916: 264). Whenever a warrior made peace, the surrender of one of his kinswomen to the victim's family enlarged his circle of affines. The remorseless killer was a wise and generous hero to those who descended from his sisters' daughters and sons.

The passage from violence to order portrayed in these stories about warriors calls to mind the clan histories described in the previous chapter. The two sets of narratives follow a formula that bears a direct relationship to the fetishization of the foreign; violence serves as a resource for figuring the unexpectedness of an encounter that gives rise to the exchanges that define social persons and groups. For the purposes of this chapter, what is significant about the warrior stories is the way they valorize a particular form of agency. Blinded by anger and inebriation, these fearsome ancestors embody through their destructively creative acts forces that originate beyond their conscious intentions. This form of agency is akin to what Benjamin describes in his depiction of "law-giving violence," a kind of harm giving exemplified in the deeds of Greek deities. "Mythical violence in its archetypical form is merely a manifestation of the gods. Not a means to their ends, scarcely a manifestation of their will, but first of all a manifestation of their existence" (Benjamin [1920–21] 1978: 294). My consultants may not have worshiped gods of the sort described by Benjamin, but they did attribute the origin of social order to a similar conjunction of force and fate. In New Order Biak, as we will see, this logic cut across diverse arenas of social action, in which not only authority and value but also prestige and pleasure were the outcome of actions indexing surprising encounters. One finds the traits celebrated in experts of various sorts expressed in a distilled manner within these legends of famous warriors, whose sudden acts of violence gave rise to new lineages and new cycles in social time.

Although my consultants were quick to insist that the islands' "dark ages" have ended, they denied that the warrior was extinct. High-ranking officials postured as modern-day *mambri*—heroes who had braved the bureaucracy for the benefit of their group. Typified in warrior stories, but also operating in other spheres, a resilient dynamic continued to link intoxicated violence with the transactions that generated social bonds. I saw it most distinctly in contemporary disputes.

One Sunday morning, in my corner of Sor, chronic squabbles over the division of clan land erupted into an open confrontation. Gripping a machete, an inebriated Marcus Rumapura began shouting insults at his classificatory brother's front door. Abe Rumapura was at church—"Luckily for Marcus!" he later growled—so his wife had to confront the angry neighbor by herself. She let fly a shrill wave of abuse. Marcus responded with a sudden swing of his machete, which sent two small fruit trees crashing to the ground. As other villagers saw it, a clear message was contained in this violent display, which destroyed part of the evidence (I: *bukti*) that supported Abe's claim to his houseplot. Marcus's enemies could count themselves lucky that they had not come as close to him as these saplings.

Staged as random, this destructive performance followed a familiar formula. By raising the possibility of intraclan violence, Marcus forced the village chief and the elders who served on the village council to intervene in the dispute. In the adultery proceedings I witnessed after a similar display, those involved continued to demonstrate their dangerous potential. Each faction's spokesman assured the elders that his good "Christian" cousins harbored no thirst for vengeance. But at the back of the room, in a volley of hissed insults and shouted accusations, the female parties to the feud gave voice to the anger that raged in silent male eyes. The tension rose to a climax, then dispersed when the two sides finally reached an agreement. A stack of porcelain and money passed from one side to the other, and everyone swore never to mention the matter again. To erase every trace of the incident, the "winners" divided the fine among uninvolved onlookers, before tearfully embracing the "losers." Oscillating between animosity and affection, inciting and relieving the danger of dissolution, the participants in such disputes performed the passage from heathen darkness to Christian light—over and over again.

In the context of historical and contemporary feuds, impulsive action appeared as the vehicle of transformation. Beside themselves in rage, warriors and disputants reconfigured the social landscape, creating and repairing relationships. My consultants agreed that there were moments when it was socially productive to give vent to violent emotions. I was told that disputants sometimes used magic to cool their opponents' wrath, so they would be less capable of pressing their case. Although my neighbors in Sor clearly valued good manners, they were quick to tell me that the capacity for righteous anger was part of what made a man a man. This conception of agency not only led warriors to be esteemed as the founders of kin groups; it also influenced the way people distributed blame. Much to the chagrin of colonial officials, the islands' disasters never happened just by chance.[4] An attack by a sea spirit (B: *faknik*) was seen as stemming from the sexual misbehavior of someone on board the stricken boat. Biaks traced accidents to actions, if not intentions. Mishaps came from "intoxicated" people who were driven by forces beyond their control.

As we shall see, for contemporary practitioners of magic, music, and dance, the automatic action that gave rise to terror in warrior stories served as a source of pleasure and seduction. Where the poetics of warfare resided in a particular narration of events, these experts positioned surprise in ritual action and verbal and visual art. Just as the warrior's violence created genealogical time, these genres punctuated temporal cycles. The implications of this conception of creativity should become clear as we move through these arenas of performance. Magicians, singers, and dancers prevented the foreign from becoming familiar, even as they used it to set local rhythms. Our exploration of the allure of the alien takes us first across the boundaries of species, to encounters between humans and fish.

Magical Feasts for Fish

I am not sure when I first realized that in Biak there was something vaguely racy about fish. It was not that first day when Sally Bidwam rejected the tuna I was about to buy from a Makassarese trader during a trip to the Biak City market. I could not understand why my new family would see something wanton in my desire to eat the strange man's fish. I only started to appreciate seafood's significance when I recorded an old woman singing a song about her brother that consisted of a list of local species. By the time my fieldwork ended, I knew how to read the glint in a young man's eye when he assured me that he too knew how to *fish*. The pointed way he mentioned this masculine gift marked his boasting as a bald attempt to flirt.

The magical methods employed by fishermen contributed to the connotations of their catch. Whereas fish in Biak seemed subtly seductive, magic was explicitly erotic. During my first trip to North Biak, I was sternly warned never to touch a man's harpoon. Treated with magic herbs, the tip contained *boryas*, a substance whose potency could raise boils on a woman's inner thighs.[5] Girls were taught never to startle a smith or a carver when he was intent upon his work. Distracted from its target, a craftsman's "heat" could flare into a burning passion engulfing the man and any potential partner who happened to be near. In the past, talented singers often had many lovers; contemporary artists were almost expected to have affairs. When men admitted to me that they had eaten magic leaves, it was never without an air of coy embarrassment. It was assumed that magic, creativity, and promiscuity went together. Few men acquired the first two properties without indulging in the third.

Magicians displayed the seductive face of the potency that took a fearful form in stories about warriors. In magic, this potency was explicitly associated with foreign lands. According to my informants, two types of magic were practiced on the island. "Black magic" (I: *ilmu hitam*) originated in places to the west, like the Bird's Head Peninsula, the Raja Ampat Islands, or Ceram. The harmful spells (I: *bahasa alam*, "supernatural language") were acquired by travelers or introduced by migrants to the islands. Local magic, I was assured, was wholesomely organic. "We use nothing but leaves and bark," craftsmen and curers always told me, before describing how they ingested, manipulated, or prescribed forest products in order to ply their useful trade. However, many beliefs and practices blurred the boundary that divided the malevolent and benevolent sides of magic. Several clans claimed to have rather nasty animal familiars, endogenous birds or marsupials that reacted to their masters' anger by invading and consuming their enemies' guts. And even though a smith ate local leaves to enhance his skills, to strengthen a machete he had to whisper a secret foreign word.[6]

A close look at any of Biak's many kinds of magic would illuminate the relationship between foreign and local sources of potency. However, the seasonal hunt for flying fish is particularly enlightening. Linking sex and the sea with the power of the Land of the Foreigners, this magical pursuit remained a focus of great enthusiasm in the early 1990s. Its efficacy validated by legends old and new, flying fish magic combined local ingredients and careful procedures with the eruption of "random" foreign speech.

During my first October in North Biak, when the breeze rose and little crabs began scuttling along the coastal road, my new neighbors in Sor told me that the flying fish would soon be arriving. Every year, during the wavy season that lasts from early November through March, a shift in the winds brings schools of flying fish to the north coast to spawn. In the old days, at the first sign of change, every family in the villages from Mara to Dwar began preparing a special boat. After a "messenger fish" soared ashore to offer an "invitation," one of the fishermen went to sea. If he returned with a good catch, the other fishermen joined in. From early in the morning until late at night, men spent each day at sea. Until the yields dropped off several months later, their departure and return set the rhythm of daily life. Boisterously greeting the canoes every night, villagers feasted on the harvest throughout the season and enjoyed smoked fish for weeks after its close.

Nutty and delicate in taste, the flying fish I saw in the nets of local fishermen were eight inches long, with sleek torsos and half-foot wingspans. When they sailed over the water, they looked, or so friends told me, just like tiny bombers on a raid. To explain how the people in North Biak started hunting this species, as well as shark, Abe Rumapura's younger brother, Bruno, who taught school in the neighboring village of Dwar, told me the legend of Madirai.

It all began in Sor. In the olden days, people did not know how to fish; they used strings and wires and caught very little. In those days, few people lived along these shores. A man named Madirai is the hero of this story. One day, as was his habit,

Madirai went to collect palm wine from his coconut tree. (Madirai was a big drinker.) To his dismay, he discovered that the bamboo containers were empty. Someone had stolen his palm wine. Madirai was furious, ready to kill, but no one would confess to the deed. Madirai decided to guard the tree. He spent the whole night awake, but saw no one. But the next morning, the bamboo containers were empty. How could this be? He decided to build a platform part way up the tree and watch from there. This he did, but the next morning, the palm wine was missing again. Madirai spent the third night at the very top of the tree, near the crown. He waited through the night and saw no one. But then, just as dawn was breaking, to his amazement, a person descended on a ray from the Morning Star, Sampari. She or he (it was an "angel" [I: bidadari] Bruno explained, thus neither male nor female) headed straight for the bamboo containers.[7] Quickly, Madirai sprang up and grabbed him/her. The sun rose. The angel struggled. "Let me go! I cannot be late!" But Madirai refused to let go until the angel told him something useful. The angel asked Madirai what he wanted. "All this time, I've been dying to eat some fish," answered Madirai, who, like the others in Sor, rarely caught a thing. "Tell me how to catch lots of fish."

So the Morning Star angel taught Madirai the art of catching shark and *inanai* (flying fish). The angel showed Madirai how to profit from the apparently useless parts of plants like the coconut tree; she/he described how to fashion the shell into a fish rattle (B: *sobekakas*), and outlined the procedures involved in catching flying fish. Every season, Madirai had to make a trap (B: *arsam*) out of the bark of the *samet*, a particular type of tree. After soaking the fibers in the ocean, he was to pound and stretch them into thread. He was to weave this thread very neatly into a net and hang it on a loop of a particular type of vine. He had to use wood of yet another variety to make the bar that would hold the ring open whenever he set up the trap.

The Morning Star angel told the old man to lay a platform of coconut fronds on top of the ring as soon as he got out to sea. This construction made the fish trap look like the floor of a men's house (B: *rumsram*), Bruno explained. Madirai was to erect a thick mast of coconut fibers on top of the platform so he could find the trap over the waves. The angel then told Madirai where to find a special "flying fish shrub" (B: *inanai prer*), whose tiny leaves resemble the species' eggs. Before releasing the *arsam*, he was to pour palm wine over a coconut-leaf pouch filled with these eggs, then pound it, repeating the procedure until the fish trap was drenched. If Madirai did everything correctly, the flying fish would flock to his trap, soaring and splashing, before making their frenzied way through its four little doors.

By way of these careful instructions, Bruno explained, the celestial being taught Madirai how to hold a dance feast for fish. Hosting such an event was no simple task. When Madirai's heirs discussed their technique, the word *sembarang* peppered their descriptions. On one level, everything about catching flying fish was "not indeterminate" (I: *tidak sembarang*; B: *fanfnomba*). The art was found only in North Biak, "not just anywhere." "Not just anyone" knew how to practice it. Only certain leaves, fibers, and liquids could be used in the trap, which had to be carried to sea. "You have to use a special canoe," Abner Sorofek, an experienced fisherman, explained to me. "Not just any boat (I: *tidak sembarang prahu*) will do." This canoe's rigging could not be tied "any which way;" the loose ends on the net and in the boat all had to point in one direction. Likewise, the fishermen had to have "straight hearts," untwisted by secret mistresses and angry or pregnant wives. While they were waiting for the fish, only one man at a time could stand to call the fish; the others had to crouch face down in the canoe. Under no circumstance, could they pollute the sea; if they needed to vomit or urinate, they had to do it in the boat.

Just as the fishermen had to wait for an invitation to open the season, they could not approach the trap until a "messenger" summoned them. A lone fish soared over the boat to inspect the rigging before fetching its fellows; later, it informed the fishermen when the trap was full.[8] When they arrived at the trap, one man carefully plucked the first seven fish from the water. After that, the others joined in. As long as they took care not to damage any gills or loosen any scales, the fish would swim willingly into the men's open hands. On shore, the first seven caught had to be smoked on a special platform, where they were left until the season ended. The fresh fish could not be eaten "any old way": they had to be grilled intact, never chopped, boiled, or fried. Nursing children and pregnant mothers could not consume the catch, unless someone ripped open a cooked fish over their heads. If any villagers broke the rules, the fish would boycott their "parties" and bring the season to a sudden halt.

The season also would end if the fishermen could not combine these decidedly determinate procedures with indeterminate, *sembarang*, speech. At sea as on shore, to draw a big crowd, a host had to circulate an alluring invitation. Facing to the east, then the west, then the south, then the north, the fishermen had to call the fish. Although anyone could learn the hunt's regulations, fish calling was a highly prized art. Those fluent in "flying fish" (B: *wos inanai*) used kinship terms to catch their prey's attention. Beckoning their "uncles" or "aunts," but above all their "cross-cousins," they urged their scaly relatives to join the party. The callers also used "funny talk" (I: *bahasa lucu*) to attract the fish. In a fast and furious barrage of words, they said anything and everything that entered their minds. Some lewdly referred to the women in the village; others even propositioned the fish. Many rhythmically extended their syllables and spiced up their speech by including archaic terms. But the most effective *wos inanai* included *wos amber*: real or imitation foreign words.[9]

The purpose of *wos inanai* was to startle and amuse the fish. If foreign words were appealing, foreign faces were irresistible. Few informants could describe the season without recalling the occasions when a foreigner had accompanied local fishermen to sea. In the 1950s, "Tuan Karels" took part in a very successful expedition. The colonial officer called out in Dutch, "Komt U binnen!"—and fish flooded into the net. The half-Chinese son of Sor's shopkeeper spent many a day at sea, borrowed by fishermen who hoped to add to their yield. Flying fish were said to act like Biak children when they saw a stranger: they did not need to recognize foreign faces or tongues to delight in encounters with the new. Even rumors proved appealing. The day after I interviewed some fishermen in Dwar, one of them thanked me for their remarkable catch. They were sure that those fish had heard that I had been around.

Flying fish magic calls to mind what happened at Biak's airport whenever a jet en route between Bali and Los Angeles landed to refuel. The fish acted like the Biak villagers drawn to the transit lounge to stare through the windows at the tourists inside. Just as the flight schedule and the building provided a ritual space for the foreign, *inanai* magic structured a zone where something novel could erupt with the same startling force every time.[10] One could turn to Mauss's *General Theory of Magic*, which describes how frequently foreign words are used in spells, to account for the efficacy of the technique. By engaging unexpected affinities between fish and people, the magic staged a "terrific confusion" of images that filled the gap between a wish and its fulfilment ([1902–1903] 1972: 62). In Lévi-Strauss's terms, the fishermen summoned up the "floating signifier," the empty sign that signifies the power of signification. Such an interpretation would approach the foreign words as a figure for the origin of Biak categories, the surplus of significance over the "universe" that Biaks had "mapped" ([1950] 1987: 56–64). If a general description of flying fish magic lends itself to such readings, a closer look reveals a more complicated dynamic. The tourists in the transit lounge may have functioned as the bait, but they were also the fish, briefly detained on their weekly migration. While the Biaks watched the tourists, the tourists, as we shall see, watched a small troupe of Biaks performing a welcome dance in the center of the hall. Fish talk elicited the same transpositions of audiences and objects of desire, as the following example should make clear.

Amandeus Marsyom performed the following fish call for me in Dwar in January 1994. In the late afternoon, surrounded by friends and relatives on a beach-front porch, the old man closed his eyes, and rapid, rhythmic words began to shoot from his mouth. I have reproduced the call in its entirety to illuminate how the setting for "random talk" was structured. Amandeus performed the long text in four parts, which he distinguished according to the position of the fishermen relative to the trap.[11] The Biak verses invite the fish to no ordinary dance feast, but one that engages every corner of the world.

Before the Fishermen Release the Fish Trap

1. Napirem romgune sinane rwamuma ro pon korafrefe kobe oser ureb mampiopero, ai biryoe, ai yanfane kobani inendai e.

1. Cross-cousin, boys, parents, come early! We will chase each other, we will join together, our white sandbar, our big white flower, our white *kabus* wood, our white *yanfane* wood way out at sea.

2. Mbo napirem wuno snono arwo ine besauo bewor siwor kabarbor bekain kabor ansya muma.

2. Yes, cross-cousin, bring along the men who sing quick and lively wor! This morning, let them sing their songs very fast! You boys who are sitting there, come on in!

3. Koberao rwai mobo au. Ausiryafa besyobo.

3. We thought you had gone far off. But here you are, close by!

4. Wunsima ne, ne, ne, ne, ne wuno wendok brandok sapupo wasyaio do sima, wunsima.

4. Bring them here! Rise, rise, rise, rise, rise! Bring the legs and arms that splash themselves with sea foam! Bring them here!

5. Kobri fuaro kinem komserido man be napirman se samamek bo spaukpau bo sorun bome narber naisinane.

5. At the base of the coconut-spine "mast," we'll drink until we are drunk, male cross-cousin of mine, then they'll grab each other, they'll pull each other, they'll jab each other with their unfolded spears.

6. Wo napirem wasusu bepak awer. Waryur iryur bo manardar bo mansun syun kukero inai romgun sya mufrum.

6. Oh, cross-cousin, don't back up too far! Gather them, he gathers them together! The man who gathers, the man who enters, let him enter with the girls and boys who are coming into the house!

7. Mangun kyon dao muniwa imnis munine imnis dow beba manomane arurui.

7. Let he himself sit on that end, which is like this end, which is like a big song with men rushing in and out.

8. Wawan mansarde imufyaie fa syade warek pampun ayabe danenda.

8. You tell the show-offs to give me a sign and I'll push myself back to sea.

9. Yasar yaposo snon in Sabado man Sabado, in Imbirsba man Imbirsba, in Aibeb, man Aibeb, mansibaber befmar ai

9. I will go out and call people: the women from Sabado Island, the men from Sabado Island, the women from

mayan dame rambon dame arɓek ram
besrono korkorɓe.

Imbirsba cape, the men from Imbirsba
cape, the women from Aiɓeb, the men
from Aiɓəb, the naked men adorned
with floating *mayan* leaves, with floating
rambon leaves, with seaweed draped
around them like necklaces.

10. Srame srama koryur siraryur siwor
diɓa ro arwo di mundi, isnai di mundi.

10. They're coming, they're coming, we're
gathering, they're gathering to sing wor in
the morning hours, at earliest light.

11. Au wawan inuni isar pyos in do
yene man do yene in do pare, man do
pare, ɓin swapor, man swapor siraryur
ma siwor diɓa ro meser di mundi, isnai
ri mundi.

11. Tell the messenger fish to go out
and call the women from the floor of
the sea, the men from the floor of the
sea; the women from the cracks in the
reef, the men from the cracks in the
reef; the women from the capes, the
men from the capes. Call them to gather
and sing wor in the morning hours, in
the early light.

In the first verse, fish and humans become kin through the union of white
things of the land and the sea. Verses 2, 4, and 5 slide between references to
the prey as intoxicated guests and as fish that spawn in a frenzied mass.
Verse 5 compares their fins to the weapons Biak warriors used to bring to a
feast. They left their spears stuck in the wall until the dancing heated up,
then grabbed them to swing as they circled.[12] Verse 7 assimilates the gathering fish to both a song form and a feast. Just as a file of dancers has a head
and a tail, as I explain below, a "big song" (B: *dow beɓa*) is sung in two parts.
Just as a dancer can join the line at any location, new voices can join the
melody at any moment. Just as new revelers can crash a feast whenever they
please, new fish should jump into the net.

Throughout the call, the voice of the text vacillates; sometimes the fisherman seems to be speaking, sometimes the fish, sometimes imagined members of a wider world of guests. Verse 6 is at once an order, a plea, and a
description. Everyone, in all modalities, must come inside. Verses 9, 10, and
11 inscribe differences oriented to the points of a Biak compass. The fishermen turn west to summon the men and women from various landmarks: an
islet down the coast, a cape on the adjoining island of Supiori, a white spot
on Supiori's highest peak. Then he turns around to call the naked inhabitants
of New Guinea's distant eastern reaches, identifying them with the fish swept
in by the current with the debris. Verse 11 complements this compendium of
spatial distinctions by substituting an underwater topography for terrestrial

zones. All positions collapse together in the frenzy of the feast, which climaxes at dawn, the cusp between night and day.

While the Fishermen Are Drifting a Distance from the Trap

12. Yasusu binkwan ba kukero yamamepen wor beba kobena nero bondi ba rya.

12. I am not moving back too far, so I can watch our big wor that isn't really too far away.

13. Kobe sa inai romgun sya san sinem rao simserido au kukero aya kosbasna nadarepen ro afsnon do rumi.

13. We want the girls and boys to eat and drink a lot and if they get drunk, you and I, we'll scold the ones that leave this bachelors' hut.

14. Wo napirem mgo pur ya mgo iyasya mgo iriyambrai koryur kofananar swan di do mangundau romgune inaie koramuma.

14. Oh, cross-cousin, you in back, you on top, you on shore. We're gathering together, we're racing together. You are the only one left at the bottom of the sea. Come on, boys and girls, let's all come inside.

15. Korama kopon korafrefe beso sram beyinem nabye beyan nabye arwo imsar arwo kobananende.

15. We're coming, we're racing, we're chasing each other to the bachelor's house where everyone drinks and eats well. By morning it will be filled to bursting; only in the morning will we go home.

16. Kopon korafref kowai ri broben kofananar abro snoman kobananendi.

16. We race, we chase each other, we run to and fro, we tear after each other to our bachelor's hut.

17. Yakofen nairo kopon korafref kofananari bon bon di ro ro ri dwas dwas ri kek dofen kek aryar inde wasamberen na wafasau na mufrum bae.

17. I say, let's race, let's chase each other, let's tear after each other on the mountains, in the valleys, over the cliffs that we climb, that we climb. Take the short cuts so you are fast, so that you quickly come inside.

18. Au ma nyanuk naiso nyanuk na nyan fai naiso nyan fai.

18. Hey you, the short cut, that's it, the short cut. The pig path, that's it, the pig path.

19. Korandum kwarido mgokafepen mgopewerepen mgosrurepen.

19. Once we're inside, cling, grab tight, hang on!

The rich vocabulary of verses 15, 16, and 17, performed by Amandeus at breakneck speed, transforms the trap into an irresistible focus of enthusiasm. The multitudes flock forth, racing and chasing, taking short cuts by land and by sea.

As the Fishermen Are Approaching the Trap

20. Wo, napirem *b*esya *ya*besya wawano mansade fa pyampun aya ro *b*ondi.

20. Oh cross-cousin of mine, tell the messenger boy to keep me away.

21. Mbude yara dau di ro snon randak mangun randak sirumyafa wer fe.

21. Lest I should chase off the first men, those arriving alone. Let them all come back into the house.

22. Yamewer yamai *b*o yamnis raris ras *b*eponja ananendai wedi.

22. I don't want to be ashamed like on those days in the past.

23. Eh, napirem *ab*ri afsnon mano *b*esero romawa kaku mano in kewuwo*b*a war pyaso*b*a sapupo*b*a war ro ro ko*b*a.

23. Hey, cross-cousin, the bachelor's hut, it's the gathering place for real boys, those male fish that jump out and play in the water with their tails in the air then in our water.

24. Eh, napirem, *b*ramsidar mankon kaderen pamber ap in di kare i*b*e *b*andum simbren mundi awer simbren mufrum.

24. Hey, cross-cousin, gather them up with your hands, the men sitting on the end of the platform, the women at the edge, he will gather them together. Don't let them run off, gather them up!

When the "guests" reach the "dance hall," the reckless abandon with which they gather congeals in a contagious masculine intoxication. In verses 20, 21, and 24, the messenger fish is urged not to let the energy disperse.

When the Fishermen Find the Trap Full and Start Collecting the Fish

25. Ari ari ari! Man be napirman ansui*b*uni suyuf *b*o supir wer made suyuf ro *b*rampin bidwom dao *b*raba*b* fuar nawandum.

25. Hey, hey, hey! Male cross-cousin, these two guys are grabbing, grabbing, and not letting go, not only with their finger tips but under their armpits, too!

The fishermen approach the net carefully, but as the fish surrender the men's excitement grows. By verse 25, they can't keep pace with their hands and start scooping with their arms. On shore, their neighbors will greet them in the same fevered state. Wild with pleasure at the hunt's success, the villagers create a new focus of enthusiasm building toward the dispersion of the catch.

Amandeus's fish call was the longest and most elaborate that I recorded, and the closest in composition to the "sea language" recorded by Feuilletau de Bruyn (1916: 317). Other experts gave me smaller samples of "funny talk." Fritz Brabar demonstrated the mockery shouted shoreward at dusk, when smoke begins rising from the gardens. Look at the sweaty women roasting taro for the feast! "They have forgotten to cover their genitals!" (B: Fikaper simam si ba!). Instead of cloth, the fish will find a "dark land" between the hot women's legs, as the sun sinks, dimming the terrain. Manase Rumsowek's call pushed back other horizons by summoning the Javanese from the west and the Fijians from the east. Facing north, Manase warned the fish that the bombers were approaching. Then he shouted some "Japanese" words that he overheard in 1944 when the Allies relentlessly strafed the northern coast, which was then under the control of Japan (see chapter 6). Luis Rumbino combined the erotic and the exotic in a call I recorded during a trip with him to sea. The old man used pillow talk to excite the fish, addressing them as female cross-cousins that he would "lie with" at the feast. After imposing and violating a taboo based on kinship, Luis confounded a dichotomy of ethnicity and class. The fishermen were hicks from the interior who still lived in caves; the fish were "civil servants," who obviously slept beneath tin roofs. The "hosts" walked or paddled wherever they went; the well-off *amber* "guests" could always fly. The most "random" part of Luis's tirade closed the gap between races, sexes, and species. Repeating a phrase that he learned as a coolie after 1944, when Allied forces occupied the islands, he gleefully shouted—in English—"Hey woman! Come on!!" Although Luis seemed to know these "American" words were "naughty," I was told that the meaning of a fish call did not determine its effectiveness. The cry seduced through the strangeness of its sounds. It was as if the incomprehensible foreign words sparked insatiable desires that spread to encompass the spawning fish.[13]

Along with foreign expressions, the calls included archaic terms that elicited another sort of "confusion." In several texts I collected, the word *mun* appeared in a formulaic plea for the fish to enter on "that side and this side" (B: *mun iwa, mun ine*) of the net. The same term was then repeated in the phrase that depicted the feast as lasting until "the morning part of the day" (B: *arwo di mundi*). This formula effected a magical conjunction of time and space. The same could be said of the entire magical ritual, which marked a shift in the seasons at the same time that it linked land and sea, thus punctuating both periods and zones. It is worth recalling that flying fish magic came from the Morning Star, the sentry that stands between two temporal circuits: the months of the year that the islands' seafarers once measured by the constellations and the hours of the day that they measured by the sun (Feuilletau de Bruyn 1940–41).

The next section examines another means of harnessing the foreign that retraces the fish call's pathway between structure and surprise. Where the fish call posits then collapses distinctions, wor begins with an eruption that elicits a song. Having survived a long history of suppression, this non-diatonic song form lived a tenuous existence at the time of my research. It was remembered by old people across the islands, but only performed collectively in a handful of communities. Where fishing magic still marked the cycling of a season, wor once marked the cycling of lives.

Vocal Feasts for Families

I first heard wor on a North Biak beach shortly after I began my research on the islands. The night before I had walked for four hours along a dark coastal road to reach the village where I would stay while exploring possible field sites. Having ended our meeting at the church, the members of the local women's union were taking me to visit the ruins of an Allied encampment. Rounding a corner, we came upon an old man in a loincloth who started singing a song that was slow and, to me, unintelligible. He stared into my eyes, repeating the verses to the beat of a drum and the wavering accompaniment of two companions. When he finished, he led me to the water, dampened my face, and presented me with a shell necklace to protect me from local spirits. Many months later, I finally got a transcription of the song.[14] At the time, I was only told that it "welcomed me back" to the place.

Given what I had read of the authorities' assault on "heathen" singing following the World War II outbreak of Koreri, I was amazed to find wor waiting for me in Biak. According to local legend, the song form originated in an equally amazing encounter. North Biak singers told me that the first wor expert was from the Mnuwom clan. Late one night, while he was hunting in the forest, Old Man Mnuwom suddenly heard voices high in a tree. In vain, he scanned the branches for the source of the noise. When he sat down to rest, the music swelled. Startled, he grabbed a vine that was coiled around the tree, and the voices divided into two choruses. The vine's flowers were singing the song! To keep the voices from sinking into the soil at sunrise, Old Man Mnuwom cut down the vine. He took it home and ate the leaves— and became the first Biak clever at singing wor.

This North Biak story presented wor's birth as a double surprise. Not only was Old Man Mnuwom startled, so were the flowers—which generated the new singing style when he tugged on the vine. A West Biak version of the tale emphasized the differences inscribed by a similar shock. According to Dominggus Adadikam and Kundrad Bonggoibo, the early Biaks only had one monotonous song, whose words, if not melody, the old men recalled.

Wo, sinan sya *be*pon sya siburi sekormbai, kormbai.	Oh, the ancestors ran off and lived any which way, which way.
Wo, siburi sepuraimuke, sepuraimuke!	Oh, they ran off without a tail, without a tail!

The song portrays the conditions of which it is a product as a world devoid of distinctions. Living "any which way" (B: *sekormbai*), the ancestors had no "tails" (B: *sepuraimuke*) and, hence, no heads, nothing to direct them toward a goal. The form of the couplet is equally aimless: the second line is simply a shortened synonym for the first.[15] This random state ended when four hunters paused to rest beneath a tree. To pass the time, the young men sang their song, in perfect unison, as was the custom. Swaying to the beat, they inadvertently disturbed that magical vine. Two leafy choruses suddenly emitted a series of melodies. Prohibited by the leaves to sing their boring ditty, the four cross-cousins divided into pairs to practice the new tunes.

The older singers who told me about wor's origin in a meeting between man and plant had much to say about the song form in its heyday. Like the vines that thrived in the islands' rocky soil, wor was once deeply rooted in every crevice of local life. As they gardened or wove baskets, women sang wor recalling dead or distant loved ones. Men sang wor at sea to calm the waves or prepare for battle. Wor served to legitimate clan claims to territory; to express demands for food and drink; to evoke sympathy, support, anger, or sorrow. Wor songs provided proof (I: *bukti*) of the experiences that gave rise to them, just as a rock might offer evidence of an ancestor's adventures, or a tree confirm its owner's claim to a particular plot. Some songs went with stories, like the myth of Manarmakeri; a storyteller's ability to sing such a wor established the veracity of his or her version of a tale (see chapter 5). An expert singer, versed in the subtleties of melody and rhythm, earned fame and fortune for his clever and sudden improvisations, as did the warriors whose praises he sang.

In the past, wor had the capacity to draw a crowd. One will recall that the word then denoted three inseparable activities: to sing, to dance, and to celebrate, all of which once came together in Biak feasts. To protect a child during a dangerous transition, the hostess's natal kin spent the night circling the dancing ground in a clump. At the front of the line were two young men, who leaped and swooped, thrusting and parrying with their drums as they pounded out the beat. Behind them came other drummers, then a knot of male singers, which gradually narrowed to the women who took up the rear. Singing an unending progression of spontaneous songs, the guests stayed in motion from sunset until dawn.

In the course of a night of feasting, Biaks once sang as many as fifteen different kinds of wor. The song form then consisted of dozens of types distinguished by melody, rhythm, and/or social function. Singers I met in the early 1990s still recalled the more common categories: the introduction song (B: *kakarem*), the narrative song (B: *beyuser*), the war song (B: *dow mamun*), and dance songs like the *yerisam*, the *sandia*, and the *dow arbur*. Within particular wor types, they allowed for regional and individual variation.[16] Yet they held that these different "dialects," like the varieties of Biak language, derived from a single complex and consistent scheme, whose mastery was central to the art of wor.

The same sort of contagion that infected the magic vine infused the performances I witnessed when I assisted in the production of an album of Biak music (see chapter 7). Every wor I encountered was divided into a tip (B: *kadwor*; also b*idwam*) and root (B: *fuar*). In collective singing, a man or woman suddenly would start a new song by singing it through as a solo. In the next repetition, another singer answered. Other singers quickly followed, forming opposing sides, with one group singing the *kadwor*, the other the *fuar*. Drummers took up the rhythm, and the volume swelled as more singers learned the lyrics. Within each group, individuals chose their own pitch, joining the chorus when they pleased, and modifying the melody dramatically before ending each line in unison. A song had no leader, and each singer varied the tune in an attempt to stand out. Likewise, each chorus attempted to seize the focus of attention, with the *fuar* singers beginning their verse before the *kadwor* was finished, and the *kadwor* singers retaliating to steal back the song. The effect was "heterophony": a rich mixture of pitches, phrasing, and volumes contained in the structure of a single song (cf. Feld 1988; 1990: 244–246).[17]

With its parallel verses, wor poetry calls to mind the ritual language of eastern Indonesian societies, known for their botanical metaphors and their penchant for "speaking in pairs" (Fox 1974, 1988). But where the structure of Sumbanese couplets, for instance, involves the metaphorical equation of phrases, wor's structure stresses the difference between two renditions of a verse (Kuipers 1990: 76–77; Keane 1997a: 101–110). Producing the effect of a riddle, with the "root" filling in words missing in an otherwise identical "tip," each text is built around a surprise. Consider, for example, this *kankarem*, sung for me by Marinus Workrar in Mara, North Biak. (I have italicized the elements added to the tip to make up the root.)

KADWOR	TIP
Woyo, wunimbare, wunimbare.	Oh, bring it here from a distance, bring it here from a distance.

FUAR	ROOT
Woyo, bin *bena wore wuno sireb bo Myam Me Ba* wunimbare, wunimbare.	Oh, *woman who is holding the feast, bring the tifa drum called Doesn't See the Mother's Brother*, bring it here from a distance, bring it here from a distance.

In the 1940s, at the party where Marinus first sang this dance wor, everyone listened closely for the words that revealed the song's target: the hostess, whom Marinus chided for waiting so long to hold a feast. (It was as if she "did not see" that her children had mother's brothers; hence the drum's name.) At stake for Marinus's fellow guests was their ability to join in the singing; for the hosts, their ability to respond to a veiled criticism or demand. Augustinus Rumapura described how audiences responded to wor's poetic structure. "There's a verse on top [that is, in the *kadwor*], that is only explained underneath [in the *fuar*]. The people listening have to figure it out. What is this guy singing about?" In their alternation between a fragment and a startling whole, the verses assume a metonymic structure of desire or interest (see Lacan 1977: 167; see also Weber 1991: 127). Forever anticipating the "closure" of the "gap," a listener is moved through the song. My recording session with Marinus Workrar suggested the appeal of this process. Children crowded around the doorway and leaned through the windows of the beachfront house, no doubt drawn by the funny sound of this old-fashioned style of singing, not to mention me, the foreign guest. But with them were older relatives who laughed, sighed, and sometimes sang along when they caught the gist of Marinus's high-pitched, warbling words.

If my consultants saw surprise as central to the mythical origin and poetic structure of the genre, they saw it as no less essential to the creation of particular compositions. The wor experts I met all described themselves as artists who could transpose a new sight, sound, or sensation immediately and automatically into a song. Their performances indexed striking moments by providing an icon of the experience on the level of both content and code. Their songs provided evidence of their composers' unprecedented encounters by describing these experiences and by subjecting audiences to the emotions they provoked. Sometimes the outcome of a chance encounter was sorrow or nostalgia, as in the case of a song that suddenly came to Manase Rumsowek after he happened upon a tree that his long-dead mother had planted for him to carve into a canoe. At other times, the focus was the pleasure of an encounter with something novel, as Gabriel Bidwam explained after listening to a wor inspired by a trip to Biak City. "He's surprised (I: *kaget*) to see the lights. But even stranger (I: *yang paling aneh lagi*) is the thing that sits on the table and sings [that is, a radio]." Functioning as a sort of booty providing proof from distant places, good songs once traveled far from their origins, enhancing their composers' renown. Wor composers, like warriors and fish callers, gained recognition for what were seen as unintentional acts. Susceptible to being carried away by their surroundings, they reproduced the sensation in the very structure of their texts.

By virtue of their poetic structure, wor lyrics posit the incursion of a stimulus that interrupts discourse, something like a question in an unknown language. This stimulus can be as simple as a singer's hunger, but it often has included foreigners and foreign things. The following texts, taken from a collection of over one hundred songs, are exemplary in this respect. As such, they illustrate the subversive side of the genre, which was apparent in the very first song I heard. It may have been my first visit to North Biak, but I certainly was not the first Westerner to walk down that beach. As much as Biaks stressed wor's dependence on novelty, what is most striking about the genre is the defamiliarizing power of its form. By repeating perceptions that elsewhere might have passed without remark, these composers confirmed the foreignness of particular experiences and things.

Wor 1. The Foreigner as Interlocutor

The most common type of wor in contemporary Biak, the narrative song or b*eyuser*, often follows the path of a voyage. The late evangelist Utrecht Wompere sang the following wor to validate a story about being conscripted during the Japanese occupation.

KADWOR

1. Koriro kora i*b*ekwan dawo *b*yasero papan byasero.

2. Kayun ro*b* ine ma yakon sajufo madui wam beso ro wam bune nanembune.

3. Ro*b* yara inandamyasi yoresi yayapansonem yaro manor wam bero wuren ya *b*o yanewem fama.

4. S*b*aren damyasi sifuken seya*b*o so*b*e, "Kora ryo, kayun da ryo?"

TIP

1. We set off from the long extended planks.

2. We sailed that night and I sat shivering in the breeze that gusted from the shore.

3. That night close to dawn I was leaning on a pole at the back of the boat when I heard something.

4. They churned up and asked me, "Where are we going, where are we sailing?"

FUAR

1. *Aryo Imem Kapisen*, koriro kora *Sebini jembesan* i*b*ekwan dawo *b*yasero papan byaser.

2. Kayun ro*b* ine ma yakon sajufo madui wam beso ro *Woi* wam bune nanembune.

3. Ro*b* yara inandamyasi yoresi yayapansonem yaro manor wam bero wuren ya *b*o yanewem fama.

4. *Rondansi* si*b*ab*y*a s*b*aren damyasi sifuken seya*b*o so*b*e, "*Naeke* kora ryo, kayun da ryo?"

ROOT

1. *Oh, Uncle Captain*, we set off from *Sebini*, the long *jetty* made of extended planks.

2. We sailed that night and I sat shivering in the breeze that gusted from the shore of *Woi*.

3. That night close to dawn I was leaning on a pole at the back of the boat when I heard something.

4. *The incessantly questioning engines* churned up and asked me, "*Brother*, where are we going, where are we sailing?"

In this, as in most b*eyuser*, the words added in the second verse include personal and place names that establish and enrich the song's field of reference (cf. Basso 1988; Feld 1990: 261–262). By specifying Wompere's imagined audience and the location of the action he describes, these terms take listeners back to the moment when the wor was conceived. Addressed to the foreign captain, the "root" puts Biak words into the mouth of his engines. Into the forbidding setting evoked in the "tip," the stranger and his machinery suddenly enter as kin. Biaks hearing this song are invited to put themselves in the position of the foreign captain, the addressee revealed in line 1 of the tip. Indeed, the very revelation of this addressee—and the mysterious interlocutor in line 4—are what count as the surprise. The imaginary identification elicited through this text constitutes both its proof and its pleasure. Members of a Biak-language audience intercept a narrative directed to a long-gone outsider, who is taught by the song that engines, surprisingly, can speak.

Wor 2. A Shock as Legacy

Inspired by memories from World War II, when, as I have noted, Biak was the focus of heavy fighting, the following song is addressed to a bird.

KADWOR

1. Wabremaie nwara bari wanda, bari wanda.

2. Nyara bar iwande, bari wande.

3. Baya besyamasa subar anya sunaibe farfyaro sarisai, farfyaro.

TIP

1. You sing on your side, the side toward the sea, the side toward the sea.

2. He has the side toward the land, the side toward the land.

3. So that these two sides will someday become the stuff for their stories, their stories.

FUAR

1. *Kowoki man bena kabui aibyayayir ro Fanindi yen Fanindiwa* wabremaie nwara bari wanda, bari wanda.

2. *Suan Amerika ine isan bom inema* nyara bari wande, bari wande.

3. Baya besyamasa *romawa* subar anya sunaibe farfyaro sarisai, farfyaro.

ROOT

1. *Oh, morning bird, with your home in the iron wood there on Fanindi, Fanindi beach*, you sing on your side, the side toward the sea, the side toward the sea.

2. *Mr. America dropped the bomb that* has the side toward the land, the side toward the land.

3. So that these two sides will someday become the stuff of *our sons'* stories, *their* stories.

Toward the end of the Allied campaign, a fighter plane flew over Sor, whose inhabitants had just returned from their hiding places in the forest. Most of the villagers knew not to move. But on Fanindi beach, a few panicked people ran for cover under an ironwood tree. The pilot saw the fleeing figures and assumed that they were Japanese soldiers. He dropped two bombs. The parachute from the first got tangled in the ironwood's branches. The second bomb hit the ground and exploded, killing seven people.

For months, the villagers waited for the soldiers to come and defuse the first bomb. Every day, the morning bird sang on its tree limb, oblivious to the danger. Well after the war ended, the ironwood reminded the villagers of the tragic attack. After a storm knocked down the tree, Jason Dasem composed this wor. Its root disrupts the peaceful scenario portrayed in the tip by repeating the shock of the bombing. But it also extends the trauma's temporal horizons to encompass the history it will have produced. The lyrics link "Mr. America" to the sons who will someday narrate the encounter. The two-sided song is a monument to the two-sided tree, which in turn is a monument to the attack.

Wor 3. Modernity as Maternal

By providing evidence of a startling experience, these first two songs served to confirm the veracity of historical events. The next wor, addressed to a steamship, moves from the epic to the everyday.

KADWOR

1. Wayun bo wayir afio nara narar ro saba sonduna, sonduna.

2. Yaranda yores yasayori yobe ra surande sukun afio yo ro bo bin Biak ansu iryano, ansu iryano.

FUAR

1. Meri bo wai amber ine, wayun bo wayir afio nara narar ro Samberi saba sonduna, sonduna.

2. Yaranda yores yasayori yobe ra awinsu surande sukun afio yo ro Maryendi bo bin Biak ansu iryano, ansu iryano.

TIP

1. You sail and puff smoke across the machete-blade, the machete-blade cape.

2. I go to the sea and gaze from afar; and I thought they were roasting tubers in the Biak women's hills there, over there!

ROOT

1. Passenger ship, foreign canoe, you sail and puff smoke across Samber Point, the machete-blade, the machete-blade cape.

2. I go to the sea and gaze from afar; and I thought the two mothers were roasting tubers in Maryendi, the Biak women's hills there, over there!

As the preceding chapter made clear, to raise a foreigner was a typical dream of Biak mothers. Taro was the privileged gift of food recalled by men and women whose mothers had brought them up to "travel far." This wor, sung by Johannes Sukan, superimposes a foreign ship onto a woman's garden, blending the smoke from her fire and the steam from its stack to blur the divide between two orders. Out of the haze of the "tip," the "foreign canoe" materializes—an uncanny disruption of a quotidian world. By replicating an error in perception, the text enacts the strangeness of an intimate truth.

Wor 4. Technology as Trope

The next wor makes modern technology into a surprising simile for relations among kin.

KADWOR

1. Wo . . . kwansi ra buki dembabyuk aya ro yen anirewa.

2. Ayama mobo sane dun da nairyama sane mura rori ya beukur boi beso be Kema mura yo.

3. Sane mura rori ya beukur boi beso be Sendano mura yo.

4. Bapak manbondi man Sobero ine ryama dobe yo, rwama waso ya ro waio bepyan yabe irawa. Kokara aimando na rao.

TIP

1. You wept as you made him coax me on the beach back there.

2. He captured my heart so my thoughts travel back like that which measures the distance to Kema.

3. My thoughts travel back like that which measures the distance to Sendano.

4. The man from abroad, the man from Tobelo came and said, "Come with me on the boat that waits at the sea." But I think of the islands endlessly.

FUAR

1. *Aryo Awino* kwansi ra buko *anak ya benababari* dembabyuk aya ro *Wai Waio Pyaka* yena nirewa.

2. Ayama mobo sane dun da nairyama sane mura rori *kawai kumora* ya beukur boi beso be Kema mura yo.

3. Sane mura rori *kawai kumora* ya beukur boi beso be Sendano mura yo.

4. Bapak manbondi man Sobero ine ryama dobe yo *sebe anake* rwama waso ya ro *Rorehi* waio bepyan yabe irawa. Kokara aimando na rao *ine*.

ROOT

1. *Oh, Mother*, you wept as you made *your favorite child* coax me on *Wai Waio Pyaka* Beach back there.

2. He captured my heart so my thoughts travel back like *the telephone line* which measures the distance to Kema.

3. My thoughts travel back like *the telephone line* that measures the distance to Sendano.

4. The man from abroad, the man from Tobelo came and said, "*You'll be like my very own child.* Come with me on *Rorehi*, the boat that waits at the sea." But I think of the islands endlessly *now*.

This b*eyuser* dates from the 1930s, when Yakonius Rumaropen was a coolie in northern Maluku. When some Tobelans asked Yakonius to sing them a song, he created this wor, which depicts his tearful departure from Biak. Its invocation doubles the reversal I flagged in the previous examples, which address a captain, a steamship, and a bird. Here, the Biak-language audience hears a song initially composed for ethnic others. Yet these ethnic others are themselves hailed as a Biak mother, in a further transposition of ethnicity and, one assumes, gender. This transposition sets us up to hear an echo between the first and fourth lines of the root, which refer to "your favorite child"—that of the Biak mother—and "my very own child," the singer himself, who is adopted by the foreign man. Between the child who coaxed the singer and the child who agreed to migrate, the simile of the telephone line, revealed in the root, makes a link. Like a cable from the Moluccas to Biak, Yakonius' divided affection mediates between distant worlds.[18]

Wor 5. Foreign Words as Poetic Code

Composers often inserted Indonesian, Dutch, or English words into wor. These were not "loan words," used to fill out a deficient indigenous vocabulary, but "art words" selected for their interesting tones. The following song was created during a recording session with the ethnomusicologist Philip Yampolsky.

KADWOR

1. Myundiso rwamandiyasa, rwamandiyasa.

2. Suworo mindima mukesepen boi muyun dandi ra *bebukayi boi* sukon surower.

TIP

1. It's a good thing you two came, you two came.

2. They will sing a wor for you to record so you can take it over there to open and play while they sit and listen.

FUAR

1. *Aryo naeko Suan Bebaye* myundiso rwamandiyasa, rwamandiyasa.

2. *Romawa* suworo mindima mukesepen boi myun dandi ra *bebukayi boi insoso* bi*n ansu iwa* sukon surower.

ROOT

1. *Oh, Brother, Mr. Big Man,* it's a good thing you two came, you two came.

2. *The young men* will sing a wor for you to record so you can take it over there to open and play while *the young ladies* sit and listen.

The composer, Karolina Amsamsyum, like the vast majority of Biaks, could speak the national language. Although she almost certainly knew the Indonesian word for "record," *merakam*, her couplet employs a complicated but poetic Biak rendering, *mukesepen*, which literally means, "you make a memorializing trace." But in line 2, forgoing *museben*, the simple Biak term for "you open," Karolina sang *mubebuka*, using the Indonesian word to depict my friend and me "opening" the tape and playing it for the young women in the United States. According to Biak listeners, *buka* sounds nicer than *museben*, which would have ruined the verse.

"Indonesian is quoted in poetry to make it more amusing," an expert singer told me. Appropriating the pleasure of translation, some songs repeat a word in both languages: the Biak *farfyar* for "story" in the tip and *sarisa* (I: *cerita*) in the root; *srai* for "coconut" in the tip, and *karapa* (I: *kelapa*) in the root (cf. Fabian 1982). These examples raise another aspect of wor language: the transformation of Indonesian to fit Biak phonology. I never met a Biak who could not pronounce the Indonesian phonemes /l/ or /t/. Yet in Biak poetry, which tinkers with all "normal" speech, these phonemes are always replaced with the Biak /r/ and /s/. Tobelo becomes "Bero," Tuan, "Suan." These transformations add another level of pleasure to Biak play with "foreign talk," as listeners have to decipher the modified Indonesian word. But the game remains within a local linguistic system. Unlike in the case described by Keane (1997d), the national language is alienated at the same time it is absorbed.[19]

These narrative songs, sung by aging men and women, represent but a fraction of the widely varied corpus of songs once sung on Biak. At the same time that the circulation of songs spread the renown of their composers, the genre turned surprising encounters into markers of the passing of social time. The types of wor sung during the course of a dance feast served as a nocturnal clock, setting the rhythm of the event. The events themselves formed the conventional cycle of feasts described in chapter 2 that punctuated the rhythm of a life. The automatic songs did more than generate surprises; they generated temporalities of varying scales.

When I came to Biak in the early 1990s, wor no longer played a central role in Biak feasting. Nonetheless, the poetics of surprise that the genre exemplified had not been lost. What I heard in wor I could see in yospan, a decidedly New Order genre, whose practitioners were by and large unmarried youth. Like wor, yospan enabled Biaks to engage in a peculiar form of submission. Characterized by the surprising circulation of foreign gestures, the dance served to mark contemporary forms of time. In this central component of Biak "feasts for foreigners," we find the principles that guided their feasts for family and fish.

Visual Feasts for Foreigners

The first time I encountered yospan was in 1988, when I joined a planeload of tourists in Bali for one of the national airline's first direct flights to Los Angeles. When we touched down in Biak, it was midnight and I had been sleeping; like most of the other passengers, I had no idea where I was. As we were herded down an endless corridor onto the transit lounge balcony, I heard drumming. Below us, a small troupe of dancers was performing. Feathers bobbing, grass skirts swishing, they jogged in a circle around a handful of musicians. Then the musicians pulled out some stringed instruments and began plucking a quick Western tune. The dancers picked up the pace, skipping and hopping in a neat line of boy-girl pairs. My eyes strayed to the darkened windows, and I suddenly met the gaze of one of the locals who were watching the tourists through the glass.[20] "That stuff with the guitars," a friend would later tell me, "*that* is Biak dancing."

I was introduced to yospan—and Biak—from within the fish trap, as it were. Earlier, I alluded to the connections between the scene at Biak's airport and the settings conjured up to catch flying fish. If Biaks lured fish with foreigners, they lured foreigners with a dance. Unlike wor, which was opaque to outsiders, yospan served as a privileged avenue for bringing them off the airplane and, with luck, out of the airport, to take in Biak's cultural riches. We could call yospan the bait's bait.

Yospan was born of two genres, *yosim* and *pancar*, which were joined by edict in Jayapura in the early 1980s at a seminar convened to select the province's official welcome dance. *Yosim*, the slow jog, is an older step from Sarmi, a regency not far from Irian's capital. *Pancar*, the Biak ingredient in the mix, is of relatively recent origin. A local authority on Biak music traced pancar's birth to the military build-up that preceded the end of Dutch colonialism, when rumors of an impending Indonesian attack swept the islands. The drills of Dutch fighter pilots inspired an "anonymous artist" to invent a step imitating an airplane entering a stall. Performing it to folk songs, some of which supposedly commemorated the "liberation" of West Irian, Biak people named the dance *pantjar gas*, literally "jet."[21]

The quick, energetic dance was an immediate hit on Biak, as was yospan, which alternates fast and slow musical passages to let dancers catch their breath. Imported from Jayapura by students on break, yospan rapidly became a staple at feasts and ceremonies, great and small. During the period of my fieldwork, most major and many minor national holidays occasioned a yospan contest. Dancers waited on the tarmac to greet every high-ranking official who passed through. The tourism bureau sponsored an annual parade that brought together teams from across the regency to perform for any visitors who happened to be in town. In Biak City and in the villages, no one could plan a wedding or farewell party without first seeking a police permit so that the guests could dance yospan—or, as they said, "play" (B: *fnak*)—until dawn.

Almost every rural community and urban neighborhood had its own yospan band, with instruments that included a pair of store-bought guitars, a couple of ukuleles carved of wood, and a gargantuan, brightly painted two-

Figure 7. A yospan band at the regent's house in Biak City

stringed double bass (see Figure 7). Some groups had recently added a "percussion set," consisting of a squat metal or wooden cylinder covered in hide and one or two of the region's hourglass *tifa* drums (B: *sireb*). At parties, the band would sit on benches in the center of the dance ground, singing in harmony, strumming, drumming, and beating the strings of the prone double bass with a stick. At the yospan parades, band members walked as they sang, rolling their basses in elaborate little floats constructed to resemble "traditional" houses or canoes.

Although some groups made modest profits off cassette sales, yospan remained more or less an amateur art, with a shared repertoire of songs circulating among the regency's groups. With the exception of an occasional hymn or popular hit adapted to a yospan beat, most of the dance songs I heard were or were derived from old Biak folk songs, anthems to the islands' beauty and the loved ones a traveler left behind.[22]

Apuse, kukon dao.	Grandmother, we sat together too long,
Yara *be* soren Doreri.	I have to leave for the Doreh seas.
Wuf lenso *ba*ninema, *be*kipasi,	Wave your handkerchief!
Arafa*bye*,	Alas!
Auswara kwar.	You're on your way!

So goes "*Apuse*," the Biak song played on the intercom before takeoff on the national airline's domestic flights.[23] I was told that the composer was a well-known teacher and evangelist who wrote the tune in the 1930s. However, most yospan songs did not hit the national airwaves, as it were, and the young men who sang them often did not know who wrote them or understand all the words.

What was important about yospan songs was that they were good for dancing. The familiar music provided a backdrop for the genre's startling steps. At a village feast, celebrants circled the band in an increasingly disorganized file of pairs. Typically, the line was led by a young man and woman, who were siblings, cross-cousins, or sweethearts. They selected and switched the steps, which were expertly followed by the pairs of teenagers directly behind them. After the aficionados came the trainees, school children who picked up the changing routine more or less quickly. They were followed by adult women, who bumbled along happily. Colliding during a tricky reverse or a sideways hop, some gave up on yospan altogether and reverted to the simpler *fier* dance. Then came the young men, often dangerously high on palm wine, who mimicked the leaders with clumsy abandon. An old man often took up the rear, prancing along with a stick or a cane, doing his best to make the onlookers laugh.

As the night wore on, the dance picked up energy. Having sung for five or six hours, singers had to strain their rasping voices to make themselves heard. The dancers sang along, and sometimes their formation would come close to disintegrating, as when the leaders doubled back to form two concentric circles of panting dancers hurtling past each other. A night of partying in the coastal villages sometimes would end in a brawl, as inebriated band members greeted the sunrise by chucking dancers into the sea. Building and releasing tension in the fashion that once characterized wor, parties ended with the celebrants dragging themselves home to sleep it off.

What wor once did in time, village yospan did in space, sending new moves like nerve impulses down a ganglion of dancers. In government-sponsored contests and performances, this effusiveness was suppressed. The better groups had a trainer, who drilled six to eight boy-girl pairs in a routine of shifting steps, set to the clean harmonies of the band. After shuffling in neat columns to the stage or the grandstand, the dancers would skip and sashay through a series of symmetrical formations in front of the jury and honored guests. Judged for creativity, costumes, but above all unity, the competitors' brief and expert rendition of the genre seemed a far cry from the playful village dances. Nevertheless, driven by a love of pleasure and a thirst for victory, yospan's poles were linked by the circulation of new moves.

The pleasure of yospan lay in its ever-changing repertoire of steps. The genre is as visually variegated as wor is vocally diverse. The basic steps are simple: *yosim* takes little concentration, and *pancar*, a forward double bunny-hop with hands thrown up in mock distress, is easy to pick up. The *jef* and its many variations are more complicated: two quick steps forward, one step back, two quick steps forward, one step back, four slow forward steps, and three hops back on each foot. Then there is the "hoe" (I: *pacul*) and a series of complicated combinations that incorporate Western dance moves: the skater's waltz, the two-step, the wedding march, the swing. At the contests and performances I attended, the announcers always stressed the autoch-thonous symbolism embodied in the latter, but it did not take a trained eye to detect borrowings. Eager to surpass their competitors, yospan teams found new and unusual moves, which showed up at village parties with astonishing speed.

The pleasure of competitive yospan also lay in an ever-changing array of costumes. In the parades, the dancers had to wear "local materials," and so they appeared in a bewildering assortment of frocks fashioned from fibers, bark cloth, bones, and feathers. Many teams wore a modified version of the highlands' "grass skirt," which they dyed a bright pastel and raised to cover the women's breasts. A contest organizer once showed me a photograph of a group of Biak women from an old Dutch ethnography he owned.[24] He told me that he planned to design an outfit that incorporated their loincloths, but for the most part, yospan's costumes reflected other peoples' "customs." This tendency became even clearer when a jury slackened the rules. On Armed Forces Day, one team appeared in bow ties, orange satin shirts, dress pants, and patent leather shoes.

That anyone could do yospan was the assumption and apparently the rule. Perhaps not surprisingly, the winner of the first annual parade was an eth-nically mixed squad of military wives. In the early 1990s, some government agencies took to organized yospan as an indigenous form of aerobics. The activity seemed to supplement "morning exercises" (I: *senam pagi*), an official routine performed to the same catchy march, at the same time each week, at schools and offices throughout Indonesia. The genre had little chance of replacing these ubiquitous national calisthetics, although the contests stressed the same conformity of body and mind. But in the end, yospan's visual openness overran the hierarchies rehearsed across the nation first thing each Friday. The dance responded to stimuli at an alarming rate, recombin-ing fragments of alien gestures, giving its observers the sense that they were seeing themselves in a twisted mirror. It seemed in yospan's logic that perfor-mances for guests always seemed to end, like so many of the "ethnic" dances performed for tourists in Indonesia, with the dissolution of the boundary between the viewers and the viewed. A lunchtime performance at the regent's mansion climaxed with the university rector linking arms with the army commander's wife and calling his Canadian funders to join the line. Dutch church delegates climbed the stage at a national women's conference; young dancers pulled tourists from their chairs. In a seductive exchange of gazes, yospan seemed destined to appropriate whatever came into "sight."

When Irian Jaya's team entered the stadium for the opening ceremonies of Indonesia's National Sports Competition (I: *Piala Olahraga Nasional* or PON) in 1993, the neat columns of athletes broke into yospan. Before the president's box, they froze, turned, and doffed their caps, before picking up the next step without missing a beat. During the soccer final, life in Biak ground to a halt as people crowded around televisions to watch Irian Jaya take on Aceh. What commentators had dubbed "the *yosim pancar* team" ended the Indonesian Olympics undefeated in soccer, wowing even a German "expert." Irian's skillful execution of "European" strategies made this the best Indonesian soccer squad he had ever seen.[25]

The yospan team's victory at PON spawned dreams of glory, in which Irian's athletes soared to ever-greater heights. But the thrill soon faded and the crowds dispersed, to remain dormant until the next Olympic year. Like wor and fishing magic, yospan marked time. But where the older practices followed the cycles of the sun, waves, and stars, yospan moved to the music of a different cosmos. The contests and parties divided the Biak year according to a calendar that was both patriotic and Christian. Independence Day was worthy of yospan; the changing of the ocean's currents was not. Communities used yospan to commemorate transitions sanctioned by national norms: people celebrated weddings, not nose-borings; the consecration of churches, not the taking of heads. Throughout a night of feasting, celebrants switched songs and steps at random; people had no need to make yospan function as a clock. In harmony with the state's ideology of "development," yospan endlessly reiterated the impression of progress. There was nothing remarkable about the ambivalence that some Biaks felt towards the genre. Yospan changed so quickly, it seemed poised to disappear.

Periodically marking Biak's place in the nation, yospan served as a token of recognition for an authoritarian state. But this token of submission was not quite what it seemed. I have recounted *pancar*'s birth in a mythical instant of shock, which recalls the beginning of wor. I have described how yospan mimetically incorporated the foreign—and foreigners—into its circulating moves. I have suggested how village dances sustained the drama of older forms of feasting. If contemporary Biaks were dancing to the beat of other drummers, they seemed to be taking their own steps. Surprise was still the stuff of repetition, as a closer look at Biak holidays should confirm.

Between the first of December and New Year's day, the Biak congregations

I visited held multiple services to commemorate Christ's birth. Everyone got their own "Christmas"—the women, the children, the families, the youth. Everyone attended everyone else's celebrations to enjoy the donuts, coffee, and yospan served up at each event. Government officials considered December a dangerous month. It opened with the anniversary of the first raising of the Papuan "Morning Star" flag, which occurred under Dutch supervision on December 1, 1961. Its many parties gave people with grudges an ample opportunity to vent their wrath. To prevent violence from erupting in the revelry, the government banned the sale of alcohol from November through January. Military patrols trimmed any coconut flowers that palm wine drinkers or sellers could tap. But celebrants found ways to subvert the prohibition, which only seemed to add to the thrill. The holidays were never as calm as they were bright.

The excitement climaxed with the arrival of the New Year. At midnight in Sor in 1994, boys began firing homemade bamboo cannons, drawing their distant neighbors into a war of noise. The random explosion of flammable vapors shattered the silence until well after dawn. There was a cease-fire for a church service before the battle raged on, to be fought to the last drop of kerosene. Marked by youthful aggression, New Year's day was also an occasion for grief. At the end of the church service, many in the congregation began to weep as they joined a long receiving line at the altar. As the villagers shook hands, their tears expressed both sorrow for the past and fear for the future. The year 1993 was gone forever, a friend explained, "and so are all the people who died that year." The year 1994 had come, with all its mysteries: "Who knows, maybe we'll die this year, too!"

Besides tears and explosions, the New Year was welcomed with yospan. Beginning at sunrise and lasting until dark, the dancing inverted the nocturnal schedule of a feast and transcended the division between hosts and guests. Attacking their neighbors with songs, roving bands circled every house in the village. They demanded drink or money from the occupants, then urged them to join the departing line. Bands from other villages flooded into the community, miming the rampages of old. Replaying old traumas, these villagers relived the New Year as a bombing raid, an assault, a sudden death. Feasting and fighting, intoxicated by spirits both liquid and spectral, the "survivors" submitted to the catastrophe of the passing years.

Surprise and Subversion

Yospan illuminates a puzzle that remained implicit in wor. The Biaks I knew celebrated the New Year on the same day as did societies all over the world. Why did their festivities register this holiday as an occasion for surprise? Since the cycles marked by yospan are so obviously imported, we can not repeat the mistake of Dutch structuralists by tracing the "instability" embodied in the genre to the natural world. Nor can we reduce yospan's ceaseless mimicry to a self-conscious effort either to resist or emulate powerful outsiders. Like the warriors of the past, contemporary artists appeared as intoxicated, animated by forces beyond their control. A Freudian reading might trace their compulsion to repeat unprecedented encounters to an unresolved trauma, which Biaks were attempting to master retrospectively (Freud [1920] 1961: 35–39). Still, it is worth recalling Freud's insight that such a trauma can be a fantasy derived from a mixture of experiences (see [1918] 1963). It is difficult to distinguish between the striking moments posited by Biak performances and those that, presumably, gave rise to the poetics I have described. Fishing magic, wor, and yospan did more than respond to shock; they recreated it in the very act of tapping the pleasure of surprise. In the early 1990s, Biak audiences and performers fetishized the foreign with the same paradoxical effects that we explored in the previous chapter. In their conventional efforts to capture the unexpected, they ensured that the foreign remained strange.

However, just because the genres I have described in this chapter worked to reproduce their own startling source does not mean they had no relation to history. Warrior stories recreated the mythical birth of the Land of the Foreigners by turning random violence into the origin of social order. Although there is no way to specify the event that gave rise to the poetics described in this chapter, critical junctures in the islands' history do present themselves as legible in terms of current chartings of pleasure and fear. In 1915, an intoxicated warrior named Aweko (the White Parrot) murdered an Ambonese evangelist on a North Biak beach. Witnesses claimed the victim stepped between the *mambri* and his target, but the Dutch colonial government and the Protestant mission suspected a plot. To find the culprit, Lieutenant Feuilletau de Bruyn "cleansed" the islands of suspected collaborators. His troops detained every man they encountered on their way to the scene of the crime (Feuilletau de Bruyn 1916: 261).[26] After marching the length of the coast wired together by their necks, some of the captives were returned to their villages after the killer's cross-cousin betrayed him. Still others were incarcerated in Manokwari or Ternate, where they remained even after Aweko was shot.

In their accounts of the episode, North Biaks described "Dekna," their nickname for Feuilletau de Bruyn, in the terms reserved for warriors as well as other notables: to them, he was the "most evil" of men. But they insisted that out of this "evil" came "good;" the crime and its punishment led to progress and light. Feuilletau de Bruyn's patrol founded a permanent military post and opened a road through Biak's interior. The improvements in security enabled the Protestant mission to serve areas that long had remained out of reach. Schools and congregations were founded, often at the urging of the warriors whom Dekna had deported. Supposedly, they had learned the importance of education during their stay in distant jails. By setting genres like wor and yospan in the context of colonial violence, one sees how this history can be inscribed in a register quite unlike the official forms of narration described by White (1987) and Dirks (1990). This past found a place in New Order Biak not only in the content of local stories but also in the genres of social action my consultants found most compelling. Feuilletau de Bruyn's campaign belonged to Biak's history, but also to its historicity; it was echoed whenever performers turned shock into delight.

Wor, yospan, and fishing magic assumed conventional forms and functions in contemporary Biak, but they also evoked the possibility of pure acts of transgression. Their formal affinities with Biak warfare reflect the weakness of analyses that attempt to oppose violence to speech (see, for example, Scarry 1985). The connections I have drawn in this chapter turn on a shared vision of agency, quite alien to those who conceive of social action as the product of self-conscious subjects. Effective action does not derive from self-interested agents but from persons who embody alien powers. The persistent valorization of this concept of creative action is surprising, in light of scholarship on other parts of the former Dutch East Indies. Among the Weyewa of Sumba, valued genres of verbal art vanished with the colonial identification and suppression of local leaders who exemplified "angry men" (Kuipers 1998: 42–66). Under the pressure of colonial interventions and institutions, Weyewa men and women came to regard the encompassing state as a center, to which they related as cunning, yet timid, subordinates. When they perform ritual speech, forceful oratory has given way to laments. With the suppression of warfare, much changed in Biak society. But the mode of action posited in Biak feuding has remained.

It is the paradoxical fact that to act, Biaks have had to alienate themselves from the sources of their agency that provides an entry into the subversive side of their complicity. The genres depicted in this chapter, on the face of it, played a central role in Biak's cultural integration into the nation. That is not to say that Biaks were unaware of the importance of wor in colonial-era outbursts of Koreri, or of yospan in the separatist struggle that followed the transfer to Indonesia. Given their association with temporal rhythms, it makes sense that these genres, along with flying-fish magic, were performed or evoked in the enormous dance feasts that accompanied these movements. Opening a utopia of endless pleasure, Manarmakeri's arrival was supposed to signal the end of time. Still, one could argue that wor and yospan's role in antigovernment uprisings mattered little; genres can always be mobilized for radically different political purposes. Through the invention of yospan and, as we will see, the revival of wor, Biaks acted as good New Order subjects. Yet, as I hope the broader context I have provided suggests, there was more to their complicity than met the eye.

In the next chapter, the unruly consequences of this conception of agency come more clearly into view. In the interpretive strategies of the leaders I describe, something untranslatable was attributed to the speech and writing of outsiders. Instead of appearing as the alien origin of pleasurable surprises, the Land of the Foreigners became, through their practices, an inaccessible source of unfathomable truths. I offer another angle on the fetishization of the foreign by examining how collaborators and rebels alike appropriated what I will call the authority of absence. Through the practices of those who claimed privileged access to foreign texts, incommensurability was not just negotiated; it was produced.

CHAPTER FOUR

The Authority of Absence

I<small>N</small> 1993, in an upscale neighborhood in Biak City, the negotiation of Decky Wambrur's marriage to Helly Karwor involved a curious deployment of "custom" (I: *adat*). Given what I knew of the Indonesian government's politics of culture, I could not help taking a cynical view of the affair. The day before the meeting in which the two families were to decide on the bridewealth, I had returned from a trip to find my home on the Ridge filled with fuming strangers. Sally Bidwam introduced them as her long-lost relatives. Young Decky had arrived the day before with his Biak father, his Javanese mother, his sister, her three children, and his aunt to ask Helly's family for her hand. The preliminary negotiations had not gone well. The Karwors had raised questions about Decky's treatment of Helly. They claimed that he had kept her from participating in campus activities when the two were in college, and that he had struck her once during a spat. The potential groom's behavior was often at issue at this stage in the process, Sally told me. She knew of one humiliated couple whose son had been forced to sign a statement swearing that he would stop drinking and fighting before formal discussions could begin. In this case, the Karwors had added injury to insult by making a series of demands concerning who should attend the meeting (that is, Decky, but not his sharp-tongued aunt) and what gifts the Wambrurs should bring to the event (that is, several antique vases and a large sum of cash). The Wambrurs were enraged at their prospective in-laws' recalcitrance. As Decky's aunt emphatically informed me, this affair was the concern of "big foreigners" (B: *amber beba*), of which the groom's family boasted no fewer than the bride's. There was Decky's father, the chief of tourism in a regency on Irian's mainland. There was his official representative, Fritz Rumorek, a high-ranking health worker like his cousin, my friend and hostess Sally. There was Dina Kapare, Fritz's brother's wife, a civil servant who was the sister of a well-known performer. And now there would be me, the American scholar, whom the Wambrurs wanted present at the subsequent events.

The next day, wearing our Sunday best, we set out for the Karwors' in a chartered van, stopping on the way to purchase an antique Chinese vase to offer as an opening gift.[1] The night before, Fritz had managed to reject, as "incorrect procedure," a demand of Rp. 500,000 and three cases of beer.[2] It did not take us long to make it through the bride's parents' front door, thanks to Sally's last-minute briefing of Decky's sister, who had to scrape her feet, turn around twice, and say the proper Biak verses before presenting the porcelain. Once inside, we found ourselves confronted with an opposing team of "foreign" figures: Mr. Karwor, the prospective father of the bride, a high-ranking official; his spokesman, a smooth-talking paramedic from another island; and Mr. Karwor's late wife, a Makassarese woman, unable, of course, to be there in person, whose wishes were voiced vicariously from beyond the grave. Some time later, our firepower would increase when the daughter of the regency's highest-ranking official waltzed in with more porcelain to present on Decky's behalf. But for the moment, the biggest of the aliens on hand for the proceedings was on the other side: the bride's father's uncle, a Biak lieutenant colonel whose stripes and epaulettes exuded an aura of command.

Mr. Karwor's spokesman opened the proceedings with a speech in Indonesian on how the vase had "opened the door," turning what otherwise would have been an unwelcome intrusion into a legitimate proposal of marriage. He then turned over the floor to the lieutenant colonel, who had "just flown in from Jakarta." The officer began by politely introducing himself to the Wambrurs, whom he professed not to know, before conversing with me briefly in English. Having thus posed as the most "foreign" of the "local aliens," the officer turned to the problem at hand. This was not a military matter, he reassured us. He was here not as a soldier but as a worried grandfather. He was disturbed by the Wambrur's failure to honor the Karwor's "traditional" requests. Not only had they failed to present the requisite cases of beer, they had refused to bring Decky to meet Helly's family. The lieutenant colonel was not familiar with the couple's relationship, but he sensed that there was cause for alarm.

> I'm Irianese but I've been in Java for a long time. I haven't really been following developments here. But I just heard that my brothers and sisters from the woman's side are pursuing a point of custom (I: *tuntut soal adat*). If we all recognize custom, there won't be any trouble. . . . If those from the men's side understand custom, "No problem" [the lieutenant colonel said this in English]. Well, every ethnic group in Indonesia has custom (I: *punya adat*). And the government protects it. No doubt, you already know. If it weren't for custom, there would be no government. No populace (I: *rakyat*), no government. This is the fundamental issue.

The lieutenant colonel was well acquainted with the customs of Java, Sunda, and Kalimantan, he went on—and that was how he knew that Biak's must be preserved.

Delivered in formal Indonesian and peppered with platitudes, the lieutenant colonel's lecture seemed to have the desired effect. The Wambrurs accepted a written request for bridewealth. It was agreed that Decky would present himself for some "advice" from the officer, and that the Karwors would keep Helly close to home. The event ended with the sharing of betel nut and small talk dominated by the officer, who held forth in a mixture of

Biak and English about his experiences in Java and the United States, whose "customs" he also professed to know well. While they smiled and nodded at the time, later at Sally's house, Decky's relatives scoffed at the lieutenant colonel's pretences. That uniform was outdated, Sally noted archly; if she had known he would be dressed that way she would have worn her nursing whites. In any case, the Karwors were only distantly related to the officer, Decky's aunt pitched in; clearly they had recruited him in a last-ditch effort to lend the family some much-needed prestige. Even if the lieutenant colonel were the big foreigner he pretended to be, nothing could disguise the shabbiness of the Karwor women's clothing or the nails in their walls, which once had been covered with precious plates. With Mr. Karwor's recent demotion to a less lucrative post, the family was in dire need of porcelain and cash, and so they had trumped up that complaint about custom and Decky's misdeeds in order to justify a higher price for the bride. But the Wambrurs would show them in five months time, when they paraded the demanded bridewealth through the streets of Biak City. Then everyone would know which family was really capable of mobilizing distinguished persons and valuable things.

The struggle between the families never reached a clear conclusion; tragically, the bride died before a wedding date was set.[3] But one can detect something important about Biak conceptions of authority by considering the strategies deployed in the dispute. It was not the substance of the lieutenant colonel's recommendations that the Wambrurs attacked when they rehashed the meeting, even though his suggestion that the prospective groom attend the negotiations went against what was generally felt to be the norm. Rather it was his "foreignness" that they later called into question: the same quality that had allowed the officer to command their attention without claiming special knowledge of the matter at hand. Just as the foreign porcelain validated the Wambrurs' proposal, the lieutenant colonel's foreign experiences validated his complaints. His years in the Land of the Foreigners (B: *Sup Amber*) were as compelling as his military resources and rhetoric. The officer spoke with authority on Biak's customs and conflicts—*because he had not been there.*

Authority and Textuality

Extracted from its context, it would be tempting to interpret the lieutenant colonel's short-lived victory as a vote of confidence in a government that posed as the guardian of tradition. This certainly was not the first time I heard Biaks voicing government rhetoric, or seen them speaking in the official register of the Indonesian state. Analysts of New Order oratory have identified a number of distinguishing traits: its impersonality, its vagueness, its unchanging themes, its recurrent deployment of key words like progress, custom, and security (Hooker 1993; Errington 1998: 51–64; Anderson [1966] 1990: 144–51). Errington, most tellingly, writes of official Indonesian as communicating the "view from nowhere," a trait that Javanese conversationalists deploy to their advantage in order to appear in a superior moral light (1998: 178; see also Nagel 1986). Official Indonesian is "textlike" in the way that *krama*, the honorific speech style of Javanese, is textlike; hence it is the perfect medium for mediating unequal relationships, for conveying commands and enlightenment from on high (Anderson [1966] 1990: 145–146; Siegel 1986: 21). In style and content, the Indonesian utterances I heard on Biak generally mirrored official models, whether one has in mind a village chief holding forth during a dispute resolution or a church elder formally greeting a guest. If Philip Karma's deposition is any indication, this separatist leader also deployed New Order models. The example of Philip Karma is, of course, the most puzzling. Karma evoked New Order rhetoric to attract an audience that, on that very occasion, had gathered to deny that they were Indonesian at all.

It is the goal of this book to make sense of the strange combination of complicity and resistance with which Biaks in the early 1990s dealt with the New Order. In this chapter, I consider the fetishization of the foreign in a context in which its political implications are particularly clear. The task at hand, to borrow from Goffman ([1974] 1986), is to find a frame that makes sense of the odd performances of Biak leaders, performances that seemed self-serving, to be sure, but slightly askew in their engagements. That is, this chapter's aim is to find the basis for an interpretive strategy that gave Biaks a coherent sense of "what it is that's going on here" (ibid.: 8) when men and women spouted government rhetoric—other than a whole-hearted, if awkward, endorsement of the policies of the state.

To take just one example of how such an interpretive strategy might work, consider the lieutenant colonel and the marriage negotiation described above. Although the officer's speech sounded like pure propaganda to me, my companions may have heard something different in his diatribe. Even though they later criticized the officer, they did not reject the basis of his claims. At the time of the meeting, the Wambrurs listened intently. The officer's constant references to his displacement from another scene highlighted the alien origins of his words. Like his uniform, his platitudes served to index his encounters in other places and times. To borrow Baker's terms, his listeners' "comprehension" of his speech—their ability to restate and evaluate his message—was overshadowed by their "apprehension" that what they were hearing derived from a distant center of power (1993: 108).[4]

In varying ways, the leaders described in this chapter appealed to the "textuality" of outsiders' discourse: those qualities that allow utterances to seem autonomous from their speakers' interests and the matter at hand. Recent scholarship has highlighted the authority achieved through "entextualiz-ation" and "recontextualization"—processes entailing the translation of "autonomous" segments of discourse from one context of performance to another (Bauman and Briggs 1990: 74; Kuipers 1990; Keane 1997a: 133; 1997c: 62–63; Silverstein and Urban 1996). This approach could provide a method for analyzing the authority of New Order oratory: "the view from nowhere" is not intrinsic to Indonesian as a language, but is the product of standardizing institutions and conventions that mark a speaker's words as transcending and encompassing particular scenes. Such an analysis would focus on an orator's ability to extend a powerful sense of presence: to achieve the spread of the regime's authority through the widespread repetition of its texts. In analyzing Biak performances, one must account for a different out-come. There is a subtle yet significant difference between Indonesian as an "unnative language," one too neutral to conjure an image of "native speakers" (Errington 1998), and Indonesian as *wos amber*, literally "foreign speech." To appreciate this difference, one must pay heed to the tendency of entextualiz-ation and recontextualization to insinuate differences into the very contexts they serve to constitute and connect.

This potential for estrangement rests on two related aspects of significa-tion. On the one hand, signification depends on the iterability of representa-tions: the fact they are "detachable from particular speakers and acts of speaking" (Keane 1997a: 25; see also Derrida 1973, 1981, 1982, 1988). It is not only when one writes that one finds oneself alienated from one's signs but, potentially, every time one speaks. It is not simply that it is impossible to express oneself fully in language. Rather, without the process of objec-tification that accompanies mediation by a code, there is no recognition of a self. On the other hand, representation in general, like writing in particular, embodies a structure of delay and distancing. The meaning of a particular segment of discourse is the product of movement through a chain of nega-tively defined distinctions. Along the axes of selection and combination used in writing or speech, we can only grasp the significance of a sign in relation to what it is not.[5] Words, sentences, and narratives are only legible through a process of anticipated retrospection: meaning only emerges in relation to what will have come before. As the basis for these interrelated qualities of the trace, the problematically material character of discourse opens the possi-bility for divergent readings and renderings. Even official pronouncements can run astray.

The stress my consultants placed on the indexical character of certain instances of discourse—taking words as impressions left by the impact of absent worlds—emphasizes aspects of signification suppressed in settings where language is taken as a transparent instrument to communicate facts and ideas. The ideology I am describing would seem the opposite of that associated with standard national languages, when they are taken as "not just infrastructural for communication within territorial boundaries and across institutional contexts" but also as necessary for "objective, context-free, 'modern' modes of discourse and thought" (Errington 1998: 61–62).[6] But one would be mistaken to take Biak perspectives as simply the inversion of some monolithic "modern" view. Work in the ethnography of speaking and writing points to the diversity of local treatments of the written word (Street 1984, 1993; McKenzie 1987; Ewald 1988; Messick 1989; George 1990; Gewertz and Errington 1991; Kulick 1992a: 168–175; Boyarin 1993; Kulick and Stroud 1993; O'Hanlon 1995; Silverstein and Urban 1996). Other research has revealed the divergent ways in which spirit mediums and orators displace the source of agency from the speaking self (see Bloch 1975; Siegel 1978; Brenneis and Myers 1984; Lindstrom 1984, 1990; Myers 1986b; Duranti 1988; Boddy 1989; Watson-Gegeo and White 1990; Cannell 1991; Steedly 1993; Keane 1997a, c). One can only make sense of these varied discursive practices by placing them within the context of a wider social world.

In the preceding chapters, I have already sketched the outlines of such a world. Recall the feasts and informal settings in which brothers presented their sisters' children with valuables acquired abroad, valuables that served as proof of an uncle's prowess. The fact that this proof could be provided through performances, as well as by way of "solid" goods, was established in my discussion of wor and yospan. These genres clearly served as a conventional means of indexing an artist's experiences in foreign lands. Although a common history underlay these different facets of the fetishization of the foreign, it is worth distinguishing among the figures of the alien that Biak practices presupposed and reproduced in the early 1990s. The practices described in chapter 2 played up the excessive character of foreign value; those described in chapter 3 highlighted the startling character of foreign acts; those described in this chapter emphasized the opaque, inscrutable character of foreign words.

Like wor singers and like participants in the ceremonial economy, Biak orators and authors fetishistically reproduced the foreignness of a wider national and global context. Their pursuit of authority gave rise to a distinctive form of translation that stressed the textuality of foreign slogans, documents, and books. I use the term "translation" in an expanded sense to refer to the varied ways that Biaks offered evidence of their encounters with the spoken and written words of outsiders. My understanding of this process highlights aspects of translation cast in shadow by approaches that aspire to the seamless transfer of meaning from one language to another (Venuti 1992; see also Benjamin [1923] 1968; Mehrez 1992; Jacquemond 1992; Niranjana 1994).[7] The men and women I consider sought renown by presenting themselves as having access to texts with no true equivalent in the vernacular. Their translations created their own impetus and object: an external realm of meaning that provided local leaders with an avenue to power and prestige.

The lieutenant colonel would have been the last man on earth to call himself subversive. And, indeed, had his superiors witnessed the negotiation that Sunday, they would not have noticed anything amiss. There were no markers internal to his performance that changed his "footing," that is, that signaled a shift in his relationship to his utterances from a straightforward to a more complexly strategic deployment of New Order terms (Goffman 1981: 128; [1974] 1986: 40–80; Austin 1976: 2n). One can only detect such a transformation by expanding the scope of inquiry to notions of authority and authenticity expressed in other contexts, and to other, more explicit instances of translation. In the following pages, I take both these tacks: first, gleaning what can be learned about Biak leadership from a comparative perspective and second, setting the performances of particular individuals in the context of collective translations of the Bible, the most esteemed and sacred of "foreign" texts. At the very least, my evidence calls into question the view that literacy inexorably leads to the changes in consciousness associated with nationalism, Christian conversion, and modernity more generally. As the interpretive strategies described in this chapter make clear, it does not always mean the same thing to read.

The Making of Big Foreigners

In colonial times, the meanings that Biaks and other Papuans ascribed to reading were frequently unsettling to Dutch missionaries and officials. Strange specimens of foreign writing often turned up in the possession of supposedly illiterate warriors and shamans. From official letters of appointment from the sultans of Tidore, to European works of theology, to the membership log of a California swim club, imported books and documents served as instruments of protection and divination for men and women who claimed to know how to tap their magical power (Kamma 1972: 222). In contemporary times, foreign texts remained potent, alluring objects, despite my informants' widespread literacy and fluency in the codes of outsiders. To understand why, one must consider first the nature of authority as Biaks envisioned it and second, the circulation of languages and literatures on the ground.

Not surprisingly, given Biak's history, the big foreigners I knew failed to fall squarely within Melanesian models of leadership, including Godelier's ([1982] 1986) typology, which focuses on "tribal" societies supposedly isolated from the impact of state-based forms of hegemony.[8] Godelier locates "great men," who exercise ascribed authority in warfare and ritual, in societies where restricted sister-exchange marriage and blood feuding follow the principle that a life must be given for a life. Found in societies with bride-wealth and the payment of death indemnities, "big men," by contrast, achieve authority by monopolizing the shells, pigs, and other commodities that served as media of social reproduction. In contemporary Biak, as one will recall from chapter 2, one found named, patrilineal, patrilocal kin groups, called "keret," and a system of marriage that traditionally included both the use of bridewealth and the occasional exchange of sisters. Unions were not permitted between first and second cousins, giving rise to a pattern of "scattered alliance" (cf. Liep 1991: 38). Although my consultants occasionally referred to inherited prerogatives, the tendency was to downplay lineage-based claims to authority. "Big foreigners" looked less like "big men" or "great men" than "men of prowess": individuals whose goal was less to follow their forebears than to become ancestors themselves (Wolters 1982, 1994; Reid 1988; Atkinson 1989; Tsing 1990, 1993; see also chapter 2).

I have already described how individuals both gained and demonstrated prowess by mobilizing the matrilateral relationships that cross-cut their patrilineal kin groups. As I explained, the bonds of love and debt that linked brothers and sisters, on the one hand, and mothers and children, on the other, perpetuated an "inflationary" economy, financed by an ongoing "raiding" of foreign wealth. Encouraging individuals to seek novel ways to stand out above their peers, this system of kinship once served to validate authority derived from an array of spheres, from distant entrepôts to the invisible world of the spirits. Dutch observers listed an array of Biak leaders from clan elders (B: *adir*), to warriors (B: *mambri*), to shamans (B: *mon*), to village chiefs (B: *mananir menu*) (Kamma 1972: 12–13; see also Feuilletau de Bruyn 1920). In the 1990s, Biak leaders ranged from government officials to pastors to traditional musicians, blacksmiths, and healers.[9] One could measure their authority as much from their success in assembling an audience for their performances as from their ability to shape the course of events (cf. Geertz 1980; Anderson [1972] 1990; Atkinson 1989; Tsing 1990, 1993). Authority in Biak, as elsewhere in the region, was a function of being known by distant others (see Munn 1986). Having a name entailed recognition of one's skills, status, and right to pronounce on matters of collective concern. My consultants also tended to describe people who enjoyed authority in a given setting as those who "had a voice," an expression I also heard with reference to Biak brides (see chapter 2). For the foreigners I encountered, this acknowledgement derived from relatives, fellow villagers, acquaintances, and strangers, who produced and confirmed the fame of leaders by repeating stories about their exploits abroad. Besides marriage negotiations, the planning of church construction projects and other community events provided arenas for the exercise of authority, as did land disputes and court cases on the village and district level. Big foreigners with connections to the military or government also proved themselves by interceding on others' behalf.

Faced with the diverse forms of leadership found in other Austronesian-speaking parts of Melanesia, scholars have divided newly emerging figures who control the flow of valued objects from older notables who control the ritual production of valued persons (Jolly 1991: 77). Biak descriptions of the prestige gained through the bestowal of foreign valuables suggest that one should be cautious in imposing such a distinction. In New Order Biak, wealth could only become a source of authority when it indexed one's access to absent sources of value and power (cf. Helms 1988, 1993). The gifts that circulated on Biak in the early 1990s embodied different histories, connecting the alien with the past and the ancestors in varying ways. A Tidoran title or an antique Chinese vase referred not only to a far land and a long history of trade but also to the forebears who brought them to Biak. A T-shirt or radio recently acquired in Jakarta evoked a less layered sense of distancing in space and time. Yet however it was configured, a displaced origin was crucial to the allure of such objects and the prestige earned in giving them. Just as warriors made their names by bringing home alien heads, traders earned renown by importing alien goods.[10] Likewise, clan elders distinguished themselves from competitors through narratives that confirmed their access to the ancestral origins of the group. Blurring the line between words and things, both titles and trade goods served as booty marking an encounter in an alien realm.

Intrinsic to the dynamics of Biak kinship, a long history of raiding provided the setting for contemporary appropriations of foreign speech and writing. Elsewhere, I have described how a tendency to treat outsiders' words as booty shaped Biak relations with the early evangelists (Rutherford n.d.). The word for the Gospel in Biak is *refo*, from the Tidoran *lefo*, "written text," indicating an exposure to foreign writing that dates to well before the missionaries' arrival in 1855 (van Hasselt and van Hasselt 1947: 190). The presence of loanwords in *wos Biak* should come as no surprise. Spoken by the interpreters who accompanied foreign expeditions to the region, and by the Dutch and German missionaries who settled on the Bird's Head, a dialect of the language once served as a lingua franca along the coasts of northwestern New Guinea. When the colonial administration expanded in northern New Guinea in the late nineteenth century, Biaks were quick to master new languages of rule, including Dutch and Malay, which, one will recall, was used in commerce and administration throughout the Netherlands Indies (Hoffman 1979; Maier 1993).

An interest in the languages of powerful others has persisted on Biak. During fieldwork, I met virtually no one unable to converse with me in Indonesian, the national language that grew out of Indies Malay. Codeswitching was common in conversations among adults, who embellished their Biak anecdotes with Indonesian, Dutch, and English words. Friends told me that "children's language" (B: *wos romawa*) was "foreign language" (B: *wos amber*), as people called Indonesian. Mothers often addressed toddlers in the national language, leaving the mother tongue for conversations amongst themselves.[11] When pressed to account for this habit, women told me that they spoke

Indonesian to enhance their children's success in school. Given the prestige women gained from raising famous foreigners, this tendency made a certain sense. Some of my informants bemoaned the impending demise of *wos Biak*; one man, half-jokingly, forecast the day when his grandchildren would have to go to Holland for lessons from the successors of the Dutch pastors who had been so fluent in the language. Although the prevalence of Indonesian in lessons, sermons, and official speeches supported this gloomy view, Biak remained the language of singing, storytelling, and scolding. It played a key role in popular genres of performance and in the bustle of everyday life.

The ascendancy of Indonesian was evident in one highly valued arena: it long has been the main language in which Biaks read and write. Thanks to the islands' long tradition of education, literacy was not new to Biak in the early 1990s. In 1947, Dr. J. V. de Bruyn, a Dutch official assigned to govern Biak after World War II, called the islanders "the most cultivated and therefore most progressive Papuans in Netherlands New Guinea, among whom illiteracy is relatively scarce and even among men under thirty-five completely absent" (1948; see also de Bruyn 1965). With most villages tracing their Christian conversion to the 1910s and early 1920s, even the oldest of my informants had completed three years of school. Some middle-aged men and women had benefited from training programs launched in the 1950s and held the equivalent of a college degree. In line with national policy, children on Biak were guaranteed six years of primary education in the early 1990s; many went on to junior and senior high school, for which their families paid nominal fees. Although de Bruyn's estimate may well have been inflated, literacy was an important value among the Biaks I knew. Many did not use their skills frequently, but they showed a clear respect for those who did.

Religious works made up the majority of reading materials I saw in Biak residences (cf. Kulick and Stroud 1993: 36). Families kept Bibles and Indonesian-language hymnals, stored in fancy leather cases by more affluent urbanites or tucked in woven bags and hidden in the rafters of a rural home. Although many households included little else in the way of texts—a marriage license or birth certificate slipped between the pages of the Bible, an outdated newspaper stapled to the wall—I was often shown more exotic treasures: certificates of honor from the Dutch army, Biak-language lesson books dating from well before the war, identification cards issued by the colonial government. Among the newer publications that people collected were Indonesian-language pamphlets based on Dutch writings on Biak culture and the history of the mission. A newly translated Biak New Testament was a popular item among pastors and elders. As I discuss below, a few of my informants boasted collections of Dutch and English books.

It was not only published texts and documents that friends on Biak were eager to show me, however; people also kept collections of their own writings. As I mentioned in chapter 2, a college dropout presented me with a poster-sized map of his family's genealogy, which illustrated the special prerogatives supposedly enjoyed by his particular line. A retired schoolteacher let me borrow his "life history," which listed the communities where he had served and some of the incidents that had occurred during his tenure. Some of the records I was shown served a pragmatic purpose; people saved requests for bridewealth and lists of contributors in order to keep track of the debts connecting relatives who had provided and divided each other's bridewealth. The same was not obviously true of the thick collection of notes that I was shown by a retired evangelist who was widely known as an expert on "custom." Interviews with this consultant often began with me and my informant taking out our respective notebooks: mine was empty, his was full of descriptions that he read aloud for me to write down. It was almost as if the old man had kept these meticulous records in hopes of someday meeting someone like me.[12]

Part of these authors' enthusiasm for my efforts, no doubt reflected the importance the Indonesian authorities—and their separatist foes—assigned to the preservation of "custom." But their eagerness to show me written documents also corresponded to a wider conception of the nature of authenticity. The written word was considered evidence (I: *bukti*) of the veracity of a narrative, like the old wor songs and named rock formations I mentioned in chapter 3 (see also chapter 5). The most reliable sources were old foreign monographs, Biaks told me, because their authors knew the "old people" before they all died. Experts on "custom" were delighted, not embarrassed, when I recognized why their stories seemed so familiar—often we had read the same Dutch books. Those who spoke without "proof" were said to be subject to whims that could lead them to add or detract from the "truth." Whether they appealed to inscriptions on the land or evidence "written in their heads," my informants tried to support their words with the authority of the written trace.

Outside of conversations with an ethnographer, reading was also presented as a crucial source of unusual knowledge. To be acknowledged as a "foreigner," men and women had to demonstrate their privileged access to the truths contained in texts that were difficult to obtain or understand. But although literacy was an important component of the repertoire of leaders I knew, they reached the realm of foreign meanings by varied means. Teachers were typical foreigners, but well-known healers, hunters, and singers also claimed the title on the basis of their ability to interpret a dream, the landscape, or the events of everyday life. People did not seem to draw a sharp divide between these traditional figures and their Westernized contemporaries—often the teacher and singer were the same man or woman. Nor did they valorize one mode of reading over another. One healer boasted that he had been called to the hospital to help with tough cases and to brief the doctors on his special brand of skills.

The New Order leaders I met on Biak derived authority from very different sources from those relied on by the shamans and warriors described by Dutch observers. Yet there is more than a vague resemblance between their approaches. Both these colonial-era notables and contemporary "foreigners" inhabited societies in which the fetishization of the foreign gave rise to an uncertain situation in which one found differing speculations about power and strategies for acquiring it.[13] These speculations and strategies made themselves felt in differing treatments of spoken and written words. In the next section of this chapter, I tease out three of the meanings implicitly ascribed to reading when particular leaders translated foreign texts. Although these interpretive strategies could and did overlap, I approach them separately by highlighting aspects of the words and works of two local historians and a contemporary prophet. I do not mean to imply that these men were typical Biak characters. On occasion, the strategies exemplified by one of these leaders might appear in the performance of another. Moreover, the stress on textuality I highlight in my analysis does not preclude the fact that these readers were quite capable of "comprehending" the contents of their books. But an alternative vision of the pragmatic functions of literacy was evident in their bid to be recognized as the holders of authoritative knowledge. Their practices serve to illustrate some of the myriad ways in which Biaks registered and reproduced difference by positioning themselves as monopolizing a key source of truths from afar.

The Meanings of Reading

Mr. Fakiar and the Possession

One can illuminate a first meaning of reading by pondering the activities of Mr. Fakiar, a former colonial official who was in his early sixties when I met him. An early participant in Dutch experiments with limited self-rule, Mr. Fakiar belonged to the first generation of Biaks to be educated by the colonial government. He resided in his home village, not far from the regency capital, where he dispensed advice on matters relating to the land disputes that had been smoldering in South Biak since the displacement of coastal communities during World War II.

In 1993, when I ran into Mr. Fakiar at the Biak City port, he gave me a good dressing down. I had first encountered the retired official in 1990, when I was researching a case study on land disputes. Since returning for fieldwork, I had seen him once on the street with his wife, who was an acquaintance from the women's group in town. He had spoken proudly then about his writings on Biak history and culture, telling me all about his inter-view with an American "expert"—a person who turned out to be me. Now he asked, in mock anger, why it was taking me so long to come and collect his valuable texts.

And so I found myself, two days later, in a sunny beachfront village, shel-tering in a cool sitting room while Mr. Fakiar rummaged for books. He had greeted me with delight, quickly changing into a government party T-shirt before launching into a monologue. I was not the first to seek him out—the regent, the mayor, and various foreign visitors all had his manuscripts—in fact, most had been borrowed, although he would see what he could find. Every day, from dawn until dark, Mr. Fakiar did nothing but write. When he wasn't writing, he was consulting his library of rare foreign texts. By way of proof, he rattled off a list of explorers—Ortiz de Retes, Jacob de la Maire, Willem Schouten. He had read about them in Dutch in a very old book, "probably the only copy outside of Spain." Like his own works, this book was in very high demand.

After sending a child scampering through the neighborhood to look for his writings on Biak culture, Mr. Fakiar ducked into his bedroom. A moment later, he emerged with K. W. Galis's *Papua's van de Humbolt Baai* (1955), opened to the English summary. I perused the disquisition on Tobati kinship and ritual, while my consultant looked for more materials. "I bet you haven't seen this!" he chuckled, placing before me a glossy guidebook to Nether-lands New Guinea, dated 1956 (see *Vademecum voor Nederlands-Nieuw-Guinea* 1956). Flipping past the pictures of smiling tribesmen and immunized babies, he directed me to a list of important historical dates.

When I pulled out my pad and began to ask Mr. Fakiar some questions, he stopped me. "Don't write!" he commanded. "Where is that boy?!" To occupy me while we waited for his corpus on culture, he read aloud from some of his other manuscripts: "The Papuan *Volkskarakter*" (a portrait of the native's temperament), "The Government of the Dutch East Indies" (a history of Old Batavia), "Biak in the War Years" (a military description of the islands' defenses during World War II). When I asked Mr. Fakiar about his own history, he pulled out another handwritten document and showed me his name on a list of delegates to the New Guinea Council. Mr. Fakiar never found the manuscripts he was looking for that day, but he urged me to take the others when I left.

Mr. Fakiar treated me the way a senior faculty member might treat a first-year student: he loaded me up with references and sent me on my way. But we should not take for granted Mr. Fakiar's performance simply because it calls to mind something that we think we know. Like scholars elsewhere, Mr. Fakiar offered his manuscripts as valued objects that he was eager to put into circulation. His writings were translations in Indonesian from Western texts, which he wanted his Western visitors to take away. In fact, I would argue that the foreign books in the library of the retired civil servant—some so rare that they were not even there—played the role of what Weiner (1992) calls "inalienable possessions": highly valued objects removed from circulation in an attempt to stabilize debt and generate hierarchy (see also Weiner 1985). Weiner has described how the production of facsimiles of precious heirlooms, such as Samoan fine mats, enables their owners to claim them as a medium of identity, represented within transactions yet absent from exchange. Realized in a combination of practice and rhetoric, Mr. Fakiar's strategy had similar effects. Letting him give while keeping his precious originals, Mr. Fakiar's ceaseless production and bestowal of brief translations allowed him to assert privileged access to a hidden foreign source.

Inalienable possessions, Weiner argues, do more than embody the past; they promise immortality to those who seek to reproduce differences against the flux of time and the threat of loss (1992: 3). Their value resides in their association with cosmological sources of authentication. If the ownership of a treasured heirloom strengthens the position of particular kin groups or persons, it is by virtue of its paradoxical ability to bring an ancestral past into the present while marking this realm's excentric relationship to the everyday world (see also Benjamin [1936] 1968; Helms 1993). Where Weiner's model tends to downplay differences in the ways that people conceptualize the cosmological, my encounter with Mr. Fakiar brought home a simple truth: just as objects gain meaning through their embeddedness in broader contexts of social discourse, transcendence and ancestrality are created in locally distinctive ways. Reflecting a tendency common among Biak leaders, Mr. Fakiar used his mastery of the foreign in an imaginative effort to act as a future ancestor himself. On one level, he proved this mastery by structuring the aura of an elsewhere into his performance. By reading aloud from his works, Mr. Fakiar suppressed his unreliable voice and made himself into the conduit for his own writing. In a sense, he let himself be possessed by these traces of his possessions, his foreign books, and thus accessed their alien power. On another level, he asserted the ancestral character of this uncanny autoinspiration by defining his texts as a legacy for his son. Transforming the foreign into the origin of a new genealogy, Mr. Fakiar tried to turn the textuality of his writings to his advantage in his quest for the recognition of future generations. By turning his books into heirlooms and his translations into a bequest for his children, he provided social figures for the absences that constitute every document in the form of an author and addressee who are never exhaustively known.

Turning from Mr. Fakiar's library to the Bible, one gets an even clearer sense of writing's role as an inalienable possession on Biak. With their leather cases and woven coverings a marker of social standing, particular Bibles were closely associated with particular persons. As I noted in chapter 2, copies of the Scriptures often accompanied their owners to the grave. At once specific to individuals and associated with Biaks as a group, the Bible not only harbored the aura of an elsewhere; it provided people with access to magical powers. Bibles were used to make prayer water by Biak healers. Holding a glass of water over the Scriptures, they breathed a prayer onto the surface, then gave the liquid to their patients to drink. The protective character of the Scriptures was well known to Biak travelers, who never set out without a Bible in their bag. The Bible appears as the protagonist in hymns and myths I recorded, describing the vanquishing of heathen darkness by Christian light. Instead of praising the missionaries for their brave devotion, these narratives credit the Bible for "breaking the warrior's spear." The magical and the ancestral come together in a story an old man told me about an encounter between some Bibles and his forefathers' *korwar*. The word *korwar*, one will recall, refers to the reliquaries Biaks once carved to hold the skulls and spirits of recently deceased relatives (see chapter 2). But the *korwars* in this tale are enormous, hilltop boulders that mark the boundaries of the clan's land. The narrative presents the Bibles as taking the place of the boulders, which vanish upon their meeting with the Book (Rutherford n.d.).[14] Like my meeting with Mr. Fakiar, this clan history illuminates a moment when the foreign and the ancestral converge to found a genealogy. But the ancestors remain encompassed by the foreign, which stays beyond anyone's control.

My encounter with Mr. Fakiar revealed just one of a repertoire of strategies for translating foreign texts into a source of authority. The next big foreigner illustrates another approach. Once again, the seemingly idiosyncratic practices of an individual find a parallel in collective treatments of the Bible. With Mr. Senyenem, the focus shifts from the foreign text as an absent heirloom, which serves as the origin of valued gifts, to the foreign text as an alien yet all-encompassing narrative, which serves as the origin of surplus meaning. Like Mr. Fakiar, Mr. Senyenem viewed his translations as an inheritance for future generations. But here, the foreign original was not only an inaccessible source of value; it was an inexhaustible source of truth.

Mr. Senyenem and the Model

The outlines of a second meaning of reading are discernible in the practices of Mr. Senyenem, a slightly older man than Mr. Fakiar, who was trained by the Protestant mission to serve as a teacher and evangelist. Mr. Senyenem spent his career teaching in primary schools across the islands, before retiring to his East Biak home village to serve as a member of the East Biak church council. In addition to his work with local congregations, he was widely known at the time of my fieldwork as a promoter of wor, the song genre discussed in the previous chapter. Mr. Senyenem was as proud of his ability to remember old wor songs as he was of his knowledge of Dutch texts on Biak's past.

"Goede avond! Ik heb U wachten!" ("Good evening! I've been waiting for you!") A voice rang out as I climbed a rocky path to a clifftop house in the village of Opiaref. This was my fourth trip to see Mr. Senyenem, and I was used to being welcomed in Dutch. The short, expressive man led me to his spacious back room, where I took a seat at a table stacked with ledgers and stencils. A small manual typewriter sat before me, poised for use.

I often went to Mr. Senyenem for help transcribing wor. Before we began, he usually gave me a progress report on his village history, which he had been working on for several years. Unlike Mr. Fakiar, who was eager to offer me samples from his opus, Mr. Senyenem kept his masterpiece under tight wraps. Whenever I asked to see it, Mr. Senyenem sighed; his book was "not yet perfect" (I: *belum sempurna*, a common Indonesian expression in such situations). But finally, one day the old man handed me a bulky volume, which was opened to a page of Biak poetry. What was this? Wor lyrics! To show me what had inspired them, he directed me to another page, where I found a complete register of every teacher who had ever served in Opiaref. Further on, I found five or six additional wor, including several that Mr. Senyenem had created as he was writing. The history also contained a hymn by a well-known Dutch missionary on the birth of Irian Jaya's Evangelical Church. "Everything will go in," Mr. Senyenem promised me. "Had to start in the beginning. In Germany." I looked at the opening chapter; indeed, Opiaref's past began in Berlin with the theologian who trained New Guinea's first evangelists. Mr. Senyenem grinned. "If I don't include everything, then the grandchildren won't know!"

By starting his story with a discussion of the Utrecht Mission Society's Pietist founders, Mr. Senyenem had organized his text on the model of F. C. Kamma's two-volume study (1976, 1977) of the New Guinea mission. But the fact that local history began in the Land of the Foreigners was not the only remarkable thing about this manuscript. Filled with editorial comments and creative compositions, Mr. Senyenem's hefty text was unlike Mr. Fakiar's succinct translations. Both men viewed their translations as a source of genealogical continuity; here the parallel ends. Mr. Fakiar's ongoing transactions enabled him to "give-while-keeping" a treasured object. Mr. Senyenem's endless epic referred less to a treasured object than a treasured narrative, overflowing with data and meanings that could never be adequately glossed. In both cases, the copy, put into circulation, produced a particular image of the original. Mr. Senyenem's manuscript exemplified how Biak translators confirmed the "foreignness" of foreign texts, even as they transformed them into a source of local truths.

It was not only in encounters with local historians that I caught a glimpse of the model that took shape at the beginning of Biak's works. The foreign original loomed large in the church history quiz contests that were a popular component of congregational celebrations during the period of my fieldwork.

Held on a local or regional level, these panel games engaged small teams of men, women, and youths in a battle of wits. During the trip to Miei described in chapter 2, I found myself, along with three Biak friends, representing South Biak in a contest with the women's group from the mainland. Luckily, Sister Sally had a fine collection of relevant materials. My teammates and I pored over the booklets and grilled each other on mission lore—to little avail, it turned out. Despite my months of research in the Netherlands, I was easily stumped.

I should not have been surprised by my poor performance in the contest. As the inquiries of rural acquaintances confirmed, the Dutch archive of the Biak imagination was not the same archive that I had consulted in Holland. As seen by Biaks, the distant repository contained an unlimited supply of information, from the middle names of the missionaries' children to the accurate dimensions of a particular village's clan land. Quiz masters could ask anything of contestants, given their putative access to an archive that told all. The impression that local knowledge was simply the tip of an iceberg of foreign data was perpetrated by the wide dissemination of abridged Indonesian translations of the most famous foreign works: *A Miracle in Our Eyes; Ottow and Geissler: West Irian's Apostles; The Slave Child; A Brief History of the Irian Jaya Evangelical Church; The Fort at Yenbekaki and the Koreri Movement.* Many of these booklets were written by distinguished "big foreigners," such as the Biak founding fathers of the native church.

But the foreign original held more than a surplus of information; it also held a surplus of meaning, as one learns when one turns to Biak glosses of the Bible. The Bible was the most fertile site of translation I encountered. It circulated in languages national and local, written and spoken, in storybooks, sermons, and songs. Whether or not they used the word, "translation," my informants made it clear that they traced their sermons and compositions to privileged encounters with the Holy Writ. During the holiday season, the faithful had a chance to offer evidence of such encounters. The Christmas services I attended in Sor lasted for many hours because everyone in the congregation had an opportunity to preach. In 1992, those participating included Solomon Pasem, an elementary school teacher; Petrus Rumsarsram, a college student home on break; Lukas Rumsur, the village chief; Dorkas Mamorba, a teacher's wife from another village; and Fritz Rumapura, a fisherman and elder. When I chatted with the head of the women's group on the day of the event, she described the fear and exhilaration she always felt whenever she mounted the pulpit. "This is God's Gospel," she informed me gravely. "It's not just any old book!" Biak descriptions of the impossible yet imperative mission of conveying God's word portrayed "witnessing" as a process of unending translation. Confronted with the task of interpreting the Scriptures, the faithful experienced the same sense of the sublime Mr. Senyenem did with his interminable village history. What began with a

plan "just to take a few words [that is, from the Bible]," as Dorkas Mamorba put it, often ended in a seemingly interminable sermon. Translation
appeared as an infinite process, since no local rendering could fully capture
the truth.

This meaning of reading was discernible not only in what lay preachers
said about the task of translation but also in the content of their sermons.
Their texts bore witness to the inexhaustible store of meaning found within
their sacred, foreign source. Given their belief in the ultimately inaccessible
character of biblical meaning, audiences were willing to accept the most
disparate performances as evidence of contact with the Gospel's wisdom.
Some preachers packaged their message in official Indonesian. A local lay
leader began one sermon with an Indonesian bible verse—"Hari sudah jauh
malam, sekarang terbitlah terang" ("It is late and the dawn is breaking")—as
the hook for a Biak-language harangue against drinking and fighting. A retired regent drew on military metaphors. "Kapal silam baru naik," he chided
his listeners in the national language, comparing them to "submarines" that
only "surfaced" once a year. A village chief glossed Christ's birth in baldly
New Order terms. "Tuhan ambil inisiatif untuk program keselamatan" ("God
initiated the salvation program"), he announced in Indonesian, before turning to "Point One" in his text. Others drew on domestic imagery to capture
Christian sentiment. Christmas is like a family reunion, one lay leader explained. A good Christian should feel the joy of an old Biak parent whose
"foreign" child has just walked through the door. Still others evoked the alien
character of the Scriptures through metaphors that highlighted the materiality of language. One minister brought his listeners to tears by playing on
the similarity of the Indonesian words for "uterus" (*kandung*) and "manger"
(*kandang*). To appreciate the miracle, Christians need not inspect Mary's
uterus, but the dirty, smelly manger in their hearts. In a sermon that met
with attentive silence, a student from the seminary portrayed sin as an indeli-
ble scribble. Life is like a writing exercise, he proclaimed. But one gets no
eraser, only a pen and some paper to fill with one's marks and mistakes. The
inexhaustibility of the original did not just announce itself through a quick
switch of codes in this performance, but through imagery that conjured the
surplus of significance inherent to every spoken or written sign.

Turning from sermons to Biak-language hymns, one finds a similar stress
on the inexhaustible meaning of the Scriptures. Here, as well, the biblical
text appears as the fount of truths that can be evoked but never adequately
conveyed. The contemporary, diatonic songs and hymns I recorded bore a
genealogical relationship to "Bible wor" (B: *wor Refo*), the most vital variety of
the older genre during the period of my fieldwork, when it was sung by
small groups of old men in church. In the case of *wor Refo*, the status of the
Scriptures as the alien original is explicit; their composers told me that they
read Bible verses or looked at biblical posters and songs simply popped into

their minds. Sung by predominantly female choirs, the haunting harmonies of Biak-language hymns sounded more conventional to Western ears. But their lyrics reveal a similar reading of the Bible, whose allure is often the central topic of a song.

Consider, for example, the following hymn. Written by Sermima Sanadi of Insrom, the lyrics use a structure of internal translation to depict the Holy Writ.

I

Hai saudara mari berkumpulkan di sini.
Supaya bersama-sama mendengar.

  Kor: Suara yang keluarlah di atas
     mimbar.
     Siapa yang bersimpan
     mendapatkan sorga.

II

Sye naik srar mgo mgora muma kam ro
  rum ari.
Manseren byedine komnaf kam wos
  manseren.
  Kor: Isbawer kwar ro nimbar ya
     kofananyar kam.
     Mansei beyun wos nabor iso
     besmai slamat.

III

Imnis japan ker dirya kada awin
  pyanggar.
Ker ya be mami ma inggo kam nggani.

  Kor: Bape slamat nanggi ima
     kopanggar i ba.
     Imboi awin kamam su kosewar
     besisye.

I (Indonesian)

I say, brethren, let us gather here
  together.
So that together we can hear.
  Chorus: The voice that emerges from
     the pulpit.
     Whoever keeps it will reach
     heaven.

II (Biak)

Hey, brothers and sisters, let's all go to
  church.
Let's all listen to the Scriptures of God.

  Chorus: What spills from the pulpit,
     let us seize it all.
     Whoever gets lots of words
     will be saved.[15]

III (Biak)

As for the taro root, mother cuts it up
  in pieces.
And divides it for father and the rest of
  us to eat.
  Chorus: But this heavenly salvation,
     we cannot share it.
     Like mother and father, we
     must seek it ourselves.

The Indonesian verse, presented in the staid idiom of the State, instructs the flock to listen to the minister and "save" what they hear. Note how the Biak rendering—which is twice as long as the original—translates this command into an incitement to something quite different from attentive obedience.

Rather than a voice, what pours from the Biak pulpit are words—*wos*—which is also the term for language or writing. The proper relation to these words is not passive listening but active seizure. Another composer explained the same Biak term (*kofananyar*) in Indonesian as "kita baku rebut" in a line that described how Biaks "snatch" at salvation. Although the next verse, which asserts that salvation cannot be shared, might be read as encouraging the emergence of an individuated Christian subject, the "word riot" around the pulpit offers an alternative. The course from the collective to the individual runs from orderly deference to disorderly desire. Just because the Gospel is not a taro root, neatly divided by mother, that does not mean it is not food—perhaps a peculiarly masculine sort of treat, inciting the free-for-all sometimes seen when an outrigger brings in a good haul. Another hymn tells us that the Bible is like a delectable smoked fish. Once you start eating it, you just cannot stop!

Within this song, the Bible appears as it was perceived by those who sought to gloss it: as an indestructible object of delectation. I have already mentioned other hymns that highlight the potency of the Scriptures; in these, the foreignness of the Bible is compared with the foreignness of warriors who are defeated in their encounter with the Word. Hymns recounting particular episodes from the Gospel assign this potency to the protagonists; in an Easter song, Christ, the King of Life, confronts Death, the King of Darkness, sending Herod's soldiers tumbling and humiliating their master. Another hymn has Jesus boldly shouting at the Devil, "Faimano!"—the Biak-language equivalent of "Jump back!" Most relevant for our purposes here are hymns that express the longing felt by believers when they think of the Bible and its promise of salvation. "Saneraro," sighs one narrator, voicing his or her yearning for the distant shores of heaven, the original home and destination. The term used in this hymn, which describes a believer sailing the "canoe" of his or her "life," is an extended version of the Biak word for "heart" or "stomach" (see chapter 2). The word *saneraro* evokes the love of a "foreigner" for a distant sibling or mother, whose nurture included both food and foreign wealth. Another song uses the word *mowi*, also mentioned in chapter 2, to express the beauty of the seascape over whose horizon lies Mansinam, the island where the missionaries first landed. *Mowi* refers to the decayed remnants of something dead, what remains behind when the *rur*, "soul," and *nin*, "spirit," leave the body. Hosea Mirino, the young composer, explained that people sometimes used the word as a noun to depict "something to throw away, something rotten, something no longer good." But as an expletive, the same word gives an observation an emphasis implying that a sight is exceedingly glorious or wretched. "It is as if you must curse," Hosea explained. "You are enraged because words don't suffice."

Significantly, in light of the strategy of the prophet described below, composers also attempted to express the inexpressible by including phrases associated with Koreri, Biak's long-standing messianic movement. Some hymns gloss "heaven" as Koreri, that word meaning "We Change Our Skin"; others repeat phrases like "K'an do mo*b* oser," "We eat in one place" (see chapter 1). Despite their use of these locally resonant terms, the composers I interviewed presented their hymns as indebted to a foreign original. But their texts set the stage for a final mode of translation, which brought the origin of truth and power back home.

Uncle Bert and the Fragment

A third meaning of reading emerges vividly in the performances of a prophet whom I will call simply "Uncle Bert," following the lead of his nephew, who was sensitive to political nature of his kinsman's activities. Whereas Mr. Fakiar and Mr. Senyenem were widely regarded as authorities, this younger man commanded a smaller sphere of influence. Uncle Bert was a relatively uneducated fisherman whose renown derived from his leadership of one of a number of "prayer groups" founded on Biak in the early 1990s. These innocuous-sounding organizations were watched closely by church officials and the military, for they were believed to be dangerous pockets of syncretism and Papuan separatism. Above all, the authorities worried about the prayer groups' association with Koreri. As I have already suggested, colonial-era Koreri prophets exerted remarkable influence over their followers, who destroyed their gardens and gathered by the hundreds, sure that Utopia was about to begin (Kamma 1972). Under Indonesian rule, Koreri imagery and rhetoric soon found its way into the Free Papua Organization (Organisasi Papua Merdeka, or OPM), that scattered yet tenacious armed resistance movement that sought independence for the province of Irian Jaya (Osborne 1985; Sharp with Kaisiëpo 1994; Kapissa 1980; see also chapter 1). Although the ritual drinking and dancing associated with Koreri did not occur during prayer group meetings, members did take part in ecstatic bouts of hymn singing and praying. Heralded as prophets, leaders like Uncle Bert claimed to owe their foresight to direct encounters with Manarmakeri, who at the time of my fieldwork was also sometimes known as Jesus or God.

I met Uncle Bert during a visit to Wundi, a small island off Biak's coast. I had come to see him with his nephew, who had promised that his uncle had many stories to tell. Accompanied by Edith, another friend, we made the trip by motorized outrigger on a stormy day with two Dutch tourists who told me that they were testing a guidebook. They seemed quietly pleased to discover that the entry on Wundi was inaccurate. Indeed, our destination was scarcely an "unspoiled paradise," as the guidebook claimed. First a command post, then a supply dump during the Allied invasion of Biak, the beach where we landed was strewn with wreckage. Wundi's inhabitants had made their homes from the marks of spent aggression. The house where we stayed was representative: the cement foundation of an abandoned warehouse formed the floor and porch; the walls were iron of roughly the same vintage; one of the tables was an old refrigerator, one of the chairs, a fighter-pilot seat; a shining airplane wing provided a bench in the back. The Dutchman returned from snorkeling to report that the sea was "full of things," including old bulldozers. The rubble even offered lodging for the fish.

On the edge of progress, among the husks of history, Wundi seemed to epitomize Biak's marginality. Yet for the man I came to interview, it was a center. The World War II ruins covered an older set of tracks, those left by Manarmakeri, the Itchy Old Man. The Biaks I knew widely agreed that the most important episodes in the long and complicated myth of Manarmakeri had taken place on this site. To anticipate the story I will relate in the next chapter, the island was where the old man captured the Morning Star, who gave him secret powers of production, and where he rejuvenated himself by jumping into a fire. In 1992, the government announced plans to take advantage of Wundi's past to develop its potential for cultural tourism. Bert saw no coincidence in this conjunction of local lore, world history, and national planning. Where Mr. Fakiar and Mr. Senyenem, in differing ways, presented their texts as indebted to a foreign original whose full meaning and value lay beyond their grasp, Uncle Bert claimed to know the "truth" behind alien narratives. No less a bricoleur than his neighbors, instead of cobbling together rusting equipment Bert worked with words.

In the late 1980s, God—a.k.a. Manarmakeri—began sending Bert signs. As soon as Edith and I were seated, Bert disappeared into his bedroom, returning a moment later with a Bible. Wordlessly, he pulled a laminated card from its pages and flipped it on the table. On one side was written, in English:

Independence Day 1943
Independent of Spirit
Depend on God

On the other side was a black-and-white drawing. In the foreground were two figures in soldier's caps. One was General MacArthur, Bert told us; the other was General Haig. Behind them, against the backdrop of what looked like an American flag, stood Jesus Christ. That was the Koreri flag, Bert corrected me: blue and white stripes, red and white stars.

Bert pulled out another card, a hologram of Christ standing atop a golden pedestal. In the clouds above his head was a white-bearded figure; below his left arm, a spiked ball, below his right arm, a crescent moon. All the components of the myth of Manarmakeri were there, Bert told us: the old man, his son, the small yellow fruit, the Morning Star—which was really the angel Gabriel. Bert brought out a bronze box—"just like the gold pedestal"—and showed me its contents: a rock, a corroded brass earring, and another yellow fruit.

We turned to the last two cards that Bert kept stored in his Bible, which looked as if they belonged to a tarot deck. The first showed an old man with a cane, who was escorted by two dogs. The second showed a young man who was carrying a child and a shepherd's staff and was leading several sheep. That was the Old Man, Bert told us, pointing to the first picture. The second picture revealed him in his other guise, that of the handsome young man he became after his baptism in fire.

Bert asked me to translate the English-language prayer printed on the back of the first card, which I did to his satisfaction. He let me copy the verses on the back of the second, which he told me was in "Dutch." He did not ask me to translate these lines, which only served to highlight the significance of his possession of this seemingly untranslatable text.[16] Written in Dutch, English, Biak, and a language Edith and I did not recognize, the poem read as follows.

> Jesus from deh langeh
> jou de vis Shoupekh
> efendi long S. werden
> grai firmen and
> webek kahat ende
> wile: From Sue
> laidmen di patnia
> ai tibk draits
> Manseren Kayan Biak
> Daite from Shop

Manarmakeri told Bert where to find the first card—in a Biak City copy shop; he gave Bert the other cards on the small island.[17] Bert was not alarmed to learn that I had seen these pictures in other peoples' possession; relatives made photocopies, which quickly got passed along. Bert had other evidence to prove that he was the initial recipient. He brought out a green plastic flashlight, which he had received on November 11, 1991, when Manarmakeri came to tell him about his second coming. Bert told me that the brand name "Technosub" meant "The Cleverness of the Irianese." He pointed to an enormous wooden cross mounted in the rafters above his head. Manarmakeri first told Bert to look for this object suspended in the sky; when he returned the next day, it was planted in the sand. The last item that Bert showed me was a foot-long iron plate embossed with the words "White Freightliner." The Old Man told Bert that this object was a "travel permit" for voyages around the world.

Manarmakeri sent the flotsam and jetsam to confirm the predictions that he communicated through his prophet. Bert's other source of proof was the Bible. Manarmakeri informed his messenger where to search in the Scriptures, in the same way that he told him where to look on the beach. Bert kept the Bible close at hand throughout his long monologue on Biak's history and the times ahead. At various points in his narrative, he cited chapters and verses, repeated them by heart, then showed me the pages for good measure.

The Bible was a gift from Manarmakeri, Bert told me, no less than the other evidence. It was the Old Man who ordered Gutenberg to print the Gospel. He wanted his people to know their history, and so he sent them the Book.

Bert's representation of the Bible superceded the images of the Scriptures depicted above by repositioning the origin of foreign meaning. Bert's Gospel was neither an heirloom nor a model; it was an abridged edition of Biak myth. No less than the signs that washed up on the small island's shores, it had to be reconciled to an original mythic text. The Land of Canaan was really this island, Bert told me, and the Israelites were really the Biaks.[18] It was also really Bethlehem, the birth place of the Lord. Manarmakeri's second coming would be revealed in Bert's village, where the world would gather to face him. From his Throne of Justice, he would sort the believers from the sinners: the saved would go to heaven, the rest, straight to hell.

Along with the Scriptures, Manarmakeri's messages incorporated the official narrative of development. Everything that the government told the Biaks confirmed a master scheme. This year's tourists belonged to the first wave of Westerners who would come to Biak. Next year, a national women's conference would attract delegates from ninety-nine nations. In 1995, all of Bali's visitors would flock to Biak for a festival to celebrate the opening of a seven-star hotel. In the years that followed, the non-Irian Indonesians all would leave, replaced by "white people" like the Allies and the Israelis. At the end of the century, the world would "leave the launching pad"—a popular New Order cliché—and Manarmakeri would appear. Articulating the New Order's futurist rhetoric, Bert contained the Indonesian government's current schemes within his prophecy. He validated his predictions by identifying Manarmakeri with the powerful others who backed the New Order regime. The Biak hero had obviously scripted the government's plans and projects—why else would they be financed by Western loans? What was returning to Biak now was simply the "dregs," merely a trace of the riches to come.

Given the all-encompassing scope of his prophecies, very little had the power to surprise Bert. He had predicted my visit days in advance; as soon as he heard our outrigger, he knew that I had arrived. As the earthly medium of Manarmakeri's messages, Bert was the first to learn of all events.[19] Yet in another sense, this position only intensified the alien character of what the Itchy Old Man revealed. In order to convey miraculous predictions, Manarmakeri had to motivate, that is, provide a rationale for, apparently unintelligible signs. Bert did not immediately recognize the codes that flowed from his pen when Manarmakeri inspired him to write in other languages. Manarmakeri had to tell Bert that a text was "Greek" and explain how to read it before the traces disappeared. In the same way, the Old Man helped him pair proper names with secret denotations: Biak was really "Bangun Ikut Anak Kristus" ("Rise and Follow the Child of Christ"), "Bila Ingat Akan Kembali" ("If Remembered, Will Return"), and "Berbiak-biaklah Kau Menutupi Dunia"

("Be fruitful and multiply"). Proper names are said to be what passes between languages without transformation (cf. Derrida 1985; Baker 1993). A powerful ancestor had given Bert access to the true message behind these seemingly untranslatable signs (cf. Becker 1995: 56; Zimmer 1998, 1999).

It is worth noting the difference between Bert's claim to authority and the strategies of Mr. Fakiar and Mr. Senyenem. Mr. Fakiar took foreign books as an absent site of surplus objects, signifying his proximity to the alien original by flooding the "market" with his circulating translations. Mr. Senyenem took foreign narratives as an absent site of surplus significance, cranking out pages in an attempt to be complete. In Bert's prophecies, the foreign source of surplus was interiorized in the guise of a secret meaning. Instead of beckoning on the horizon, the truth became autochthonous: it lay within the parameters of Biak myth. This transformation of the foreign text implied a reconfiguring of the relationship between mobility and authority posited in the practices of most big foreigners. Where others spoke on the basis of their privileged access to distant places and times, Bert claimed to be recognized where he stood. He bragged that he never left his home. He did not need to, for the tourists knew where to find him; even Western faith healers came asking him to be blessed.

Bert's radical reframing of outsiders' discourse drew on the authority of Manarmakeri, a figure who, as we will see in the next chapter, explicitly embodies the connections between the alien and the ancestral. Although there were signs that outsiders were coming to recognize Biak's true importance, the prophet's predictions would only be confirmed in the impossible event of the Itchy Old Man's return. Just as Manarmakeri's arrival would spell the end of the world, it would also spell the end of Biak's big foreigners. Bert's future had no room for local aliens—only "Papuans," white people, and the Indonesians whose removal would satisfy all desires. Koreri, defined as the final encounter with the foreign, would put an end to the practices through which Biaks created their identities. No longer in the distance, the foreign would be present, closing the quest for value and prestige. Manarmakeri's return would eliminate the uncertain, excessive quality of the foreign, that instability that was a fetishized product of and precondition for the practices of Biak leaders. The alien and the ancestral would be as one.

Given the cost to other aspiring leaders, it took rare talents and special conditions for prophets like Bert to attract a broad-based following. Even though she shared Bert's desire for Koreri, my educated friend Edith, for instance, had her doubts. As this female foreigner saw matters, Bert was not misled about Biak's secret place in the world; he was mistaken about the Bible. "What about Herod?" she mused, when we were alone. Bert's attempt to encompass the Bible in Biak myth had failed, given his inability to find a meaning for all the Gospel's strange details. With this simple question, Edith restored the untranslated to the foreign text, thus reinstating the grounds for her own pursuit of status. Without discrediting the dream of Koreri, she undermined Bert's predictions.[20] Edith did not doubt the divinity of Manarmakeri. She simply wanted to keep him out there.

Collapsing Distances

Kept at a distance, the Land of the Foreigners offered my consultants multiple sources of authority. By closing the gap between Biak and the alien sources of local power, Uncle Bert explicitly sought to displace big foreigners like Mr. Senyenem and Mr. Fakiar, not to mention the lieutenant colonel with whom this chapter began.[21] Bert's prophecy undermined claims to authority that posited access to an inscrutable surfeit of significance. His rhetoric reduced the strange character of alien texts by demonstrating his mastery of the local meanings of foreign words. But as I hope the preceding pages have made clear, Bert and his opponents were not mutually exclusive characters. His messianic practices took to an extreme the logic that oriented the "normal" pursuit of power. Although this chapter has not dealt with millenarianism per se, my findings call into question the view that such movements necessarily signal a radical break with "earthly authority" (Bloch 1992: 91). In their recourse to the foreign, officials who seemingly supported the status quo anticipated prophets who openly opposed the state.

By bringing an expanded set of evidence to bear on the analysis of speeches like the lieutenant colonel's, I have sought to set Biak responses to the New Order in the context of a longer history of confrontation. In doing so, I have called attention to the limits of accounts of ideology that posit uniform responses to shared words. Be these words located in the newspapers and novels so central to Anderson's ([1983] 1991) analysis of nationalism or in the "strips" of social activity that, for Goffman ([1974] 1986), make up everyday life, every text is subject to multiple interpretations. What is remarkable about the disjunction between national and local understandings explored in this chapter is not simply the fact that it occurred but the fact that it was so stubbornly sustained. According to Goffman, it is the exception, not the rule, for participants to diverge in their definition of an interaction (ibid.: 444). Deception, fraud, and error are illuminating because they reveal taken-for-granted mechanisms for the grounding of social reality, the markings that social actors tacitly interpret in order to stay on the same page (ibid.: 445). If Biak were an "out-of-the-way place," only sporadically exposed to the institutions and agents of the state, the mismatches depicted in this chapter would seem less surprising (cf. Tsing 1993). But Biak was and remains one of the most cosmopolitan locations in Irian Jaya, a group of islands with high rates of literacy and widespread fluency in the national tongue. The interpretive strategies described in this chapter were not the product of isolation but the outcome of a long-standing tendency to fetishize the foreign. Social relations on Biak fueled a stance on distant authorities that was sometimes subversive, sometimes openly supportive, but always corrosive of a lasting submission to their power.

Through an ethnographic exploration of diverse arenas of social action, from the family to fishing, from oratory to song and dance, in these three chapters I have accounted in part for Biaks' ability to deflect New Order efforts to integrate them into the Indonesian nation. The task remaining is to investigate the utopian limits of this dynamic by analyzing how Biaks created a context in which they obliquely acknowledged perspectives obscured through their pursuit of the foreign. These perspectives revealed that the foreign was a local creation, and that national and local forces had thoroughly permeated this local world. The disavowal implicit in the practices described in these chapters calls to mind the pattern Abraham and Torok identified in the symptoms and stories of the Wolf Man (see chapter 1). According to their (1986, 1994) analyses of the materials surrounding Freud's famous patient, the Wolf Man's dreams and hysterical ailments stemmed from his overhearing of a disturbing conversation, whose repressed components found expression in Russian, English, and German words with tangentially related meanings and rhyming sounds. Although it also plays on the problematically material character of discourse, the fetishization of the foreign evident on Biak is certainly not to be equated with the dynamic that these psychoanalysts discerned in the Wolf Man. But in both cases, the end of fetishism assumes the same dimensions: the collapse of the barriers that conceal outsiders' viewpoints is not just a catastrophe; it leads to an eruption of unbearable pleasure and the utopian closure of space and time.

One gains a sense of the utopian limit inherent to the practices I have depicted by considering what these genres of social action prevented: something like the accession to a novel form of identity that theorists influenced by Lacan have described. In the preceding pages, I have focused on the way the fetishization of the foreign enabled Biaks to avoid submitting to what Errington (1998) describes as the "unnative" authority of the Indonesian state. But one finds an equally stark subversion of the "view from nowhere" when one considers how Biak treatments of the Bible reproduced an image of divinity that diverges from what others have taken as the Christian norm. If mainstream hymns set the stage for the "heresies" of prophets like Uncle Bert, it was by presenting a particular portrait of "orthodox" faith. The image of heaven as a tranquil harbor where believers "eat in one place" differs subtly from that which has been attributed to the modern ideology of Christianity, where, as Durkheim put it, "the dissociation of nature and the divine becomes so complete that it even degenerates into hostility" ([1893] 1984: 231). One might think of heaven as a reward for souls who have renounced sensual pleasures. By contrast, in the vision presented in these hymns, Biaks who follow the Gospel are led toward a salvation that is less a release from physical demands than a stalling at the point of their satisfaction. "Eating in one place" is both the destruction and the climax of desire. It joins a surfeit of food with an insatiable appetite in a moment of consumption that never ends.

In the anthropological literature on Christianity, much is made of the tension between immanence and transcendence (see Leach 1983; Parry 1986; Cannell 1999). Christians elsewhere are said to draw moral and ontological boundaries between this world and the next, creating in turn the problem of the "unhappy consciousness" that yearns for communion with an other-earthly God (Hegel [1807] 1977; see also [1907] 1977). In the comparative light shed by such studies, it is tempting to conclude that Biak's conversion never really occurred. The Biaks I knew insisted that their forebears left behind the errors of heathen "darkness" in the early years of this century, no less than they insisted on their own membership in a global order of nations, if not as Indonesians, then as West Papuans. But at the same time that they engaged in these global conversations, they participated in activities that both presupposed and sustained very different conceptions of the nature of space and power. To understand how they coped with the dissonance between such highly divergent "frames," one must move beyond the everyday to the dynamics of transformation. One must consider how Biaks learned to speak the languages of church and state without irreversibly acceding to the identities that these institutions are said to promote. The task is not to document stasis but to elucidate continuities in the ways that people experience change.

In this chapter, I have challenged the assumption that literacy automatically gives rise to new forms of identity. The recruitment of national subjects entails recognition, and not simply reading; people must suddenly come to see themselves from a new point of view. In the next three chapters, I speak to the problem of recognition more directly. Over a long history of contact, Biaks experienced conditions that elsewhere promoted the emergence of new conceptions of self: that of the native believer subjected to God, and that of the native subject subjected to the colonial state. Where the first half of this book has dwelt on the recent New Order past, the second half focuses on myth and history. More specifically, the next three chapters explore the myth and history associated with Koreri, the millennial movement that, as we have seen, still has a place in contemporary affairs (see chapter 1). In these chapters, I attend to a particular set of moments: moments when the gaze of outsiders was acknowledged, then reversed; when the violence of recognition was felt, but deflected; when the interiority held to characterize modern identities was experienced, but kept strange. I begin by examining how the violence of conversion has been incorporated into Biak myth.

CHAPTER FIVE

Messianic Modernities

TIP

The sand, here on the shore, the sand that covers the bone-handle
   knife, so that we don't know where it is.
The cape, there at sea, the cape that hides the canoe that is
   approaching, so that we don't know that it is coming.
It doesn't belong to him, it doesn't belong to him.
He takes it as his own, and I myself have nothing!

ROOT

The sand, here on the shore, *Karobi beach*, the sand that covers the
   bone-handle knife, so that we don't know where it is.
The cape, there at sea, *Sobari ("First to Appear") Cape*, the cape that
   hides the canoe that is approaching, so that we don't know that
   it is coming.
That nightstalking witch, it doesn't belong to him, it doesn't belong
   to him.
He takes it as his own, and I myself have nothing!
   —*Erisam epdorem/bekoker*, sung by Dominggus Adadikam,
      Mandenderi, West Biak, October 1994

WHEN I was doing fieldwork in Biak-Numfor Regency in the mid-1990s,
it was difficult to avoid being swept up in the sentiment that something
dramatic was about to happen. At the beginning of the decade, during my
first trip to the islands, a Javanese businessman had explained Biak's "strategic" role in the central government's recently unveiled Go East policy. The
gateway to both the province and the nation, its international airport a step-
ping stone between Jakarta or Bali and the United States, Biak was ripe for
development. The blueprint was already in place. In East Biak, just in time
for Visit Indonesia Year 1991, President Suharto would officially open the
first in a complex of luxury hotels designed to make the islands into a tropi-
cal playground, "just like Bali." West Biak would become a handicrafts production center; South Biak would be the site of an export-processing zone;
North Biak would house a satellite launcher and another resort. The businessman had told me these things after striking up a conversation in the
threadbare lobby of the province's oldest accommodations, a single-story,
oceanfront hotel, built of teak and equipped with private verandas and cov-

ered walkways, which was opened across from Biak's airstrip in the early 1950s. Amidst the fading splendor of this monument to the Netherlands's broken colonial dreams, it was difficult not to take his prophecy as an utter flight of fancy. It seemed nothing short of miraculous three years later when a fraction of his predictions appeared to be coming true.

Years behind schedule and millions of dollars over budget, the first hotel was approaching completion (see *Cendrawasih Pos* 1993d, g). Located twenty kilometers to the east of the airport, the colossal structure was being built into a raised coral cliff that looked out over the Padaido Islands. The residents of an entire village had given up their clan land and rights to the shoreline to make room for the compound, trading in their breezy seaside homes for a row of concrete units along a hot, dusty road several miles from the coast. Theirs was not the only displacement associated with the project; plans were in the works to bring a hundred Javanese transmigrants to Biak, to set up a handicrafts industry in the regency (see *Cendrawasih Pos* 1994). Along with the provincial government and a foundation of pension funds held by Bank Exim and Bank Dagang Negara, the Bali Tourist Development Corporation was a major investor in the project, which bore more than a passing resemblance to Nusa Dua, Bali's own compound of luxury hotels. Few of the Biaks I knew had been permitted to visit the building site, which lay just beyond the last minivan stop in East Biak. But at the Annual Development Exhibition and Night Market held to commemorate Hari Pancasila, a holiday chosen to coincide with the anniversary of the aborted coup that began Suharto's violent rise to power, men, women and children stood in line to see a scale model. For the young friends I accompanied to the abandoned airfield where the exhibition was held, the Hotel Marauw tent was almost as exciting as the one sponsored by the Department of Forestry, which spiced up its graphs and flowcharts by posting them above cages filled with deadly lizards and snakes.

The hotel project was not the only evidence that Biak might soon be "leaving the launching pad," as government propagandists put it. The satellite launcher remained a twinkle in the eye of then minister of research and technology, B. J. Habibie; the tax-free processing zone, as well, was still in the planning stages. But improvements in infrastructure necessary to these projects were well under way. Bridges now spanned the River at Korem and the straits dividing Supiori from Biak Island, opening the scenic north coast to private cars carrying tourists and well-off town dwellers. Trips to the market from Sor no longer entailed an overnight sojourn; the old truck, "Safety Two," had been replaced by a fleet of shining minivans that whisked women and their produce to Biak City and back in less than a day. Although the roadwork in West Biak was proceeding more slowly, by the end of the decade, a similar bridge would span the river at Wardo, providing trucks, minivans, and jeeps with access to the supposedly "dangerous" (I: *rawan*) subdistrict. Along with improvements in the regency's telephone service and additions to the fleet of passenger ships that served the islands, the new roads accomplished locally what the hotel promised to achieve globally: it brought Biak communities into closer proximity with hitherto distant worlds. The government's openness to foreign tourists, not to mention foreign anthropologists like myself, served as proof of the success of national integration in Biak; it was a way of telling outsiders that the regime had the islands under control.[1]

Curiously, even Biaks with good reasons to mistrust the authorities greeted the new projects and policies with little cynicism. Just as a sandy beach, according to this chapter's epigraph, could hide a knife, just as a cape could hide an approaching fleet, just as a familiar face could hide the nightstalker who had stolen the beloved's form, the changes in the islands' physical and cultural topography marked and masked an approaching transformation whose effects could far exceed the planners' goals. Confronted with an uncertain yet imminent future, pregnant with promise and fraught with threat, the regency's inhabitants contemplated "development" with a certain wonder. The Biak they now knew would soon be no more.

In Biak in the early nineties, development appeared as an event, not an ongoing process—an abrupt and total rupture with the current status quo.[2] The Koreri prophet Uncle Bert, whom we met in the previous chapter, was not the only one to link talk of Biak's "takeoff" to the impending return of the mythical hero, Manarmakeri. Sightings of the Itchy Old Man—recognized only in the wake of an encounter—were rampant during my period of fieldwork. Sometimes the encounters were more or less mundane. Villagers described chance meetings on the road or beach with strange old men, who accompanied them then abruptly disappeared. At other times, the anonymous ancestor was associated with more spectacular events. A fire in the market that destroyed several Sino-Indonesian shops reportedly followed a sighting of Manarmakeri. A year later, when another fire destroyed the offices at the East Biak construction site, people once again exchanged meaningful glances. But it was not simply the obstruction of development that brought the mythical hero to mind; others saw him as the source of progress. Manarmakeri had promised to return from the West after seven generations; the end of the Cold War and the opening of Irian Jaya to foreigners proved that the time might be nigh. A former regent ended a portrait of his plans for Biak's future with a "secret" metaphor. When Manarmakeri's parrot died in Holland, where the ancestor supposedly settled after leaving New Guinea, the tree planted on the bird's grave bore valuables instead of fruit. Like the bird, today's pleasures must be sacrificed for the sake of tomorrow's miraculous comforts and wealth. A potential candidate for governor told me another secret story. An old Biak had come to his office to describe a dream that represented the official as Manarmakeri's favored choice. Whether or not they deviated from the official trajectory of development, leaders and followers gave change an ancestral name.

Modernity and the "Indonesianization" of Indonesia

In the context of New Order Indonesia, Biak's imagined future was a familiar one. In the early 1990s, throughout the Indonesian archipelago development was collapsing distances and consolidating the state's control. On the one hand, the "blueprint" for Biak bore witness to changes in the central government's strategy for integrating Irian Jaya into the nation. Officials and villagers spoke of the projects as evidence of a shift from the "security" to the "prosperity" approach to the troubled province's governance (Djopari 1993: 154–166). With the armed opposition firmly suppressed, and a plethora of development programs under way, the Melanesian traits that had validated the separatist struggle of the Free Papua Organization (Organisasi Papua Merdeka, or OPM) were being recast as the makings of *kebudayaan daerah*, a decidedly Indonesian "regional culture." Through special programs and contests, experts sifted out the undesirable aspects of Irianese custom, while selecting "peaks" consisting of picturesque dances and costumes for the province to contribute to the development of national culture (cf. Picard 1993: 93). For the first time in recent memory, the word "Papuan" was no longer taboo. On the other hand, the plans for Biak reflected a national trend, in the aftermath of the mid-1980s collapse in oil prices, to extend investment to new sectors and sites. The fact that tourism was a major component of the blueprint was no accident. On Bali alone, between 1970 and 1994 the number of foreign visitors rose from 30,000 to over 1.5 million—an outcome that reflected global trends as well as deliberate efforts on the part of the regime (Picard 1997: 182).[3]

The stage was set for the project fever that I witnessed on Biak by a national Tourism Consciousness Campaign, which was launched in 1989 in preparation for Visit Indonesia Year 1991, an undertaking inspired by the success of Visit Thailand Year 1988 (see Yamashita 1994: 80). As part of the campaign, which was designed to help Indonesians "form a strong and sturdy identity and to maintain national discipline," regional groups were urged to cultivate what the minister of tourism, post, and telecommunications proclaimed as the Sapta Pesona (Seven Charms): security, orderliness, friendliness, beauty, comfort, cleanliness, and memories (Adams 1997: 157). Biak was not the only island being touted as the next Bali in the early 1990s; across the archipelago, officials and ordinary citizens alike assessed their locality's "charms" and dreamed of acknowledgment on a national stage. As the minister's comments reflect, the tourist gaze, as felt by Indonesians, passed through the lens of official ideology, which presented the industry as an instrument of nation building as well as a source of national wealth. This perspective was evident not only in literature on domestic tourism, whose promotion was "aimed at strengthening love for country, instilling the soul, spirit and high values of the nation, improving the quality of the nation's cultural life, and promoting historical sites" (ibid.). It was also evident in the very effort to attract international visitors, as Yamashita aptly notes:

> "Visit Indonesia Year" in this sense was intended to allow the Indonesian people to internalize "the beauty of Indonesia" of which they are proud. Therefore not only foreign tourists but also Indonesians themselves could share and feel the beauty of the nation. Seen in this way, tourism is a new form of Indonesian nationalism. By carefully situating ethnic cultural heritages within the regional framework of the nation, tourism in Indonesia can work internally as well. In this sense, tourism is an attempt at the "Indonesianization of Indonesia." (1994: 80)

In retrospect, tourism was the perfect site for development, given the New Order ideological imperatives. In using development (I: *pembangunan*) as a key legitimating value, New Order authorities were able to profit, both materially and ideologically from a global discourse of development, which cast the relationship between the Third World and its Western benefactors in messianic, salvationist terms (Escobar 1995: 25, 30; see also Nandy 1987: 3). But at the same time, the regime evoked older, late-colonial meanings of *pembangunan* in taking nation building as the aim and even meaning of the term (Heryanto 1988: 9). The goal of development was not for Indonesians to become more like Westerners, but rather to become more like themselves. Development would effect spiritual as well as material transformations. Indonesian citizens would come to see within themselves a national essence that was immune to the vagaries of politics and time (Pemberton 1994; Picard 1993, 1997). The promotion of tourism combined the construction of costly edifices—which reaped rich rewards for bureaucrats able to skim from their budgets—with the construction of authentic cultural selves. Despite the transformations and displacements entailed in particular projects, development was offered as a way of reviving tradition, through a radical suppression of both the future and the past.

The New Order was, of course, not alone in justifying its authoritarian rule by presenting the regime as the bestower of development (cf. Coronil 1997; Pigg 1992). Nor was it alone in representing ethnic and regional cultures by a few emblematic "peaks." Scholars have long recognized the role of tourism in promoting the "staging of authenticity," a process that works in concert with the policies and practices of host states (MacCannell 1976; Picard and Wood 1997). This is not to say that New Order national ideology was not distinctive in some respects. The promotion of regional culture was combined with the demand, enshrined in the official doctrine of Pancasila, that all citizens subscribe to a world religion. According to Acciaioli, this expectation had the effect of evacuating local custom of living meaning, thus transforming culture into art (1985: 161–162). But in focusing exclusively on the impoverishing effect of this ideology, one risks overlooking a more striking phenomenon: by and large, official notions of culture were embraced by Indonesians of different regions and walks of life.

The literature on tourism and cultural politics in the early 1990s is full of evidence of what Siegel, referring to Pemberton (1994), has described to as the "enhanced power of quotation" possessed by official representations of national identity (Siegel 1997: 3; see also chapter 7). Siegel uses this phrase to describe the capacity of New Order icons of traditional places, persons, and practices to project greater authenticity than the originals themselves. Picard, in his (1993) discussion of the emergence of Balinese regional culture, states the case baldly. The Balinese take the interest of tourists—and the support of the government—as evidence of a revival of Balinese culture. Not only the elite who serve as cultural brokers, but also the villagers who flock to official events have internalized the abstract notion of a culture that finds its locus in a clearly defined set of cultural arts. As Picard notes, quoting Vickers, "no one on Bali would seriously challenge the idea of Balinese culture. Even people who oppose tourism and see themselves as defenders of tradition are supporters of the idea" (1993: 87). In her work on tourism in South Sulawesi, Adams documents a similar acceptance of the validity of New Order categories. Adams quotes a Makassarese tourist agent who complained about the licensing of Torajan villagers as guides (1997: 164). In the absence of officially sanctioned courses, they could not possibly be acquainted with their culture's authentic ways. For the Torajans who demanded a share in the profits of tourism, the same appeal to authenticity prevailed. Communities whose tourism potential was overlooked by the government did not criticize the official model of culture; rather, they competed for acknowledgement of their own versions of cultural "peaks" suitable for raising into the national heritage (ibid.: 171). Few seemed to question the ability of improved versions of local rites—or even miniaturized versions of traditional houses—to express their cultural essence. It is this ability of New Order replicas to compel commitment to an abstract realm of tradition that Pemberton (1994: 159) illuminates in his analysis of the national theme park, Taman Mini. The elite Javanese Jakartans he interviewed found the heightened abstractness of the Java pavilion comforting. Spared the "complications" of an actual trip to their homeland, they felt right at home in their New Order selves.

In the early 1990s, the New Order authorities envisioned tourist development as a means not only of exploiting Irian Jaya's resources but also of winning national souls. The hoped-for outcome of the state's policies was the emergence of an orderly Irianese subject, as Biaks and others came to see themselves from the perspective offered by the national-cultural discourses of the state. Althusser, whose writings I touched on in chapter 1, provides one way of approaching the regime's stated goal in Irian Jaya. Through a process of "hailing" or "interpellation" described by Althusser (1971: 174) as key to the recruitment of cooperative state subjects, the province's population would come to acknowledge official categories as expressing their most intimate sense of self. In the first half of this study, I have suggested some of the reasons why Indonesia's "ideological state apparatuses"—and, indeed, Althusser's model—appear to have met their nemesis in Biak. They have to do with the fetishistic gesture by which the foreignness of the regime was reproduced as Biaks raided it for value, pleasure, authority, and prestige. Although my analysis so far has suggested what was at stake for Biaks in this particular representation of the state, to account for its resilience I must widen my lens.

For the Dutch officials who governed western New Guinea after World War II, the colony's development was seen as involving many of the same social, economic, and political changes as those associated with the modernization of Europe: the spread of literacy and wage labor, improved communications, urbanization, religious conversion, and the widespread acceptance of the rule of law. These transformations were expected to promote the changes in worldview and understanding that would enable the "Stone Age" Papuans to step into the modern world. Repeatedly throughout Biak's colonial history, observers forecast the end of the islanders' primitive beliefs and customs. And repeatedly the joyous moment of conversion returned in the form of Koreri, an unsettling repetition in which what vanished was not Biak but the world. Koreri, one will recall, is the name of the messianic movement that recurred in the region whenever a prophet was able to convince local inhabitants that the Biak ancestor, Manarmakeri, would soon be with them. Heralding a final collapse of time and space, the movement always erupted at moments when the indigenous order seemed to foreign observers to be doomed. Repeating the past as a series of unfulfilled prophecies, this study's final chapters examine how desires for a messianic ending have coincided with outsiders' efforts to modernize the region. They focus on a cultural logic that is no less history's symptom than it is its script.

In these chapters, I use the notion of modernity in a strategic fashion to pinpoint the dynamics through which Biaks have diverted colonial and postcolonial interventions. This is not to say that these dynamics had their origin only in an exposure to colonial and postcolonial regimes. As I argued in the introduction and elaborate in the following chapter, this fetishization of the foreign bears the traces of a much longer history of engagements with a dangerous and alluring outside world. Yet by placing the utopian narratives and practices associated with Koreri against the backdrop of supposedly modern forms of hegemony, we gain an understanding of how this mode of relating to centralized polities has been sustained. If the logic I have described in this book is, in the New Order context, antinational, it is also antimodern, in the sense Sakai (1989) gives the term. What we find in Biak is not a negation of the modern, in the sense of its defining opposite, the traditional. Biaks fully participated in the modern practices of New Order citizenship, yet in a fashion that dislodged the identifications that would have situated "Indonesianness" in their souls.

Modernity is commonly considered from two perspectives; the first takes it as a novel apprehension of time, the second as a novel structuring of identity and authority. In both cases, modernity is often said to represent a rupture from the past. First, the emergence of the concept of modernity is said to have entailed a break with the notion of doomsday. No longer does the end of the world seem imminent; signs of change are free to signify something other than that the Day of Judgment is at hand (Osborne 1995: 11). Second, the emergence of modernity is taken as entailing a breaking of the bonds of kinship. Persons conceive of themselves as belonging to new collectivities—"imagined communities" moving in concert through homogeneous empty time—joined through an identification with faceless others instead of debts borne of patronage, nurture, and blood (Anderson [1983] 1991: 9–36). The decline of what Anderson calls the "dynastic realm" dovetails with a third, related rupture: the break with magic through the division of religion, science, and art. Marx, Durkheim, and Weber each offered an account of the links between the individualization of belief, the rationalization of society, and the progressive disenchantment of the world. Whatever they make of the differences between these classical thinkers, many contemporary—and not so contemporary—theorists of modernity follow them in specifying a fourth rupture: a break with the gift as a "total social phenomenon" (Mauss [1925] 1967: 1). Read subtly or loosely, Marx's analysis of the commodity illuminates how capitalism's emergence entails new conceptions of God, sociality, and time (Marx [1867] 1967: 48–62; see also Parry 1986; Strathern 1988; Anderson [1983] 1991: 22–46; Pietz 1993).

To approach postcolonial Indonesia as the product of a straightforward rupture with tradition would, of course, be misleading. Yet certain aspects of the New Order's policies and practices embody traits associated with classically modern forms of power. To approach Biak responses to these policies and practices as the resistance of tradition would be equally misleading. Just as it is hard to deny that the New Order cultivated modern conceptions of identity and authority, one must appreciate the degree to which people on Biak in the early 1990s expressed a modern openness to the new. Although some might be tempted to speak of such complexities in the language of hybrid modernities, my aim here is not simply to argue for new labels (see Osborne 1995: 18). It is to explore what Biak's history reveals of the process of recognition through which modern identities are assumed—and of the vicissitudes to which this process is prone.

From Hegel on, recognition has been depicted as entailing two moments:

one characterized by the sensation of being seen by another, the other by acknowledgment of what the other sees as oneself (see [1807] 1977: 111; see also Siegel 1997; Keane 1997a; Ivy 1995). What I hope to show through an analysis of Koreri is a restaging of this drama. One will recall that to explain his notion of "interpellation," Althusser uses the analogy of a policeman shouting "Hey, you there" at a suspect (1971: 172, 174). Koreri, as it were, intervenes in the interval between the moment when the suspect turns and the instant when he or she answers, "Who, me?" Koreri's millennial plot line turns on the alterity always entailed in the assumption of an identity. Seeing oneself from the perspective of another, one experiences oneself as foreign, momentarily other than oneself. The imperatives that have led Koreri followers to fix on this alienating aspect of recognition find their basis in a social order underwritten by the valorization of the foreign. But at the same time, Koreri plays upon the limits of this order, a fact one can only appreciate if one considers the conditions that have led to outbreaks of the movement in light of the aspirations and assumptions articulated in the associated myth.

My analysis in the following chapters approaches Koreri from two angles. The present chapter focuses on the myth of Manarmakeri, that wandering Itchy Old Man, the ancestral hero whose return will inaugurate Koreri. It sets this myth in the context of Derrida's (1995) reading of Kierkegaard's *Fear and Trembling*, a text that questions the scope and conditions of possibility for the emergence of the modern Christian self. By comparing the biblical figure of Manarmakeri with the biblical figure of Abraham, I show how the Biak myth can be read as deferring the emergence of a modern Christian subject—at least until the ancestor returns.

This textual analysis sets the stage for a second approach to Koreri, one that seeks to connect the myth with the movement. I have already referred on numerous occasions to the movement, called a "cargo cult" by some, which repeatedly erupted over the course of western New Guinea's extended colonial history. Undertaken in the concluding chapters of this study, my reading of Biak's past attends to the "microphysics of power" that Foucault depicts in his history of the modern European subject ([1975] 1979). In chapter 5, I focus on the disciplinary regimes introduced by colonial authorities and the changing notions of civility they sought to impose. But I do not assume the inexorability of the modern or the singularity of its structures. Viewed from the vantage point of both Biak and a series of modern states, failure, not success, is the focus of my investigations. The story that follows is less an effort to depict what happened than an attempt to reflect on what did not.

This exploration of the distant past provides a context for chapter 6, in which I consider Biak responses to the New Order's efforts at constituting a modern Biak subject. In the early 1990s, Biaks seemed to be on the brink of accepting a place in the order of Indonesian regional cultures. Yet in celebrating the revival of Biak's "true" traditions, the individuals I describe anticipated a modern national-cultural future envisioned in distinctly millennial terms. In affirming continuities in a series of responses to the interventions of outsiders, I do not mean to discount what has been lost in the collisions between societies that have constituted contemporary Biak. I hope that the following pages do fleeting justice to a particular history's wreckage—as well as to its stubborn remains.

Mythical Limits

In the early 1990s, it was not easy to get informants to agree on what might constitute the "core" of Biak culture. Although most people followed the official line in asserting that such an entity must exist, their versions of the rules of Biak "custom"—and even the names of Biak "rituals"—varied by region, village, and sometimes person. Just as different villages had different ways of speaking Biak language, different kin groups had different ways of narrating their past. As I explained in chapter 2, there were virtually no cosmogonic myths of the sort documented in societies to the east and the west. The closest thing I found to an origin myth was a clan narrative that cited Thor Heyerdahl's *Kontiki* as proof that the ancestors could have crossed the ocean by boat. But there is one narrative that proves a striking exception to this tendency to contest all claims regarding the normative center or starting point of Biak culture. That is the myth of Manarmakeri. Throughout the regency, young people and their elders were familiar with the narrative. Communicated through whispered asides or late-night conversations, documented in the writings of foreign scholars and local historians, the story circulated widely, even if certain clans had the right to relate the most valid version of episodes believed to have occurred on their land. The mythical feats of the so-called "Itchy Old Man" provided one body of authoritative, if somewhat dangerous, knowledge that Biaks felt they could share.

In the language of Kenelm Burridge, an expert on "cargo cults" at a time when Europeans still viewed colonial New Guinea's modernization in optimistic terms, the song and story that follow recount a "primal myth" (1960: 154; see also 1969). One could approach this narrative as the intellectualized crystallization of what Burridge calls a "myth dream": "a body of notions derived from a variety of sources, such as rumours, personal experiences, desires, conflicts, and ideas about the total environment which find expression in myths, dreams, popular stories, and anecdotes" (ibid.: 27). Reflecting a "collective daydream," the narrative "formulates connexions between various kinds of experience, and attempts to express relations between past, present and future." The events recounted in it reveal "the validity of moral principles," however fanciful many of the episodes may appear (ibid.: 150). For Burridge, as for more recent analysts of Melanesian millennial thought, questions of morality lie at the heart of cargo movements. Sparked by the natives' exposure to the values of the modern colonial world, these movements sought to redress imbalances in power and prosperity set in place by what appears in these treatments as the natives' "original sin." Like the narratives analyzed by Burridge (1960), Worsley (1968), Lawrence ([1964] 1971), Tuzin (1997), Lattas (1998) and others, the myth of Manarmakeri simultaneously depicts the birth of local sociality and the transgressions that led locals to lose their power.

But there is more to the myth of Manarmakeri—and, indeed, to the Koreri movement, more generally—than this quick comparison reveals. For Burridge, millennial movements, like origin stories, provide a template for a movement between moral universes. To reach the new regime from the old, followers must place themselves in a liminal position, much like that experienced by the "free-moving" entities depicted in myth. Between the old order and the new lies a "lawless" state that mythical protagonists can only overcome "at the point when articulate awareness makes them subject to explicit rules," which they "think of as derived from a divine source" (Burridge 1969: 166). Although the myth of Manarmakeri portrays the limits and grounds of Biak sociality, the form of the error that leads to the loss of wealth and power complicates Burridge's model. As we will see shortly, a refusal to gain "articulate awareness" leads to Manarmakeri's departure and, hence, to the dreams of his return that have inspired Koreri prophets. And the deferral of the new order brought by the ancestor is also the gesture that generates Biak's social world.

To appreciate the relationship between the myth of Manarmakeri and everyday sociality, on the one hand, and state intervention, on the other, one must consider the various ways in which the narrative figures limits. First, one must place the myth in the context of the limits inherent to the fetishization of the foreign. The themes addressed in the narrative are not simply the product of a clash between worldviews of the sort described by Burridge; they follow from the practices through which valued persons are produced. Even without reading the myth, several widely known attributes of its hero suggest linkages to key features of these practices. As I have noted, the return of the "old man," as Biaks call him, is envisioned as inaugurating Koreri, literally "We Change Our Skin," the utopian state also described by the phrase "K'an do mob oser," "We eat in one place." Van Hasselt's (1889: 268) description of Koreri still rang true in the 1990s: "The dead will rise, and there will be no more planting and harvesting, for everyone will dine richly on Mangundi's magical fare. The old will become young, and a golden age of endless eating and drinking, and dancing and leaping will dawn, for there will be no more death." Manarmakeri's role as an anonymous grandfather

who promises the pleasure of unending consumption brings him into relation with the economy of Biak kinship. In this economy, one will remember,
the Land of the Foreigners' status as the origin of inexhaustible wealth rested
on the deployment of a gendered language of love and debt.

In chapter 2, I highlighted the importance of the gifts that bound "foreign"
children to their mothers, who, in this patrilineal system, nonetheless remained members of their natal clans. Through the food they produced and
the money and imported valuables they elicited from their brothers, the
mothers I knew not only transformed their children into "foreigners"; they
also helped constitute the Land of the Foreigners as a source of surplus
goods. Giving what they did not have, that is, a "foreignness" that they conveyed but did not create, they both demanded and deflected their children's
reciprocity. Recall the angst felt by a dying woman's successful adult sons and
daughters, who saw themselves as eternally indebted to the mother who gave
them both "life" and the ability to stand out above their peers. The debt
children owed their mothers cannot be viewed in isolation, however. The
wealth and talents that contributed to a person's success came not just from a
mother but also from a mother's brothers. For the mother was also a sister
whose marriage, for her clan, led to an irresolvable sense of loss. Expressed
in songs, stories, and personal anecdotes, the unending love between
brothers and out-married sisters underwrote a system of exchange in which a
bride's brothers repaid in excess what they received in bridewealth. Their
ongoing gifts to their sister's children confirmed in practice their oft-stated
assertion that their affines could never fully repay them for the value their
sister would produce. It was not only the desire of a woman's brothers—and
her children—to stand out above their peers that compelled them to raid
alien spaces for the goods and powers that fueled this inflationary economy.
It was also their longing for lost sisters and mothers: alienated sources of
value that, of necessity, had to remain out of reach. At once incestuous and
utopian, this longing had the effect of commemorating debts that could neither be forgotten nor redeemed.

Or, rather, these debts could only be redeemed with the return of Manarmakeri. In the myth, we see how the fetishized limits of this economy can
appear in the guise of a "grandfather" who belongs to no particular clan. Biak
genealogy, I have argued, was characterized not by the stable transmission of
clan property but by an ongoing disruption of patrilineal descent. Biak men
cherished the dream of creating a legacy for their sons and grandsons, but
few were able to leave a lasting mark. Children inherited clan names and
land rights from their fathers, but the resources and talents crucial to their
prestige and authority came from their mothers and mothers' brothers—and,
ultimately, from foreign lands. In this context, it makes sense that the figure
personifying foreign value should take the form of an anonymous forebear.
Manarmakeri is not a father in whose footsteps children might follow. Rather,
he is the repository of powers and pleasures in which any Biak might par-

take. The ancestral yet indeterminate character of foreign sources of value finds expression in Biak narratives such as the story of Doberok, which depicts an itinerant skull as an inexhaustible source of meat and porcelain (see chapter 2). As we will see, Manarmakeri provides an endpoint, as well as an origin, for the pursuit of the foreign: the paradise of "eating in one place."

But Manarmakeri is not simply an anonymous grandfather who offers maternal gifts; he is literally an old man who itches. In addition to sexuality, death, and debt, the myth also foregrounds another aspect of the fetishization of the foreign touched upon in earlier chapters, namely, the strange corporeality of foreign value. In its visible forms, value appeared as "proof" of an encounter with outsiders. Yet value also appeared as the generic potency conveyed in the gifts of food and porcelain that enabled Biaks to brave distant lands. Epitomized in the invisible *barak* that adventurers absorbed from the sultan's floor and rubbed into their relatives' faces after a trip to Tidore, this potency resided in an invisible yet corporeal realm. The importance of this feature of Biak practices should become clear when we consider the figure of Manarmakeri, whose power literally resides in his skin.

Second, to understand the myth, one must take seriously its relationship to Christian doctrine, whose normative limits the narrative also explores. It was not only prophets like Uncle Bert who drew connections between Manarmakeri and the Christian God; one pastor I knew told me that he politely declined when his examiners at the seminary asked him to explain the difference between the two. The myth is not simply a traditional society's reaction to the monotheism introduced by missionaries; it is a central aspect of Christianity, as Biaks experience it today. Yet in making the argument that Biaks are, indeed, Christians, one must not underplay the specificity of their beliefs. If Koreri evokes an experience of "redemption," as Burridge's formulations would suggest, the aspirations underlying the movement diverge from those associated with Christianity's "economy of salvation," its "curious ability to renounce this world and announce another, more compelling and true" (Hefner 1993a: 34). Writers who have considered the relationship of millenarianism to Christian doctrine have tended to describe millennial movements as attempts to overcome what Cannell describes as "the problem Christianity poses for people in ordinary life" (1999: 197). Millenarianism appears in these treatments as one of several strategies of "mediation," designed to cope with "the fate of humanity when power is seen to withdraw from immanence in the material world to a transcendent world beyond, leaving mortals, as it were, orphaned" (ibid.). According to Leach (1983), a widely cited proponent of this viewpoint, millennial prophets in the West have tended to build on heterodox conceptions of God's nature that make it possible for humans to embody the divine. Christianity in Biak complicates this formulation: in a setting where Christian divinity is associated with the foreign, it is not clear that God is "otherworldly" at all.

It is my argument that more is at stake than theological niceties in this difference. The image of transcendence proposed in these accounts of Christianity is accompanied by a particular image of the self, one sheltering a bit of the unworldly in the form of the believer's immortal soul. Intimately associated with the person, the soul is ideally immune from social scrutiny; the only one who can truly know it is God. In deflecting recognition of an interiorized Christian soul, the fetishization of the foreign also subverts the emergence of an interiorized national cultural subject. Without conflating church and state, one must appreciate the historical and logical connections one often finds between the practices by which these institutions have compelled submission to higher powers. If Christianity did not appear in a familiar guise in New Order Biak, it was not for lack of effort on the part of the Protestant missionaries who brought the Gospel to northwestern New Guinea in the mid-nineteenth century. They were well aware of what was at stake in the Papuans' conversion: peace, order, prosperity, and the acceptance of colonial law. In the next chapter, I will have more to say about the history of Christian evangelism in the region and its entanglements with the history of colonial rule. For the moment, I want to propose a reading of the myth of Manarmakeri that shows how the narrative's enactment of the limits of Biak sociality interacts with its staging of the limits of Christian doctrine. I want to show how these two aspects of the myth come together to provide a portrait of conversion as an event that is both longed for and endlessly deferred.

At the forefront of my analysis is the relationship between the intimate dynamics of families and the emergence—or subversion—of new identities. When we place the myth of Manarmakeri against the backdrop of more familiar myths of conversion, the relationship between intimacy and transcendence becomes particularly clear. In the next section, I begin by recounting the myth of Manarmakeri, which explicitly thematizes the question of recognition: who will recognize the messiah and, as a result, see themselves anew? Then I turn to Kierkegaard's account of Abraham's sacrifice of Isaac, the Old Testament story the philosopher read as anticipating the founding of Christian faith. Kierkegaard's narrative shows how a space is made for this faith when a transcendent God demands the sacrifice of a "worldly" order of relationships. The Biak narrative shows how a "worldly" order incorporates the shock of divine recognition and postpones the sacrifice that transcendence demands. Where Abraham's ordeal is an encounter of fathers and sons, Manarmakeri's involves mothers, daughters, and sisters, a factor that proves crucial to both the myth and the movement, as we will see.

Two Tales of Conversion

In the early 1990s, there were three authoritative sources for the myth of Manarmakeri. One was Kamma's *Koreri*; another was the Bible, of which the myth was held to be the secret source (see chapter 4); and the third was a wor. I collected four versions of the song during my research: one in South Biak, one in East Biak, one in West Biak, and one on Wundi. Just as Manarmakeri is held to have written the Scriptures, he is said to have composed this narrative wor or b*eyuser*, whose first-person narrator is the hero himself. Those who performed it for me claimed to have inherited the song from their ancestors, who heard the hero singing it as he paddled past their shores. Although the wording and details differed slightly from place to place, the episodes included were remarkably consistent, as were the stories that explicated the wor.

In October 1993, I recorded the following version of the song in Sopen, West Biak, where Manarmakeri's peregrinations began. An older wor expert, whom I shall call Nikanor A., sang the long text, along with a shorter text that provided a prologue to the myth, then spent the next two evenings transcribing and explaining them. Nikanor was a young man at the time of the Koreri uprising of 1939–43, the longest and largest reported by colonial observers; it is likely that he, like the singers of the other versions I recorded, learned the songs he sang for me at that time.[5] In the following pages, I combine a prose rendition of the myth with excerpts from Nikanor's sung performance. Thus I offer the poetic "root" to be read in conjunction with my informants called the "tip," the explicated tale.[5]

Wo*be* fawi *bo* fawi naranem.	You said you recognized, you recognized the betrothed maiden.
Mbo ma *be*wori kyaren do fawi yo fawi ya *ba*.	Yes, but those who held a wor feast did not recognize me, did not recognize me.
Yado yamasasi yo mare piryar yano fawi yo, fawi aya *b*va.	I descended and bathed at my spring, they did not recognize, did not recognize me.

Kamma's version of the myth of Manarmakeri begins with a prologue (1972: 7, 23–25). Chasing a pig he had just speared in his garden, the hero, then called Yawi Nushado, found himself following human footprints to a cave. Having recovered his weapon, Yawi ventured inside, where he saw a miraculous sight: a subterranean world, vast and luminescent, in which all the dead ancestors had come to life. A voice told him that this was Koreri, "The Changing of Our Skin," the flip side of the illusion of worldly existence. Yawi would enter in his own time if he obeyed instructions: walking backward, he was to leave the cave quickly. But when a snake slithered across his path, the startled hero dropped his spear and sprinted to the entrance. By virtue of this error, Yawi withdrew from society and eventually became Manarmakeri. Despair at losing Koreri was what made the old man itch.

As Nikanor told the story of Manarmakeri, it all began with a woman, a pig, and a crusty old man. One day, while a young man was fishing near

Sopen, a cassowary bird emerged from the forest with a beautiful young woman riding on its back. The young woman waited on shore while the bird submerged, then waded out to pick small fish from its feathers. The next day, the bird and the girl came back to fish; again, the young man watched, unseen. He was amazed. He was also in love.

The young man was the son of Sopen's regent (B: *sanadi*), a wealthy, powerful village leader. He simply had to have the Cassowary Girl to marry. One day, with his father's approval, he made an announcement to the villagers. Any man who could catch the girl would receive the regent's daughter as his wife.

Nikanor stressed the difficulty of this task. Cassowaries are large and quick birds, although flightless, with sharp claws and powerful legs. For seven days running, Sopen's men struggled to catch the girl who rode on the cassowary's back. The boys went first, then the adolescents, and so on through all the age groups in the village. Finally, the old men tried their luck. The young warriors jeered at their elders as they hobbled to the beach where the cassowary was swimming. How could these feeble characters succeed where their sons had failed?

One particularly unsavory old fellow did not join the others. He had cascado, a chronic skin condition endemic to Biak, and was covered with oozing, scaly welts. Followed by a swarm of flies, he limped to the forest's edge to hide behind a tree. With the maiden astride it, the cassowary plunged through the ring of would-be captors and trotted toward the path. At just the right moment, the old man held out his cane. When the bird tripped, he grabbed the girl and clung to her while the bird kicked and scratched. The cassowary finally gave up, and the old man turned over the young woman to the regent's son. In return, instead of the regent's daughter, he was given a pig.

The old man had absolutely no wealth, not even a plate. To make the most of the windfall, he decided to ask his cross-cousin, who lived deep in the forest, if he would trade some porcelain for a leg of pork. In his absence, the villagers grew impatient. Knowing that the old man would probably share some of his meat, they decided to go ahead and hold a feast. Their appetites got the best of them, for when the old man returned, all that was left of his pig was a knuckle. What was more, his garden had been gutted. His neighbors had ripped out his squash plants for leaves to wrap the meat, and his fence posts for the fire to roast it.

Fankoryaye *bo* dawamnai *be* rya dawamnai *ba* rya.	The ridicule that would not end, that simply would not end.
Yadoi yakon do wai ka*b*asa ya *bo* yasyesye sandima yapyar yakakir ro rayam bekoro, Uri, ye, aryare.	I went down and boarded a single-outrigger canoe and followed the coast. I floated and gazed down at the shellfish to be broken open near Uri's pillow.

Yasyesye sandima yawakwaker ro yom bekeruko besomufe sirewa.

I followed the coast and gazed up at stone penis that dangles there.

Yasyesye sandima yararyo iro Baryaisabari naraiyamama yakin be wendui bewansoso indai ye indai manyenefo.

I followed the coast and floated with the current at Baryaisabari Cape. I grabbed my harpoon to throw at a fish, a blue parrot fish.

This old man was Manarmakeri, and this transgressive feast was the "humiliation" (B: fankoryaye) that prompted his travels. In debt to his cross-cousin and mocked by his juniors, Manarmakeri decided to leave Sopen for good. Taking an abandoned canoe, he set out along the coast on the lonely journey recounted in the main song's opening four lines. His eastward course towards what is now Biak City, Nikanor told me, remains etched in the natural environment. On the coral flats at Maundori, he drank from a well, which he bored by pressing his cane on a rock. He stopped to look for shell fish near Uri's stone pillow, a trace of the giant that was Biak's first man. Further on, he paused to gaze at Uri's stone penis, hanging above him in the cliffs. He drifted with the current; he spotted and speared a fish.

This blue parrot fish enabled Manarmakeri to reestablish social contact. He left half with the locals near Baryaisabari Cape, and took the head for his relative, Old Man Padawakan, who lived farther down the coast.[6] This masculine gift yielded him his cross-cousin's "pity" in the form of two coconuts to drink on his trip. After polishing off one, he turned toward the Padadaido Islands. He passed Auki, which henceforth would shield him from Sopen's scornful gaze. By the time he landed at Sokani Bay on the island of Wundi, the other coconut had sprouted and was ready to plant.

Suiso sane beso ya bo bebuko aimani bon ine fyaryam yaranda ro Sokani baro dorei irawa.

Those people there, they loved me so they gave me a coconut to eat on the way over to Sokani bay.

Romawa koriyaye subena naibebewari Auki sura dauwaso, dauwas.

The boys' ridicule caused Auki to block them, to block them.

Naibebewari yado yarakaki yo sarai sasuf anya.

That caused me to go and inspect the coconut I was tapping.

Sarai sasuf anya ibebewari indwari in beyan baf ine siryuri sipyan do kamboye kambo yenai iro.

That coconut that I was tapping caused the indwar fish, the fish that eat seaweed, to swarm incessantly in my room, my bedroom.

Naibebewari yakin be maresi bonoma yabuk syosaserefo insoso sesasewar anya susan simaker.

That is what caused me to pick a fruit from the mares tree and throw it to seek the so sought-after young maiden so that her breasts would itch.

In the song, the mocking youths, the sprouting coconut, and the subsequent transgressions are links in a crucial chain of events. Making his home at a distance from the village, Manarmakeri planted the coconut, which grew into a tree, whose flowers provided liquid solace to the lonely vagrant. Every morning, Manarmakeri crawled up the trunk to collect the palm wine that had dripped into his bamboo tubes. But one morning, Manarmakeri, like Madirai, the ancestor we met in chapter 3, found the containers empty. To catch the culprit, Manarmakeri stood guard at the tree's base, then on a platform halfway up the trunk, then, finally, perched in its crown. On the third and final night, close to daybreak, the thief descended.[7] Manarmakeri sprang from behind a frond and grabbed Mak Meser, also known as Sampari, the Morning Star.

The Star struggled and begged; the eastern sky began to glow; the old man refused to loosen his grip. Nikanor reported their conversation verbatim.

> *Manarmakeri, shocked*: Bah!!! *You're* the one who made me curse at the villagers for drinking all my palm wine!!
>
> *Star, afraid of losing his celestial job*: The sun is rising, look. You have to release me so that I can go home. Come on, what do you want? Wealth?
>
> *Manarmakeri, unsatisfied*: Wealth? I already have it all.
>
> *Star, getting nervous*: Come on, let me go. I've got to get back. What are you asking for? Brains and beauty?
>
> *Manarmakeri*: Brains and beauty? I already have them all.
>
> *Star, stumped, falls silent.*
>
> *Manarmakeri*: Quick, make me another offer!
>
> *Star*: If you want one of the girls in the village, then pick a fruit from the *mares* tree and throw it towards her while she's bathing.[8] It will float up and strike her in the chest. Her breasts will start to itch, then her stomach will swell.

Finally, the Star had promised Manarmakeri something he did not have—a woman. He let go. By the time the Star had risen to the sky, dawn was in its full glory. The encounter with Manarmakeri accounts for how the Morning Star became the Morning Star, a trace of the night sky that persists until dawn.

The episode also accounts for how Manarmakeri received the secret of Koreri. Enraged at the Star for inciting him to further alienate his fellows, Manarmakeri demanded compensation. Nikanor called the scene the kernel of the myth. "Our ancestors were afraid to tell this part of the story carelessly. Because humans originated here." Nikanor's version of the *beyuser* alludes only briefly to the episode. In the line repeated above, the coconut tree Manarmakeri is tapping causes "the fish to swarm incessantly in his bed-room," which Nikanor explained was a trope for the miracle of "eating in one place." It was not simply the acquittal of a debt—the receipt of the woman/ pig that Manarmakeri lost in Sopen—that released the Old Man's power. To go from his self-contained, self-directed state—the paradoxical torment of "having it all"—Manarmakeri had to receive the power to surprise, which in this case involved a process of contagion. The key to Koreri was getting a woman to itch.

Manarmakeri immediately followed the Star's instructions. Hiding by the beach, he waited for the village's most beautiful maiden, the Korano's daughter, Insoraki (Woman Who Joins the Raiding Party). After Insoraki slipped into the water, Manarmakeri tossed the small, round *mares* fruit. It floated up and tapped her right breast. She cast it off. It floated up and tapped her left breast. She cast it off again. It floated back again. Shocked at the fruit's persistence, Insoraki cried out, "Ye-sus!"—"My breast!" This cry was the moment of conception. She dried off, went home, and started to scratch. Her nipples turned black; the rash descended; she clawed at her belly, and it started to swell. These signs of pregnancy were followed by the reality. Nine months later, she gave birth to a son.

Insoraki's parents were not pleased at their daughter's condition. The young woman was an *insos*, an initiated virgin, whom the Korano and his wife had guarded very closely. Insoraki's inability to identify her lover infuriated them. It also troubled the child, who wailed for his father incessantly for the first five years of his life. Finally, Insoraki's parents had had enough. They decided to host a feast for all the villagers to see if the boy would find his father in the crowd.

Ibebewari bewori kyaren do ai saninem yano. "Yamambabiryo yayo, yaye isya baim."	It caused them to hold a wor and sing at the drinking tree. "I don't recognize father, father is not here yet."
Ibebewari bewori kyaren do yen wukem yano. "Yamambabiryo yayo, yaye isya baim."	It caused them to hold a wor and sing at my stretch of sand. "I don't recognize father, father is not here yet."
Ibebewari wai o sumunda sukin aryab bo bo subuki ryab aninek.	It caused them to push all those canoes into the sea and to grab sticks to beat off the fingers with stinging blows.
Ibebewari wai o sumunda sukin aryab bo bo subuki ryab aninek.	It caused them to push all those canoes into the sea and to grab sticks to beat off the fingers with stinging blows.

The feast repeated in modified form the structure of the hunt for the Cassowary Girl. Male villagers from every age group danced past Insoraki and her son; the young men failed to catch the little boy's eye. Finally, the old men hobbled out, once again greeted by youthful taunting. Again, Manarmakeri was set off from the others, jerking along clumsily at the end of the line, waving a twig to brush off the flies. The onlookers' surprise at seeing the stranger quickly turned to horror. Struggling free from his mother, the Korano's grandson dashed over to embrace the decrepit old man.

The boy clung to Manarmakeri. Fury swept through the village at the thought of this creature having had sex with the beautiful Insoraki. As the song goes, "it"—an unmentionable violation—caused the villagers to fill in all the wells, tear up all the gardens, and prepare to abandon the island. As the canoes pushed off, Insoraki clung to the gunwales, frantic not to be left behind. Again and again, she was beaten back, her fingers stung by the blows. The only person to feel any pity was Insoraki's younger brother, who happened to look back at his weeping sister. "We'll die together," he told his family, leaping from the boat, accepting his beloved sibling's fate. He joined the doomed castaways in the midst of the rubble, thus completing the key positions of Biak kinship: a brother and a sister, two parents and a child.

Simewer ko, simewer ko ker rorya rwama kukain, rwama kukain insa yado yarande yakun aikun ya *bo* yaranda yari*b* yen dirawa da*be* sampan bo ukure orase na*be* nararone.

They don't want us, they don't want us, so let's just stay, just stay so that I can go inland to light an ironwood fire and go toward the shore to draw a small ship in the sand that in a split second will be in the water, afloat.

Ku*b*uki iyom musero *indwami* kawer yakon dori *b*o.

We will make it chase them, the *bark cloth* swaddling-cloth I sat in.

At this point, the song changes voices to depict a series of miracles. "They don't want us, they don't wants us," reads the first line above, in which the narrator continues to speak from the perspective of Manarmakeri, but the pronouns used are the plural and dual inclusive forms of "we" (B: *ko, ku*), the first presumably referring to the entire group of outcasts, the second to Manarmakeri and Insoraki. The new family took shelter in a hut. Refusing to let the old man near her, Insoraki stared out the window at the departing flotilla. The child tugged at her sleeve. He was hungry—already!—and of course she had nothing to give him. All she could muster is a bitter joke. "Go tell your father to let you eat some of his crusty skin!" Which the boy immediately did.

Manarmakeri listened to the request, then bade the boy to enter one of the bedrooms. In it, the child found a table laden with every sort of food known to Biak. He ate his fill, then grabbed a banana to take to his mother. "Mother, the room is filled with food of every kind," he reported, using the same word, *fyos*, that signifies age groups or generations of the dead. Sceptical, Insoraki sent her younger brother to check out the story. The siblings ate together, then the food disappeared.

After enticing his wife to swallow food made of his skin, the object of her scorn, Manarmakeri strolled into the forest. Finding some ironwood, he built an enormous fire. He leapt into the blaze, spinning around as his old skin peeled off of him. The cascado fell away, transformed into shell bracelets and porcelain plates. Now a beautiful youth, Manarmakeri stepped from the fire, naked and glistening. Nikanor claimed that his skin was white; another version has him returning to roast it to an attractive brown (see also van Hasselt 1914: 94). In either case, the change was dramatic: Manarmakeri now appeared as Manseren Mangundi, "the Lord Himself."

Beside the fire, the hero found a mirror and three sets of clothing. In his hair, he put an *asisom*, a gaily decorated bamboo comb. Slipping on the first ensemble, he looked into the mirror. This would not do. The shirt and trousers did not go with the ornament. Then he tried on the bright red cotton loincloth, made of a sort of fabric long imported by Arab and Chinese traders. Still, he wasn't satisfied. Finally, he grabbed the last article, a supple piece of brown bark cloth called a *marbui*. This locally produced garment looked just right.

After collecting the ceremonial wealth from the ashes, Manarmakeri walked to the beach. He picked up a stick and drew in the sand. As soon as he had completed the ship—a small steamer—he filled in the crew. He stamped his foot beside the drawing; instantly a real vessel was floating in the sea before him. Leaving the ship at its moorings and grabbing his harpoon, Manarmakeri strolled along the water until he spotted a school of *indwar* fish. After loading his line in a single cast, Manarmakeri returned to the house to fetch his family. With his fish, beauty, and fine transportation, Manarmakeri now offered everything a woman would want in a man.

Manarmakeri's son recognized his father immediately. But Insoraki could not believe her eyes. Could this beautiful youth really be the same person as that disgusting old man? Once she was convinced, her doubt turned to rage. If Manarmakeri had only revealed his power earlier, her family never would have left! Nonetheless, she cooked Manarmakeri's catch, then the four exiles boarded the ship. Chasing Insoraki's mother or "bark cloth swaddling cloth" (B: *indwami kawer*), they headed for Yapen or "Yobi," the fertile island where the Wundi people had settled. Viewed from dry land, the steamer that shimmered on the horizon turned into a canoe as it neared the village. Presumably so he could test his in-laws' faith, Manarmakeri changed from the Lord Himself back into the Itchy Old Man.

Manarmakeri sent Insoraki's brother to shore with a request. The Old Man wanted his mother-in-law to lie down at the water's edge to serve as a slide for the heavy canoe. The Korano's wife scoffed at her son. "Who could do that and survive?" She rejected this proposal, despite Manarmakeri's promise to bring her back to life, rejuvenated. Among the villagers, news of the interloper's arrival spread quickly. Following Insoraki's brother back to the canoe, they spat at Manarmakeri. Cursed and defiled, the hero and his family left.

Kirawi do robeyan simewer kunibo
  kuranda ku*b*e wombon bo kufafawaso
  romuno Ayawi siriwamumyas.

At Krawi where there is abundant food, if
  they don't want us, we will become
  like dolphins and join up with the
  sharks that swim from Ayawi.

Yaranda yasoro *Mamberamo* kiye
  kawairon ya*b*e *mandepo* syoso
  *b*emungi nawama *b*ero kobansiso
  ayasan isyun ya e ra isyun ya *b*o.

I'll go to sea and follow the
  Mamberamo's current, to the final
  layer *of clouds* where our dead are
  piled in layers like roof thatch.

Arasai yakon kuker anya iso *Meri* ryama
  dun kaker, dun kaker.

The wealth I had, *the steamship* will
  come, bringing it back again, bringing
  it back again.

In Nikanor's long b*eyuser*, the final episode of the myth was brief. The young
family became like dolphins, speeding along in their gleaming vessel, following the coast east before returning to the west and vanishing into the land of
the setting sun.[9] From the crowded villages—in the clouds, of the dead, the
generations layered like roof thatch—some day Manarmakeri's wealth would
return on a passenger liner bound for Biak.

Nikanor's story proved more complicated. Creating various islands as a
playground for his son, Manarmakeri set off with his family for Numfor,
where the scene of rejection was repeated. Appearing to the villagers in his
humble form, Manarmakeri tried to convince them to cancel a trading trip.
They were to stop plaiting mats and carving paddles; if they stayed on the
island, they would "eat in one place." In Kamma's (1972: 36) version of the
episode, after creating Numfor's four founding houses, Manarmakeri told the
islanders not to mourn those who died, for then he would revive them with
his powers. The Numfor islanders lost Koreri when a disbelieving woman
refused to stop weeping over a child's corpse. In Nikanor's story, a disbelieving woman killed Manarmakeri's proposal, which in the midst of the "hungry
season" would have spelled certain death. When the "spokeswoman" (B: b*in
fadweren*) rebutted him, Manarmakeri turned away, offended. The family returned to the canoe/steamer and sailed away.

Babara yun bo yabur ansya siso yabuki
  kyamara *more2* *b*am ya ma *naeko*
  insoso mumam bo *b*ori yaye, mu*b*ori
  ya wer.

Taking *my crusty skin*, I'll leave them
  and use it to decorate the *more-more*
  vase's surface. *Boys and girls*, you will
  see me, but you will not know me,
  will not know me any more.

Manarmakeri proceeded west, now magically inscribing the features of a
human landscape. In Sorong, the steamer docked briefly, and Manarmakeri
dismissed some of the crew. He stopped in Tidore and Ternate, and others
got off. These crew members became the ancestors of the inhabitants of the
Raja Ampats Islands and the Moluccas. Further west, more crew members

got off, founding the ethnic groups who people the archipelago that later became Indonesia. Through this process, instead of the surface of a map, the progress of a journey provided the principle that organized a cultural order. It is almost as if the "unity" in the national motto, "Unity in Diversity," was born on Manarmakeri's moving ship.

Leaving Asia, Manarmakeri set in motion other histories. Some versions of the story depict his son's ministry in Palestine, the basis for the second half of the New Testament. Nikanor cut to Europe, where the family, now in a canoe, landed at a small Dutch village. Back then, the Dutch lived just like the Biaks, fishing, hunting, and raising taro and yams. So it was no surprise to find the houses empty; everyone was working in the garden. The only person on hand to greet Manarmakeri was a cripple. When Manarmakeri asked this villager to fetch the others, he scoffed; he could not even stand. So Manarmakeri told the cripple to rise—and miraculously, the Dutchman was healed.

The Dutch villagers were shocked to see the cripple climbing up to the gardens. "Waranda," he called to them, "Go down to the shore"—thus giving the Dutch people their Biak name (Woranda, a cognate of the Malay Belanda). The villagers followed him back to meet Manarmakeri, who had set out all the valuables that he had plucked from the fire. According to some versions of the episode, the Biak hero invited a villager to try on the shirt and trousers, then held up a mirror to let the Dutchman admire the fit. He thus became the source of European identity. In Nikanor's story, the villagers simply took all the beautiful things.

Soon all that was left was Manarmakeri's *mandwam*, his tattered loincloth, which he had placed in the center of the pile. Insoraki turned to her husband. "That thing, if they don't want it, why don't you let me have it? Someday, I'll take it back to my people, beyond the rising sun." And so the Europeans got their knowledge and affluence, Nikanor concluded. But they rejected the true prize, the bark cloth, which both stood for and was Manarmakeri's dead skin. Western wealth and technology are simply the "dregs" of Manarmakeri's abject potency. It is the "accursed share," to borrow a term from Bataille ([1967] 1991: 9), which Insoraki is saving for Manarmakeri to deliver when he returns.

Mythical Differences

What can this "traditional" narrative tell us about Biak responses to the "modernizing" projects of Protestant missionaries, colonial officials, and the postcolonial state? The myth's conclusion offers an explanation for the islanders' resilient desire for the foreign. What Biaks want is not just Western commodities but the ancestral remnant at their source.[10] The myth of Manarmakeri offers an origin and endpoint for differences; instituting the inequalities that divide Biaks from outsiders, the hero provides the measure of value, space, and time. Providing a figure for what is in turn a fetishized figure, the foreignness that orients and originates from the genres of practice this book has described, Manarmakeri provides a distinctly corporeal—and hence "worldly"—source for the distinctions that define this social world. Still, the story's ending leaves us with a paradox. If Manarmakeri already had the scaly basis of his potency, why did he need the Morning Star?

In the tracks of Kamma, many Biaks, including Nikanor, have found it easy to assimilate this question to a conundrum of Western Christian theology. Manarmakeri is God, the omnipotent Father, and yet he had to send the world his Son. But the story reworks the problems of sin and redemption that have exercised many Christian thinkers. Instead of asking what sort of person could be the subject of faith, the myth asks what sort of person could be God. It turns out to be someone deeply entrenched in the dynamics of Biak kinship. Biak's Bible may end with the Lord himself, but it begins with an itch.

If Manarmakeri is the Lord, then the myth is his prehistory. The story opens with an apparently autonomous individual—an old man who gardens by himself. Soon enough, we see that this singularity is an illusion—the old man is split by desire. He has cascado, a chronic and repulsive disease, which has him stalled at a strange sort of climax. Instead of "eating in one place," he is scratching himself: a gesture that both satisfies and stimulates an urge. The cycle is excessive—often interminable—in its unbearable conjoining of pleasure and pain. The "remedy"—scratching—inscribes marks on the sufferer. With no means of deferring the compulsion, the sufferer transforms his body into a cipher, wearing his libido, as it were, on his skin (cf. Turner 1980). By portraying Manarmakeri as the origin of foreign power, the myth reverses everyday standards for evaluating a person's stature. One might consider scratching as the negative counterpart of raiding the Land of the Foreigners. Instead of distant spaces, the hero's own body is the focus of desire and enjoyment; the "booty" from this action is a cutaneous wound. In contemporary Biak, the Old Man's condition was a focus of amusement. During a skit held as part of a conference in Biak City, I watched an audience collapse in laughter when an amateur actor, playing a healer with cascado, compulsively scratched himself on stage. In the myth, the scaly skin marks its bearer as unassimilable to the community. Manarmakeri is less like Jesus than the demons in the lepers. He is written in the imperative: "Cast me out!"

To grasp the significance of this vision of divinity, it helps to compare the myth of Manarmakeri with Kierkegaard's commentary on the Old Testament story of Abraham's sacrifice of Isaac. Shared by the three so-called "religions of the Book," the story of Abraham is familiar throughout the world, including Biak. The first religious work translated into the Numfor dialect of Biak spoken at the mission post was a Bible history that included the story as it appears in Genesis 22 (Zahn 1870).[11] In the 1920s, a missionary in Korido distributed a vernacular tract entitled *Abraham* for Biak's growing ranks of literate Christians to read at home.[12] The story would have struck a chord with the early missionaries and their successors, who struggled to free the Papuans from the bonds of heathen society. Significantly, like Manarmakeri, they tested the piety of female converts by asking them endure their children's deaths without the ritual weeping that traditionally accompanied such a loss (see, for example, *Berigten van de Utrechtsche Zendingsvereeniging* 1904: 4–5). For my purposes in this chapter, these historical connections are less important than the conceptual insights one gains by pausing to consider Kierkegaard's commentary and Derrida's analysis of its underlying tensions. By rereading the myth of Manarmakeri in conjunction with *Fear and Trembling*, one gains a sharper sense of the implications of this Biak rendering of the demands of Christian faith.

After the Flood and the fall of the Tower of Babel, we learn in Genesis, God came to Abraham and promised to make of him a great nation. His name would be great, his descendants as innumerable as the stars in the heavens; through him the earth's families would be blessed. At God's command, Abraham left his home and moved to the land of Canaan, where he waited until the twilight of his very long life for his wife, Sarah, to bear him a child. Abraham was one hundred when Sarah gave birth to Isaac; he was even older when God told him to sacrifice his only, beloved son. Telling no one of God's command, Abraham traveled to the land of Moriah and led the child to the top of a mountain. He bound the boy and laid him on the altar.

> Then Abraham put forth his hand, and took the knife to slay his son. But the angel of the Lord called to him from heaven, and said, "Abraham, Abraham!" And he said, "Here am I." He said, "Do not lay your hand on the lad or do anything to him; for now I know that you fear God, seeing that you have not withheld your son, your only son, from me." And Abraham lifted up his eyes and looked, and behold, behind him was a ram, and Abraham went and took the ram, and offered it up as a burnt offering instead of his son. So Abraham called the name of that place The Lord will provide (Or *see*); as it is said to this day, "On the mount of the Lord it shall be provided (Or *he will be seen*)."[13]

Kierkegaard's commentary on the Old Testament episode encourages us to read it as an account of the paradoxical origins of modern Christian consciousness. In *Fear and Trembling*, Kierkegaard takes up the story of Abraham in a reflection on faith in an age when doubt came cheaply ([1843] 1985: 41). There have been three kinds of heroes in history, Kierkegaard writes: those who strove with the world and conquered the world, those who strove with themselves and conquered themselves, and those who strove with God. Where the first and second figures owed their glory to the poets who sang their praise, the third needed no one to glorify his name. Such a figure was Abraham, Kierkegaard announces, in a text that resounds with wonder at the magnitude of the prophet's ordeal. Throughout his long life, Abraham never gave up on the Covenant, never took comfort in the conclusion that "this was not meant to be" (ibid.: 51). He did not set his sights on the dim horizon of the afterlife; he held firm in his initial belief. When God fulfilled his promise, only to demand Isaac's death, Abraham bore the burden alone. He offered no excuses or explanations; instead of comforting his son, he turned on him in rage.[14] Caught between the demands of the "ethical" and the "absolute"—the moral dictates of his community and the unfathomable purposes of God—Abraham took the "leap of faith." Forsaking recognition as a leader and a father, Abraham made an offering with no guarantee of a return, a gift rendered unforgettable by the absurdity of his hope.

As Derrida (1995) suggests, the nineteenth-century philosopher's reading of the Old Testament story of Abraham's sacrifice shows how a gift of death might lead to the birth of the modern Christian subject. Derrida traces the conditions for this impossible event to an interplay of secrecy and sight. In silence, Abraham departs to obey the Absolute Other. A novel structure of subjectivity is born when Abraham sees himself in an invisible gaze. In answering, "Here I am," Abraham accedes to the irreplaceable identity held to characterize the modern Christian "soul." His deed, at the limit, is an encounter with the possibility of the extinction of all that constitutes his identity. God's demand forces him to envision a breaking of all bonds of worldly duty and debt. Hating what he loves, that is, the son who defines him as a father, Abraham is given his own death in the immeasurable interval between the moment when he raises his knife and the moment when God stays his hand. According to Derrida's reading, this violent instant allows for the emergence of a new plane of existence that frees the self and the divine from worldly contingencies. Envisioned from the perspective of an omnipresent deity, the world no longer holds any surprises; this topography literally subtracts Abraham's soul and his God from space. Divine recognition generates a subject oriented to an inaccessible object: the self of the possessor, not the possessed. What Derrida calls the gift of death results in a situation where earthly exchanges and relationships no longer seem central to the production of personhood, where one no longer gives because one owes oneself to others, to paraphrase Mauss ([1925] 1967: 45). Where relations with God take precedence over earthly intimacies, the gift of death spells the death of the gift.

To arrive at this sense of subjectivity divorced from space and time, Derrida's reading draws out two moments in *Fear and Trembling*. One speaks of the general dilemma of discourse, in a world where to give to one is to sacrifice all others. Where resources and lives are inevitably limited, choices of the type endured by Abraham are always, in some sense, the rule. The other speaks of the Christian response to the paradox: the heavenly economy that reinstitutes the logic of exchange. Kierkegaard's Abraham may not have gained his generation's recognition. "But he who loves God has no need of tears, needs no admiration, and forgets his suffering in love, indeed forgets so completely that afterwards not the least hint of his pain would remain were God himself not to remember it: for God sees in secret and knows the distress and counts the tears and forgets nothing" (Kierkegaard [1843] 1985: 143–144). A new economy emerges on the plane of the transcendent (see Derrida 1995: 101). The gift of death is rewarded with the gift of eternal life.

According to Western Christian theology, Abraham's sacrifice of Isaac prefigures God's sacrifice of Christ. According to Biak Christian theology, Manarmakeri is the author of both acts. Like the Old Testament narrative, the myth of Manarmakeri tells of a man blessed with a son in the deepening twilight of his years. Like the New Testament refrain, it depicts a virgin birth. But despite certain parallels, Biak's plot unfolds differently, under the impetus of promises broken and orders disobeyed. The Itchy Old Man is an outsider who institutes a local order, not an insider who transcends it. A mother's scepticism as to the desirability of immortality disrupts the paternal moment of recognition, postponing Manarmakeri's gift of eternal life. In the course of Derrida's analysis of Kierkegaard's essay, he asks whether its "logic of sacrificial responsibility . . . would be altered, inflected, attenuated, or displaced if a woman were to intervene in some consequential manner" (1995: 76; see also Delaney 1998). If we can approach the myth of Manarmakeri as a retelling of the Bible, the answer to Derrida's question would have to be yes.

Like the story of Abraham, the story of Manarmakeri recounts the founding of a novel economy of relations, based on a new articulation of sites and modes of exchange. At the story's start, Manarmakeri's rejection takes him nowhere; he is kept at a distance in the midst of society. "You did not recognize me!" the first song reminds Sopen's residents; the hero is a stranger in his own land. For this condition to change, something supplemental must interrupt Manarmakeri's static suffering. This supplement turns out to be the sudden stimulus of something incommensurate or unexpected: beginning, in Kamma's version, with the cave that held Koreri; in Nikanor's, with the beautiful woman riding the bird. The story of Abraham turns on the hero's unstinting belief that God will fulfill all his promises. By contrast, a mixture of startling events and unbalanced exchanges propels the Biak hero through the myth. He trips the cassowary, surprising both the bird and the villagers.[15] He gives a man a bride, but does not get a woman; instead he is offered a pig. He promises his cross-cousin some pork in exchange for some porcelain; he loses the meat and incurs a shameful debt. The villagers are not satisfied to consume his prize; they destroy his means of production, as well. A breach in reciprocity sparks the anger that marks the start of the main narrative song. Abraham, remember, is obeying God when he leaves his camp and begins the long trek to Moriah. Manarmakeri is literally launched into space by the villagers' "scorn that won't stop."

The first leg of the journey features moments that seemingly add little to the story. Beyond a local field of discourse, in an empty ocean, the hero drifts like a bit of debris. Yet this space is not so vacant; it holds elements of nature and history. What Manarmakeri sees and does exerts a force that sets him back into orbit. His first sight is of the "proof" of another Biak narrative: the giant's headrest, the rocky memorial of a myth. Then he sees the giant's phallus etched into stone. Called in some renditions *"genitals for/of a woman"* (B: *yom binsai*), the outcrop designates what the hero lacks: the supplement of a woman's desire. Inscribing borders in space and time, these mythical markers reinsert the hero into a circuit of exchange, which is structured by sexual difference. The Old Man reenters social discourse through the doorway created by an out-married sister. After seeing the giant's penis, Manarmakeri catches a fish; giving away the tail, he elicits his cross-cousin's "love" and gets the extra coconut that holds the key to his power.

While the reference to sexuality is subtle in these lines, it proves central to the subsequent events in the narrative. An outcast becomes divine through the founding of a kin group, which entails an extension and displacement of the ancestor's itchy condition. Moving to Wundi, Manarmakeri returns to an isolated state, shielded from the scorn of Sopen's villagers. The scratch and the itch give way to Manarmakeri and his tree, joined in a relation of addiction. A theft of palm wine, not pork, sets off a new series of events that are explicitly presented as surprises: Manarmakeri startles the Star, the Star startles Manarmakeri, Manarmakeri obtains the power to startle the world. Arguably, this power comes to earth from the realm of nanggi, the firmament, said by colonial observers to be the most powerful spirit in Biak's pre-Christian cosmos (Feuilletau de Bruyn 1920: 67; van Hasselt 1921: 113; Kamma 1976: 247–249). Yet this encounter with the celestial does not lead the hero to recast his relations with terrestrial others, whose significance to his identity is somehow diminished. Rather, his exchange with the Star is inserted into the circuit of transactions that defines his standing back on earth. Where the Sopen villagers are indebted to Manarmakeri on account of their misdeeds, the thief's unmasking leaves Manamakeri indebted to the villagers on Wundi; he must get something to give back to those he falsely accused. With this sudden insight comes a breach in Manarmakeri's auto-erotic circuitry, the self-enclosed itching that gives him his name. Transferred to Insoraki, shock and desire become productive. Startled by the fruit, she produces a sign—"Ye-sus!"—a child conceived as an expletive, then scratched into her skin.

What the boy gives Manarmakeri is acknowledgment—in his decrepit form, at the dance party, and later, on the beach, when he appears as a beautiful young man. Initially, this acknowledgment does not raise the Old

Man's status; the child's embrace results in an upheaval. Brides and grooms should be similar in age and different in origin. By claiming the young girl as his wife, Manarmakeri confounds categories; the repulsive old hermit is impossible to place. With the addition of a brother to this divinely incestuous scene, the group left on Wundi has the elements of Biak kinship but lacks its alignment. Manarmakeri remains an outsider until the child asks for his scales in a moment of mockery gone awry. His stigma nullified through coprophagy, the eating of excrement, Manarmakeri reenters exchange. But when he stops being a stranger, he does not simply become a father. In this strange Communion of skin, not flesh and blood, the Old Man appears as a Biak mother. His very first gift is food.

This ambiguity is striking, given Biak attitudes toward gender crossing. According to my consultants, a "male woman" (B: *snon bin*) was once considered a particularly valuable wife or sister (see chapter 2 n.47). Although the most famous *snon bin* were ancestral warriors, the term also served as a compliment for contemporary women who displayed unusual bravery or strength. Conjuring a boy who enjoyed housework more than hunting or fishing, the term "female man" (B: *bin snon*) was generally reserved as a taunt. In Manarmakeri, we see the most loathed of genders ascend to the pinnacle of power and prestige. In Sopen, Manarmakeri trades pork for porcelain, taking a feminine position in a familial exchange. On Wundi, it is a matter of garb, not gifts: rejecting men's imports he selects a woman's product, the *marbuk*, to stand for his skin. This choice allows for a slippage in the Old Man's identifications. The next line of the wor conveys two actions: a steamship chasing the bark cloth or the bark cloth chasing "them." An origin that always remains foreign to its creations, Manarmakeri is alternatively a mother and an uncle. The divided deity who institutes differences appears in the form of a maternal man.

When we reach the ordeal that decides Biak's fate, the trial analogous to God's test of Abraham, the Old Man's appearance as a maternal man becomes critical. Like the meeting between the outcast and the Star, the encounters between the disguised deity and the old women are nonoriginary points of origin. That is, these encounters give rise to the context that determines their outcome: a society in which the debt that binds children to their mothers is both the model for and the mediator of hierarchy. In the economy of kinship described in chapter 2, a woman's prestige depends on her brother's recognition, in the form of the foreign gifts she receives for gifts of food. She uses these foreign gifts to make her children into foreigners, valued persons who owe their status to her. A man's standing depends on his ability to appear as the source of foreign wealth, but this ability in turn depends on capacities acquired through his mother's gifts of nurture and the valuables she elicits from her natal kin. The myth brings into convergence mothers' and brothers' divergent pathways to distinction, which rest on an individual's ability to demonstrate privileged access to visible objects and invisible capacities that originate in a realm beyond the here and now. In the myth, the God of foreign power becomes the privileged creditor without effacing the feminine character of the position. In social life, debts to the feminine appear as irredeemable by virtue of their origin in the foreign—and hence in God. In contrast with the story of Abraham, where obedience to a heavenly Father overrides the prophet's duty to his wife or son, the story of Manarmakeri shows how kinship can provide a model for the divine without obligations to God cancelling obligations to worldly others. This is because there is not simply a metaphorical relationship between relations with God and relations with mothers and uncles; exchanges across the limits of the local are crucial for constituting the most intimate relations among kin. The loss of Koreri results from the very dynamics Manarmakeri's departure sets in motion, dynamics that continually displace the sources of prestige, pleasure, and potency onto an alien scene.

By keeping this entanglement of the worldly and the divine in mind, we can better understand why mothers are the ones who cling to death, the "most known unknown thing," when Manarmakeri promises endless life.[16] It is not simply their refusal that distinguishes these Biak mothers from Father Abraham; it is the nature of God's offer. In Biak's version of the divine test of faith, the hidden Lord tells the chosen person what is at stake. Belief seems cheap; if the wager works, Insoraki's mother—and the Numfor mother and child—will live forever. All they have to lose by lying beneath the canoe, by refusing to travel or mourn, is an earthly kind of dying, one that comes in its own time. But to lose that, precisely, would be to lose everything—everything that gives them a position in exchange. For in Biak it is death that creates the debt that ensures a mother's hold on the "foreigners" she has created. Death is the horizon where her children acknowledge what she has given and by the same token has the power to take away. In chapter 2, I described how dying mothers transformed their offerings to their children into a source of lasting recognition from their descendants. Remember the death-bed scenes that my Biak consultants found so compelling. Remember Bruno Rumapura's gentle joke about his children's obligation to care for their mother's grave until the end of time. Like the Trobriand women described by Weiner (1976), the mothers in the myth "need" death as the conjuncture at which their reproductive power is realized and displayed.[17] Against a rival who would openly efface this horizon, the old women insist on a determinate sacrifice. Willing to stop neither living nor grieving, unready to accept the extinction of distinctions, they insist on their own death and the death of their children. They insist on remaining the givers of the gift.

What structures this mythical moment is the fetishistic logic that I described in the first three chapters of this study. To understand the importance of death in the story, one must consider how mortality might confirm the irredeemability of the debts created by gifts of foreign wealth and potency.

The dying mother evokes the inexhaustible character of the Land of the Foreigners, the quality that makes it a place one can raid for excess wealth. Her own death, which deflects all attempts at reciprocity or response, puts her on the far side of a boundary not unlike the horizon that separates Biak from foreign worlds. In asking the Biak mother to give up death, Manarmakeri demands what one could think of, following Bataille ([1933] 1985), as a limitless expenditure.[18] This burnt offering would consume even its altar; nothing recognizable would remain in its aftermath, no point of origin to be acknowledged. An infinite authority would arise from such a sacrifice, but only at the instant of annihilation. The lure and limit of the foreign as fetish lies in the impossibility of intentionally inhabiting such an instant. To think or to name the foreign, as Biaks do, in their pursuit of power and pleasure, is already to set local limits on something that, by definition, should remain impossible to define. The most successful leaders cannot avoid anticipating what should not be anticipated in their effort to place themselves at the gateway to foreign worlds.

This fetishistic limit, which is implicit in Nikanor's story, is expressed explicitly in a version included in a detailed study of Koreri by a Biak civil servant. When Manarmakeri tells the people on Numfor not to travel—not to seek the surprise, the obscurity, the excessiveness of the foreign—a woman contradicts him: "If we change our skins and eat in one place, we'll have no prestige," literally, "we will have no names!" (B: Korer kando mob oser kobe snon-snonba!; Mampioper 1976: 47). The outcome of her refusal recalls the stories I mentioned above. At the end of my visit, Nikanor confirmed this connection when I begged him to tell me the beginning of the myth. I expected him to repeat Kamma's prologue, depicting the discovery of Koreri in a cave. Instead, he recounted how Sopen had lost utopia by insisting on a determinate surprise. If Manarmakeri is Doberok, as Nikanor quietly told me, then his departure was not unprecedented. The Noisy Thing, one will recall, withdrew his gifts when a young boy peeked out the door and shouted in amazement at the walking skull and the trees hung with valuables. Likewise, Manarmakeri withdraws immortality when mothers refuse to submit to a power they cannot domesticate, a shock that they cannot circumscribe.

The outcome of this withdrawal is to locate beyond the horizon an ancestral reflection of the intimate dynamics of Biak families. On both sides of the divide, one finds persons caught up in ongoing efforts to redeem irresolvable losses, to satisfy indestructible desires. Nowhere does one find an autonomous subject. Even Manseren Mangundi, the Lord Himself, lacks a singular soul. With his secret power residing on his surface, he is always divided in two. As the myth tells us, Manarmakeri's skin must circulate for the Itchy Old Man's power to be expressed. By infecting Insoraki, Manarmakeri does more than win recognition; he redoubles his already doubled desire. The out-married bride, as well as the alien mother, participates in the agency of the Lord. Insoraki's longing draws Manarmakeri from Wundi to chase her family. In offering his mother-in-law endless life, Manarmakeri does more than test his mother-in-law's faith; he repays her for the life the old woman gave his wife. The importance of Insoraki's yearnings becomes clear in the Netherlands, when she pledges to bring the skin back to Biak, a messianic act that represents the only way she can cancel her debt to her kin. Working through different characters, each stage in the narrative gives expression to Manarmakeri's predicament: the itch that produces the scratch that produces the itch. The only way to escape this torment and this pleasure is literally to leap from one's skin.

To leap from one's skin, in the case of this myth, is to put it back in circulation; it is not to leave bodily existence behind. Manarmakeri's skin represents a materialization of the invisible capacity for acquisition conveyed in *barak* and the foreign valuables a mother gives her daughters and sons. As the creator of foreign value, the anonymous ancestor, who is identified with God, embodies power at its most abstract. Yet this God does not transcend corporeality, as we have seen; he replicates earthly passions in other registers and scenes. The myth of Manarmakeri works at cross-purposes with Kierke-gaard's myth of conversion: it keeps divinity spatial. The Lord Himself is the unseen figure who sees, an unrecognized viewer, as we hear quite clearly in the wor. But Manarmakeri is imperfectly omnipresent; the horizon (Auki) can block him from view. What the island blocks is the gaze of society—a society that rejects him, not one that he transcends. Just as "the world" is not simply the stage but an agent in the myth, so too is the feminine. The virgin is more than a blessed receptacle; the movement of the narrative, as we have seen, depends on her desire. It is critical not only to the Virginal Conception but to the events that displace the Crucifixion—Manarmakeri's baptism in fire. Manarmakeri's resurrection as Manseren Mangundi is no less sexual than spiritual; he remakes himself as the object of Insoraki's gaze. Even when the Old Man wins her child's recognition, sexual difference disrupts the dialogue between Father and Son. Insoraki's refusal to give up her kin explodes the static utopia on Wundi. Her mother's refusal to give up death opens the horizon that keeps the hero's potency at large. Denied by these women who would not believe, somewhere Manarmakeri remains in motion. Paradise will begin when the world's gaze turns to the island and the old man suddenly reappears.

From Myth to Movement

Like the cargo "myth dreams" recorded elsewhere in Melanesia, the myth of Manarmakeri opens itself to a straightforward reading. With their garbled messages and enticing trade goods, the nineteenth-century missionaries presented the natives with a puzzle. The myth projected Papuan faithlessness into the past to explain why these white men had so much stuff. A more nuanced reading might draw on Knauft's (1978) argument that the widespread value of "existential equivalence" predisposed the region's cultures to cargoism. Exposed to Europeans, but excluded from their ranks, Melanesians formed a negative self-image—not because they were inferior by Western standards, but because Westerners were superior by their own. Knauft's analysis jibes with the historical record. It was not simply belief that Biaks denied the mission; they refused to see themselves through a new Other's eyes.

But one could add another wrinkle to the reading of the myth of Manarmakeri, one that gives a stronger emphasis to the feminine intransigence at the roots of Biak's "faithlessness." Just like the Biak hero in his rejoinder to the Star, Biak society, through its women, claimed to have it all. The ancestors refused to sever their bonds to an order in which mobility gave them a name. Through the remorse and longing that the loss of Koreri evoked, their refusal ironically reproduced the urge to move. "Eating in one place" became the impossible object that incited both work and travel. Through a conversion both registered and postponed in Biak myth, "worldly" concerns were transposed; they were not transcended. Prestige on Biak remained the reward for those who ventured to the West and brought the foreign back.

This mythical paradox has profound implications when translated into the dreams that have driven the Koreri movement. The old man's return has been taken as meaning that the recalcitrant Biaks are finally going to get another chance. This repetition reverses the sequence posited by Western theologians. According to Western Christianity, believers gain redemption when God repeats Abraham's sacrifice by sending the world his only son. According to Biak Christianity, believers gain Koreri not when the "divine" repeats the "human," but when the "human" repeats the "divine." The effort of the faithful to follow Manarmakeri's prescriptions does not present itself as an unconditioned "leap of faith." The question is not whether what they sacrifice will be restored, but whether what they recognize is really the Lord. Manarmakeri's arrival is unpredictable, but its implications are not: the end of the world, infinite wealth, eternal life. Through the fetishistic logic that shapes their longing for the foreign, Biaks displace a contradictory desire onto an unattainable object. The gaze that finds something unexpected in Biak is instantly drawn into the messianic narrative that reserves for a lowly grandfather the power to astonish the world. While waiting for the millennium, Biaks make do by transforming themselves into "foreigners." This startling "conversion" will endlessly repeat itself—that is, until the cargo comes.

Beyond Comparison

And so we return to the question of recognition. The myth reveals how Biaks resist the "emptying" of space and time. But, more than that, it shows how Biaks subvert the forms of authority associated with modern identity. Theorists who stress the self-avowed secularism of Western modernity tend to underplay its metaphysical moorings. But it can be argued that it is only from the transcendent viewpoint of an omnipresent God that the world's clocks appear to run in synchrony. The shock of envisioning oneself through an invisible gaze allows one to conceive of one's autonomy from the estimation of one's kin. The emergence of forms of identity like those associated with "nation building" under the New Order entails something more than the march of science. It entails a transformation in the representation of power.

In this chapter, I have used Derrida's analysis of Kierkegaard's text to provide a point of comparison with Biak's version of the Bible. Manarmakeri is veiled in a sort of secrecy different from than that attributed to God in Western Christian theology. The Lord in Biak remains in the realm of the visible; he is manifest in more than his angels or his voice.[19] Father Abraham must see himself seen by an invisible viewer, whose reasons forever remain obscure. Biak's prophets must recognize an unrecognizable alien as the source of an offer once refused. If we consider the mythical depiction of this offer in the context of what we know about Biak sociality, we see that it was not simply a sceptical mother who sealed Biak's fate but also the instability of the divide between what Kierkegaard called the "ethical" and the "absolute." In a society that highlights a tension between principles, there is no homogeneous moral order against which "transcendence" might be posed. Every time a man must choose between a son and a nephew, every time a woman must decide whom to feed, Biaks find themselves "hating what they love." It is not that Biaks do not live what Derrida calls the "aporia" of responsibility, the impossible structure that makes the choice of one always the sacrifice of another (1995: 67–69). One might say that the Biaks I knew in the 1990s lived this dilemma closer to the surface. The predicament was both relieved and reinstated by constant excursions to "foreign" worlds.

Although it resembles versions of the story recorded by colonial observers, one can scarcely deny that the myth I have recounted in this chapter is of recent origin. The first mention of Manarmakeri in European documents dates to 1854 (Kamma 1972: 105–106); over the decades, new details emerged that updated the tale.[20] Still, it is safe to venture that the features of the story I have highlighted in this chapter are relevant to the next task of this study: to move beyond abstract comparisons to consider the conditions that might have given rise to this distinctive "translation" of Christian doctrine. As I hope to show, the dream of Koreri both shaped and was shaped by local responses to the missionaries and administrators who attempted to reform this distant frontier.

At what historical moments has Manarmakeri seemed ready to return to a Biak prepared to do his bidding? In broad strokes, my findings confirm the results of Knauft's (1978) essay. In Biak, as in other places on New Guinea's colonial fringes, the most dramatic uprisings coincided with the departure of Europeans. But the force of my argument rests on a careful inspection of the baggage they brought with them from the West. To make sense of those moments when Manarmakeri's arrival seemed imminent, one must begin with an understanding of the Dutch colonial project. If the effort to master New Guinea followed the trajectory of "state building" elsewhere, it met with a particular set of challenges in this "unprofitable" hinterland. Not the least of these was Manarmakeri's impending return.

CHAPTER SIX

The Subjection of the Papuan

> The sand, here on the shore, the sand that covers the bone-handle knife, so that we don't know where it is.
>
> The cape, there at sea, the cape that hides the canoe that is approaching, so that we don't know that it is coming.

Doubly puzzling, resolving one riddle only to pose yet another, Doming-gus Adadikam's "very old" wor both elicits and resists periodization. Who was that coming around Sobari Cape? Given an acquaintance with northern New Guinea's past, one might replace the canoe with any number of vessels. Could it be the Ternate, bringing the Protestant missionaries and the Book to Mansinam, an island off the Bird's Head peninsula, a three-day paddle from Biak, in 1855? Could it be HMS *Tromp*, on its way to avenge the murder of a sea captain on Biak in 1886? It could be *Wai Meri*, the Biak-language term for one of the subsidized steamships that helped to bring the island under effective colonial rule during the first two decades of this century. It could be the Japanese fleet, which in the fifth decade of this century suddenly swept that rule away. It could be MacArthur, the Allied general, carrying weapons of mass destruction and a cargo of inexhaustible wealth. In the social memory of Biaks, as in their poetry and prophecy, epochs begin with surprises that come by sea.

Since 1730, when Corporal Enoch Christian Wiggers accompanied a Ti-doran *hongi* fleet to the Schouten Islands, the crafts silhouetted on Biak's horizon have carried agents of increasingly modern regimes. Shaped by the dynamics of global trade, Biak's relation to precolonial Tidore was probably in no sense exceptional. Elsewhere in Tidore's uneven sphere of influence, one may well have found stories analogous to the Biak myth that made the hero, Goeroe Besi, into the founder of the sultan's court (Andaya 1993: 104–106; see also Kamma 1947–49: 542). The authorities that came later sub-scribed to different conceptions of sovereignty, as similar as their practices might have appeared on the ground. Since 1828, when the Netherlands made its claim to western New Guinea, Biak has stood within the imagined borders of a modern territorial state. In objective terms, the islands' integra-tion into the global order of modern nation-states seems indisputable. But by virtue of a turn of phrase that insistently displaces Biaks' post-colonial iden-tity, this wider order is always "foreign," *amber*.

It should be clear by now that this displacement cannot be understood as the product of isolation. The myth of Manarmakeri, which was in some ways the most "indigenous" of the texts I collected, maintains a link between the modern and the messianic by incorporating discourses of transformation introduced by outsiders into a narrative that turns "conversion" into the focus of utopian desires. In the preceding chapter, I examined this incorporation of conversion through a reading of the myth that set it in relation both to the limits of Biak sociality and the limits of a particular version of mainstream Christian doctrine. I bracketed the necessary companion to such an analysis: an exploration of the historical encounters that shaped this translation of Protestant belief. The myth of Manarmakeri may well have emerged in the general form we find it today in the aftermath of the mass conversions described in chapter 2 (see Rutherford n.d.). Through the story, coastal Papuans, who had long transformed the missionaries' sermons into "booty," developed a new way of appropriating mission words as elements of their narratives, and not just as objects to put into exchange. In this chapter, I touch on this history, but with the aim of exploring the forces that sparked the messianic movement associated with contemporary renditions of the myth. As I have speculated, given the testimony of my consultants and comparisons with Dutch sources, the versions of the Koreri song sung to me in the early 1990s probably dated to the major uprising that lasted from 1939 to 1943. To make sense of this uprising, I move from the mythical to the explicitly historical, from abstract to concrete expressions of modern power.

Where the previous chapter involved a strategic comparison of the myth with Kierkegaard's account of the modern "leap of faith," this chapter entails a strategic contextualization of the movement in a set of discourses and practices akin to the formations examined by Foucault in his genealogies of sexuality and the modern prison (see [1975] 1979, 1980). For Foucault, the modern subject is the effect of a "profound subjection": the product of historically specific "methods of punishment, supervision and constraint" ([1975] 1979: 29). Foucault's explorations of the emergence of a "body imprisoned by a soul" have become familiar, even banal, among contemporary scholars of colonialism. It is difficult to describe the colonial birth of new forms of consciousness without some reference to the attributes of the so-called "modern regime of power." Historians have stressed the long-term implications of the initiatives of the late colonial state—its schools, prisons, barracks, and workshops, its laws, its censuses, its programs in health and housing—all mechanisms for "disciplining colonial bodies" and "regulating the growth of colonial life." Analysts have related such interventions to the cultivation of bourgeois European identity (Stoler 1995) and the emergence of the nationalist subject of the postcolonial state (Anderson [1983] 1991: ch. 10). The exclusion of the colonized from full civil status in no sense detracts from the post-Enlightenment character of the apparatus. Modern natives were the analogue of modern children, who had to be trained to partake in their "natural" rights (Stoler 1995: 141; Gouda 1993; 1995: 118–157). Although the literature on western New Guinea easily illustrates these themes, my aim in this chapter is different. By exploring the vicissitudes of Dutch colonialism at the limits of its reach, I hope to bring to light a historical drama that unsettles easy assumptions about the coherence and consequences of colonial regimes.

As we will see in this chapter, a key factor complicating efforts to establish colonial authority in Biak was the interaction of mission and government projects of reform. For the Indies, this alliance was unusual, given the Dutch government's tendency to discourage Christian evangelism in areas with a Muslim majority (Hefner 1993b). But when we compare western New Guinea with other colonial settings, this interaction should come as little surprise. From a variety of angles, scholars have documented the relationship between Christian conversion and the consolidation of capitalism and colonial rule (Horton 1971, 1975; Bond 1987; Comaroff and Comaroff 1991, 1997; Ranger 1993; Rafael [1988] 1993; Hefner 1993a, b). But this linkage is more than historically specific to colonial contexts; there is an affinity between depictions of the process of conversion and the process of submission to a modern disciplinary regime.

It proves enlightening to consider the transformations described in *Discipline and Punish* in relation to Kierkegaard's description of Abraham's encounter with God. Enacting an ordered emplotment of time and space, modern disciplinary power generates an individuality with four seemingly secular characteristics: "it is cellular (by the spatial distribution), it is organic (by the coding of activities), it is genetic (by the accumulation of time), and it is combinatory (by the composition of forces) . . . it operates four great techniques: it draws up tables, it prescribes movements, it imposes exercises. . . . In order to obtain the combination of forces, it imposes tactics . . . the art of constructing, with located bodies, coded activities and trained aptitudes, mechanisms in which the product of the various forces is increased by their calculated combination" (Foucault [1975] 1979: 167).

These mechanisms do not function in isolation. The exercise of modern power entails a moment of recognition that calls to mind Abraham's faith in the face of the divine. The panopticon captures the moment's visual geometry most explicitly. Divided from their fellows, the inmates turn to the central tower of the prison, the visible source of an invisible gaze (Foucault [1975] 1979: 200–203). The violence of the anonymous watcher's unpredictable intervention also makes itself felt in the "hierarchical observation" that defines the modern classroom. Foucault quotes the inventors of the "signal," an apparatus for training school children, which contained "in its mechanical brevity both the technique of command and the morality of obedience." "The first and principle use of the signal is to attract at once the attention of all the pupils to the teacher and to make them attentive to what he wishes to impart to them. . . . Whenever a good pupil hears the noise of the signal, he will imagine that he is hearing the voice of the teacher or rather the voice of God himself calling him by his name. He will then partake of the feeling of the young Samuel, saying with him in the depths of his soul, 'Lord I am here' (Foucault [1975] 1979: 166). The sudden sense of recognition conveyed by this signal offers an entry for the fetishization of the foreign that characterizes the practices described in this study. Transformed into the valued medium of social identity, a violent intrusion is repeated as a desirable surprise. So pervasive in Biak songs and stories, this insistence on surprise prevents the "normalization" that would come of seeing oneself through the eyes of an observing other. In doing so, it destabilizes hierarchies of the sort Foucault associates with modern regimes. This response to modern authority raises the possibility of a "soul" that subverts at the same time that it submits.

The analysis of the Koreri movement undertaken in this chapter shows that the emergence of the "modern soul" need not follow from the imposition of modern technologies of the body. Erupting with the crumbling of Dutch authority in the Indies, the outbreak that began in 1939 enacted a startling response to the colonial gaze. The movement followed the mission's revival of the "heathen" musical genre of wor for use in Christian worship. In previous decades of Dutch involvement on Biak, officials and missionaries often blamed their problems on the criminality of local "customs," including some of the practices described in chapters 2 and 3. The revival of wor to express the essence of the authentic Biak Christian coincided with changes that consolidated the government's rule on the island and integrated Biak workers into a growing regional economy. It will be my argument that the Koreri movement of 1939–43 was, in many respects, a response to these transformations. This analysis calls into question the belief that colonial regimes exert a uniform force with universal effects.

My goal, however, is not simply to challenge scholarly presumptions; it is to trace the colonial roots of Biak responses to the New Order state. In setting my sights on the conditions that gave rise to the 1939–43 movement, I do not mean to obscure the long history of uprisings that preceded it. As I noted in the previous chapter, Manarmakeri first appeared in European records in 1854, a year before Protestant missionaries settled in northern New Guinea (Kamma 1972: 105–106). The first reported movement occurred in about 1855, when a Papuan "impostor" claimed to have brought the ancestor to Numfor from Tidore, which at the time nominally governed the region on behalf of the colonial state (ibid.: 106–107). Manarmakeri's sudden visibility to Dutch observers was a direct result of the broader changes arguably registered by his prophet—changes that brought increasing numbers of Europeans to New Guinea's northern coasts. In 1828, Holland fixed the Indies' eastern boundary at the 141st parallel, a line running down the center of New Guinea (van der Veur 1966). Although the Dutch based their claims on those of the sultan of Tidore, colonial muscle-flexing hastened the native ruler's decline, a decline that had begun in the seventeenth century with the enforcement of the Dutch East Indies Company's spice eradication policy. This intervention had destroyed the already weakening global trade that was once central to Tidore's power and prestige (Andaya 1993: 214–239; see also van Fraassen 1987; Reid 1993; Lieberman 1995: 797).

Clearly, any analysis of the 1855 Koreri movement on Numfor, about which we know very little, would have to begin with an assessment of this changing regional context. In approaching the 1939–43 uprising, for which the data is more complete, I have likewise attempted to open a wide setting for considering coastal New Guinea's colonial past. I begin with an overview of late colonial history, as depicted by scholars focusing on the heart of the Indies. Revealing some of the assumptions and expectations that informed colonial practice in New Guinea, this snapshot provides a context that wrests Koreri from the depoliticizing discourse of cargoism and the politicizing myths of Papuan nationalism. Then I turn to the particularities of colonial experience along the northern coasts of western New Guinea. The Dutch colonial project in New Guinea adhered closely to the plot of *Discipline and Punish*: the Papuan "pirates" were to change from the enemies of the state into the objects of humanitarian reform. Yet this furtherance of "life" was thwarted by vexing questions of sovereignty, which were exacerbated by what officials and missionaries viewed as the Papuans' refusal to admit the dominance of higher powers. From the viewpoint of nineteenth-century officialdom, the Papuans' Christian conversion seemed a precondition for their transformation into docile colonial subjects. From the viewpoint of the mission, the Papuans' pacification seemed crucial if Christianization was to proceed. Yet both the mission and the government had to contend with a chronic shortage of resources. They blamed the Papuans' failure to become a disciplined work force for the lack of investment and a tax base to finance the introduction of reforms. The massive uprising that erupted on Biak in 1939 ended a brief interlude when the prospects for prosperity, peace, and order finally seemed to be brightening in New Guinea. It was not simply the region's distance from the colony's center that kept its "modernization" seemingly stalled.

In 1883, Resident Haga of Ternate, whose administrative unit included western New Guinea, ended a history of the territory on this sour note: "When we think of how many sacrifices of money and human life the Netherlands has already given for western New Guinea, without reaping any profit from them, then one comes to the conclusion that it is a dubious privilege to be known as the sovereign of New Guinea" (1884, vol. 2: 435). It would not be easy to civilize the Papuans "because nowhere do we find it noted that human authority is properly honored or that awe for a God or gods is interwoven into the people's character" (ibid.: 430–431). Although conditions improved for the authorities in the following decades, missionaries and officials remained haunted by the prospect that the coastal Papuans' submission was only skin deep. In this chapter, I find myself in the strange position of suggesting that colonial observers were right to be concerned. Biak went through major transformations during the period between the 1855 outbreak of Koreri and the 1939–43 movement. But patterns emerge across these discontinuities. When we return to the recent postcolonial past, in the following chapter, the relevance of these patterns should become clear. The dream of Koreri not only informed local reactions to shifts in colonial practice; it shaped local responses to the gradual consolidation of New Order hegemony—and the New Order's sudden collapse.

Colonial Contexts

Given New Guinea's location in the Netherlands Indies, one can understand why Biaks have long imagined modernity as traveling in the hold of a ship. Founded in 1602, based first in Ambon in the Moluccan Islands, and later in Batavia on Java, the Dutch East Indies Company (VOC) functioned as a mercantile state, intervening in local politics and extending its sphere of influence whenever necessary to protect its lucrative trade. Bankrupt in the eighteenth century, it was replaced in the nineteenth century by a colonial government with growing means and ends.

To appreciate how these means and ends played out on the frontier of the colony, one must know something of the history of its center. For historians of Java, where the late VOC concentrated its efforts, the founding of the Culture System in 1830 represents a watershed. After the English interregnum and the Java War, Governor General van den Bosch designed a regime of forced cultivation modeled on an older tributary order (Furnivall 1944; [1948] 1956: 217–467). Through an intensified system of "indirect" rule, the Indies government controlled the production of raw materials and the distribution of commodities, creating a machine for the extraction of export profits. Local social relations were profoundly transformed (Breman 1983: 5–38; see also Geertz 1963). A range of intermediaries upheld the scheme: from local nobles or *priyayi*, who forced peasants to cultivate indigo and sugar for sale to the state, to Chinese "farmers," exempted from pass laws, who managed the state-controlled sale of opium and monopolized local trading networks, to underworld enforcers or *jago*, who trafficked in protection and surveillance (Onghokham 1978; Rush 1983). At the system's helm were European managers and officials, often married to local women, who assumed the trappings of privilege attributed to the "traditional" Javanese courts and built a sumptuous world on the spoils of the system.[1] But by the end of the century, changing policies, as well as new technologies and economic conditions, had rendered this world obsolete.

In 1870, the Dutch government abolished the Culture System, an act with more impact in the Dutch capital than in Java's villages (Breman 1983: 31). In the same Liberal spirit, leaders in the Hague repealed laws restricting European migration to the Indies. Some of the Europeans who arrived by the faster, more frequent steamships turned their attention to the Buitengewesten, or "Outer Territories." Using the land of local sultans and the labor of Chinese then Javanese coolies, planters in East Sumatra paved the way for multinational corporations, building fortunes in the production of tobacco and rubber (Stoler 1985). Other new arrivals joined an expanding colonial administration, financed by government enterprises and taxation on private concerns (Furnivall [1948] 1956: 225–226). The new officials took part in the development of a state that increasingly sought to achieve a uniformity of governance. On the one hand, this entailed an extension of "peace and order" to the Indies' more unruly corners (van Goor 1986; Locher-Scholten 1994); on the other, a penetration into the depths of native life (Shiraishi n.d.). Although the first project left the government bogged down in a protracted war in Aceh for several decades, at the turn of the century, politicians in the Netherlands proclaimed an "Ethical Policy" that would dispel the Indies' "darkness" and bathe the colony in modernity's "light" (Furnivall [1948] 1956: 226–467).

The Ethical Policy gave expression to older ideologies in a rationalized form. Building on the practice of indirect rule, experts undertook the study of customary law (I: *adat*) to ensure that justice was served on what were supposedly authentic local grounds (Spyer 1996: 27–28). The codification of tradition and the normalization of villages were seen as essential to the implementation of "humanitarian" programs in health, education, and welfare. These initiatives did little to improve native welfare. But the new policy succeeded in creating a Western-educated elite from the expanded pool of trained natives needed to carry them out.

Joined by mission-educated Christians and reformist Moslems, Dutch-speaking natives, Chinese mestizos, Eurasians, and Europeans translated the language of Western progress into an evolving local idiom (Shiraishi 1990; Adam 1984). "Market Malay," the precursor to Indonesian, had been the language of rule; now it became the medium of the vernacular press and mass rallies attended by thousands of Javanese peasants (Hoffman 1979; Maier 1993). In the Indies' growing Dutch community, pleasure turned to fear as the "native awakening" yielded a series of popular uprisings in the 1920s. The government's response was to jail or exile countless "subversives" to remote parts of the colony, including New Guinea, and to reinforce the position of "traditional" leaders (Shiraishi 1990: 216–228). What Shiraishi has called an "age in motion" gave way to an "age of parties," in which officially sanctioned organizations represented interests conceived along racial or ethnic lines. In the 1930s, colonial repression set the terms for a new phase of politics, now limited to an urban elite.

In the wake of Benedict Anderson's seminal writings, analysts broadly agree that it was within a tiny, privileged group that the colonial Other named the subject of Indonesian nationalism (Shiraishi 1990; Anderson [1983] 1991: 113–140; Mrázek 1994; Siegel 1997). Late colonial society was fractured by two chasms: that dividing Western-educated natives from the vast majority of their compatriots and that dividing educated natives from Europeans. The latter gulf haunted the new leaders who came to dominate the mainstream. Seen through the lens of a new language, Indonesian, the imaginary object of the colonial gaze was transformed into the imagined citizen of a nation. The Indies "native" became the Indonesian, one of many formally equivalent members of this, one of many formally equivalent nation-states. Following the collapse of Dutch authority in World War II, a turbulent marriage of social and political forces energized the revolution that resulted in Indonesian independence (Kahin 1985a: 12). Yet those with an interest in order harnessed these energies. The postcolonial order would be shaped by inherited hierarchies, sustained against the impulse to sweep them away (Anderson [1983] 1990).

One can imagine a number of ways to insert Biak into this scholarly narrative of Indonesia's inception. One might think of modernity as taking the slow boat to the territory, arriving, like the clothing sported by local leaders, always already out of date (Spyer 1998: 168). While Java's villagers were being "uplifted," Biak's were supposedly being "pacified." Local clans never underwent the dramatic changes in land tenure that elsewhere accompanied state rule (cf. Kahn 1993: 187–223). Plantations were opened on New Guinea's mainland at the height of the Depression, when elsewhere they were bankrupt or in decline. Whereas in the late 1930s, Batavia (now called Jakarta) was a thriving metropolis with close to a million inhabitants, without telephones, electricity, or any "Western comforts," North New Guinea's administrative capital, which was then Manokwari, "could not even be called a town" (Derix 1987: 67). Limited to the coasts, the effective topography of authority in New Guinea bore more in common with the precolonial than the late colonial order. Yet the image of New Guinea as lagging on an evolutionary path obscures, among other things, the way in which the Indies' modernization rested on the shortening of distances. In the late colonial period, what happened on New Guinea's coasts was often the effect of a much broader set of colonial interests. Sometimes discussions in and about New Guinea radically diverged from the dominant conversations of the day. But occasionally, they even appear to have anticipated what would later become more general concerns.

Such is the case for the period of the Koreri movement of 1939–43, the

episode that is the focus of this chapter. One could view Biak's history during
World War II, when Japan occupied the Indies, as a reflection of what might
have happened elsewhere in the colony. Biak lay within the region overseen
by the Japanese Navy's Southwestern Fleet after the capitulation of the
Netherlands Indies government. The Great East was to be a Japanese territory, not a "self-governing" protectorate, as was promised to leaders in Java
and Sumatra, areas under the Japanese army's command (de Jong 1985, part
2: 497–513; Kahin 1985a: 6; see also Kahin 1952: 102, 115, 121). Exposed
in the east to the advancing American forces, and with its southern settlement at Merauke never taken by the Japanese, western New Guinea stood on
the front throughout most of the war. Biak became the front in mid-1944
after the border town of Hollandia (now Jayapura) fell in a massive assault by
the Sixth U.S. Army, Fifth U.S. Airforce, and Seventh U.S. Fleet (Derix 1987:
127). What would occur in the colony's west at the end of the occupation
took place on Biak at its start: violent uprisings swept away the vestiges of
colonial rule and obstructed its reestablishment on the island.[2] From the
perspective of the Dutch government in exile, what should have happened
on Java did happen in New Guinea—the colony's former rulers were swept
back into power on the coattails of victorious American soldiers. Indonesia's
history would have unfolded quite differently if General MacArthur had kept
his promise to help reinstate the Dutch colonial regime elsewhere in the
archipelago, as well (Anderson 1988: 86–87; Derix 1987: 129).[3] Biak's might
have, too. Dutch scholars and politicians would have been far less likely to
view the Koreri movement as a primitive outburst of "anti-Indonesian" sentiment. They might have seen it as it appeared from the angle of the officials
who served in its immediate aftermath—as a revolt against the colonial state
(de Bruyn 1948; see also Worsley 1968).

When the Netherlands insisted on the retention of western New Guinea in
the aftermath of Indonesian independence, they built on a consensus that
emerged among certain right-wing Dutch activists, scholars, and officials in
the 1930s (Rutherford 1998). In his 1989 memoirs, Jan van Baal, anthropologist and former governor of Netherlands New Guinea, stated the consensus plainly: anyone "conversant in the literature" and "experienced in
the region" could see that the Papuan and the Indonesian had "nothing in
common" (1989, vol. 2: 153). Although Indonesians saw the Papuans as
"brothers," the Papuans saw the Indonesians as strangers. For van Baal, the
reason for this discrepancy was clear; while other natives had circulated as
members of the Indies bureaucracy, the Papuans had simply stood still (ibid.,
vol. 2: 166–67). In characterizing western New Guinea's past in this fashion,
van Baal downplays the long-standing involvement of Biaks and other north
coastal groups in the colonial system. In the following pages, the Koreri
movement of 1939–43 appears in a light different from that cast by this
official's memories. So does New Guinea's history as a "neglected" frontier.

Pacifying New Guinea

"Discovered" in 1528 by Tidore's Spanish governor when his galleon was blown off course between Mexico and the Moluccas, New Guinea found a place on European maps during a period often depicted as the dawn of Western imperialism.[4] Whatever their stance on the legitimacy of Indonesia's claims to the territory, most observers agree that European colonialism gave little more than a name to the western half of the enormous island (Salim 1973: 39; van Baal 1989, vol. 2: 139). The "savage" land was a "backwater," purposely kept that way by the Dutch East Indies Company. Through agreements with Tidore in 1660 and 1779, the Company claimed the "inhospitable" territory as a bulwark against the Spanish and the English, powerful rivals to the lucrative Indies' trade. In 1828, the secret extension of the colony's border to the 141st parallel in southern New Guinea and the Cape of Good Hope in the north had little immediate effect on the region's governance.[5] Plagued by disease and hostile natives, those who pioneered new settlements in western New Guinea soon threw in the towel; Fort du Bos limped along from 1828 to 1836, but other stations survived for less than a month (Haga 1884, vol. 2: 10–13). Even after the opening of permanent posts at Manokwari (1898), Fakfak (1898), Merauke (1902), Hollandia (1909), and Sorong (1915), the government's influence remained severely limited (van Baal 1989, vol. 2: 145). Even after World War II, the campaign to develop the new colony of Netherlands New Guinea left much of the interior relatively undisturbed. To this day, many in the province live in mountainous areas only accessible by steep and slippery paths. If a single adjective sums up most assessments of the Netherlands' performance in New Guinea, it would have to be "neglect."

There are reasons why the Dutch colonial state neglected enormous New Guinea—its vast swamps, dense forests, and rugged terrain; its infertile soils and apparent lack of oil and minerals; its scattered population, indisposed to wage labor and bereft of the "native chiefs" through whom the authorities preferred to rule. Even if investors had known of the interior's massive reserves of gold and copper, the technology needed to exploit them did not yet exist. The sheer size of the territory and its distance from Batavia, the colonial capital, made the cost of its governance far outstrip any foreseeable return. These factors are as obvious in officialdom's early writings on the territory as in scholarly postcolonial postmortems. But what is striking in the colonial record is less the intransigence of these constraints than the tenacity of the dream that things could be otherwise. The colonial government more or less "neglected" other corners of the Indies, but in New Guinea the agents and critics of Dutch rule were particularly cognisant of the government's shortcomings (cf. Locher-Scholten 1981: 194–200; 1994; see also van Goor

1986). Colonial practice in the region was shaped by a contest between hard-headed calculation, dreams of glory, and a recurrent fear of loss.

On the face of it, the Netherlands' fear of losing its share of New Guinea is easy to explain. Ending an era of imperial conquest on the African continent, in 1885 the Berlin Conference yielded an agreement that apportioned the spoils. Besides setting boundaries, this agreement stipulated that a European nation-state's claim to a colony was contingent on its ability to protect free trade and passage in the territory and to "civilize" its native population. Although the Netherlands did not participate in the conference, Dutch leaders were aware of its implications with regard to New Guinea (van Baal 1989, vol. 2: 143). From the day that the Netherlands claimed the western half of the island, Dutch policy makers tried to create, at the lowest possible price, an adequate impression of Dutch authority. At the beginning of the century, when European visits to the territory were rare, this task had been fairly simple. But by the end of the century, the experiences of Europeans on both sides of the border had fueled demands for more intensive intervention (van Baal 1989, vol. 2: 143–144; van der Veur 1966: 79–81). It was not simply that the region's "Papuan" inhabitants had been left "uncivilized"; the safety of traders and missionaries could not be guaranteed.

One can trace the evolution of efforts to present a "pacified" New Guinea, which mostly targeted coastal populations, including Biak speakers, who had a reputation for plundering villages and ships. In the eighteenth century, the Company urged the Tidorans to punish the Papuan "pirates" more rigorously. *Hongi* expeditions were launched with greater frequency, with Dutch officers sometimes accompanying the fleet.[6] By the mid-nineteenth century, it was Tidoran princes who accompanied Dutch warships as they toured the distant islands and coasts. On widely scattered beaches, the Dutch commanders erected escutcheons—iron plates embossed with a coat of arms and the label *Nederlandsch Indië*—then shot off canons and tossed out trinkets to impress the Papuan onlookers.[7] They punished coastal troublemakers after the fashion of their Tidoran counterparts: ambushing villages, burning houses, and seizing anyone who failed to escape (see, for example, Haga 1884, vol. 2: 107). It was only after the opening of the post at Manokwari on the Bird's Head Peninsula, across Doreh Bay from Mansinam, that the authorities began to insist upon the apprehension of individual suspects. In chapter 3, I described how Lieutenant Feuilletau de Bruyn took a warrior's entire family hostage after the murder of an Ambonese teacher on Biak in 1915. The attempt to capture the suspected culprit ended in the warrior's death at the hands of his own kin (Feuilletau de Bruyn 1916: 261–267). The native officials who replaced the Dutch lieutenant continued his campaign to incarcerate Biak warriors. Some suspects were sent to Ternate; others were "exiled" to Java; it is said that still others were imprisoned in southern New Guinea at the "colony" for subversive natives at Boven Digoel.[8]

On the one hand, the Netherlands's colonial counterparts on the other side of the border prompted the promotion of "law and order" in Dutch New Guinea. When Tugeri headhunters—erstwhile Dutch subjects—committed "atrocities" on the coast of the British colony of Papua, the diplomatic uproar forced the Dutch to take action (van der Veur 1966; van Baal 1989, vol. 2: 143).[9] On the other hand, ground had been laid for the decision to apply a "firmer hand" by decades of complaints from the leaders of the Utrecht Mission Society (Utrechtsche Zendingvereeniging), which, as I have noted, was the sponsor of New Guinea's Protestant mission. In the early 1850s, when Brothers Ottow and Geissler sought permission to settle in the territory, Dutch officials in the Moluccas, then ruling New Guinea from a comfortable distance, tried to dissuade them from such folly.[10] Well aware that the state had little control over the Papuans, they would not have wanted witnesses publicizing the fact. The resident of Ternate finally assented to the missionaries' plan, no doubt expecting them soon to despair of converting these primitives, whom the Tidorans called "apes without tails" (Kamma 1947–49: 267).

In the short run, Ottow and Geissler's presence in northern New Guinea was of benefit to the government. One will recall that they settled in Mansinam among natives who spoke a dialect of Biak. For several decades, the evangelists supported themselves by serving as local agents for the owner of a shipping firm in Ternate (Bergsma et al. 1889; Beekman 1989: 45; Rutherford n.d.). The firm delivered provisions three times a year in return for a steady supply of bird skins, massoi bark, and other goods. The missionaries augmented their trade earnings with a dispensation from the resident, whom they saved from embarrassment by ransoming stranded Europeans (Kamma 1976: 96). Working against the local conviction that shipwreck victims should be killed, the evangelists set out for distant villages to "buy" foreign nationals and deliver them to safety. Soon, the missionaries found themselves intervening in local "wars," many of which, arguably, they themselves promoted by purchasing captives taken in such raids (Kamma 1976: 269; see also chapter 2). If it was in the interest of the colonial government to turn a blind eye to these disruptions in *rust en orde* (peace and order) as long as foreign victims were not involved, it was in the interest of the missionaries to play them up, exaggerating the barbarity of this "dark" heathen land to cast a brighter light on their struggle. Then, as in the years to come, the failure of the colonial government to "make something" of New Guinea was attributed to a lack of funds, understanding, and political will. The fact that no European evangelists were killed during these decades was taken more as an indication of the allure of their wealth than as a sign of the Papuans' acceptance of their message. From a handful of lonely posts along the Bird's Head's eastern shore, Ottow and Geissler's successors made it clear that they expected to make little headway unless the government strictly upheld colonial law in the region, forcing the Papuans to behave—and to believe (Beekman 1989: 84–88).

The Papuans' behavior was indeed important to the Protestant evangelists. Ottow and Geissler, New Guinea's mission pioneers, were a pair of German cabinetmakers, dispatched under a scheme to save souls and alleviate urban poverty by sending unpaid "Christian workmen" to the colonial east (Held-ring 1847; Rutherford n.d.). Themselves the beneficiaries of the era's spirit of reform, at the post at Mansinam the evangelists devoted much of their energy to instilling discipline among the heathens. Trade served both as the carrot and the stick: those who showed up for church received tobacco; those who worked on Sunday could sell no produce the following week (Bergsma et al. 1889; Beekman 1989: 46; Kamma 1976: 143). But for the role of exchange in enforcing the evangelical regime, the following scene, as described by a visiting Dutch official, might be taken to exemplify the production of "docile bodies." J. H. Tobias attended services in Mansinam in 1857: "If the sound of the gong, the signal that church is beginning, rings through the village, men and women come in their best clothing and enter the missionaries' house, where they respectfully kneel for the service, even though they don't understand anything about worship. Through all their gradual language work the missionaries have found themselves in a position to win the Papuans' trust, for the latter are now more properly clothed and have even begun to attend to their gardening" (Haga 1884, vol. 2: 110).[11]

Although this strategy allowed the missionaries to generate faint signs of pious living, it took more than trinkets to take the project further. A more daunting challenge was posed by the Papuans' *zwerfzucht*, the "lust" for "wandering" off to trade elsewhere or, worse, to raid, which emptied services as quickly as it filled them.[12] At the end of the century, the Utrecht Mission Society's supporters in the Netherlands contributed to the pressure that compelled the Dutch parliament to finance an expanded government presence in New Guinea (Haga 1884, vol. 2: 86–87). In 1892, the head of the civil administration department in Batavia lent support to the cause: "The prestige of our nation among foreigners does not allow us to leave the population of [western New Guinea] in their miserable and depraved condition" (Locher-Scholten 1994: 107). "Pacification"—disciplinary action that would teach the natives to respect authority—was seen as the precondition for the Papuans' salvation. "Civilization" and "Christianization" would go hand in hand.

At the turn of the century, the Utrecht Mission Society celebrated the "breaking" of a new Christian dawn, as requests for evangelists began to pour in from distant coastal communities. The "great awakening" in northern New Guinea—and the increased government involvement that accompanied it—was the product of a range of factors. The 1880s brought a jump in trade to the region, as growing numbers of Ternatan schooners scoured Papuan harbors for resin and bird skins (Haga 1884, vol. 2: 375, 399, 406).[13] In the

1890s, with the long and taxing war in Aceh finally winding down, the colonial military could attend to other "rebellious" regions; in the same decade, the founding of the subsidized steam line, the Koninklijke Paketvaart Maatschappij (KPM), and its immediate extension of services to northern New Guinea, made the project of pacification both easier and more pressing.[14] But if the government moved to pacify New Guinea in the spirit of "ethical imperialism" then sweeping the Indies, mission concerns set the tone of the campaign (Locher-Scholten 1981, 1994). Again, the treatment of the Papuans diverged from that of other natives. What might have passed elsewhere as custom (I: *adat*) was for the missionaries a sign of sin and a legitimate target for reform.

The lawlessness of Papuan culture, as seen through the spectacles of the Utrecht Mission Society, is evident in its emissaries' earliest letters. Night after night, the missionaries in Mansinam were kept awake by thunderous drumming from the native houses that were perched precariously over the bay (Kamma 1976: 146). The brother who braved the rickety logs that led from shore to a clan house to call a halt to the racket met with laughter, derision, and sometimes threats. In the eyes of the missionaries, every feast was held to celebrate a bloodbath; every song was an incitement to a raid. In the first decades of the century, the mission and the government cooperated to stamp out infelicitous customs. For the missionaries and their native assistants, local ceremonies, celebrations, artwork, and music were obstacles to the emergence of a truly Christian Papuan (see, for example, Jens 1915; Agter 1921; Hartweg 1925b, c, 1926; see also van Baal 1952; Kijne n.d.). For colonial officials, the same "wasteful" practices obstructed the emergence of the Papuan worker, a truly productive subject of the state (Feuilletau de Bruyn 1920: 49–50; 1936–37: 169).

The Colijn Note of 1907, which called for greater involvement in New Guinea, inaugurated a decade of exploration and assessment.[15] Whereas the expansion of state control faltered elsewhere due to a lack of funds, Biak's "pacification" proceeded apace. By the 1930s, despite some resistance, the missionaries and government officials had made considerable progress. The arrival of Petrus Kafiar in 1908 was followed in 1912 by the posting of a Dutch missionary on Biak. Brother Jens settled in the government center at Bosnik, on the island's east coast, and supervised a growing cadre of Ambonese, Sangirese, and Papuan teachers (Jens 1915; Kamma 1977: 743). By 1931, virtually all of the coastal communities had churches and subsidized schools. Most children studied for three years in their villages; the brightest boys went on to boarding school at the new post at Korido and from there to the teachers college on the mainland at Miei. Conversion had entailed the destruction of reliquaries, the abandoning of men's houses, and a sharp curtailment in the extensive series of life cycle feasts. Male circumcision no longer took place; female initiation slowly vanished, as well (Jens 1916:

406). Local officials enforced a ban on palm wine and dance parties with the help of a regiment of armed police.[16] Older forms of heroism gradually faded, as the last of the warriors were carted off to jail.

For ambitious young Biaks, by the mid-1930s, new voyages to New Guinea's western reaches were filling in for the older journeys to Tidore. A brightening in the region's economic prospects had accompanied the improvements in security. In the early 1930s, a Japanese firm called the Company for South Sea Development (Nanyo Kohastu Kaishu, NKK), won concessions in northern New Guinea for the production of cotton and damar resin.[17] In 1935, the Netherlands Nieuw-Guinea Petroleum Maatschappij (NNGPM), a joint venture of the Bataafsche Petroleum Maatschappij and the Nederlandsche Koloniale Petroleum Maatschappij, began drilling for oil in western New Guinea (Klein 1935–38, vol. 3: 50). The NNGPM undertook an aerial mapping project, and Dutch investors founded a mining company to prospect for gold (van Baal 1989, vol. 2: 148). Biaks were prime recruits for the Dutch oil fields and the Japanese plantations, which suffered from a chronic lack of ready labor.[18] Although a bit "outspoken" for some captains' taste, the islands' youths also made suitable dockhands who toured the coasts with the KPM steamers and earning a pittance for loading and unloading freight (Klein 1935–38, vol. 2: 764). The government had introduced forced labor and taxation in New Guinea in 1912 in order to stimulate the natives' "development" (á Campo 1986: 176). Now, with more Biaks working as coolies, the effort to impose a head tax was finally paying off. Although officials still had to guard against smiths melting coins to make silver bracelets, Biaks were participating in the cash economy. Right-wing colonials who bemoaned New Guinea's backwardness during the 1930s might have found a bright spot on Biak, had they bothered to look (van Sandick 1934).

That is not to say that Biak's missionaries and colonial officials were without their worries. At the turn of the century, the new horizons opened by steam travel appeared as a mixed blessing to the Protestants. Instead of paddling a canoe, a "modern" trio of Biak-speaking brothers took the passenger liner to Ternate in 1896. After popping over to Tidore for an audience with the sultan, who gave the eldest brother a title, they bought thirty-six cases of wine for the enormous party that was held on their return (Kamma 1977: 527). In the early 1920s, warriors in northern Biak staged a revolt when a new Dutch officer tried to force the locals to build a road through an impassable stretch of the interior (Agter 1922a, b, c). Their attacks on cooperative villages horrified the missionaries, who everywhere saw signs of a weakening of Christian belief. The fear that the islanders' "faith" was only a veneer had long been haunting the Utrecht Mission Society's leaders. From the start, the missionaries had viewed Islam as a threat; in the 1920s, a few began to worry about secularism and even nationalism, a force that colonials elsewhere were working hard to suppress.[19] By the 1930s, the decision to limit "custom" was causing some uneasiness: had the policy left a gap for other evils to fill?

New Guinea's Dutch officials and aficionados were asking themselves similar questions (Kepper and van Sandick 1937). Was Western Christianity really enough to give meaning to the lives of former pirates and headhunters? From the viewpoint of the government, the native evangelists' insistence on forbidding customary practices now represented an overstepping of their duties (Beets [1938] 1991: 100–102). With much of coastal New Guinea finally under government control, the secular state should take sole responsibility for making and enforcing the law. Scholarly studies of the degeneration of acculturated "primitives" may in part have prompted New Guinea's government chief to call a series of meetings with the missionaries. Afterward, Assistant Resident Beets circulated a proposal calling for the following change in policy.

1. (Hulp) bestuursassistent ([adjunct] government assistants) are forbidden to arbitrarily interfere with the holding of dance and other feasts by the indigenous population.
2. All functionaries of the mission are forbidden to interfere with the holding of dance and other feasts by the indigenous population.
3. Should the persons in provisions 1 or 2 be of the opinion that the holding of a dance or other feast in a particular village or area at a particular time will constitute a disturbance to public peace and order or a threat to public security, then they should immediately approach the presiding European official, who after an investigation shall take whatever measures he deems necessary for the preservation of public peace, order, and security.
4. Unless a disturbance of public peace and order or a threat to security is expected (e.g. a head-hunting raid, etc.), all at present extant prohibitions with regard to dance and other feasts, issued by the government as well as the mission, are immediately repealed. (Beets [1938] 1991: 102–103)

Although the Utrecht Mission Society never seems to have endorsed the assistant resident's new guidelines, on Biak the discussions apparently had an effect. The Dutch missionaries at Korido had long promoted the use of the vernacular in prayers and sermons (Utrechtsche Zendingsvereeniging 1926). It was a short step from this policy to a new plan to turn local music toward Christian ends. At the end of the decade, as the "rehabilitated" warriors were returning from prison, Biak "tradition" was revived.

Thus, the world's discovery of New Guinea's untapped potential was accompanied by recognition of Biak "custom." In a certain sense, this concern with Biak's cultural essence fit snugly into a wider project of colonial categorization (Anderson [1983] 1991: 170; Benda 1958). As I mentioned above, the effort to suppress nationalism in the 1930s entailed the promotion of ethnic elites and a tightening of the connections between identity and place.

But the new policy, as we will see, met with disaster when Biak's march to modernity took an unplanned turn. Biaks had accepted colonial education and employment, but not colonial authority. No more than the adventurers who delivered tribute to Tidore had internalized their position in the sultan's hierarchy had Biaks internalized their role in the colonial order. The episode that follows portrays their audacity most vividly, but in subtle ways the stage was already set.

In 1849, Second Lieutenant G. F. de Bruyn Kops visited the Biak village of Sowek, on the island of Supiori, in order to erect an escutcheon (*wapenboord*). As at earlier stops, the Dutch officer distributed gifts to impress upon the Papuans the value of belonging to the Netherlands Indies.

> The population was very familiar; men, women, and children surrounded us during our stay on shore. Some beads were strewn around, upon which everyone greedily fell. The same peace and order appeared to reign as was noted earlier on Run. Then the pole was planted on the right bank of the river, on a small rise under some coconut palms. To all those who helped, knives were distributed. Toward this end, Mr. Gronovius stood in a ring chatting with the various heads with the knives set near him. All of a sudden, a man forced his way through the thick circle of bystanders, fell upon the knives and took as many as he could carry, then pushed his way out between the onlookers and fled across the river without anyone moving to stop him. Remonstrances regarding this did not help, and the people even showed signs of displeasure when as a result of the robbery they could not get any more knives. (de Bruyn Kops 1850: 229)

The sign's erection was supposed to be followed by an explosion of trinkets and gunfire, the startling surplus with which colonialism seduced its subjects. But the sudden raid reversed the surprise. Ninety years later, at the end of almost four decades of "peace," another bold Sowekker was ready to snatch the potency of the state.

The Revival of Wor I

She was arrested two times. Three times the authorities laid siege to her village and burned every house to the ground. Her followers were admonished by the missionaries, mocked by local leaders, beaten by the police. Her close relatives were imprisoned, interrogated, tortured, shot. And yet the crowds kept returning to Insumbabi and Rani, small islands close to Sowek, to join Angganeta Menufandu, the Queen of Peace. They returned after her release from a Dutch colonial prison on nearby Yapen in late 1941. They remained after a Japanese gunboat took her away to be killed in the middle of 1942 (Kamma 1972: 160, 168). Suppressed at one site, only to arise at others, drawing in communities throughout the islands of Biak, Supiori,

Numfor, and nearby Yapen, the movement centered on her persisted for five long years, lasting almost the duration of the Japanese occupation. It began with a woman who sang wor.

In F. C. Kamma's painstakingly researched study of Koreri, we learn that Angganeta Menufandu was an "uncommonly gifted" poet (1972: 157–158). Born in roughly 1905 in Sowek, a village long known for its traders and traveling smiths, she was widowed in her early thirties. According to Kamma, the loss of her husband and a child during a trading trip in the Moluccas led to the illness and miraculous recovery that transformed Angganeta into a prophet. As in the myth of Manarmakeri, Angganeta's sorrow led to a skin disease that worsened, leaving her paralyzed. On Aiburanbondi, the deserted island where the widow had gone to die, a mysterious old man brought her food and medicine (ibid.: 156).[20] After curing and blessing Angganeta, the visitor—Manarmakeri—appointed her as his messenger. Angganeta's descendants told me in the early 1990s that, just like Jesus, the prophet had returned from the dead. They placed her meeting with Manarmakeri at the Japanese plantation at Waren, where her cousin had taken her to cultivate cotton. In both versions, Angganeta's tidings were the same. New Guinea—and the world—were to be renewed.

One of Kamma's informants repeated Manarmakeri's message to Angganeta.

> I have seen thy misery and all thou had to bear, the sorrow and the persecution, and all the foreign oppression. I shall give thee a reign of permanent peace and therefore thy name shall be: *Bin Damai* or *Nona Mas ro Judaea* (Woman of Peace or the Golden Lady of Judaea [The latter title is a hybrid of Malay and Biak]). Today I send thee forth to lead thy people to *Koreri*. In order that this may come about thou shalt never shed blood, for blood bars the way to *Koreri*, since I know thy people is one that likes to wage war. And this shall be the token to thee all, the flag that shall fly over all New Guinea in blue, white and red—faith, peace and courage—or, from above comes peace or war. I am *Kayan* Sanau who came from the West and who wages all the wars of the world. Do not fear, for great peoples will wage war but that people that shall do right to thee all shall conquer the whole world. But if, o Irian, thy right and thy flag are not recognized, if again thou art oppressed, then a third world war shall destroy the whole world. But I, *Kayan* Sanau, shall lead the world war, do not fear. (Kamma 1972: 158)

News of Angganeta's recovery spread quickly. Although the first visitors to seek out the widow may have come to be healed, my consultants stressed the appeal of her songs and prophecies. On the small island of Insumbabi, not far from Sowek, where Angganeta settled with her family, an encampment grew, bringing together villagers from Biak, Supiori, and further afield. Day and night, encouraged by the prophet's endless stream of compositions, they drank palm wine and sang wor, waiting for Manarmakeri to appear.

Angganeta's appearance was not unprecedented. Her inverted Dutch tricolor belonged to a long lineage of symbolic reversals of hierarchy. Kamma lists forty-two separate movements, culled from mission and colonial records, for the period from the 1850s to World War II (1972: 102–156). Seventeen took place on Numfor and Biak proper; the rest among migrant groups of "Biak-Numforese." At least one involved a female leader (ibid.: 132–133). Each outbreak followed the same pattern of "proof" and expectation, but the contents of Koreri discourse reflected the changing times. Arising at the twilight of Tidoran influence, the earliest reported movements entailed the delivery of tribute to leaders who claimed to have usurped the sultan's position.[21] A subsequent group set the "prophet" (*konoor*) in competition with the missionaries, who challenged them to prove their mastery over death.[22] With Biak's increased integration into the colonial system, later prophets foretold a reversal of racial hierarchies, depicting the transfer of potency as a switching of skin.[23] Although many movements ended in the prophet's death or flight, a few resulted in the government appointing their leaders as headmen, a "tactical" move meant to dampen local ambitions.[24] Set off by earthquakes and epidemics, the movements coalesced around leaders who promised eternal life at moments that heralded a transformation in regional relations. Embracing foreign practices, yet rejecting foreign domination, the prophets appealed to dreams that long outlived their own demise.

More violent and tenacious than any of the preceding eruptions, Angganeta's uprising occurred at a significant conjuncture for the entire colonial world. World War II was casting its shadow on New Guinea when Angganeta met Manarmakeri. The Netherlands fell to Germany in May 1940; European women and children were evacuated from New Guinea to Java in 1941; with the bombing of Pearl Harbor in December of that year, a Japanese invasion seemed imminent. When the government on Java capitulated in May 1942, the Japanese navy had already taken the islands of Timor and Celebes (de Jong 1985, part 1: 862). As one Biak explains in an unpublished study of the movement, "Among people who believe very strongly in ancestral spirits, invisible powers beyond the ordinary world (in the ground or sea, or above the earth), in a situation where the visible world thus seems to be a mere appearance (I: *seakan-akan semu*), natural disasters, disease, and war can be interpreted as implying an impending transformation in the inhabited world" (Mampioper 1976: 52). In this case, the coming chaos coincided with an array of changes, one of which was the revival of wor.

As I suggested above, this revival was part of a colonywide promotion of "traditional" identities during this period, a trend with repercussions throughout the Indies. On Biak, it entailed a dramatic shift in perspective for those who staffed the Protestant mission. The teachers who founded the island's first schools frowned upon Biak's "heathen" music. The new Christians were only permitted to sing wor in order to stay in unison while paddling their enormous outriggers to deliver mission staff members and supplies. As the government improved its coverage of the region, new dilemmas presented themselves to the missionaries. The exodus of young Biaks for wage labor elsewhere left only their elders on hand for Sunday services. Reversing a long-standing policy, Brothers ten Haaft and Agter began permitting wor singing in church, in hopes of attracting older worshipers. In 1937, popular lyrics began to circulate in the mission newspaper, *Sampari*; that year and the next, at the yearly convention in Korido, each delegation performed its once-forbidden songs.

Like the New Order revival of the genre, to be discussed in the next chapter, wor resurfaced at precisely the moment when "modernity" seemed to be undermining "traditional" ways of life. As coolies, felons, and ship hands, Biaks were exploring new worlds. Their adventures exposed them to new technologies; radios, telephones, movie theaters, a golf course, even airplanes were to be seen at the sites where Biaks worked.[25] The coolies picked up more than porcelain plates to use as bridewealth during their travels; they also gathered global rumors.[26] Angganeta's forecast, so uncanny in retrospect, found fertile ground in a changing local context. For the prophet and her followers, it was no coincidence that the missionaries' discovery of a Christian core in Biak's "heathen" practices coincided with other surprising developments. This discovery confirmed the suspicion that a Biak ancestor had a hand in these global events.

A short paddle from Korido, Angganeta's gathering may have resembled the encampment of congregations set up for mission conventions. As far as what seems to have been the policy on wor was concerned, the only regulation that the followers violated was the ban on singing with more than six drums.[27] The followers clustered by village, setting up dance circles where they performed biblical songs. They were accompanied by the throbbing of hundreds of drums, whose heads were made by local men from a special species of lizard, which miraculously flocked to their shores.[28] If the party began with Angganeta's relatives, it expanded quickly as news spread of amazing happenings. The prophet's house and body shone with a miraculous luminescence; watery points of light circled the island every night; mingling with the singing, people heard the voices of the dead. Soon everyone of any standing throughout the region felt compelled to come to the island to find out what was going on.

Angganeta's followers welcomed the newcomers. At sundown, everyone gathered on the dance ground. Kamma describes the performance of a series of wor enacting the return of Manarmakeri; my informants who were present recalled a mixture of older and newer tunes. Christian wor gained a compelling new significance in a setting christened with biblical names: Yudaea, Bethlehem, Gadara. Although anyone could raise a song, the newest compositions came from Angganeta—now known as "Mary"—who remained isolated in her "radio room" during most of the dancing. Receiving "transmissions" from the distant and the deceased, she conveyed them to her followers by way of a kinswoman known as her "wire." Dressed in white loincloths and *asisoms*—"traditional" bamboo combs, now used as "antennae"—initiates could also tune in for amazing communications. The main qualification for membership in the movement was possession by the spirits of the foreign and the dead.

For some people, possession occurred automatically during the course of the singing. Kamma explained the phenomenon as follows.

> The combined singing of men and women is stirring, by the way the deep male voices sound the lower registers, while the female voices or the higher male tenors seem to tear the melody from the sombre grip of the deep basses of the men and the drone of the drums. It is reminiscent of the struggle of a canoe on the waves of a turbulent sea. This kind of singing always makes a deep impression, even on strangers. It is particularly moving when there are hundreds of singers.
>
> Participants asserted: "When we join in the singing, after some time it seems we are dwelling in a mysterious world." An informant's words translated into Indonesian from the Biak dialect were: "*Oleh karena pergerakan dengan lagu2 yang sangat menarik perasaan orang, maka achirnya ada roh yang menggerakkan lidah orang akan berkata dengan rupa2 bahasa*" (in consequence of movements together with melodies that stir the people's emotions to a high degree, there is eventually a spirit—which comes over the people—which loosens their tongues so that they can speak in several languages). (Kamma 1972: 163)

Others became possessed through their contact with Angganeta. When darkness had fallen and the dancers had begun to succumb to the music, the Woman of Peace emerged from her shelter to greet new followers.

> Those who want to participate rise and go meet her. One by one she takes their hands and literally says to them: "Ye-sus Christus and liberty." Firmly clasping their hands she slowly moves the upper part of her body to and fro and makes strange sounds. The body of the disciple begins to tremble and eventually to shake. It is the spirit who has come and whose name Angganeta will presently pronounce. It may be Saul, David, Adam, John or some other biblical figure, and this becomes the disciple's *Koreri*-name. Sometimes it is the name of one of the candidate's deceased relatives. The disciple, who has lost consciousness, then begins to sing in a strangely high-pitched voice and says words that only Angganeta can explain. (Kamma 1972: 163)

Kamma goes on to describe how some people were possessed by evil spirits—"snakes, crocodiles, pigs, sea-spirits, the spirits of rocks"—which Angganeta then had to exorcise. Others who failed to respond had to confess their "sins"—their violation of the taboos Angganeta imposed on her followers. These taboos gave the followers a chance to set right their ancestors' offenses against Manarmakeri. Believers were not to shed blood or get in fights—lest the whole world be destroyed by wars; they were not to eat pork, labu (a kind of squash), or blue parrot fish—all important elements in the myth; nor were they to harm animals that shed their skin. Finally, they were not allowed to build fires at night "for that is the time when the glory of *Koreri* is manifest and the *Manseren* ship will come" (Kamma 1972: 159).

The first phase of the movement ended in mid-1941, when Brother Agter contacted the Ambonese assistant district officer in Bosnik, who sent a police patrol to destroy the encampment. When fire proved insufficient to end the gathering, the patrol returned to arrest Angganeta (Kamma 1972: 160; see also Mampioper 1976: 55). Her relatives followed her to Serui, where she was jailed, and convinced the Dutch district officer to release her. Angganeta returned to Insumbabi in late 1941, as the war with Japan was beginning. With the authorities distracted, disputes broke out between the movement's supporters and critics. The activities took on a more formal character, a "reaction," Kamma reasons, to its opponents' harsh response (1972: 165–166). Now it was potential officers who came to seek Angganeta's blessing. In each case, the candidate had to come to Insumbabi in a large canoe. The craft had to circle thrice in front of the harbor, then land with the paddlers "standing stiffly at attention." The guards saluted, then greeted the party, saying "Hail! Peace be with you" (B: *Jow! Damai kien so mgo*). After the proper welcome, the supplicant received an appointment to appear before Angganeta, whose name had grown: Star of the Mountains (B: Makbon), Woman of Peace from Judaea (B: Bin Damai Judaea), The Golden Queen of Judea (I/B: Ratu Mas ro Judaea). At that appointment, the guards repeated their greeting then led the supplicant to the throne. Raising one hand, he or she addressed Angganeta, "Peace be with you"; if allowed to come nearer, he or she responded, "Hail to you, Queen." The supplicant sat on the floor, below Angganeta and her functionaries, and presented the request. He or she then rose and repeated the greeting, before backing out the door. Unfolding like an episode in the myth's prologue or an audience at the Tidoran court, the visit ended with a deferred bestowal of gifts. Not unlike the Tidoran sultans and their colonial successors, Angganeta's lieutenants presented successful candidates with a title and a flag to carry ceremoniously home.

Angganeta was the sultan, according to this report received by Kamma; in my interviews, she sometimes appeared as Jesus Christ. I asked those who remembered her how this could be—how could a woman become the master of such overwhelming power? My informants did not stress Angganeta's role as a healer; they never mentioned her genealogy, which, according to Kamma, connected her to Manarmakeri by way of his mother's clan (1972: 157; see also Sharp with Kaisiëpo 1994: 26–27, 44). What they did stress was the fulfilment of all that she foretold. Angganeta did not simply have a radio; she became a radio, conveying meaningful messages "without adding or subtracting." Everything that she described quickly appeared to her followers: in drawings of ships, airplanes, and houses; on a ghostly movie screen that sometimes shimmered before the dancers; in dark waters where submarines circled at night. Here was the "proof" that had been missing from the mythical promise that the Old Man first offered to his in-laws. Here were followers eager to believe. Like Uncle Bert and the other leaders described in chapter 3, Angganeta assumed the authority of absence—and took it to astonishing extremes.

The prophet's descendants went further in responding to my question; the fact that Angganeta *was* a woman was key to her legitimacy. Angganeta's cross-cousin frowned when I mentioned Stefan Simopyaref, one of the prophets who came after her. "He was a man. But before, when it was just a woman, there was no [armed] movement (I: *tidak ada pergerakan*). Just singing and dancing. Because she was a woman, all the people were amazed. What's up with this woman? They came to witness everything up close." He went on to tell me that her male underlings had "ruined everything" by using her power to "make themselves into war chiefs" (I: *kepala perang*). The prophet's practices made her the embodiment of feminine liminality; she crouched in isolation, like a teenage initiate; like a dying mother she drew together distant kin. She surrounded herself with scores of foster children. Her transmissions reported the birth of infants; she summoned their mothers, who gave her their babies to raise. Again, these practices are significant in light of the myth; by performing as a mother, Angganeta made up for those mythical women who refused Manarmakeri's offer. As a result, the prophet not only welcomed Manarmakeri; she partook of his hybrid powers. Like the ancestor, Angganeta combined the "alien" powers of mothers and uncles, collapsing the differences that oriented social action on Biak. Marking the border between the future and the past, the living and the dead, the newly born and the dying, her practices anticipated the messianic moment that would end all histories and redeem all debts. "Only a woman could have given birth to these revelations," her cross-cousin told me; only the "Peace Woman" could have borne this destruction and these dreams.

The world did not end in 1942 on that little island of Insumbabi. Despite the ghostly voices, despite the miraculous visions, Angganeta's followers never reached the climax that they desired. By force and persuasion, the faithful convinced doubters to join the fold by holding dances in their villages and obeying the taboos. And still Koreri failed to appear. Yet few Biaks, past or present, have accused the prophet of lying; from the beginning, she had posited two paths. If the movement did not end in Koreri, she told her followers, it would end in Korore—a Biak gloss for Tidore—a term that meant "progress," "warfare," and "bloodshed" all at once (Kamma 1972: 164). If not with the end of history then as the wreckage in history's path, Biak would enter a new world.

On May 8, 1942, this time joined by Assistant District Officer Tilly, the police returned to Insumbabi (Kamma 1972: 168). They burned the encampment and arrested Angganeta, this time jailing her in Bosnik. Three days later, the Japanese fleet passed Biak on its way to take control of Manokwari. On June 29, Western New Guinea's new Japanese administrator, or resident, returned with a ship to take the prisoner away (Kamma 1972: 168).[29] Following Angganeta's departure, the movement's emphasis shifted. With Angganeta now at a distance, new forces arose to act in her name. Angganeta had given Rani, a small island adjacent to Insumbabi, a new name: Gadara, the island of unclean spirits. In the first phase of the movement, she used it as a site of banishment for "those who wanted war and had shed blood" (ibid.: 161). After her arrest, Rani became the new center of activities. Instead of the Peace Woman assisted by warriors, warriors surrounded by peace women heralded Manarmakeri's return.

There is much agreement on the origin of the second phase of the movement. My conversations confirmed Kamma's observations: the new leaders got their start in jail (1972: 168–170). Stephanus Simopyaref of Manswam, East Biak, met Biromor Boseren of Wopes, North Biak, in the Manokwari prison. According to Kamma, Stephanus was a convicted murderer who had just been transferred back to New Guinea after serving time in Ternate and on Java. Biromor, "the Impenetrable Grove," was among the last of the *mambri*, a warrior tracked down many years after his crime. In the weeks leading up to the Japanese invasion of Manokwari, both men had visions. Biromor saw a strange man walking unscathed through a downpour of bombs and bullets and heard him proclaim that New Guinea would be his kingdom. Stephanus saw the old man leaping and singing a wor ahead of the invading Japanese. The Japanese attack on the district capital deeply impressed the two prisoners; not only did it fulfil what they had seen in their dreams, it demonstrated the fragility of the Dutch colonial system (Kamma 1972: 170). Armed with foreign magic—potions and knowledge acquired abroad—the men returned to Biak to join Angganeta's movement. Stephanus took over in Supiori in June 1942, hoping to free Angganeta. Biromor started his own uprisings in West and North Biak in August 1942, after Japanese officials took Stephanus away.

According to Kamma, Stephanus made earthly use of Angganeta's messianic predictions. To the movement he brought military power—in the form of "invulnerability water" (I: *air kabal*)—and a carefully crafted political program. He also brought an aura of Islam—"carrying himself with the dignity of a prince of the Moluccas"—along with some biblical posters that he found strewn on the ground during the looting that followed the invasion of Manokwari. He was well schooled in the Gospel, lacing his speeches with verses from the Sermon on the Mount (Kamma 1972: 170). Having fled from prison in the confusion, Stephanus headed south along the mainland toward Miei, the site of the mission seminary and an important stop on the route to

Biak from the oil fields and plantations. There, he met up with a group of laid-off workers, who, with the students, were on their way home. Calling for "traditional dances" to put the returnees "in the right frame of mind," Stephanus persuaded many of them to join him for a planning session (ibid.: 171). On the island of Wabruk, on June 8, 1942, Stephanus laid out his vision of Manarmakeri's new kingdom. Angganeta would be queen, but Stephanus would serve as her general, organizing an army to protect her and implement her plans. Kamma lists the points formulated during the "elaborate" discussions:

A. To achieve a firm unity, as much propaganda as possible is to be made.
B. Angganitha Menufaur [Angganeta Menufandu] must be liberated and return to Judaea.
C. 1. All those who are hostile toward the movement must be destroyed.
    2. Those autochthones who are not willing to join will be forced to do so. The following categories will be put in prison:
       a. All foreigners (*Amberi*).
       b. Indonesians who are in the Japanese army.
       c. All government officials.
       d. Native preachers who do not join the movement.
       e. Teachers, Papuan as well as *Amberi*, who insult the movement.
    3. Autochthonous teachers will be allowed to become officers, or to hold other important posts. Those who are reluctant will be coerced.
    4. Imprisoned preachers must not be maltreated. If they confine themselves to their real task, the Church, they will not be molested.
    5. *Amberi* who want to join the movement may stay.
    6. Schools must not be destroyed but will be closed for the time being.
    7. Religious services shall not be interfered with. Churches must be saved even if they must be fought for.
    8. Any ruffians must be kept in check.
    9. Robbery and theft are strictly forbidden and will be severely punished.
D. The *Koreri* army will be named A.B. (America-*Blanda* or America *Babo* = New America). Eventually the army will help the A.B.C.D. Front (America, Britain, China, the Dutch). The army will be composed as follows:
    1. *Muris Swan* (the fleet).
    2. *Muris Sup* (the army).
    3. As a weapon to coerce autochthones the *karbere* (an ironwood club . . .) will be used.
    4. Real weapons such as hatchets and spears can be used against the Japanese.
    5. The people will be allowed to use the magic powers they have inherited from their ancestors. (Stephanus himself was an adept.)
    6. The A.B. army will be composed of members of all the peoples of New Guinea.

E. *Symbols*
  1. The *Koreri* flag—blue, white, red (faith, peace, courage, or From Heaven comes peace or war).
  2. The Peace flag. A blue cross on a white flag.
  3. A white headcloth is to be worn.
  4. A white star (Sampari) will be put in the blue bar of the *Koreri* flag, and a blue cross in the white bar.
  5. All will wear white loincloths.
  6. The bamboo comb with the cock's feathers will be introduced.
  7. The Biak *sirep* (hour-glass drum), gongs, and triton shells will be the instruments to call the people to war.
  8. The *Do mamun* (*hongi* songs) will be sung.
F. The Japanese army will not be molested except in extreme necessity. Efforts will be made to persuade Japan to recognize the movement to unite the whole of New Guinea, and its flag.
G. The whole of New Guinea, from Gebe to Hollandia and Merauke, will fall under the protection of the new flag.
  1. All tribes will be one.
  2. Each tribe will have its own leaders.
  3. All the leaders will meet in Rani (Gadara), the center.
  4. The local wars that formerly used to occur must not be resuscitated. Now is the time for the people of New Guinea to make peace with each other. The name *Angganitha Bin Damai* (Woman of Peace) will exemplify the pacifism of all the people.
H. *Positions*
  1. *Angganitha Menufaur Bin Damai ro Judaea* will be recognized as queen of the whole of New Guinea.
  2. To this end the Biak people must work very hard.
  3. *Stephanus Ronsumbre Simopyaref Rumgun Kababur Tuan Damai Ro Gadara* will be general and leader of the A.B. army.
  4. Three of Stephanus' brothers will be appointed commanders of the fleet.
  5. Any functionaries appointed by Angganitha will be acknowledged by the other members and by the officials of all grades. (Kamma 1972: 171–173)

It is scarcely surprising that this document, culled from Kamma's notes, has functioned as a charter for Papuan nationalism (Sharp with Kaisiëpo 1994; Osborne 1985). After the fall of Manokwari, the Japanese general made a speech promising to recognize "all existing organizations and their functionaries." "This seemed to Stephanus the chance to fill in the Koreri ideal with political substance," Kamma notes (1972: 170). Stressing the leaders' hostility to *amber*—a word he defined as "non-white foreigners"—Kamma's interpretation supports a reading that would take Koreri as an eerily prescient expression of separatism. Forty years after the publication of Kamma's book, many of my informants saw the movement quite differently. Some told me that Stephanus and Biromor had been in Boven Digoel, the prison camp in southern New Guinea. A few claimed that Biromor had received an amulet from Indonesia's first president; Sukarno gave the warrior a tiny Bible to wear on a chain around his neck. With less dramatic yarns, others made the same point—an encounter with the Indonesian "struggle" (I: *perjuangan*) had given these leaders their radical ideas.

For our purposes, what matters more than this contest over memories of the movement is the way that it played out on Biak. Outsiders from Ambon, Sangir, Java, and Japan all came under attack when Stephanus stepped in to represent the absent Angganeta. In the middle of 1942, having ordered the beating of Koreri followers at Samber village, Tilly, still the island's chief civil administrator, was caught by surprise when the police boat carrying him landed at the village of Sorido (Kamma 1972: 176). A crowd of angry Biaks killed the Ambonese official and delivered his guards to Stephanus's prison on Rani. In late 1943, in North Biak, Biromor slew a Japanese officer sent to arrest him, first stunning his victim by unveiling his tiny Bible (ibid.: 201; Mampioper 1976: 93–95). Before Yosimoto could raise his sword, the warrior had lopped off his head. Flying the reversed Dutch flag, followers on Numfor reversed the colonial order. A leader named Adam forced Assistant District Officer Diponegoro to trade places; he slept in his bed, ate his food, and relaxed "in an easy chair" while the *amberi* did the onerous tasks (ibid.: 188–189).

The stories that I collected made just as much of the aggression directed at Biak's *local* aliens. On Numfor, young followers smashed antique porcelain and proclaimed the end of bridewealth. "With the cry 'the old harta (valuables) bar the way to Koreri,' they pounced on everything they could find" (Kamma 1972: 182). All of North Biak's teachers were locked in a pig sty. Biromor's followers refused to release them until they revealed the secret written on the Bible's "stolen" page. In South Biak, another teacher recruited his relatives to stand guard over his Bibles and books. To save himself, he exchanged his uniform for a loincloth and joined the dancers; other teachers, including some non-Biaks, became the secretaries to those in charge.[30] Those who refused to join the movement faced mounting pressure. The Japanese had to evacuate Wardo, in West Biak, to save the villagers from Biromor's wrath (ibid.: 199–200).

The witnesses with whom I spoke tended not to blame the movement's leaders for these abuses. They saved their animus for anonymous individuals who turned Koreri's power toward evil ends. By going into trance and speaking in tongues, a participant of either gender assumed the office of b*in damai,* a "peace woman" with the right to command other followers. Today, people say that many of these "peace women" were deceivers, who sought the position in order to denounce their neighbors. The authority that they gained by feigned possession became a weapon for settling old scores. Thus contemporary memories stressed the movement's heterogeneity, a quality also stressed in Kamma's finely detailed rendering. Kamma describes a man on Numfor who claimed he was Manseren Mangundi and traveled across the island performing the Holy Communion (1972: 192). When Stephanus Simopiaref got wind of this, he summoned the rebel to Rani and cut him down to size with a new name. The villager was no longer "The Lord Himself"; now he was Koki, "the Cook." Koki took the punishment well, but his contrition did not last; back on Numfor he changed his title to Kapten Koki, Captain Cook. A more lethal "pretender" was Stephen Wanda, the "King of Supiori" (ibid.: 188, 190–192). Wanda, a former deacon who called his wife Mary and spoke with her in the "language of the new world," also claimed to be God. His trip to Numfor to exorcise evil spirits ran afoul of Kapten Koki, whose followers took up arms to fend off this competitor. After this setback, Wanda found a new source of authority: the Japanese officers at Manokwari, who promised him a palace and a warship if he would recruit plenty of coolies for the Japanese cause. At this uncertain moment, the same logic that allowed for a radical reversal of colonial hierarchies prompted followers to try to seize a share of their leaders' potency for themselves.

As heated as was the rivalry among different heralds of Koreri, the proof of the potency concentrated at the movement's centers took the form of a tense state of peace. The abandon with which Biromor's "army" attacked non-believers is said to have contrasted with the order that prevailed among his followers. His "city" at Wopes featured a dance ground for each northern village, arrayed according to their placement along the coast. In its center stood a church, a warehouse, and Biromor's residence, which opened onto a clearing where the followers danced and drilled (see also Kamma 1972: 193). Each day, the villagers would rehearse at their dance grounds for the mass performances that were held every night. Newcomers brought food, which the officers distributed among the populace; especially appointed security guards kept the peace. Some leaders built replicas of airplanes or submarines on their dance ground; Biromor built a disciplinary regime (cf. Lattas 1998). No less than the magic with which he won converts, the strategy proved him to be a master of foreign power.

In the end, the dynamics that encouraged Biaks to raid the potency of distant others led to the movement's bloody conclusion. Kamma traced the tragedy to the absence of a unified vision. "The leaders, with their aim of liberation in mind, made a mistake in thinking that *Koreri* would unite the people," Kamma wrote. "When it comes to the point a Biak man will only accord with his group or his clan, in fact only with himself" (1972: 195). A widow who lost her husband to a Japanese bullet told me that if the followers had obeyed Stephanus, the deaths would not have occurred. On July 12, 1942, the eve of the leader's surrender and departure to Manokwari,

Manarmakeri told Stephanus to send home all his followers. But rumors spread subsequently of the invulnerability of the guards who had paddled Stephanus to the ship. Taking the potion said to have turned the Japanese bullets into water, Stephanus's deputies—Jan, Zadrach, and Kaleb Ronsumbre—moved home to Manswam, South Biak, and started afresh. Their Koreri "city" responded to a changing context. In August 1942, following defeats at Midway and the Coral Sea, the Japanese military sought to consolidate its forces both at the front and directly behind the lines. With New Guinea's new rulers busy reenforcing their defenses, the movement went unchecked for over a year. In January 1943, after Biromor's followers attacked Bosnik and terrorized its inhabitants, the administration pulled out its officers and closed the post (Mampioper 1976: 86). But when the Japanese commanders decided to build an airstrip near Manswam, their patience for the disturbance grew short. On October 10, 1943, after repeated warnings from the administration had gone unheeded, the Japanese fleet opened fire on a beach lined with men, women, and children. Believing to the last that Manarmakeri would protect them from harm, from 600 to 2,000 Biaks died (Kamma 1972: 201).

Biromor's movement self-destructed following the fall of Manswam. In early 1943, the Amerika Babo Army's campaigns in Numfor and Bosnik cost scores of his followers their lives. When the Bosnik police opened fire on Biromor's God, Jesus, and Holy Ghost Brigades, wooden clubs and magic vials could not save the soldiers.[31] Those who survived the bullets vented their rage on Biak bystanders, who grabbed machetes to protect themselves from the "troops." When news of the defeat reached the soldiers' families at the camp in North Biak, divisions arose within the movement. With the South Biak massacre, the tensions kept in check by the dream of Koreri exploded into the open. After their prophet fled to the forest, leaders and followers brutally turned on each other; former allies hacked each other to bits. Japanese leaders sent supporters of a pro-occupation faction of the movement to finish off Biromor's supporters. The mayhem did not stop until Biromor was killed. Kinsmen lured the prophet from the forest to dig his wife's grave—and delivered the blow that brought the bloodshed, temporarily, to an end.

But the violence was not over. In 1944, when the Allied forces invaded western New Guinea, further atrocities were in store for Biak. Lasting almost two months and leaving thousands dead, the battle for Biak is widely regarded as one of the most brutal in MacArthur's campaign (Smith 1953: 280–396). In April 1944, following the fall of Hollandia, Allied fighter planes darkened Biak's skies. The landing in late May was followed by weeks of fighting, as American forces tried to secure Biak Island's airfields. In July, hundreds of Japanese soldiers perished when flame throwers and firebombs were used to drive them from a cave not far from Manswam (ibid.: 375).

After the carnage came the cargo, as elsewhere in the Pacific, when the victors unloaded tinned meat and crackers for the islands' hungry inhabitants and a dazzling stockpile of supplies for the troops (ibid.: 394). The islands' use as a support center for the drive toward Japan seamlessly found its place in Biak mythology. Before the invasion, Biak coolies had returned from Manokwari with rumors that equated General MacArthur with Manarmakeri (Kamma 1972: 194). It was no accident that the naval supply center was located on Wundi, the site of Manarmakeri's rebirth.

In the wake of the massacres, many Boserens changed their family name to evade the wrath of the slain and the bereaved. The catastrophe that closed the movement that had been opened by Angganeta seemed to bear out the wisdom of her prophecy. "Koreri" proved elusive, but the dream of it lives on; this episode of "Korore" ended with Biromor's death. In North Biak and Supiori, my informants took the fate of the two prophets' respective offspring as a measure of the validity of their messages. Biromor's line has dwindled, say even his relatives; Angganeta's descendants have multiplied and thrived. Biaks base this comparison not on sheer numbers but on the *amber* produced by each family. The local grade school near Wopes just graduated its first sixth graders; a leading delegate to the national parliament was among Angganeta's "foreign" heirs. Greater "progress" was thus paradoxically ascribed to those descended from the seemingly less "modern" of the prophets. The specific aims of the uprising mattered less than its underlying vision. As Stephanus said to his followers as he boarded the Japanese ship, "The shell must leave you, but the kernel remains" (*Pis ya i bur mgo, fama krafya kiein*) (Kamma 1972: 179).

The embers of Papuan nationalism that still smoulder in many Biak hearts were lit as much by Angganeta as the men who followed her. During the 1960s, some North Biak villagers took to the forest to resist the Indonesian army. A Biak man may well have been their "general," but a Biak woman was their "queen." At her "palace" hidden deep in the island's interior, Yuliana Workrar's female soldiers sang and danced to wor and yospan (Kapissa 1980). High above them, alone in her treetop house, the widow communed with the Lord. In the separatists' struggle, as in earlier outbreaks of the movement, Koreri and Korore were intertwined. Philip Karma, the most recent of Biak prophets of transformation, has continued to link aspirations for political change to a drama of divine intervention. In postcolonial Biak, the dream of Koreri has proven difficult to leave behind.

Rupture and Renewal

It is hard to exaggerate the depth of the ambivalence with which the Biaks I interviewed recalled the 1939–43 uprising. So much about Koreri still seemed right; so much went tragically wrong. Following the war, it was not simply Dutch fears of native subversion that led to the banning of anything associated with the movement (Galis 1946). Biak leaders themselves proposed draconian measures to suppress the performance of wor. The prohibitions were scarcely needed for the war-weary populace. Few wished to awaken the dangerous dream.

Still, in the 1950s, Biaks did not completely abandon the aspirations associated with Koreri. During this period, thanks to Dutch efforts to constitute an educated Papuan elite, more and more Biaks had a chance to become "foreigners" themselves. The sons and daughters of fishermen and farmers, as well as evangelists, traded the dream of changing their skin for the prestige of serving in the colonial bureaucracy, not to mention close relations with the Dutch. That the allure of "foreignness" did not fade as Biaks rose to positions of Papuan leadership was evident in the way my informants spoke of one of the luminaries of the period. In his autobiography, Markus Kaisiëpo, self-proclaimed president of West Papua, calls himself a "Koreri man" and boasts of his struggle against Dutch colonials who would not accept "our traditional religion." He recounts how he fought the mission to bring back wor, "our way of singing," "the spirit of what was already in the minds and culture of the people" (Sharp with Kaisiëpo 1994: 84–85). On the strength of his "Biakness," Kaisiëpo sets himself apart in this text from the Dutch teachers who, he claims, later betrayed him. But back on Biak, it was his "Dutchness" that gave luster to his name. To his relatives, Kaisiëpo was the famous "Dutch uncle" (I: *om di Belanda*). Even as he embraced a modern notion of tradition, he remained a Biak *amber*.

In the aftermath of Koreri, Biaks did not stop raiding the Land of the Foreigners. As the first three chapters of this study suggest, their efforts continued in ways that were both more explicit and subtler than the piracy that once occurred. In this sense, the 1939–43 movement was not simply an episode of rebellion; it was an episode of renewal in a pattern of dealing with outsiders with deep roots in the region's past. Tidore represented a source of both violence and value to Biak seafarers. These two faces of the foreign remained linked in the practices of nineteenth-century officers, missionaries, and traders, who combined sudden shows of force with excessive offerings of wealth. Pacification enacted a battle between officialdom and the Papuans for the right to wield lethal violence. Furthering and complicating official efforts at reform, the early missionaries' campaign against heathen vengeance entailed a constant commerce in tobacco, trinkets, and lives. With gold, the missionaries purchased stranded foreigners; with rifles, they redeemed captured natives; with threats of government reprisal, they rescued communities targeted in a feud. But the crucial entry in the ledger book was Papuan souls. Faith in the afterlife would end the Papuan practice of avenging every fatality; bereaved relatives would no longer need to mourn (Kamma 1976: 376; 1977: 485, 491). The mission and the government presented coastal people with the extravagance and violence of two conflated "Others": a Christian God with the power to grant "eternal life," and a government with the right to grant death.

In the Koreri movement, as in the myth, Manarmakeri became the source of both these gifts. Just like the mythical ancestor who forbade Biaks to mourn, Angganeta incorporated the missionaries' message in offering immortality to her followers. The movement promised what the state sought to create in New Guinea: discipline, prosperity, and peace between clans and tribes (cf. Lattas 1998). Contra Kamma, in Koreri, as in the colonial project, the political and the religious overlapped (cf. 1972: 183–187; see also de Bruyn 1951–52). But to understand Koreri, it is not enough simply to appreciate Biak's distinctive colonial experience. One must also understand the social order that this experience shaped. If the notions of justice described in chapter 3 applied at the time of the movement, the leaders' achievements in approximating a utopian limit are all the more striking. In a setting where misfortune was always attributed to another's misdeed, they suspended all efforts to even the score. I have noted the dynamics of Angganeta's performances, which, in the tradition of Manarmakeri, aligned divergent pathways to the foreign. I also noted the competition that followed her arrest, as aspiring prophets strove to present evidence of their own privileged access to millennial truths. But ultimately, the prophets could not sustain the new order. Although warriors like Biromor sought to displace the sources of their authority, their own interests could never be "absent" enough.

As I have noted, Biak's position on a colonial frontier sustained a situation in which there were competing conceptions of power and strategies for acquiring it. But this situation was not simply a reflection of regional conditions; it was the product of practices—including wor—that constituted the Land of the Foreigners as the origin of value, pleasure, and prestige. When the missionaries found wor at the heart of Christian Biak, they fixed their gaze on a genre that evoked the foreign by indexing unprecedented encounters. The Protestant reformers placed the heathen custom in a startling new light: now wor itself was the source of surprise. This moment of recognition is registered in the myth of Manarmakeri, which holds out the possibility for a startling revalorization of the degraded. After the fashion of wor, the surprise would be reciprocated with the return of the ancestor, an event that would astonish the world.

On the eve of World War II, Biaks responded radically to radical changes. In the mid-1990s, with armed rebellion apparently behind them, Biaks faced challenges of a different sort. Instead of "true conversion"—and submission to colonial authority—they were being asked to join the ranks of the Indonesian nation. West Papuan separatists have long claimed the 1939–43 movement as a founding moment. But on Biak, millennial activity has not always taken an explicitly nationalist form. This should become clear in the following chapter, when we turn to the second revival of wor.

CHAPTER SEVEN

The Subject of Biak?

> *That night-stalking witch*, it doesn't belong to him, it doesn't belong
> to him.
> He takes it as his own, and I myself have nothing!

CARRIED out in Dr. F. C. Kamma's footsteps, limited by visits, memories, and lives that were always too short, my research on the Koreri movement ended in resignation; there were some things that I never would know. My Dutch predecessor, doubly bound by the demands of science and faith, also came up against an impenetrable kernel.[1] Asked to describe how they reconciled their belief in Koreri with their Christian faith, Kamma's informants smiled gently, but kept their counsel: some things were impossible to explain (Kamma 1972: 210–211).[2] But whereas the Dutch missionary could draw upon his exposure to village wor feasts to imagine the events of 1939–43, I lacked even this sense of what the movement might have been like. Most of the wor singers whom I met were well over sixty; some could only muster a reedy echo of a once-powerful voice. In my mind, I had to multiply a singer's voice by six thousand and his or her melody by sixty to imagine the ambience at Insumbabi, Wopes, or Manswam—six thousand voices at boisterous play, the melodies from sixty dance circles in collision. My data seemed bereft of what Benjamin ([1968] 1984: 194) called "experience"; had the "aura" of Koreri been lost?

Then one night, I received a faint taste of Koreri. In August 1993, after three years of construction and six months of fundraising to finance the celebration, the residents of Sor, my North Biak home base, were finally ready to consecrate their new church. When I first visited the village in September 1992, my hosts took pleasure in forecasting the splendor of this momentous event. All of Sor's "foreigners," I was told—and the village's *amber* numbered in the hundreds!—would return to the coastal community for the party. All of North Biak's congregations, from Warkimbon to Sansundi, would be invited to attend. The festivities would be crowned by a visit from the governor of the province of Irian Jaya, who would officially cut the ribbon to open the new building. The chairman of the Irian Jaya Evangelical Church would preach; visiting choirs would sing; the guests would party until dawn for days on end.

Although the gathering did not quite reach the duration and dimensions projected by my friends, a considerable crowd was in attendance on the big day, August 27, which was the anniversary of the previous church's consecration. As luck would have it, this auspicious date fell after the opening of a bridge over the Korem River, an improvement in the regency's infrastructure that suddenly made it possible for Sor's inhabitants to travel to Biak City and back in less than a day. From dawn until deep into the night, a steady stream of minivans and trucks rumbled up the road to deliver people and provisions. On the eve of the ceremony, I offered to help with the preparations for the communal meal that would follow the service, a massive project for the women of Sor, who spent the entire night in makeshift kitchens peeling taro, cleaning vegetables, and boiling rice. They had amassed a huge quantity of supplies, for it was a matter of pride—no one must go home hungry from this feast.

It was well past sundown when I set out from my home at Sor's center, for the cooking tent that had been set up on the far side of the village. From my hosts' front yard, I could hear voices; from the path that led from the cluster of houses to the road, I could see the glow of torches flickering at intervals in the distance. Each of the dozen or so visiting congregations had a separate encampment where their members slept, ate—and now were dancing. Boys had brought their guitars, and some village yospan bands had brought their large double basses. As I turned onto the pavement, a cacophony of singing and strumming filled my ears. Closer to the beachfront clearing where the women had agreed to meet, the mixture was augmented by the rumbling of drums. A low-pitched voice pierced the chaos, and I managed to pick out a melody that was familiar from my previous research; someone, somewhere was singing wor.

At first, I did not recognize the Rarwaena wor troupe, which I had helped to record months earlier for an album of Biak music (Yampolsky and Rutherford 1996). Swelling the troupe's ranks were thirty or more dancers who trailed behind the singers in a bobbing line. At the front were three young men, glistening with perspiration, who leapt and thrust their tifa drums into the air. I joined the end of the file, quickly realizing how different wor sounds from within the performing group. The melody swept down the column of dancers, then forcefully rebounded as the front and back sections took up the two-part verse. After a few songs, I made my way to the kitchen, but the villagers from Rarwaena continued through the night. At four the next morning, singing at the top of their lungs and drumming with all their might, the singers descended on every house in the village, startling awake those of us foolish enough to expect to get some sleep.

In August 1993, the drummers who led the Rarwaena troupe were anomalies—young men who could call themselves experts at wor. As quick to brag of their prowess with a lance or a carving knife, Kaleb, Yesaya, and Augustinus Burwa took great pride in what many Biaks regarded as an old-fashioned art. There were good, if somewhat unhappy, reasons why the three young men, born of the same parents, excelled at music, hunting, and sculpture. These reasons also accounted for the astonishing fact that Kaleb, aged 34, had never learned how to read. Like other members of the clans who now resided along Biak Island's main north-south thoroughfare, the brothers' family had fled from the authorities in the late 1960s, shortly after western New Guinea's transfer to Indonesia. With a long history of resisting Dutch attempts to resettle their remote villages, many of the people who made their homes in Biak Island's northern forests had resisted the Indonesian government and supported the Biak branch of the OPM, the Free Papua Organization. It was not until the late 1970s, after an attack by Indonesian soldiers that cost their village chief his life, that the fugitives agreed to descend from their hiding places deep in Biak's rugged interior. This decade in hiding put the young Burwas beyond the reach of Indonesian schools and government agencies. But it also provided them with privileged access to the genre of wor, which, as we saw in the previous chapter, some in the movement mobilized for the separatist cause.

Despite Rarwaena's history, the subject of subversion never came up when talk turned to the village. It was not Rarwaena's "underdevelopment" that struck my friends in the coastal villages and in town, but its inhabitants' remarkable skill at singing wor. Even "big foreigners" shook their heads in wonder. They all ate magic leaves! I was told. Even the little kids in the troupe that welcomed delegations to the village! By the time I visited Rarwaena, I knew the rumors by heart. It was impossible to avoid adding the community to the itinerary when Philip Yampolsky, an American ethnomusicologist, arrived in Biak to record wor.

Philip came to the island in March 1993, at my invitation, as the editor of the Smithsonian Institute/Folkways Records' Music of Indonesia series. Philip's goal in Biak, as in the other places in Indonesia where his project took him, was to document and publicize lesser-known musical genres. On Biak, as elsewhere, he worked against the government's tendency to impose a single standard by representing as much variability as possible within each form he recorded. When we undertook the project, the provincial government was paying far more attention to yospan, the relatively younger dance genre discussed in chapter 3. Various agencies promoted yospan by sponsoring parades and contests on the local and provincial level, an endeavor in line with New Order efforts to promote regional cultures. At the time, it was easy to see wor, a vocal form less accessible to a wider public, as the victim in a scenario in which the government imposed a tidier identity on the unruly Biaks. The fact that the best wor singers on the island were, by some measures, among the least disciplined, only added to the poignancy of our endeavor to memorialize this dying art. But when our efforts apparently backfired, sparking a government-sponsored revival of wor, it was also easy to blame our unintended complicity with state power.

For as it turned out, the wor singing that took place at the church consecration scarcely represented the genre's last gasp. Less than a year after
Philip's visit, wor, stripped bare of its musical and poetic complexity, was
resurrected as an official emblem of Biak ethnicity. The speed with which the
islanders adopted the cleaned-up version of the genre appalled me at the
time. The government's domestication of wor seemed emblematic of Irian
Jaya's ongoing integration into the Indonesian nation. Signaling a willingness
on the part of Biaks to embrace national standards, the success of the campaign sparked by our recordings seemed to spell doom for the fetishistic
logic this study has described. Instead of reproducing the foreignness of national spaces, Biaks seemed ready to see themselves through national eyes.
Wor was no longer a mechanism for raiding the Land of the Foreigners for
pleasure and potency; it was an element of the heritage of a nation that was
culturally varied, yet monolithic in its interests and fate. At first glance, the
revival of wor looked like a symptom of Biaks' acceptance of their status as
New Order subjects. But a deeper understanding of Biak history and sociality
casts this episode in a somewhat different light.

As I pointed out in the previous chapter, what I witnessed in 1994 was the
second revival of wor. The enthusiasm Biaks showed for the Indonesian government's discovery of the genre must be set in the context of changes in
official strategy not unlike those that preceded the outbreak of Koreri that
swept the islands at the dawn of World War II. In both cases, these changes
in strategy occurred at a time when Biak and the rest of the region were
becoming more thoroughly ensconced in wider economic and political systems. In both cases, outsiders with capital and means of coercion called for
the rehabilitation of previously prohibited genres of performance. Crucial to
the dynamics of both revivals was the surprise Biaks experienced when powerful others suddenly saw something of unexpected interest and value in
their practices. But although my argument in this chapter hinges on parallels
between recent events and the incidents described in the previous chapter, it
would be wrong to equate the colonial and postcolonial settings in which
these responses to the recognition of outsiders occurred.

In the 1930s, the mission's effort to promote wor singing in Biak churches
coincided with a colonial strategy aimed at suppressing nationalist sentiment
by reinforcing the traditional differences that divided the Indies' natives. New
Order strategies designed to integrate the nation mobilized tradition toward
different ends. Suppressing history through taxonomies that mapped identity
onto space, the cultural discourse articulated in New Order performances
and institutions hailed Indonesian citizens who recognized the state's authority in recognizing themselves. This discourse effectively suppressed the vast
inequities that divided the national population along the lines of class, ethnicity, and region. Made a matter of custom, not wealth and power, differences that potentially divided the archipelago's inhabitants were portrayed as
uniting them, as members of structurally interchangeable cultural units

within a higher-level national whole. In the case of Irian Jaya, one will recall, this project was complicated by the territory's extended colonial history and the secessionist movement it spawned. During the years immediately following western New Guinea's transfer to Indonesia, Irian Jaya's indigenous inhabitants were seen as too "primitive" for their practices to count as culture (Kipp 1996: 115; see also Gietzelt 1989). Moreover, religion, ethnicity, and region lined up in a fashion that made the risk of promoting a provincial identity outweigh the benefits the regime enjoyed in places where the authorities could play these differences off one another and against affinities based on class. It is no coincidence that officials welcomed the resurrection of an authentic Biak custom at a time when the military had eliminated the last remnants of armed opposition on the islands. Just as the first revival of wor occurred shortly after the last heathen warriors were captured, the second occurred when the majority of Biak rebels were dead, in exile, or in jail. Along with the opening of new shipping lines, new factories and resorts, the promotion of Biak culture appeared as a way of bringing former Papuans into the Indonesian fold.

On Biak in the early 1990s, official agencies promoted this new sense of national-cultural belonging through various means. In variety stores in Biak City, one could purchase a poster entitled *Bhinneka Tunggal Ika*, "Unity in Diversity," which featured a map of the nation and three rows of couples, each sporting their province's traditional dress (see Figure 8). Beginning with Aceh at the upper left and ending with East Timor at the lower right, the poster belonged to a series of similar diagrams designed for the classroom, which defined diversity as a function of variation across a set of fixed categories. School children learned from such representations that Indonesia's regions were separate but culturally equivalent; each province had its own traditional wedding costume, house, and dance. Then there were government-sponsored contests, which included competitions to design traditional apparel of the sort the poster portrayed. Rewarding local artists for their ability to rework the "shreds and patches" of local aesthetics, these events served as a source not only of renown for the winners but also of cold, hard cash (Gellner 1983: 56). Finally, and most compellingly, governmental agencies and state enterprises sponsored troupes of traditional dancers, who performed in national and international venues. On Biak, I met several members of the multiethnic yospan squad sponsored by Garuda Airlines and the Tourism Service. These young, attractive sons and daughters of elite officials boasted of their extensive travels overseas.

In the case of wor, the event that did the most to spark official interest in the genre was a free trip to Indonesia's national capital, Jakarta, awarded to fifteen singers who were invited to perform at a national festival and seminar. The voyage diverged in important respects from the New Order norm for such journeys; for one thing, the singers and their fellow performers were

Figure 8. "Unity in Diversity"

practitioners of lesser-known genres and, for the most part, elderly; for another, the focus of the event was oral tradition, not dance. Still, against the better intentions of some of the organizers, the trip did follow a distinctly New Order plot. Berlant (1997) has written of narratives of national pilgrimage in contemporary America. Depicted in film and on television, these journeys engage "infantile citizens" in encounters that play upon the contradiction between the idealized abstractions of what Berlant calls the "national symbolic" and "everyday life in the national locale." The Biak dancers who traveled to Jakarta played a role in a drama highlighting the vicissitudes of national identification in a very different political scene. Brought from "backward" villages to the modern capital, they were given a chance to embody "Unity in Diversity" by sharing the stage with other previously neglected regional acts. But if the dancers were directly engaged in an effort to "grasp the nation in its totality," the very complexities of this endeavor opened the way for a different mode of narration. Jakarta may well have been for the singers a site of "national mediation, where a variety of nationally inflected media came into visible and sometimes incommensurate contact" (Berlant 1997: 25). But this place of national mediation also proved susceptible to an antinational interpretation—one that made Jakarta into a place to raid.

In this chapter, I do what I could not do in the last; namely, I explore the particularities of the experience of recognition that led some Biaks to anticipate a utopian transformation. I consider the trip to Jakarta through a strategy of double reading, showing how the very processes that seemed to be leading Biaks to see themselves as Indonesians proved legible from a millennial point of view. I approach the rich and varied narratives inspired by the voyage not simply as a corpus of written or spoken texts but also as "action organized by culturally situated meanings" (Feldman 1991: 14). The reports and anecdotes I consider not only provided a frame for the past but also oriented the perspectives of the singers and their varied audiences, shaping the horizons of possibility in which their practices unfolded. I divide these narratives into two groups, one reflecting a New Order national perspective, the other a millennial viewpoint. Subject to the double bind that characterizes a narrative's relation to its origin, both groups of stories at once create an originating moment and mark it as occurring at a distance in space and time (Stewart 1993: 23). Finding a point of intersection in the notion of a surprising discovery, the plots that structure these national and millennial narratives generate divergent objects of narrative desire. The former turn on a longing to recover missing elements of a national-cultural identity; the latter, to merge with a power that is excessive, startling, and unknown. Reflecting and reproducing different imaginings of a national geography, these plots interact according to a principle of supplementarity, not plurality; to borrow Bhabha's (1990: 313) turn of phrase, the millennial reading of wor's revival stems from a form of knowledge that "adds to" nationalist discourse but does not "add up."

As I suggested at the end of the last chapter, a key feature of this intertextual moment is that it engaged Koreri's utopian plot structure in a context that was not explicitly oppositional. Dreams of rupture emerged with the recognition of an Indonesian cultural identity, not the Papuan national identity with which Koreri has often been linked. According to Biak prophecy, Koreri's arrival is to be heralded by the global acknowledgment of the hidden power of Manarmakeri, a figure who appears as the opposite of a "big foreigner": aged, infirm, and unattractively self-contained. By encouraging Biaks to identify with the seemingly most impotent of figures, this plot confirms a stereotype that my informants otherwise rejected—one that makes western New Guinea into a land of backward, impoverished tribes. As such, the narrative appears to register the degree to which local life on Biak has long been dominated by wider political and economic orders. But this acceptance of outsiders' perspectives proves fleeting; it is taken as signaling the dawning of a utopia that collapses the distance between the foreign and the local, the gap that leads Biaks to raid alien lands. If this narrative continued to be compelling in New Order Biak, it was not simply due to its association with open rebellion. Even seemingly harmless episodes of communal action could bring the script into play.

At the time of my attendance at the church consecration in Sor, for example, wor's appearance conjured a strange afterimage of Koreri. The colliding voices from the different dance grounds—and the all-night performance of wor—gave me a sense of what the movement might have been like. Instead of the messiah, in this case, it was the governor who failed to materialize, thwarting if not expunging the revellers' hopes and dreams. On a modest scale, the church consecration reactivated the millennial plot of Koreri; first the gaze, then a multitude of long-lost outsiders would return, revealing their hidden allegiance to a local source. During the New Order revival of wor, a similar spirit swept communities across the regency. Although the outcome of this mildly messianic moment may have been to confirm New Order authority, it would be wrong to ignore its historical and mythical echoes. To attend to these, one must consider the circumstances surrounding wor's second revival from more than one perspective. In effect, one must take the trip to Jakarta twice.

The Revival of Wor II

On the face of it, the story of the second revival of wor is a straightforward one. In April 1993, Philip Yampolsky and I recorded five different wor groups, from the subdistricts of South, East, and North Biak, documenting wide variations within the genre. The youngest of the singers were the Burwas, still in their early thirties; most of the other men were at least fifty, if not older. The style of the oldest singers, not surprisingly, was the most heterophonous; individuals who had learned wor under colonial conditions made the greatest effort to make their personal versions of a melody heard. Philip's enthusiasm for the unusual, variegated genre proved contagious. Not long after the ethnomusicologist's departure from Biak, I heard from one of his associates, the American director of the Lontar Foundation in Jakarta, who was organizing a festival and seminar showcasing Indonesia's oral traditions. On the strength of Philip's recordings, I was invited to assemble a troupe of wor singers to travel to Jakarta in December 1993. I was asked to give a paper; the Biaks would perform, along with storytellers, singers, and actors from Riau, Aceh, West Sumatra, Central Java, East Java, West Kalimantan, Jakarta, and South Sulawesi. Both the seminar and the festival, entitled Lisan, an Indonesian word meaning "oral" or "spoken," were to take place at Taman Ismail Marzuki (TIM), a renovated zoo that was the premier national venue for artistic events. Organized by the Lontar Foundation and the Faculty of Letters at the University of Indonesia, funded by the Ford Foundation and AT&T, the endeavor enjoyed the support of high-ranking national officials: Joop Ave, the minister of tourism, post, and telecommunications; Wardiman Djojonegoro, the minister of education and culture; Intan Suweno, the minister of social affairs. The Steering Committee included Mochtar Lubis, a famous Indonesian author, along with Western and Indonesian scholars and activists associated with the arts.

When I showed the list of patrons to Sam Kapissa, the Biak arts activist who had collaborated on some of the Biak recordings, he was deeply impressed. Immediately, he agreed to act as my partner; we would coauthor the paper and work together selecting and rehearsing the troupe. I was lucky to have Sam's assistance, for this was precisely the sort of endeavor through which he had carved out a freelance career. An accomplished musician who had recorded several albums of Irianese Pop, Sam had a long history of participation in the arts scene in the province. In the late 1970s, along with Arnold Ap, the widely known Biak curator of the provincial university's anthropological museum, Sam participated in a project supported by the Department of Culture and Education that was designed to promote the development of regional performance genres (Osborne 1985: 148). Part of the effort involved the documentation of traditional non-diatonic genres, like wor, along with Western-influenced music associated with the Christian missions. In Jayapura, Sam participated in two of the folkloric troupes Ap organized to perform compositions based on these older forms.[3] But this effort to create a provincial culture ended abruptly with Ap's arrest in October 1983 and death in military custody in April 1984, following a wave of Free Papua Organization (OPM) actions and political demonstrations by students and members of the urban elite (Tapol Bulletin 1984a, b, c; see also Budiarjo and Liong 1988: 126–36).[4] Although there is some evidence that Ap was directly supporting the OPM, those I spoke with on Biak in the early 1990s about Ap's murder saw it as a direct result of his effort to promote "Papuan" traditions.[5] By returning to Biak at the beginning of the crackdown, Sam managed to avoid sharing Ap's fate. Back on Biak, Sam successfully ingratiated himself with a series of regents, military commanders, and department chiefs, who were sure to call on him to organize welcome dances, festivals, and contests. He served frequently enough on official committees to confirm his status as a "foreigner"—and to earn him a modest income, as well.

Based on this experience, Sam knew how to handle the government agencies we approached for funding to cover transportation to Jakarta. He advised me to make sure the festival's organizers listed our names and those of the two groups from which we planned to pick participants in the official letter of invitation. If not, Sam told me, officials from the Department of Education and Culture would fill the slots with their own employees and kin. This official letter also relieved us of the burden of appearing to have favored particular communities; news quickly spread that big foreigners in Jakarta had invited the singers on the basis of Philip's tapes. As it was, we based our decision on more or less pragmatic considerations. The members of Samsena and Kwonbora, the groups we selected, were from the adjacent villages of Warkimbon and Rarwaena and shared more or less the same repertoire of songs. Equally important, the best singers in both groups, which included the three young drummers I ran into in Sor, were young and active enough to weather the trip. Sam and I picked seven individuals from each community. For the fifteenth member, we added Ones Krarwor, a spry old composer who was living on the coast but who originally hailed from the same stretch of the interior as the other singers. Sam and I met with the troupe for weekly rehearsals during October and November. We also arranged for the singers to undergo health examinations and acquire official residency cards in preparation for the voyage. We traveled by passenger liner to Jakarta, where we stayed in the TIM dormitory with the other performers. Sam and I presented our paper on the history and future of wor, and the singers performed twice—once on opening night, when they provided the minister of tourism, post, and telecommunications with a raucous escort from the auditorium to his car, and again on the second evening of the three-day event, when they performed a medley of fifteen wor on stage. During the second performance, Sam translated the Biak lyrics into Indonesian and provided a running commentary on the songs.

The voyage certainly qualified as an exercise in New Order citizenship. After all, the trip began with members of the troupe obtaining national identity cards, documents required for translocal travel and government employment that affirmed their holders' status as citizens of the territorial state. Between rehearsals and performances, the singers visited national attractions. They rode an elevator to the top of Monas, the acronym for Monumen Nasional (the National Monument), the obelisk at the heart of official Jakarta.

After taking in Jakarta's skyline, they toured the museum in the basement, which featured dioramas depicting key events in national history—many of which, ironically, were battles that occurred before the Netherlands Indies was formed. A few days later, the festival organizers chartered a bus to take all the performers to Taman Mini Indah Indonesia (Beautiful Indonesia in Miniature), a national theme park that features replicas of provincial architecture, art, and dress. But central to the singers' encounter with the "national symbolic" was Lisan itself, which vividly enacted the transformation of marginal practices into elements of a national culture, a shared heritage from which all Indonesians could draw.

The proposal for Lisan revealed the contradiction on which this transformation turned. The organizers envisioned Lisan as a "concerted effort" not only to "document traditions" but also "to promote their continued existence" (Lontar Foundation and Faculty of Letters 1993: 2). On the one hand, the event would target genres that were languishing, due to the effects of modernization. Along with neglect by the institutions responsible for cultivating regional cultures, Indonesian-language schooling, popular music, and television were rendering these vernacular traditions obsolete. On the other hand, in identifying and salvaging such traditions, the event would contribute to the wider project of defining "a common cultural identity" for Indonesians, which would "link diverse ethnicities and histories on the path to 'national development'" (ibid.: 1). The numerous newspaper articles written on the festival elaborated upon this interplay between loss and recuperation. Oral tradition was both "threatened with extinction" and an element of what the minister of education and culture referred to as the Indonesian nation's as yet untapped "spiritual wealth" (*Kompas* 1993a, b; *Republika* 1993b; see also *Republika* 1993a; *Jakarta Post* 1993b; *Kompas* 1993c; *Media Indonesia* 1993; *Tempo* 1993; *Editor* 1994; *Travel Indonesia* 1994).[6]

This image of tradition as a vanishing yet forever retrievable store of national value was central to the discourse that made traditional culture such a compelling focus of New Order interest (Pemberton 1994; cf. Ivy 1995). One could think of the plot articulated in these reports as charting a course from oral tradition as a souvenir, indexing an authentic but absent past, to oral tradition as an element in a national collection, in which the principle of organization held the promise of completion.[7] Denuding genres like wor of their historical context, this transformation focused the longing of national citizens on "an order beyond the realm of temporality" (Stewart 1993: 151). Even a seemingly subversive article penned by one of the participants could not escape this domesticating rhetoric in attempting to portray Lisan as a challenge to "cultural hegemony" (*Republika* 1993g). It might have seemed as if the celebration of "populist" forms bore a radical charge; indeed the author went so far as to describe the event as a "demonstration" (I: *aksi unjuk rasa*). But the notables who constituted the audience were scarcely critics of the regime, and the wor they heard, as the author admitted, only sounded "as if" they expressed sorrow and rage (ibid.; see also *Jakarta-Jakarta* 1993). New Order cultural discourse rested precisely on the identification and integration of margins; through the festival and seminar, something hitherto overlooked in the inventory of cultural traditions was rediscovered and incorporated into a national-cultural self.

The publicity Lisan generated was central to the stated aims of the enterprise. Given the focus of the event—on genres that depended on living voices to pass them on—the attention paid to the performers was particularly intense. Through the press reports, as through the event itself, the Biak singers became living icons of a recently recovered element of national heritage. Recapitulated in print, on national television, and in the very structure of the festival and seminar, the nationalist narrative framed the singers as characters confronting and transcending a triple contradiction: between modernity and tradition, between the national and the local, and between the abstractions of citizenship and the contingencies of everyday life. In some respects, the singers' experiences engaged the nationalist plot almost too well. The festival transformed wor, quite literally, into wealth, in the form of the honoraria they received and exchanged for modern commodities, as well as the money they earned by selling their tifa drums to an art dealer after the event. These transactions confirmed the minister's thinking; one could resolve the tension between culture and development by making heritage into a resource to exploit. Moreover, the participants' history as performers attested to the wisdom of those who suggested that the government get involved in promoting threatened oral genres. As the grade school teacher who coordinated the Rarwaena group explained to me on the way to Jakarta, wor would not have lasted long following the singers' resettlement in Rarwaena if local officials had not started sponsoring arts events. The younger members of the troupe may have heard wor in the forest with the separatists, but they first sang together in an Indonesian school.

On the day Lisan opened, an edited version of the paper Sam and I wrote for the seminar appeared in the English-language newspaper, the *Jakarta Post*. Those who revised our manuscript had appended an optimistic prognosis. "Perhaps the performance by the wor troupe at Lisan will stimulate interest in wor and children will inherit the secret of the vine leaves" (*Jakarta Post* 1993a). These words turned out to be prophetic; in the case of wor, the "concerted effort" seemed to work. Whereas Sam and I had trouble drumming up support from the regency government before our departure (although other groups had local sponsorship, the Biak group had to be funded by the organizers), upon our return from the well-publicized event, official interest in wor increased sharply. On the day of my departure, at the end of my fieldwork in February 1994, the Jakarta troupe, as they were now informally dubbed, played for a group of provincial officials and some Canadian guests at the new regent's residence. By the time I returned for a month of follow-up research in October 1994, village officials had organized wor troupes throughout the islands. In my absence, the regency government had sponsored two wor contests, with sizeable cash prizes; officials had designated wor as Biak's official "welcome dance." As it happened, my visit coincided with a national conference of church women, so I had a chance to observe the new policy's effects. What the regent proclaimed to me during a courtesy call appeared to be true: thanks to my efforts, supposedly, yospan was finished; Biak's "true" tradition had returned.

This transformation of a dying genre into an element of regional culture followed the plot charted by those who reported on Lisan. This resemblance should not be surprising, for the civil servants who spoke with me about the effort no doubt saw and read national coverage of the event. This is not to say that wor was resurrected in precisely the form envisioned by Lisan's organizers. Kenneth George has described the appropriation of *pangngae*, a ritualized headhunt practiced in an upland area of South Sulawesi, as a form of performance (1996: 250–258, esp. 254). Wor underwent the same transformation as envisioned by the tour operators George depicts; a predominantly oral genre came to be seen as a dance. The newly organized troupes I observed that October sang the same repertoire of brief, simple songs, focused on "traditional" topics; their style lacked the heterophony and spontaneity that had been the hallmark of wor. The young performers, many of them school children, danced in neatly spaced lines, moving and singing in unison (see Figure 9). Instead of the mixed-up dress favored by yospan dancers, they wore perfectly coordinated "traditional" costumes—bark-cloth or red cotton loinclothes and sarongs with bamboo head ornaments, beads, and plumes.

Like the highly regimented camp established by the North Biak Koreri prophet, Biromor, New Order wor, as I dubbed the transformed genre, seemed to indicate a general willingness on the part of Biaks to submit to imposed forms of discipline. Officials and villagers alike followed the minister's prescriptions and unearthed a rich vein of "spiritual wealth." The very forces that supposedly threatened tradition—education, television, economic progress—turned out, through the husbandry of international organizations and the state, to hold the promise of wor's restoration as an element of the collection of local cultures that defined the national self. There is no denying that the shift from yospan to wor entailed a suppression of a mechanism for producing representations of the foreign. As readers will recall from chapter 3, what wor does vocally, yospan does visually—it creates a conventional space in which the surprise of something novel is reproduced. Wor's visual elements lacked any reference to the foreign; its incorporating function lay in its words, the medium least accessible to the foreign visitors for whom Biak's "traditions" were to be performed. Yet the islanders' rapid adoption of this

Figure 9. School children practice New Order wor in Sor, North Biak

novel tradition did not simply indicate their submission to national hegemony; rather, like Biromor's village, it represented a local reaction to the
recognition of foreigners who seemed to see in Biak something unexpected
and new. What seemed imminent in the late 1930s may also have seemed
imminent in the early 1990s, given the often messianic tone of talk about
Biak's "development"—a repetition, through mass action, of a surprising revelation, heralding the dawning of a new world.

My evidence for this reading is, admittedly, circumstantial. The day I came
to Rarwaena to tell the singers about the invitation, the oldest members of
the group regaled me with songs about Manarmakeri that they had initially
heard in the late 1930s.[8] For these expert singers, who remembered visiting
Biromor's encampment at Wopes, the utopian narrative of Koreri remained
familiar. Though they arrived at their knowledge through more circuitous
channels, Sam and the officials who led the revival were also versed in the
tale.[9] As was the case with all the older wor experts I consulted, the singers'
memory of wor's heyday was colored by an understanding of the genre as a
powerful mechanism for accessing the potency of distant worlds. Wor, from
this perspective, was not simply an outmoded tradition; it was a potentially
subversive practice, which colonial and postcolonial governments had under-

standably done their best to suppress. For experts like Ones Krarwor, who was jailed in the 1950s for singing wor at a feast, outsiders' interest in the genre's revival—as in its suppression—was an indication of the songs' secret capacities. Against the backdrop of this particular history, and through the lens provided by the Koreri narrative, the selection of old, uneducated Biaks for the honor of singing in the cosmopolitan national capital set off something more than an accession to New Order identity. For the singers, as for their audiences on Biak, the journey to Jakarta held out the promise of a transformation that would change their homeland's place in the world. In a gesture that followed the pattern posited in wor, those who revived the genre reciprocated the surprise they experienced when outsiders "rediscovered" this forbidden tradition. As a result of the revival of wor, foreigners soon would be flocking to Biak, which would regain its rightful prominence in a globalized realm. The singers' actions would hasten the radical change in perspective that would restore Biak as a center of wealth and power.

Perhaps the strongest indication that such a narrative was evoked during the period of wor's revival lies in the informal stories the singers and others on Biak told concerning the voyage to Jakarta. Instead of depicting the event as encouraging the singers to envision themselves and their practices as Indonesian, these tales highlighted the allure and danger of distant lands. Like Biromor and Angganeta, the singers related narratives that situated themselves in encounters that confirmed the threat and seduction of spaces beyond Biak's western horizon. Thus they affirmed the alien nature of the terrain that would merge with the local at the moment when Biak's secret centrality was revealed. The link the singers forged between place and identity differed dramatically from the one posited in New Order collections that charted culture onto a synchronic grid. Like the other practices I have described in this study, these narratives generated an imaginative geography that played up the friction of distance. For members of the Jakarta troupe to inspire widespread emulation in Biak, they had to be able to construct a narrative of travel that kept the aura of foreignness alive.

Raiding Jakarta

A familiar ambivalence pervaded the stories I heard about Jakarta and other destinations to the west before, during, and after the trip to the nation's capital. In the examples I discuss below, the Land of the Foreigners appears as the site of sudden violence and startling reunions; being attacked by a stranger and meeting a long-lost relative were equally plausible outcomes of a walk along Jakarta's crowded streets. The air of foreboding that pervaded the wor singers' discussions about the upcoming trip came, in one sense, as little surprise. During the turbulent 1970s, when Papuan separatists battled the army in Biak's forested interior, the communities from which the troupe's members were drawn had first-hand experience of the New Order's dangerous potency. Although in some ways the Indonesian military was engaged in completing the region's "pacification," it used violence for pedagogical purposes different from those pursued by the Dutch. Unlike the colonial authorities, the national army took action not to educate the punished but to educate witnesses; villagers who fled to the forest were not treated as unschooled children but as enemies to be eliminated before their influence spread.[10] Although they were not alone in their concern with the dangers of city living, the singers had personal reasons to recognize the threat underlying the paternalistic public face of Indonesia's long-standing authoritarian regime. Yet their fascination with the dangers of Jakarta went further, I propose; this was a case in which the cultural production of fear was in the interest less of the rulers than of the ruled.[11]

Well before I took on the task of accompanying the wor troupe to Jakarta, I had a taste of Biak conceptions of Indonesia's distant, densely populated "Inner Islands."[12] My two closest friends on Biak had each spent several years studying and working on Java. Sally Bidwam had gone to nursing school in Bandung, a West Javanese metropolis; Edith Noripuri had attended a social work course in Solo, a Central Javanese city and former sultanate. Their stories of the Land of the Foreigners differed, but they shared a single theme: whatever national stereotypes might lead one to believe about the relative advancement of Java and Irian Jaya, the opposite was likely to hold true. Sally Bidwam repeatedly told me the story of how she had mastered Bandung's urban novelties immediately upon her arrival in the city. As a result, on the first day of classes, when the new students took a tour, Sally had the pleasure of showing her colleagues from rural Java how to get on and off of escalators and across busy streets. Edith Noripuri dwelt less on her innate sophistication than on her calm courage in facing the seamier side of Javanese poverty. She described visiting a government barracks for prostitutes wearing heavy eye makeup and cherry red lipstick, a measure she took in an effort to put the women and their clients at ease. Both women made much of the poor Indonesian spoken by Java's inhabitants; luckily, they themselves had quickly mastered Javanese. With such experiences to back them up, both these bin amber (female foreigners) could scoff with authority at the government propaganda clips that frequently aired on the televisions owned by wealthier town dwellers. "Don't be deceived," they announced to their less worldly companions, as gleaming highways and prosperous villages flashed on the screen. "You can be sure that they are not showing us the whole truth!"

The same inversion of popular stereotypes characterized the comments I began to hear after word spread of my involvement in the trip to Jakarta. Sam and I were frequently approached by excited acquaintances who had heard about the upcoming voyage. The most common question they asked us was "Aren't you afraid?" This query struck me as ironic—the Javanese bureaucrats who had arranged my first visit to Irian Jaya in 1990 had asked me the very same thing. Sam and I, supposedly, had the most to fear, since as the leaders of the expedition we would be responsible for ensuring that everyone returned alive. Some interlocutors went so far as to compare our liability to that of the Biak "captains" who took young men on their first expedition to Tidore.[13] If the perils of Java did not kill us outright, a bereaved relative of one of the singers might.

To prevent the latter eventuality, we were advised not to take anyone elderly—a tall order, considering the average age of most competent wor singers; nor should we take any women. The most vociferous opponents of women's participation turned out to be the husbands of the three female singers selected for the trip, men who were themselves included among the troupe's members. Festus Rumbrawer took me aside before one rehearsal and softly explained his wife's predicament. "Laurensina was shot," he earnestly told me, neglecting to mention that the middle-aged woman had been carrying the bullet for nearly twenty years, ever since Indonesian soldiers had ambushed her family while they were hiding in the forest. It struck me as odd that Festus should be so concerned about a condition that had not exempted Laurensina from arduous tasks like gardening and hauling wood. The dispute was quickly resolved when Laurensina got wind of Festus's maneuvering. "If I don't go," she told me darkly, "neither will he!"

Laurensina's response to Festus's objections reflects another feature of the Land of the Foreigners, as envisioned through this frame: the opportunities it offered for wanton behavior. For the moment, however, I would like to dwell on the dangerous face of points west. The leaders of the groups we brought together for the event did much to inculcate seriousness among the singers by invoking the threat of random violence. Besides strange diseases, anonymous strangers would threaten anyone who acted carelessly. "I've heard that the Javanese," Otto announced gravely after one rehearsal, "will walk up and stab you without uttering a word!" Again, a common stereotype was turned on its head. Despite the fact that among Irian Jaya's exports to Jakarta were bouncers, men recruited by gangs and club owners for their "frightening" appearance, it was the tough Biak singers who would have to watch their backs.[14] As the date of departure approached, the singers told these frightening stories with growing frequency. The tension rubbed off on the singers' families, who tearfully bid them farewell, as if they might never see the travelers again. I was told later that one group of women had come to Biak City every time a ship was due to dock, just to see if their loved ones had made it home.

As I noted above, we traveled by passenger liner to and from Jakarta. Traveling west, we stopped at Manokwari, Sorong, Ambon, Dili, Kupang, and Surabaya; returning east, at Ujung Pandang, Bau-Bau, Buton, Bitung, Banggai, Menado, Ternate, Sorong, and Manokwari, a series of names the singers quickly memorized, some copying the schedule as a keepsake to take home. On the way to the capital city, we enjoyed the amenities of a new German ship, the Dobonsolo, which featured gleaming wooden decks, color televisions, and hot showers. Sam rushed ahead as we boarded to reserve a block of berths on the economy deck, which was equipped with aisle after aisle of low wooden platforms, each of which held two rows of ten thin plastic mattresses. The wor troupe commandeered an entire platform, which was soon laden with baskets, bundles, thermoses, and drums. Before setting out to explore the ship, the singers took care to assign someone to guard the group's possessions. The strangers in the immediate vicinity seemed friendly enough, but in a day or so we would be leaving Irian, and who could say what we would find.

One of the responsibilities Sam and I shouldered during the voyage was to keep the singers healthy and well fed. In addition to watching for signs of malaria, we had to lead trips ashore to forage for familiar food to supplement the meager fare served on board. The latter task sometimes conflicted with our other responsibility: making sure not to lose anyone in a strange port. None of the singers had ever been outside the province, and the temptation to go exploring each time the ship docked was only enhanced by talk of the perils associated with these strange places. We generally spent about four hours at each destination, which gave Sam or me enough time to venture out with a small team of companions to search for the nearest market. The singers took turns participating in these excursions; quiet and watchful, four or so of us would proceed in a cluster to the street, carefully counting the minutes it took to reach the city center, listening as we shopped for the fog horn that was blown to announce Dobonsolo's imminent departure. When we docked at Dili, in Indonesian-occupied East Timor, it was the women's turn to accompany me to town. In the first light of dawn, we wandered the cool streets, which were lined with crumbling stucco buildings and were empty except for an armed personnel carrier that passed us near the town square. Both the women and their companions breathed an audible sigh of relief when we made it back to the ship with several hours to spare.

By the time we reached Dili, however, we were due for a close call. The dialectic of risk-taking requires that the stakes wagered be constantly raised; one cannot sustain the specter of danger without continually testing one's control over the threat (Bateson 1972: 327–328). Not long after I had returned to the ship, I was leaving it again, this time to accompany the group leader from Warkimbon, who had discovered a fellow Biak among the bystanders who had gathered to greet the ship. This distant cross-cousin swept us off to visit a Sino-Indonesian baker who had moved to Dili from Biak a decade or so earlier. After tea, we took a tour which ended with our hostess's driver speeding to the port, arriving just before the gangplank was pulled away. This near miss confirmed what the singers had known all along—in strange lands, one must remain on one's toes.

During our stay in the nation's capital, a series of misadventures kept up the tension between safety and danger. On the first night in the TIM dormitory, one of the singers, having been served at dinner what he thought was a rotten piece of fish, exploded in fury once he had the group alone. He had come very close to dashing his plate to the ground, he told us, an outburst that surely would have ended in a fight. A handful of other singers, one of them a respected teacher, also took part in testing the envelope of safety. On the first day, Sam advised the singers not to leave the TIM compound at night. By the fourth day, three of the men, including the teacher, found their way to a streetside canteen that served beer and snacks directly outside the gate to the performance center. The teacher, inebriated, ended the evening on the curb singing the Wilhelmus, the Netherlands' national anthem, with a Dutch tourist who was in a similar state.

As if their encounters with revolving doors, escalators, and freeways did not provide enough stimulation, the women on the trip conspired to keep each other alert. Each of the singers received an honorarium. Fearful that they would spend the cash too quickly, the men decided to give their money to the women for safekeeping; they took advantage of kinship ties where possible or, lacking these, stored their money with me. A few days before we set sail for home, two performers from Riau, clearly disturbed, took me aside and informed me that they had seen one of the Biak women stealing money from another. As it turned out, Laurensina, the culprit, had returned the money of her victim, Willemina, as soon as her older colleague had noticed it was gone. "That old lady acts like a little girl," Laurensina sniffed, insisting that Willemina had had it coming. From its inception, all three of the women agreed, the heist had been a pedagogical ploy. It was designed to teach Willemina, who had absent-mindedly left her bag untended while she was taking a shower, to take greater care with her things.[15]

Through their actions and the stories they told about their experiences, the singers constituted the journey as a series of narrow escapes, quick brushes with danger that kept them alert whenever safety seemed overly assured. But the singers' view of the Land of the Foreigners, as some of these examples also suggest, was complicated by a dichotomy: these distant places were both the lair of threatening strangers and the abode of future affines or long-lost kin. The episode in Dili obviously played up this aspect of their fascination with the foreign; the thought of finding a Biak in this unlikely locale was the source of much amazement and pleasure. The singers seemed equally pleased and startled by less direct indications of kinship. Several of the singers were delighted to discover that the group of West Timorese artisans who boarded in Kupang used bridewealth, chewed betel nut, and smoked

Figure 10. Some wor singers make new friends on their way to Jakarta

shag tobacco. I took several photographs of the singers posing with the Timorese men, who were on their way to the Taman Mini theme park to build a traditional house (see Figure 10). "I look at them, and I'm filled with love and longing!" Otto Burwa sighed, squeezing the hand of a new friend who had promised to give Otto a finely woven sarong. "They have the same customs as we Biaks! Share some betel nut and then we're fast friends!" The myth of Manarmakeri, as we have seen, offers an explanation for what the singers saw as a striking resemblance; the Timorese were the descendants of the travelers who followed the culture hero to the west.

The other variety of relationship posited between the Biak singers and the "foreigners" they met in their travels was potentially affinal—the eventuality that concerned Laurensina when she refused to let Festus travel without her. The Biak men's meetings with a variety of "non-Irianese women" (B: bin amber) sparked embarrassment, amusement, and, upon their homecoming, bravado. Yesaya Burwa, the youngest man in the group, pulled me aside during the journey home to show me the address he had received from a Javanese student who had interviewed the singers. In the case of Isak

Arwam, one of the group's skilled composers, the "proof" of an encounter took a humorous form. Thinking back on the Javanese merchants who tried to sell the singers some cheap perfume, Isak composed a wor.

KADWOR

Kabido bone, kabido bone a o a.
Kabido bone, kabido bone a o a.

TIP

Kabido tree fruit, kabido tree fruit.
Kabido tree fruit, kabido tree fruit.

FUAR

Kabido bone, kabido bone a o a.
Insoso sebin Jawa ine sus besya seyo
    kabido bone, kabido bone a o a.

ROOT

Kabido tree fruit, kabido tree fruit.
Young miss, this Javanese woman has
    breasts like kabido tree fruit, kabido
    tree fruit.

This ditty threw his companions into fits of laughter. The men's stories of actual and potential liaisons grew bawdier over time. By the time we had been back in Biak a month, even Ones Krarwor, the oldest of the singers, had been roundly teased for having "snacked"—had adulterous liaisons— abroad.

As much as they enjoyed this good-natured ribbing, the singers derived more than humor from these narrated brushes with adultery; pathos pervaded some of the tales. Kaleb Burwa, Yesaya's brother, was particularly touched when, on the return trip, the ship anchored off a remote village in Sulawesi, where the vessel was quickly surrounded by canoes filled with begging children. Most of the passengers made a game of throwing money to the beggars, watching from the deck, high above the water, as the paddlers scrambled for their coins. But the Biaks were deeply touched by what they saw. One baby, held aloft by a teenage girl, brought to mind Kaleb's young daughter. "We have plenty in Biak," he later told me he felt like telling the young mother. "Why don't you come and live with me instead?" While such comments sometimes struck me as more whimsical than serious, I learned that they could have significant effects. Also on the return voyage, Fransina reacted dramatically to a playful rumor that her husband, who was late in fetching Fransina's breakfast, had run into a b*in amber*. On a self-imposed hunger strike for the next four hours, Fransina refused to speak to her husband, whom she assumed had fed a stranger her meal.

In his analysis of the dynamics of political violence in Northern Ireland, Feldman argues against narrow concepts of narrative that distinguish too sharply between action and inscription. *"The event is not what happens. The event is that which can be narrated"* (1991: 14).[16] The experience of the Biak singers seems to confirm Feldman's dictum. The singers' horizon of expectation, shaped by deep-seated assumptions about the nature of the Land of the Foreigners, defined the kinds of encounters they could have. But it was not only on the level of explicit storytelling that the "foreignness" of points west was reconfirmed; this foreignness was also, in the fashion I described in chapter 3, a product of the structure of wor. As the singers had forecast before our departure, the minds of the group's most prolific composers were constantly filled with songs. On the way to Jakarta, the wor created by Ones Krarwor and Zeth Burwa focused on the ship's capacity to swiftly breach the horizon. On the way back to Biak, the older singers expressed a sudden surge of nostalgia for Jakarta, their temporary home.[17] The Land of the Foreigners, for the singers, who now basked in its aura, had become an object of longing instead of fear.

In dwelling on the ways the singers framed their journey to Jakarta, I do not mean to imply that other travelers have not partaken of similar fantasies of danger, intimacy, and adventure. As de Certeau points out, in the contemporary world there are always two "symbolic and anthropological languages of space," one associated with the map, and the other with the route or itinerary. Taking the form of the unfolding of a narrative, the latter is a "discursive series of operations," as opposed to the former, which is a "plane projection of totalizing operations" (1984: 119). In walking through the streets of New York, or some other mapped region, one acts in a fashion akin to speaking. One enounces elements from an exhaustive order, in the same way one enounces a word, creating "space" by practicing what de Certeau calls "place." The opposition between New Order mapping and Biak raiding drawn in this chapter coincides with de Certeau's dichotomy. But there is something distinctive about the way that the singers narrated their walk through the nation. Where the language of the map is dominant in the situations de Certeau describes, the social order described in this study privileged the language of the route.

In reproducing a particular image of the Land of the Foreigners, the singers were doing more than engaging in what de Certeau describes as a form of resistance (1984: 96). In the act of recreating the foreignness of distant worlds, they were also recreating themselves. This transformation cut across the barriers faced by these lower-class farmers. Through their travels, they confirmed what they long had claimed—that their forms of magic were no less effective than those wielded by wealthy civil servants for raiding prestige from foreign worlds. Upon their return to Biak, the singers enjoyed a brief period in the limelight, as gossip about their feats in Jakarta spread. The trip quickly became a topic of conversation on porches and street corners, in offices and minivans, and in other settings where friends and relatives stopped to chat. The younger men met their public decked out like Indonesian film stars; on a trip to visit their sister in another village, the Burwas sported sunglasses, watches, and fancy jeans. But, like the other singers, they spent most of their honoraria on gifts for others; children's clothing, radios, and air rifles were particularly popular. The female relatives of some of the singers were soon wearing Lisan T-shirts on trips to the market, adorning themselves at the same time they enhanced their kinsmen's renown (cf. Munn 1986: 112). It took more than the possession of foreign commodities to transform the village dwellers into foreigners; it took the circulation of stories and valuables from afar. It seems likely that wor's newly confirmed association with the prestige of foreign travel was key to the genre's revival on Biak. The singers' newfound stature led to emulation—and in one case, dangerous envy—as others responded to the interest of Jakarta's "big foreigners" by forming their own groups to sing wor.[18] Having endured the shock of distant lands, the singers gained the power to impress their fellows, who in turn pursued this new avenue to influence and fame.

Elsewhere, I have described how the Irian Jaya pavilion at the national theme park, Taman Mini Indonesia, inspired the Biak singers to break into wor (1996: 601–602). According to nationalist ideology, each ethnic group was supposed to feel right at home in their designated identity (Pemberton 1994: 159); this action on the part of the Biaks conventionally signaled that they did not. Under New Order conditions, the Land of the Foreigners survived in Biak imaginations through anecdotes resembling the ones I have related. Repeating the logic of wor in a subtler idiom, these stories of travel discursively created the very dangers and opportunities for intimacy on which the singers' prestige came to rest. Such narratives were critical at a time when more and more of the islands' inhabitants were gaining direct experience of distant lands. Where rarity and danger no longer seem "given," a particular mode of emplotment can recreate these qualities. If the trip to Jakarta provided Biaks with an experience of national identification, it also provided them with a heightened sense of the foreignness of the New Order regime. The rhetoric that made wor into a dying tradition, calling for rescue by the state, provided just one way of telling the story. In reviving wor, Biaks briefly acted as New Order cultural subjects—but, in doing so, they anticipated a transformation of the national geography that would break Jakarta's monopoly on power and wealth.

Waiting for the End

The utopian expectations aroused by the second revival of wor dovetailed with official forecasts that predicted a rapid growth in tourism in Biak. The officials and singers I spoke with during my visit in 1994 conceived of the wor contests as providing entertainment for burgeoning numbers of foreigners. Wor was intended to serve as a replacement for yospan, which, one will recall, was performed at the airport for the tourists traveling back and forth to Bali. By mounting more authentic cultural productions—and completing a range of other "improvements"—development planners would finally lure the visitors beyond the terminal's walls. The association of wor with foreign visitors was already evident before the trip to Jakarta. When the singers gave a demonstration in Biak City on the eve of our departure, the Tourism Service asked me to provide a commentary in English, even though there was only one European in the enormous crowd.

For those not directly involved in the promotion of tourism, the events described in this chapter also gave rise to vivid fantasies. During our absence, rumors swept the island as news of the festival spread. The inclusion of wor in Lisan was simply one indication of the fact that Biak culture would soon be in great demand. One of the choirs Philip Yampolsky and I recorded nearly split over the suspicion that I had offered to take some of the women to perform in another festival in Jakarta, and that the leader was concealing the list. These dreams of foreigners coming to Biak, and Biaks traveling to foreign lands, which raised the prospect of new opportunities for individuals of limited means, coincided with the official discourse of development quoted by village chiefs and provincial dignitaries alike. But official talk of an impending collapse in the distance between Biak and the outside world also evoked older millennial expectations. Those who joined the rapidly multiplying wor troupes across the islands saw their novel actions as ushering in radical change.

In the years following my fieldwork, events conspired to dash many of the hopes raised by this revival of Biak tradition. In 1994, the national airline abolished the refueling stop that had brought tourists to Biak on their way between Bali and Los Angeles. Well before the massive resort in East Biak opened, Garuda Airlines added to the national fleet jets capable of flying longer distances without landing. In 1998, when I returned to Biak for a brief visit, Hotel Marauw, as the resort was christened, stood virtually empty. The management had turned off the air conditioning and most of the lights to save on costs; moss was already growing on the peeling walls. I toured the huge complex with the regent's wife, who had invited me to join her for an outing. In the entire resort, the only person we encountered who even vaguely resembled a guest was a subdistrict chief (I: *camat*) from Supiori who had brought his family to see the sights. Although the regent's wife was clearly proud of the project, she admitted that it was running at a loss. It was not simply the rescheduling of flights that had held up the development of tourism in the regency. Shortly after the announcement from Garuda, an earthquake and tidal wave hit Biak, destroying several villages and part of Biak City. The financial crisis that led to Suharto's resignation came on the heels of this setback in Biak's path to prosperity. With the economy in shambles, and foreign embassies warning of unrest, the onslaught of tourists seemed more or less permanently on hold.

By 1998, a road to Biak's forested interior was opened, and the singers from Rarwaena had all returned to their clan land to build houses and open gardens. The privileges they enjoyed during the trip to Jakarta still made for happy memories; yet they recognized that they were no longer at the center of attention in the regency. They told me they had fared relatively well during the crisis; now that they could plant cash crops, they had plenty to sell at the market, at prices more responsive to changing exchange rates than civil servants' salaries could be. Still, many in the community felt neglected by the government. Well-connected coastal villages had received a great deal of aid after the earthquake; despite the damage their village had suffered, they had received very little help. When I spoke with the singers, three weeks had passed since the flag raising in Biak City; although few of the villagers had participated, they sympathized with those who had. "We Papuans are not 'rupiah lovers,'" one joked with me, when I asked them about the central government's ill-fated campaign to prop up the national currency. It was no surprise that one of the village teachers had joined Karma's movement, as they saw it. "He didn't receive his salary, so up went the flag."

This is not to say that the flag raising—or the revival of wor—can simply be explained in terms of their participants' self-interest. Both incidents engaged a horizon of expectation that was rooted in an intersection between national and international forces and the dynamics of local social life. Each event took place at the crossroads of divergent sets of narratives: those that oriented the New Order's cultural policies and practices, those that fed the islanders' utopian hopes, those that shaped the experiences of foreign tourists out for adventure in this supposedly "Stone Age" land. In the revival of wor, Biaks responded to the prospect of greater foreign involvement on the islands with dreams of a radical transformation. The subversive potential of this dream lay not in the content of the utopia but in the means by which it would be reached. In the case of the flag raising, Biaks responded to a different set of imperatives, at a moment when global investors and institutions intervened in Indonesia with different effects and toward different ends. Here, international recognition boded not Biak's dramatic achievement of "development," but its dramatic extraction from Indonesia's national map. In Philip Karma's movement, the prospect of acknowledgment of a repressed Papuan nation sparked visions of a startling transformation. Now the foreigners poised to arrive were not tourists but peacekeepers from the United Nations. Still, the basis of Karma's authority did not differ radically from that claimed by those who led the New Order revival of Biak tradition. Like the singers, this provincial official exercised authority gained through access to the foreign—and anticipated a moment when near and distant forces would converge.

The sudden rise of Papuan nationalism in the regency calls into question the conclusion that, through reviving wor, the Biaks I knew became Indonesians. Despite their very different outcomes, the flag raising and the revival followed a similar plot. This coincidence reflects Biak's distinctive history and politics. But it also reflects the limits to which nationality—like every identity—is prone.

Epilogue

On Limits

In July 1998, when he walked into the sitting room where I was waiting for Sister Sally, wearing a tan uniform and twenty more pounds than when I had seen him last, Yoel Bidwam could not suppress a grin. In 1994, when I finished fieldwork and took leave from the household, in a quiet neighborhood high on the Ridge, Yoel, Sally's classificatory brother, was a lean and lanky taxi driver, one of the multitude of young Biak men who spent their days traveling in and out of the Biak City terminal. Having discovered this long-lost clan member in 1993, Sally slowly drew Yoel into her family. She offered him lunch, then a place to live, and finally, useful connections through her employers at the hospital. Clearly Sally's plan to make something of this distant Bidwam relative—which had entailed, somewhat tumultuously, extracting him from the household of his widowed mother—had borne fruit. Yoel was now a government employee, the official driver of the regency's new ambulance. Yoel beamed with pleasure, when I announced the obvious, while warmly shaking his hand: "Yoel, you have become a foreigner (B: *amber*)!"

In the preface to his study of the emergence of Indonesian nationalism, James Siegel offers evidence of the deep sense of identification with the nation felt by many Indonesian citizens; when they receive a number designating them as civil servants, they weep (1997: 7). Although it would not have been my hostess's style to break into tears, Sally would have greeted the news of Yoel's admission to the civil service with pride. She certainly seemed proud when she explained to me how she had arranged for Yoel to get his new job, cutting through the bureaucratic obstacles by mobilizing her friends in high places. But if my analysis in this study has been correct, this pride had little to do with Yoel and Sally's nationalist sentiments. After all, our reunion occurred at a moment when Indonesia appeared as doubly alien to Biaks like Sally and Yoel. I arrived shortly after Philip Karma's demonstration and the killings by the security forces that followed, shortly after protesters began to demand that the province's "Papuans" should have their own nation-state.

In the context of scholarly depictions of other parts of New Order Indonesia, the story that I have told in this study illustrates a limiting case. One can define a limiting case as an instance marking one end of a continuum of different configurations that can be taken by a particular set of dynamics.[1] The practices described in the previous chapters privilege functions of discourse that are downplayed in other ideological contexts; out of a range of ways of pursuing value, construing agency, and constituting identities, what one finds in Biak represents one possible extreme. The idiom in which the Biaks I knew in the early 1990s spoke about intimacy and rivalry, the strategies through which they pursued authority and prestige, the narratives through which they charted personal and collective pasts and futures—none of these features of social life were unique. And yet they added up to a relation to national authority that violated what then seemed to be the norm. I have argued that one must approach the fetishization of the foreign, the logic underlying this relation to wider worlds, as the product of these islands' distinctive history. But does this mean that what I have charted is simply an aberration, that there is nothing to be learned from this case about the nature of dominant forms of sociality and authority, of dominant fashions of thought?

What is the place of a limiting case in current thinking about society and culture? In contemporary anthropology, it sometimes seems that there is little interest in such a question. The research agenda that once drew ethnographers to remote communities, where they could explore beliefs and values assumed to be highly alien to their own, has lost its appeal in most quarters. For very good reasons, today's anthropologists feel the need to set their analyses in the context of the broader institutional contexts and economies that have, in varying ways, penetrated the entire globe. Where their predecessors might have looked for pockets of tradition, either thriving in isolation or languishing under the pressure of the new, today's investigators look for manifestations of modernity. Even when they explore the local, their impulse is to isolate manifestations of the global and the national. I do not wish to criticize this trend unduly; it set the stage for this study, which is fueled by an urge to historicize and contextualize ethnographic findings. But I do wish to point out the new forms of blindness it can promote. Can today's ethnographers pay heed to commonalities without ignoring distinctions? Is it possible to deconstruct dichotomies—the West and the rest, modernity and tradition—without suppressing differences, without positing an unbroken global landscape where one only discovers what one sets out to find?

I will admit that I am somewhat overstating my argument. It is relatively uncommon to find this homogenizing tendency expressed as boldly as it is at the end of Handler's otherwise enlightening study, where he notes: "The culture of cultural objectification is shared throughout the modern world of nation-states and ethnic groups. . . . The desire to appropriate one's own culture, to secure a unique identity places one in the mainstream of a modern individualist culture to which national boundaries are irrelevant" (Handler 1988: 195).

The irony of this claim is obvious, in Handler's case; Handler refers to the logic that gives rise to the desire for bounded cultural identities as a bounded totality, a uniform culture that pervades the modern world. This slippage takes his argument down the path laid out by theorists who echo Berman's claim that modernity, simply and straightforwardly, encompasses us all (1983: 15; see also Giddens 1990: 149, 151, 175; Habermas 1990). More careful, recent treatments have left open the possibility of alternative paths to the culturalist project Handler describes, paths that present the emergence of the interiorized forms of subjectivity associated with national identity not as the product of a sheer and abrupt break with the past but as the contingent outcome of engagements between emergent social worlds (see, for example, Rafael [1988] 1993; Pemberton 1994; Ivy 1995; Brenner 1998). This more discerning approach overcomes the shortcomings of analyses that assume that modernity represents a rupture from tradition, yet those who subscribe to it should be aware of the range of possibilities such a framework should be able to encompass. If the emergence of modern identity is in each case the product of a particular history, divergent histories can have different effects. In other words, the field must have room for cases like that found in Biak, where the particularities of history and context have lead to unexpected continuities. If one is willing to allow for alternative paths to modernity, one must also be willing to allow for a route that does not lead to this destination, at least not in the form one has been led to expect.

But a limiting case can do more than brake the slippage into unilineal history one sometimes finds in recent ethnography. It also offers a way of imagining in concrete, historical terms something akin to the differences at once evoked and foreclosed in the founding texts of European social thought. Spivak has recently criticized colonial and postcolonial studies for failing to take on the task of envisioning forms of alterity that do not adhere to the conventions of contemporary identity politics (1999). Taken to their logical conclusion, the approaches promoted in these fields leave the analyst with the choice of embracing the culturalist projects of Third World elites, or implicitly accepting the universalism of the West. "To steer ourselves through the Scylla of cultural relativism and the Charybdis of nativist culturalism," Spivak writes, "we need a commitment not only to narrative and counternarrative, but also to the rendering (im)possible of (another) narrative" (ibid.: 6). Spivak approaches this project by way of readings of Kant, Hegel, and Marx that recover, in varying forms, the perspective of the "native informant" each evokes and dismisses in the course of their texts. "A name for that mark of expulsion from the name of Man," the native informant plays a critical role in the constitution of the universal; s/he is both "needed and foreclosed."

One can speculate as to how this study's findings might support this difficult endeavor. Consider, in light of Spivak's project, Derrida's analysis of Hegel's treatment of fetishism in *The Philosophy of History*, a text in which Africa is dismissed as having "no history 'properly so called'" (Derrida 1986:

207). As Derrida points out, Africa, the home of the Hegelian fetish, serves as the setting for a process that both mimes and defines, by opposition, the coming to rational consciousness that Hegel depicts as the progress of Spirit. For Hegel, despite the African's movement through stages that define this progress in the Judeo-Christian West, from a form of communion, that is, cannibalism, to the objectification of desire, that is, fetishism, this "savage" remains stalled on the threshold of history. As Hegel puts it, the African lacks

> the principle which naturally accompanies all *our* ideas—the category of Universality. . . . [I]n the fetish a kind of objective independence as contrasted with the arbitrary fancy of the individual seems to manifest itself; but as the objectivity is nothing other than the fancy of the individual projecting itself into space, the human individuality remains master of the image it has adopted. . . . Such a Fetich has no independence as an object of religious worship; still less has it aesthetic independence as a work of art; it is merely a creation that expresses the arbitrary choice of its maker, and which always remains in his hands. In short there is no relation of dependence in this religion. (Hegel [1822] 1991: 93, 94; see also Pietz 1985: 7)

Hegel supports this vision through evidence drawn from earlier visitors to African Guinea, who, as Pietz has noted, depicted the *fetisso*, as the fetish then was called, as a thing of "irreducible materiality" (1985: 7). Rather than serving as the image of a transcendent deity, the fetish was the site of a singular power. The contingent nature of the choice of a particular object as fetish was also clear in these observations. European writers portrayed the fetish as the first thing the African came upon in setting out on a mission; and an owner supposedly would abandon his fetish just as hastily when his or her fortunes took a turn for the worse (ibid.: 8). As Pietz points out, in stressing the lack of "dependence" indexed by this arbitrary treatment of the fetish, Hegel paradoxically puts African kings and priests in a position of absolute power; with no dependence on the Idea, there is no independent basis on which to criticize those who represent it. According to Derrida, Hegel locates the paradox on a deeper level; the African is mastered by what he presumes to master—Nature. In either case, "the function of this view of the African as an ideology justifying the slave trade by explaining the African as slavish by nature is obvious enough" (ibid.: 7). Clearly, the African perspective is foreclosed, in a blatantly racist fashion, in Hegel's narrative; yet might there be another way of confronting Hegel's Africa without dismissing the possibility of difference? This denigrated social order, cursed for its birth in what Pietz calls the "chaotic principle of contingency"—could we reimagine this "fiction" in relation to the fetishistic logic one finds in Biak? Just as there is nothing "natural" in Biak's notion of the foreign, there can be no unmediated relation to "contingency" or, for that matter, "matter." Does not the very demand that a "principle" be "chaotic" call forth the split consciousness engendered by the fetish? Might one find here, as in Biak, a particularly resilient "Universal"—an ideology that elevates an alternative sort of "consciousness," not of a fixed sign, but of the startling experience of the new?

These speculations on Hegel's "native informant" are not intended to suggest how a "real" Africa might have looked. Rather, my comments are intended to show how this study enables us to envision features of the alternative narrative "rendered (im)possible" in Hegel's text. In the preceding chapters, I have portrayed a sociocultural economy oriented by principles that a particular European tradition of thought has expelled to its margins, an economy that is distinctive yet not divorced from the wider orders that encompass it. For this task of imagining the perspective of a native informant involves us not only in the delineation of difference but also in the acknowledgment of unsuspected affinities. Although Hegel projects into Africa "an unconsciousness that does not let itself be dialectized as such," "this non-dialecticalness, this ahistoricity can always be interpreted as negativity, as resistance proper to the dialectic economy, and consequently interned in the speculative process. A certain undecidability of the fetish lets us oscillate between a dialectics (of the undecidable and the dialectical) or an undecidability (between the dialectical and the undecidable)" (Derrida 1986: 207). When one stops approaching the fetish as the substitute that enables the critic to claim a source of value that would be real, and instead pays heed to its productivity as a site of indestructible desires, we can begin to appreciate the extent to which Hegel's system is itself fetishistic. Hegel's "mind" is stuck in a repetitive cycle: it keeps circling back to moments of negativity—like death—that the system can neither define nor supersede (see also Bataille [1955] 1990). Once one strips the dialectic of its metaphysical moorings, this reading implies, the opposition between African fetishism and European rationality breaks down.

Unexpected affinities also emerge in Spivak's treatment of Marx's notion of the Asian Mode of Production. Marx takes the Asian Mode of Production as the Other against which the dynamism of European modes of production is defined. Yet the principles ascribed to this supposedly "static" formation are discernible in the current world order: in the "debt bondage and tribute system promoted by foreign aid . . . and foreign trade" (Spivak 1999: 101). From this perspective, what appears in Marx's theory as a stage in an evolutionary progression becomes legible as a feature of a global geography, a terrain of heterogeneous yet interconnected spheres and sites. As this example suggests, by paying heed to the power of a limiting case to unsettle conventional assumptions about consciousness and sociality, one can do more than simply offer novel ways of reading classical theory. By way of this unsettling, one can bring classical theory to bear in the search for new ways of reading the contemporary world. A major group in a demographically minor province, the residents of Biak-Numfor can scarcely claim much attention on the basis of their numbers alone. But far from representing an isolated anomaly, the dynamics described in this study illuminate possibilities inherent, if suppressed, in the production of more hegemonic conceptions of identity, value, space, and time. These possibilities are systemic, but they are also historical. An ability to think the limits of modern society is needed today more than ever, when the conditions that shaped the narratives inherited from Hegel, Marx, and others seem poised radically to change.

Watching Television with Sister Sally

Indeed, changes already have begun to register. In recent years, more than a few academics and popular pundits have begun to wonder whether the "regime of representation" associated with the modern nation-state has reached its limits (Cohen 1998: 10; Mann 1996). Not only can analysts point to the internal limits of totalizing narratives of the nation; they can also point to the forces that are depriving national polities of forms of sovereignty with which they have long been associated. But to take this state of affairs, signalled by the growing importance of institutions like the United Nations, the International Monetary Fund, and the European Union, as utterly novel is to obscure the particular history of contemporary political formations. As Tilly (1990) has sought to demonstrate, the Western model of the nation-state can itself be approached as the product of historical and geographical contingencies that led to the recognition of one of an array of alternative political constellations as the most effective for the acquisition and retention of power. It is not my aim to evaluate Tilly's thesis but merely to point out that an argument like this necessarily becomes possible once we move beyond the evolutionary paradigms that have shaped conventional treatments of the nation. Others who have attempted alternative methods of modeling the history and structure of the contemporary global order point us to similar conclusions. It is less that the world of nation-states is just now giving way to a globalized order than that this world never existed in the form classical theorists presumed it to take (see, for example, Cohen 1998; Mann 1996; Sassen 1999). It may seem that the national order whose limits New Order Biaks mobilized has reached its limits; but then again, this order may never have enjoyed the autonomy some analysts presumed it to possess.

This is not to say that significant changes are not afoot in the broader contexts that shape political affiliations in places like Indonesia. One cannot understand what is happening in Indonesia today without taking into account the force of international opinion, which holds the threat that a return to the repression of the past will lead to the loss of much-needed aid. Like people elsewhere, Biaks and others in the newly renamed province of Papua have begun to participate energetically in global conversations about the environment, self-determination, world trade, and human rights. In assessing the impact of these conversations, one can no longer follow the protocols of earlier theorists of global processes, who assumed a homology between economic, cultural, and social transformations, accounting for the lingering of "traditional" forms of production through an appeal to the "needs" of world capital (see, for example, Wallerstein 1976). The effects of globalization, however widespread, are highly variable; one is unlikely to find political, economic, technological, and cultural changes proceeding in the same fashion or direction. Unpredictability, Appadurai (1996: 35) has argued, is in particular the challenge faced by analysts in forecasting the course of ethnic relations. But to Appadurai's account of how various communities create new imaginings of identity out of the global and national narratives to which they are exposed must be added an account of how communities not only choose different narratives, but also adopt different strategies of reading. Against those who assume that culture has become less a "habitus" than "an arena for conscious choice, justification, and representation" (Appadurai 1996: 44), this study has demonstrated that divergent systems of practice can implicitly shape how these self-conscious processes are approached. If the inhabitants of post-New Order Biak have anything in common with the men and women I came to know, they are appropriating global narratives in their own distinctive ways.

I cannot forecast the future of the antinational dynamics described in this study in the face of this changing global context. But my understanding of New Order Biak has given me a sense of the possibilities such an inquiry would need to take into account. Before turning this study's final page, I invite you to return to Sister Sally's household, to the guestroom I knew so well in the early 1990s, to join neighbors, relatives, and the visiting anthropologist in watching my hostess's television. Television, Appadurai notes, is one of the most powerful forces in the constitution of global "mediascapes," terrains of shared images and ideas. Mixing "the world of commodities and the world of news and politics" in their repertoires of "images, narratives, and ethnoscapes,"

> (m)ediascapes . . . tend to be image-centered, narrative-based accounts of strips of reality, and what they offer to those who experience and transform them is a series of elements (such as characters, plots, and textual forms) out of which scripts can be formed of imagined lives, their own as well as those of others living in other places. These scripts can and do get disaggregated into complex sets of metaphors by which people live . . . as they help to constitute narratives of the Other and proto-narratives of possible lives, fantasies that become prologemena to the desire for acquisition and movement. (Appadurai 1996: 35–36)

In broad strokes, Appadurai's model seems applicable in Biak. Yet in suggesting that televised images always fit into a narrative, he passes over a possible mode of consumption: a mode that stresses not the content but the structure of a story, offering a local evaluation of what counts as a plot.[2]

During the eighteen months I spent living in Sister Sally's house, I saw a range of programs on her black-and-white set. Some shows I watched with Henny, Sally's teenage niece, who seemed particularly enamoured of "Album Minggu," the hour-long pageant of Indonesian popular music videos, featuring a rich hybrid of Western production values and stereotypically "traditional" frills. Watching this show with a mesmerized Henny was a very different experience from watching the national news with her aunt, the constantly scoffing Sister Sally. The reports projected a false image of progress, Sally insisted; they never showed us Java's impoverished villages or Jakarta's slums. On such occasions, the guestroom was more or less empty; during other programs, Sally's house was full, sometimes to bursting.

The privatization of television in Indonesia was proceeding apace during the period of my research. But in provinces like Irian Jaya, unless one could afford a satellite dish one's choices were more or less limited to the offerings of the government network, a schedule dominated by documentaries on development or culture, with a plethora of Indonesian-language dramas thrown in for good measure. But late in the evening and on Sunday afternoon, the network showed programs produced in Europe or America; most of the Biaks I knew preferred these series, which drew the largest crowds to our house. So I sometimes joined a transfixed Sally in the wee hours of the morning to watch the European football matches that were periodically broadcast live.

The largest audience of neighbors and relations that ever assembled in Sally's guestroom came to watch Irian Jaya play Aceh for the gold medal in PON, the national competition described in chapter 3. But a crowd almost as large convened regularly for a program that Sally and others had named "Rosalia," after the drama's heroine. The show was a period soap opera produced in Brazil, dubbed in colloquial Indonesian. Our household was not alone in reserving Sunday afternoons for "Rosalia"; Biak City's streets and yards were empty between two and three P.M.; even the public minivans did not run.

"Rosalia" appealed to Biak audiences for perhaps understandable reasons. Those with whom I watched seemed to relate to the heroine's predicament, given their own experiences of arranged marriages and domestic strife. With their talent for tracing obscure ties of kinship, they had no trouble keeping Rosalia's complicated relationships straight. Less understandable, perhaps, was the appeal of other foreign programs—the British detective shows Sally and her family regularly devoured and "Three Fingers" (I: *Tiga Jari*), as we affectionately came to call an obscure American series about the invasion of long-digited aliens from outer space. Biak viewers seemed to identify in an unlikely fashion with the characters in such dramas, as evidenced by one friend's reaction to her first episode of "Twin Peaks." Delighted to spot a familiar Biak snack, she exclaimed, "Oh, so you have donuts in America, too!"

It was Sally Bidwam, the owner of the television, who most explicitly accounted for her taste in viewing. What she liked about foreign programs was not the wealthy lifestyles or novel gadgetry displayed on the screen but the fact that these programs followed a meaningful plot. The events of the narrative unfolded logically; Sally could follow what was happening, even to the point of anticipating the outcome. Indonesian movies and dramas seemed incoherent by comparison, jumping as they did from one theme to another. Sally simply could not figure them out.

At first glance, one is likely to be struck by the contradiction between Sally's pride at being a successful civil servant—and an adoptive mother who could make civil servants out of others—and her open disdain for Indonesian national culture. She may have criticized the images that flashed on her screen, but her willing participating in the Indonesian bureaucracy undoubtedly served the interests of the state. But as I hope the preceding chapters have demonstrated, this contradiction dissolves when one takes a closer look. At the same time that Sally's response to the national media expressed a self-conscious resistance to the forces of integration, they also illuminated the inadvertent outcome of the practices this study has described. By transforming the foreign into a source of power and value, people like Sally inscribed a sharp distinction between local, national, and, one might venture, dominant global perspectives. From their particular position in a national and global terrain, they demonstrated "the rendering (im)possible of (another) narrative." In raiding the Land of the Foreigners, New Order Biaks did more than create new meanings; they prevented other scripts from making sense.

Notes

Preface

1. On the establishment of the Indies' eastern boundary, see van der Veur 1966; Haga 1884, vol. 2: 28, 78. Through agreements with Tidore in 1660 and 1779, the Dutch East Indies company claimed the territory as a bulwark against the Spanish and English, who were then powerful rivals for the lucrative Indies trade. See van Baal 1989, vol. 2: 139.

Chapter One
On the Limits of Indoneasia

1. The New Order term for the separatists in Irian Jaya and Aceh was Gerakan Pengacau Keamanan (GPK), literally "Security Disrupter Movements." See Robinson 1998: 127. For a description of a flag raising attempted under the New Order, see *Tapol Bulletin* 1984a, b, c.

2. See Human Rights Watch 1998 and Rutherford 2001a.

3. Compare, for instance, a quote from Mydans's article with one from another article on Indonesia published in 1996. The same breathless commentary serves very different purposes.

> The elegant, taciturn princes of Java seem to have little in common with the otherworldly dancers of Hindu Bali, the long-eared Dayak tribesmen of Borneo, the seagoing pirates of the Spice Islands, or the Chinese traders who control the country's ports and warehouses . . . the idea of Indonesian unity is so elemental that it is defined as much as anything simply by the superimposition of a common tongue. (Mydans 1999: 3)

> Smoking volcanoes, rare animals, Sultan's palaces, mesmerizing gamelan music and puppet theaters, a fast growing economy that has transformed city skylines—no dearth of attractions here. (Crossette 1996: 1)

4. Statistics from the regency's department of information were also displayed at the annual development exhibition held in Biak on October 1–6, 1993. Official sources do not list Biak's population by ethnicity. However, the regency's population by religion was stated as 80,273 Protestants, 9,979 Moslems, 1,975 Catholics, 217 Buddhists, and 126 Hindus. Biaks are predominantly Protestant, as are immigrants from Ambon, Menado, and other parts of Irian. At the very most, Biak's population is 66 percent "local." See Anonymous 1992: 66.

5. In 1947, one colonial official claimed that illiteracy was "relatively scarce" on Biak and virtually nonexistent among men under the age of thirty-five. See de Bruyn 1948: 7. He later revised this estimate downward. Although Protestant missionaries published materials in Biak, the language in which literate Biaks read in the 1940s would most frequently have been Malay.

6. Garuda Indonesian Airlines suspended these stopovers in Biak in 1994 after acquiring jets with greater fuel capacities. For more on the development of the pro-

vincial economy in Irian Jaya, see Garnaut and Manning 1974, and Manning and Rumbiak 1991.

7. See Steedly 1993: 51, 53–54. The first missionary to the Karo highlands of Sumatra arrived in 1890; final authority in the region was ceded to the Dutch in 1907. The coastal region of Deli, which became a lucrative site for European plantations, did not have a "significant European presence" until 1863. See also Keane 1997a: 42. The first posts in the interior of West Sumba were not opened until 1908; the first missionary did not arrive in Anakalang, the setting of Keane's study, until 1933.

8. Anthony Smith lists Indonesia in the company of "some third world states that clearly cannot be termed nations" (1986: 7–8). By this, he means that Indonesia, like Nigeria and India, lacks a dominant "ethnie" around which a nation can coalesce. Hobsbawm's analysis is somewhat more complicated. Third-world movements discovered the nation too late, as it were. Real nationalism emerged by way of the interests of a nineteenth-century European ethnic bourgeoisie seeking to partake in the spoils of an emerging capitalist system by insuring that the state's language of commerce and rule would be their tongue. With English now the dominant transnational language of business, nationalism in its authentic form is a thing of the past.

9. See O'Leary 1998 on Gellner's evolving "philosophy of history."

10. For critiques of Weber, see Tilly 1979; Margadant 1984.

11. For a discussion of the assumptions about language and identity prefigured by nationalist ideologies and "downloaded" into the work of theorists like Anderson and Gellner, see Kroskrity 2000, esp. 30; see also Silverstein 2000. Anthropological studies of literacy have much to tell us on the divergent meanings of reading. See chapter 4.

12. The following account is culled in part from the depositions collected in Anonymous 1998.

13. Orlove and Bauer distinguish the "appeal of the alien," a widely encountered predilection for the novel, from the "allure of the foreign," which they describe as a modern phenomenon implicated in colonial relations of power.

14. Swadling (1996: 109–110) goes so far as to suggest that Tidore's claim to New Guinea was a colonial invention, dating from the Netherlands' first formal treaty with the sultan in 1660. For more on Tidore and the neighboring sultanate of Ternate, see van Fraassen 1987; Henley 1993. See also Reid 1993.

15. Lindstrom (1993) analyzes the interest in cargo cults as a symptom of Western commodity fetishism. See also Kaplan 1995. Placed in the context of a long history of anticolonial activism, the so-called Tuka movement was "neither [after] cargo nor [was it] cult." For a similar reframing of the Koreri movement, see chapter 6.

16. My understanding of the term "figure" draws on Marin's (1984: 23–24) discussion of several passages from Husserl's *Ideas: A General Introduction to Pure Phenomenology*, which focus on possible perceptions of Dürer's "The Knight, Death, and the Devil." On the one hand, one can engage in the "normal perception of which the correlate is the 'engraved print' as a thing, this print in the portfolio. This perception is positional: it is the certainty of belief whose correlate is the real." In contrast to the form of belief associated with this perception—one that would either affirm or negate the perception as reality or "mere illusion," Marin, following Husserl, posits another mode, that which would fix upon "what is portrayed 'in the picture'—more precisely,

in the '*depicted*' realities." As an example of what Husserl calls "the neutrality modification of the perception," the mode in which a representational figure is perceived escapes the sheer alternatives of negation and affirmation.

> The figure is literally the product of the utopic figure. It does not "cancel" the other thing it depicts while positing it in the certitude of the "not." But neither does it affirm it completely in the stronger reality of acceptance. When I contemplate aesthetically "the Knight, Death, and the Devil," I perceive the figures neither as the negation of the objects they depict as positing them as not being, nor as the affirmation of their very being, in the way psychologizing or objectifying thought might do regarding Death and the Devil. I perceive them as objects depicting *other* things, as this by which something else is depicted, as the replacement implying "presence and absence" of what is figured, using Pascal's terminology, excluding both reality and nothingness. (Marin 1984: 24)

In using the term "figure" to describe the European concept of Utopia, Marin emphasizes this characteristic of "neutrality," that which lies between affirmation and negation, as something that is an effect of the fictional character of More's text. But he also argues that historically specific social contradictions are bridged within the figure. In the same way—if not as an effect of the same processes—Koreri can be approached as a figure, a depiction of the "neutral" space of contradiction between the two modes of producing identity in which Biaks engaged.

17. Bull (1999: 76) explicitly refers to the myth of Manarmakeri in this regard.

Chapter Two
Frontier Families

1. For more on the activities undertaken by Johannes van Hasselt Society, see Kamma 1977: 534.

2. Founded in 1878, the Depok seminary was funded by Dutch Protestants and run in collaboration with a consortium of mission societies active in the Indies. A total of seven "Papoeas" attended between 1892 and 1915; they had classmates from Sunda, Java, Madura, Nias, the Batak highlands, the Dayak areas of Borneo, and Sangir (Het Seminarie te Depok 1895). In the seminary's 1892 annual report, we learn that the students spent their free time playing cricket and croquet and maintaining the grounds, and that each young man was issued a violin upon arrival (Anonymous 1892: 15).

3. Petrus traveled to Biak with Philippus, another native evangelist. The warm welcome they received reminded the young Christians of Paul and Barnabas's reception in Lystra and Derbe, as described in the Bible; the people "asked questions and listened tirelessly until deep in the night" (Kamma 1977: 618).

4. Ibid. See also Utrechtsche Zendingvereeniging 1909. Children's books included Hoog and Bassecour Caan 1917; and van der Roest 1921. Petrus's story also figured prominently in the society's external and internal journals, *Berichten van de Utrechtsche Zendingsvereeniging* and *Handelingen der Utrechtsche Zendingsvereeniging*.

5. But see McKinnon 1991 and 1995 for a far more nuanced account of mother's brother's daughter marriage and its implications for social status.

6. In Adatrechtsbundels 1955a: 149, Kamma points out that many kerets are

named according to their position in the village. One man told me that his keret's name meant "House Next to the W.C." Other keret names for which I obtained glosses include Rumsowek (House from the Village of Sowek) and Womsiwor (Slave Who Sings). Many keret names derive from Tidoran titles, such as Kapisa, Sanadi, and Mayor. See Adatrechtsbundels 1955a: 149; 1955b: 536.

7. And in some cases, female descendants had the same right. Some consultants told me that a woman gained rights to land at her brother's discretion. Others told me that daughters automatically received a share.

8. Cf. Platenkamp 1984 on how a "cognatic" principle destabilizes the duality established by marriage.

9. Unlike the Biaks, however, the Waropen believed that "the son of a sister should marry the daughter of a brother" (Held 1957: 119). On the use of foreign goods among groups in the Bird's Head, see Elmberg 1968; Miedema 1984; Haenen 1991.

10. "They take the house by surprise. No one expects an attack. Chaos, shrieking. The women flee, grabbing little children; the old-timer left to tend the house does what he can. He speaks persuasively, threateningly. The men sail off. After their departure, when the inhabitants gradually assemble, they are missing someone. It is Nosseni [the boy later named Petrus]. They search, they call all in vain, for Nosseni is and remains gone" (van Hasselt n.d.: 14).

11. But see van Gendt 1954: 19. The *Kankain Karkara Biak*, Biak's regional council, ordered the subdistrict's villagers to move their houses onto shore. G. J. van Gendt disagreed with this policy.

12. Shiraishi interprets the multiplication of Java's sitting rooms as the sign of a finely graduated hierarchy of masculine positions, noting that she has never seen a Javanese home with a front and back kitchen. By contrast, many of the Biak women I knew had three or more hearths, where their families spent much of their time. Note, however, that Javanese houses often have a narrow passageway beside them leading to a back door used by close friends and family (Ben Zimmer, personal communication).

13. Kamma (1972: 74–75) includes a version of this legend recorded by a Biak evangelist.

14. Unusually for an Austronesian language, the Biak term for "person" is gendered. *Snon kaku* means literally "a real man."

15. Besides sago, a semidomesticated palm whose marrow is a popular starch, Biak farmers cultivate taro, a low-maintenance tuber with a long growing period. Taro takes from six to nine months to ripen and can be picked for up to eight weeks. Between harvests, women feed their families sago and taro provided by relatives. Families plant fruit and betel-nut palms to mark their former plots, which ideally are left fallow for six years. Although Biaks also grow cassava, sweet potatoes, spinach, squash, and peppers, taro is Biak's principle crop. On Biak's "broadly-based, diverse, and seemingly rather prosperous non-monetary or subsistence economy," see Engineering Consulting Association, Japan 1990: 32.

16. This mother's appeal to her indebted children matched the motto that stood over a village church built in the 1950s: "Yafrur au radine—rosai wafrur be aya?" ("I made you as you are—what have you done for me?").

17. These are the terms of reference for ego's relatives related through *srar*: *me* (mother's brother or father's sister's husband), *mebin* (father's sister or mother's brother's wife), *fno* (sister's child [male ego] or brother's child [female ego]), and cross-

cousins or *napirem* (mother's brother's children or father's sister's children). Those related through same-sex siblings or *naek* include *kma beba* (father's older brother), *kma kasun* (father's younger brother), *sna beba* (mother's older sister), *sna kasun* (mother's younger sister), *romawa* (brother's son [male ego] or sister's son [female ego]), *inai* (brother's daughter [male ego] or sister's daughter [female ego]), and parallel cousins, who were equated with *naek* (father's brother's children or mother's sister's children). Terms for affines included *inbanyo* (wife's mother or husband's mother), *manbanyo* (wife's father or husband's father), *inbansus* (son's wife), *manbansus* (daughter's husband), *rifio* (wife's brother or sister's husband), and *rifiobin* (husband's sister or brother's wife). I should note, however, that my informants tended to use terms of address when discussing the workings of Biak families in the abstract.

18. Kamma (1972: 11) refers to Biak's marriage system as "bilateral house exogamy."

19. Many of the polygamists I encountered were successful civil servants. These men also were the most likely to violate the New Order's family planning policies. The Dutch government, eager to expand the Papuan elite, instituted salary policies that promoted fecundity. The largest families I encountered were remarkably successful by local standards, with nearly every son and daughter a student or civil servant.

20. A young Biak who sought political asylum in Holland in 1984 fled from Jakarta to Singapore by bus, foot, and motorboat. He told me that he was willing to risk such an odyssey because he knew that his sister would help him once he reached Europe.

21. Jens (1916: 410) could only guess at the meaning of the ceremony. "The sisters eat the blood from the boy's penis; would this not suggest (given the fact that matriarchy exists on Biak) that all the offspring engendered by the young man will belong to the women who have rights to them?" Jens referred to places in Biak where adult men drank the initiate's blood mixed with palm wine, a practice he viewed as strengthening the masculine solidarity of the keret. The boys who survived the painful operation without crying out were known as *k'bor*. My consultants never mentioned blood-letting, although they did describe other components of what they called the *wor kabor-insos*.

22. Forty-four such rituals are described in Kamma 1976: 220–250.

23. Kamma (1939–41: 4:326–328) describes the Biak migrants of Besewer as dancing in a "magic circle" to protect children during dangerous transitions.

24. Feuilletau de Bruyn (1920: 52) includes examples of child marriages arranged for "economic reasons" during times of scarcity.

25. *Fan-fan* bears the connotation of using food for domesticating purposes. One calls a dog that belongs to someone a *rofan*, literally "thing that is fed."

26. Male heirs usually inherited a *binawe*. A man from West Biak explained that the "keret chief" should oversee the collection and distribution of bridewealth for his keret, but he could not describe an instance when this had occurred. Another West Biak man told me that the "divider" (I: *pembagi*) had to relieve the parents of their claims to their daughter by presenting them with two gifts of porcelain: a breast washer bowl (B: *inbansus*) and a big-belly vase, shaped like a pregnant woman (B: *sabaron*). People in North Biak said that the *pembagi* could forgo this prestation as long as he or she gave half of the bridewealth to the woman's parents. In the marriage exchanges I documented, practices varied. I heard of a South Biak bride's representa-

tives requesting an *inbansus* of Rp. 300,000 (roughly $150) in cash from the groom's parents. Supposedly, the family needed the money to put a tombstone on the woman's grandmother's grave. See also chapter 4.

27. Parents sometimes granted an unmarried daughter the right to the lion's share of her younger sister's bridewealth. An average woman's bridewealth at the time of my research included one *ben bepon*, one *ben ahemer*, 21 *ben beba*, 10 *sarak*, 40 serving bowls, 50 dinner bowls, and Rp. 500,000; a more prominent family might demand 5 *ben bepon*, 25 *ben beba*, 10 *sarak*, 200 mixed serving and dinner bowls, and Rp. 3,000,000. In 1992, porcelain dinner bowls cost roughly Rp. 2,500 ($1.75); serving bowls cost Rp. 4,000 ($2.00). A *ben beba* may cost from Rp. 60,000 ($30) to Rp. 200,000 ($100) in the local antique shops. Biak City merchants charged as much as Rp. 1,000,000 ($500) for a *more-more* vase. Given the limited circulation of money on the island, the collection of bridewealth was a communal effort. In the 1950s, fearing a drop in birth rates, zealous civil servants and customary leaders called on families to destroy their *samfar*, the increasingly rare shell bracelets that once constituted the highest-ranking items.

Occasionally, a bride's family demanded an appliance. Sewing machines were a fairly common component of bridewealth, although most Biaks drew the line at "johnsons": the outboard motors used in the large outriggers that had taken the place of the trade and war vessels of the past.

28. In West Biak, each member of the groom's entourage took home a porcelain plate filled with refreshments.

29. Rarely, families held a non-Christian *wofwofer* ritual instead of a church wedding. In such cases, people tended to assume that there was something shameful about the union, as when an old man married a young girl he had seduced.

30. Kamma (1976: 227) reports that some families used to tie up their daughters to deliver them to their new husband's home just to show their affines how much the bride hated to leave her kin.

31. See Kamma 1972: 12. Kamma gives the Biak terms for "the part that returns," *bar bekaber*, and "the part that sinks," *bar bemsar*. He reports that roughly three-quarters of the *ararem* is not returned during the wedding feast.

32. In West Biak, members of the bride's retinue reportedly carried cardboard figures of valuables: the hosts had to replace a mock machete with a real blade, an image of a vase with a real piece of porcelain. See van den Berg (1981: 38–43) for a description of the festivities commemorating the Dutch queen's birthday in the 1950s, which included a night parade with special lamps shaped like churches and boats.

33. Kamma (1981, vol. 1: 288) suggests that those who waved sticks were young men with whom the bride had flirted as a girl.

34. When my consultants described the exchanges conducted at wor and umbanbin, they usually used the Indonesian word *ganti*, which roughly means to replace, to substitute, or to compensate. They distinguished among the following Biak expressions: *yabob* (B: I sell); *yakobes* (I buy); *yabuk* (I give), a form also used in the sentence "Yabuk saswar ma swaruser yena" ("I give my love and my thoughts"); *yasmai* (I take, find or get); *yasuba* (I give an offering with both hands outstretched).

35. My friend Ricky went so far as to associate female adultery with the lasting bonds between women and their families, which prevented young brides from feeling fully absorbed into their husbands' keret and left them freer to do as they pleased.

36. I frequently encountered this tension between perspectives, as when another man described a ceremony needed to sever the ties between an uncle and his dead sister's children—and added as an afterthought that with the payment of the sister's bridewealth, this had in fact already been done.

37. Not to mention couples. Kamma (1976: 221) reports that some parents were forced to sell their children to pay their debts to their siblings.

38. Pieces of porcelain in Biak were classified but not individually named. Weiner (1992: 102–103) suggests that this factor could serve to limit the life span of social rankings.

39. See also Malinowski [1922] 1961: 170. Sahlins (1972: 174) raises then dismisses the possibility that Mauss was depicting the potlatch as "sublimated warfare," before turning to the end of Mauss's essay, which better supports his argument that the gift is the guarantor of reason and peace.

40. Cf. Weiner 1976: 225; Munn 1986: 140; Battaglia 1991: 38; McKinnon 1991: 110; Hoskins 1993: 18. Despite the references to "ties of blood" mentioned above, I encountered nothing resembling these accounts of conception, which stress the contribution of matrilineal and/or patrilineal "substances."

41. Land sales often pitted village men against brothers working or studying in distant cities. "Tribal war" (I: *perang suku*) was a term some officials used to describe the inter- and intra-keret disputes that rocked the outskirts of Biak City in the early 1990s.

42. Cf. van Gendt 1954: 2. "I must point to the danger that exists for every new government official. . . . In the first months he is deluged with '*asal-usul.*' . . . He is asked to sign these texts as 'seen.' If a text is signed, the person concerned spreads the story that the government has sanctioned these origin stories. Before he knows it, he is entangled in a long-standing feud between two kerets, which each claims the honor of being '*Mansren Manu*' [Lord of the Village]."

43. Cf. Barnes 1962; de la Fontaine 1973; Keesing 1987: 439–440.

44. Women also tended to be versed in the location of rocks and trees that, along with these narratives, validated their children's claims to land.

45. No master narrative linked the various clan histories I collected. In Sor, I was told that the Rumaikiek keret was a long-lost branch of the Yensenem keret in Opiaref, East Biak. In Opiaref, the Yensenems told me that the opposite was true. Clans still living in the interior offered the only narratives that traced keret ancestry to an animal: a pig or a tree marsupial that had drunk human sperm in a garden where a couple had just had sex. Nothing in Biak compared to what Weiner (1976: 46) found in the Trobriands, for example, where a clan's ancestors are said to have emerged from holes in the ground.

46. The South Biak Women's Union (Persatuan Wanita Biak Selatan) was part of the Irian Jaya Evangelical Church, or GKI (see chapter 1). There were Women's Union branches in virtually every village on Biak.

47. This sort of gender crossing was not uncommon. One woman told me that her younger sisters often praised her for being just like a brother: extravagant and strong. I knew one lesbian couple on Biak. One of the women was a civil servant; the other, a farmer, was known as a *snon bin*, a "masculine woman" whose dress, body language, and talents (fishing, hunting, building houses) marked her as male. For more on *snon bin*, see chapter 5.

48. Cf. Lacan 1988: 170 on the aggression that can prevail between unmediated equals.

49. See de Clerq and Schmeltz 1893: plates 34–36; van Baaren 1968. Biaks believed that each person has two spirits: the *rur* or "soul" and the *nin* or "shadow." Through sorcery and in dreams, *nin* detached themselves from living persons. My informants suggested that one of the reasons their grandparents made *korwars* and destroyed property was to contain the dead person's wandering *nin*. Eventually, the *nin* retreated to join the *rur* in the firmament or *nanggi*.

50. See de Bruyn Kops 1850: 194. "At the news that the hongi fleet was coming, women and children fled in little boats, taking everything of any worth to the inner bay or the mainland in order to elude the rapacious passengers and crew."

Chapter Three
The Poetics of Surprise

1. Compare Michelle Rosaldo's treatment of a similar incident (1980: 68–69, 92–98).

2. The closely related word *sembarangan* is given the following definition: "1 at random. *Jangan ~ buang sampah* Do not throw garbage anywhere you feel like it. *Cakapnya ~ saja* He says anything that comes to his head. 2 just anyone, anything. *Ahsan bukan pelukis ~* Ahsan is not just any old painter" (Echols and Shadily 1989: 496).

3. Feuilletau de Bruyn (1916: 391) includes a list of women's insults and the fines demanded of those who employed them; cf. Kulick 1992a: 114–117.

4. In the early twentieth century, Feuilletau de Bruyn (1933: 514) observed that landowners were liable for any mishap that might befall a visitor. This practice led Feuilletau de Bruyn to conclude that it would be better for Biaks not to own land at all. See also van Gendt 1954: 144–145.

5. Van Hasselt and van Hasselt (1947: 170–171) define *boryas* as "The packet containing 'or' which is affixed to spears and other weapons." *Or* is "[m]agical power. An invisible power, which protects and helps someone and, at the same time, does harm to others by making them sick and so forth. An 'or' is also attributed to trees and animals. . . . This 'or' helps the hunter by making the prey stand still and the fisherman by making the fish come to the surface of the sea, but when the catch is poor punishes anyone who laughs at the aforementioned hunter or fishermen with swollen arms and legs. It is then said: 'or biedi min i' = his 'or' has struck him. Or is to be compared with the better known 'mana.'" See also van Hasselt 1929.

6. One man furtively told me his magic word, which I recognized as an Arabic term from an Islamic prayer.

7. Others told me the spirit was male. Kamma's data casts the star as a feminine force. Called *samfar*, the shell bracelets once used as bridewealth stood for the feminine figure of Sampari (Kamma 1976: 224).

8. Interestingly, my informants use the Indonesian verb *kontrol* (inspect) to describe the messenger fish's responsibilities. This term is common in the idiom spoken by government officials.

9. The literature on speaking in tongues refers to this practice as xenoglossia (Bauman 1983: 27, 82–83; see also chapter 6).

10. Passengers leaving or coming to Bali via Biak went through immigration in Denpasar. After landing on Biak, they walked from the tarmac up a stairway and across a walkway to the international transit lounge. Passengers were not allowed to leave the building, which no one could enter without a special pass.

11. I have divided each part into utterances, according to when Amandeus paused to take a breath.

12. Cf. de Bruyn Kops 1850: 231–232 for a description of such a dance.

13. Cf. Siegel 1978: 25.

14.

Kadwor	Tip
Myundiso rwamandiyasa yakofen bayir ro mob byarek roro.	It is a good thing that you have come so I can tell you about the place he stayed.
Fuar	Root
Awino inonaye myundiso rwamandiyasa yakofen bayir ro *Amerika* mob byarek roro.	*Mother, young woman,* it is a good thing that you have come so I can tell you about the place *America* stayed.

15. If anything, this original song negates forward motion by dropping words.

16. Compare Fox 1974; Keane 1997a: 100. Dialectal variants are deployed in these settings as a means of evoking a lost linguistic unity; they also allow ritual speakers who have mastered more than one to demonstrate their knowledge of nonlocal knowledge. I thank Ben Zimmer for this point.

17. Feld (1990: 245) notes that the Western assumptions embedded in the term "heterophony" have led some analysts to adopt the term "echopolyphony" "to describe styles involving overlapped repetition of similar melodic and textual elements, just split seconds apart." Wor differs from the ritual wailing described by Feld in that the entire chorus sings a single text. For a more detailed discussion of wor music, which "shows little obvious relationship to singing reported and published from elsewhere in Irian Jaya," see Yampolsky and Rutherford 1996: 10–11.

18. *Kawai kumora*, the singer explained, means "radio" or "telephone"; the term is derived from *kawat gumola*, Indonesian for "fish barb wire," the pieces of heavy cable that Biak anglers tie close to a hook.

19. Keane (1997d: 53) argues that the use of Indonesian in ritual speech may "undermine" Anakalangese priests "in ways they do not recognize" by treating local institutions as "instances for which there are equivalents in the vocabulary of the nation."

20. There was something surreal about the scene in the transit lounge, in the sense described by Bruner and Kirshenblatt-Gimblett (1995: 464). "If farm laborers were to dance in the performance, if bus drivers were to be on the lawn, or if the Maasai were to have tea with the tourists and talk to them in English or to graze the cows on the lawns, then the 'picture' would be operating on different principles, not in a realist mode so much as a surrealistic one—that is, a mode predicated on jarring juxtapositions following the logic of dreams."

21. People made up new songs about Trikora, the Indonesian campaign to "liberate" West Irian, a local announcer reported in the history of yospan he read at the

beginning of contests. I have never heard any yospan songs or read any lyrics on this topic. I was told that Papuan separatists on Biak had sung yospan (and wor) to prepare for their attacks on Indonesian troops.

22. In the early 1990s, many different kinds of music could be heard in Biak. In most of Biak's music stores, one could purchase anywhere from three to six different cassettes of yospan songs. Irian pop music, a subset of the thriving Indonesian music industry, was extremely popular among people of all ethnic backgrounds. Professionally produced, these cassettes included songs in local languages transformed into reggae or soft rock. Pop Irian, along with Western rock and reggae, blared from public vehicles whose young drivers were either Biaks or migrants from Sulawesi or Java. Drivers in town worked hard to keep up with musical fashions to attract homeward-bound urban shoppers to their named and gaily decorated minivans.

The church music I encountered ranged from locally composed hymns, to selections from the ubiquitous *Nyanyian Rohani dan Mazmur* (the Indonesian Protestant hymnal compiled by Isaac Semuel Kijne, a hero of western New Guinea's Protestant mission), to complex choral arrangements of Western classics like Handel's *Messiah*. Music was a central component of worship and presented yet another dimension to the circulation of musical texts—among the island's predominantly female choirs. For an example, see chapter 4; also see Yampolsky and Rutherford 1996.

23. For a transcription from the pre-yospan Biak musical group Mansyouri, see Anonymous 1978: 1.

24. My friend had a photocopy of Feuilletau de Bruyn 1920.

25. On the *yosim pancar* team, see *Cendrawasih Pos* 1993e, f, h, i, j.

26. In Feuilletau de Bruyn's discussion of "native warfare," the Dutch lieutenant describes how Biaks used stealth to overcome their enemies. During the hours when most adults were gardening or fishing, raiders would sneak from the forest and take hostages. Feuilletau de Bruyn's patrol had "much success," he admits, with a similar method. Not surprisingly, Biaks mistook his expedition for a slave raid (Feuilletau de Bruyn 1916: 264–266).

See also van Hasselt 1916. As a result of the military action, ninety prisoners were jailed in Manokwari, and another sixty were sent to Ternate. Besides instilling "fear of the government" in Biak hearts, Feuilletau de Bruyn managed to unearth a conspiracy that accounted for the murder. It was the *mon*, or shamans, who supposedly arranged to have the teacher killed to drive the Ambonese evangelists from the island. That way they could continue their "deceitful" vocation without further interference. My Biak consultants injected some humor into the brutal episode. When the patrol came to Sor, one man escaped the lieutenant's notice by climbing a tree. However, he foiled his own escape when the soldiers pulled out some tobacco and started to divide it. "Hey! I get some, too!" he called down, forgetting where he was.

Chapter Four
The Authority of Absence

1. In the event, the household we visited did not have any porcelain to sell. Instead, Fritz Rumorek offered one of his own, which the Wambrurs promised to replace at a later date.

2. The Wambrurs rejected this request on principle—"not, of course, because we couldn't afford it," Fritz was eager to assure me.

3. I will not go into the commentary generated by Helly's death. When she told me about the tragedy, Decky's aunt alluded to the way in which the sins of the young woman's father and stepmother had been visited on the daughter. The Karwors, no doubt, would have contested this account. In the end, Decky married a woman who was Javanese, like his mother.

4. It is worth noting that the case that Baker analyzes comes from Tidore, a place with long-standing historical relation to Biak; see Andaya 1993.

5. See Jakobson 1987: 71 on selection and combination as "the two basic modes of arrangement used in verbal behavior." Although this approach to signification is generally associated with Saussure, who focused on semantic meaning, the broader functional modes of speech addressed by pragmatic analysis are no less dependent on conventional distinctions, in the form of what Silverstein (1976: 25) refers to as "rules of use." See also Benveniste [1958] 1971.

6. Errington (1998: 63) characterizes Gellner's understanding of the relationship between national languages and modernity thus: "Modern national languages are by this account exoteric, contextually uninflected means for autonomous thought and discourse, the verbal grounds for distinctively modern stances and the perspective of what Nagel (1986) has called a 'view from nowhere.'" This view "can be thought of as keying to the referential capacities of language, and as corresponding to what Michael Silverstein calls standard languages' ideologically privileged 'functional utility . . . as a means of representation or instrument of denotation' (1996: 285)."

7. On the possibility of multiple linguistic ideologies concerning translation, see Rafael [1988] 1993. On translation, untranslatability, and authority, see Benjamin [1923] 1968 and Derrida 1985. On the difficulties of translating Christian texts, see Renck 1990.

8. For the results of efforts to apply the model in Austronesian-speaking parts of Melanesia, see Liep 1991; Jolly 1991; Battaglia 1991; for a critique based on comparisons among southern New Guinea societies, see Knauft 1996. I consider Biak social organization in the context of Southeast Asian and Melanesian models in chapter 2.

9. "Business" is not an important sphere of action for contemporary Irian Jayans, as it is in Papua New Guinea. See Rutherford 2001b.

10. It is telling that the most valuable component of the porcelain used in bride-wealth is called the "head" (see chapter 2).

11. Those who reflected on the tendency also described the need to prepare youngsters to talk with visitors. Nonreciprocal exchanges between Indonesian-speaking children and their regional-language-speaking parents are, of course, quite common in Indonesia.

12. Mr. Wampur was one of several Biaks I met who told me that they had served as an informant for F. C. Kamma when he was conducting research on Biak during the early 1950s. His notebooks may have dated from this work (Kamma 1972).

13. John Comaroff (personal communication) has usefully pointed out that the multiplication of images and strategies that I observed in Biak is inherent to the workings of hegemony, as Gramsci (1971) formulated the concept.

14. The potency associated with the Bible in this story recalls the agency that Biaks sometimes attributed to antique porcelain and ancestral skulls; cf. Hoskins 1993: 127.

15. An Indonesian word, *slamat*, is used for "saved."

16. Benjamin ([1923] 1968: 70) refers to the dual nature of the question of whether a work is translatable. "Either: Will an adequate translator ever be found among the totality of its readers? Or, more pertinently, Does its nature lend itself to translation and, therefore, in view of the significance of its mode, call for it?" But he also notes in the same essay that it is the "hallmark of bad translation" when the translator's goal is to do nothing but transmit information. For Benjamin, it is the "nucleus of pure language" which is the ultimate target of translation; what calls for translation and at the same time resists it is a kernel of untranslatability, residing in the bond between content and code. In Bert's poem, the resources of linguistic difference provided a figure of incommensurability—the historically situated, fetishistically elaborated site through which, I am arguing, claims to authority in contemporary Biak were made.

17. Bert told me to disregard the Biak names scribbled on two of them: Mr. Fakiar and Bert's cousin had somehow managed to sign these signs. Mr. Fakiar had taken the first card from Bert's aunt, along with a letter that Manarmakeri had written to Bert's ancestor. Scratching out the name of this nineteenth-century Koreri leader, Mr. Fakiar had replaced it with his own. Manarmakeri told Bert to go to the copy shop to find evidence that would help him retrieve the letter.

18. The original inhabitants of the small island were like the original inhabitants of Canaan, who were chased away by the Israelites. Others would say that the Land of Canaan was really Biak as a whole. A slippage between local and global versions was very common when it came to the myth of Manarmakeri. Uncle Bert was not, of course, the first to identify his group with the Israelites; see, for example, Markowitz 1996.

19. Bert gave me many examples of local and global events the mythical ancestor had helped him to predict and understand. According to Bert, Manarmakeri had made the "smart bombs" by which the Americans won the Gulf War. Visits to the small island were never without significance. An Italian had a dictionary that listed the first Bethlehem as this place. An Israeli whose surname sounded like Bert's turned out to be "Grandfather" in disguise. Bert had been ready for my visit well in advance. When he heard the noise of our outrigger, Bert knew that "Grandmother" had arrived.

20. Historically, the belief in Koreri has tended to survive the disappointment with which uprisings on Biak have ended; criticism of a particular prophet does not imply a critique of the dream (cf. Kermode 1967: 8).

21. See chapter 5 on the animosity of earlier Koreri prophets toward teachers, church leaders, and government officials.

Chapter Five
Messianic Modernities

1. Cf. Picard 1993: 95 n. 15: "To some extent, the way the Indonesian government used international tourism was not unlike the way it had been used earlier by the Dutch colonial government: in both instances, tourism turned out to be one of the most effective means to restore a respectability badly discredited by the turmoil that had given birth to the new regime."

2. Cf. Kulick 1992b: 23; Dove 1988.

3. Between 1969 and 1989, the number of foreign visitors to Indonesia as a whole increased from 86,000 to 1,626,000. In 1989, the Indonesian economy earned US$1.28 billion in tourism receipts; as of 1989, the central government was forecasting that by 1993, Indonesia would host 2.5 million tourists and receive US$2.25 billion in tourism receipts (Picard 1993: 80).

4. Nikanor's song shared many elements with wor I recorded in Opiaref and Ambroben, and on Wundi. These contemporary versions bear strong similarities to the three versions of the song included in Kamma's unpublished papers at the Hendrik Kraemer Institute. In addition to these texts from Biak, Numfor, and the Raja Ampat Island, Kamma drew on Hartweg's (1932–33) German translation of a song transcribed in Korido for his 1972 study.

5. I include excerpts from both the kadwor and the fuar of the two songs. Following the convention established in chapter 3, the words added to make the fuar are italicized.

6. Some versions of the myth add an episode in which Padawakan and his family anger Manarmakeri. In one, the cross-cousin offends the Old Man by refusing to save any fish for his wife. In another, the wife herself offends the hero by expressing resentment at the bother of having to serve him. In still another, Manarmakeri's relatives fail to follow his instructions in cooking the fish. If they had shown Manarmakeri more respect, these relatives would have been able to throw the skeleton in the water then watch it transform itself into a school of living fish.

7. According to Bert, the prophet discussed in the preceding chapter, the Star descended on an iron ladder, perhaps like Jacob's ladder in the Bible.

8. Van Hasselt (1914: 92) translates the Biak term mares as "Mal.: njamplong, Calophyllum Inophyllum, L." My informants used the Indonesian term bentangur, "k.o. tree growing on the sea shore." See Echols and Shadily 1989: 70.

9. Kamma (1972: 63, 79) suggests that the reference to the Mamberamo River in this part of the song testifies to the great age of the verses. Mamberamo means "those who have become mon (in this case: dead persons)" or the "gate to the underworld." His informants told him that Biaks originally came to the island from a coastal area far to the east, near present-day Jayapura. At that point, the Mamberamo would have lain on the western horizon.

10. Studies of cargoism have often taken for granted the value of Western commodities; see, for example, Lawrence [1964] 1971: 223–232.

11. A translation of the book of Genesis followed in 1875. The New Guinea mission's first Papuan-language publication was a "Mefoorsche" hymnal, produced in 1860, five years after the first missionaries' arrival (van Hasselt 1888: 61). The first chapters of the Bible to be translated were Psalms and the Gospel of Mark, which were both published in 1871 (ibid.: 63). Given their frequent encounters with Moluccan and European traders, it seems possible that the inhabitants of Doreh Bay were already familiar with elements of the Islamic and/or Christian tradition when the missionaries began their work there. Along with a version of the myth of Manarmakeri, Goudswaard recounts two other Papuan legends, whose characters reminded him of Adam and Eve and the Virgin Mary (1863: 84–92).

12. Brother Hartweg sold his Biak students copies of this and other storybooks written or translated by F.J.F. van Hasselt (Hartweg 1925a, 1926).

13. Genesis 22:10–14, Revised Standard Version. The text in parentheses appears as footnotes in the original.

14. Kierkegaard puts words in Abraham's mouth. "Foolish boy, do you believe I am your father? I am an idolater. Do you believe this is God's command? No, it is my own desire" ([1843]1985: 45).

15. In some versions, this action in and of itself demonstrated Manarmakeri's power (Thimme 1976: 18–19).

16. This is how Cixous (1993: 38) refers to death.

17. See Weiner's (1976: 235) speculations on the relationship in Western societies between the rise of religious institutions and capitalism and the decline in "symbolic referents to individual concerns with origins and death." "Within this trend, I suggest that, when men seek avenues to create their own transcendence that are free of assurances for the perpetuation of life, the value of women declines, tied to the decline in the value placed on life itself." See also Bloch and Parry 1982: 18–27.

18. See Bataille's discussion of the potlatch in [1933] 1985: 120–123, esp. 122. "'The ideal,' indicates Mauss, 'would be to give a *potlatch* and not have it returned.'"

19. "What your ears hear can be a lie, but what your eyes see is true." Such was the response of Mansinam's heathens to Brother van Hasselt, Sr. In the 1870s, when the missionary tried to convince erstwhile converts of the reality of heaven and hell, he found himself besieged by questions. Had he ever seen these places? Was the food any good? "A naughty rogue's eyes glistened," Kamma remarks, as van Hasselt told him of the golden harps, the white clothes, the gold crowns. When the missionary asked the man if he would like to go to this place, he replied, "Sure sounds a lot better than getting thrown in a fire" (1976: 291).

20. Goudswaard (1863: 84–88) includes a version of the myth that mentions the hero's departure from "Soping" on Biak, but begins with the old man's encounter with the Morning Star. In this version, the star gives the hero a magical stick and a piece of fruit. Konor's birth follows, along with the dance feast where the boy recognizes the old man as his father. Goudswaard locates the baptism in fire on "Mafor" (as Europeans then called Numfor), shortly after the hero created the four houses that became the island's original clans. From Mafor, the hero and his family sailed for Soeb Kalingga, which Goudswaard associates with Kalingga, or the Coromandel coast of India (ibid.: 88).

Johannes van Hasselt (1889) begins the story on Wundi, with the episode with the Morning Star, who, again, gives the hero a magic stick and a piece of fruit. In this version, Korano Konori is a "wonder child," who is born able to speak. Manarmakeri flees the "unpleasantness" on Wundi after the child's paternity is discovered, with his wife, Konori, and the hero's sister-in-law, a discrepancy that could be due to the missionaries' tendency to translate *srar* as "sister." Despite the plenty the hero offers the Numforese, they insist on taking an expedition to buy sago. Angered at their disobedience, Manarmakeri takes his family and leaves.

Tijdeman's (1912) version, collected on Biak, contains many elements of the earlier renditions: the theft of palm wine, the receipt of a magical stick and fruit from the Star, and the dance feast where the boy recognizes his father. But it also describes the destruction of the village by the angry villagers, who then flee. The hero renews himself in the fire, then creates a large canoe so that he can take his family away to see the world. He creates Numfor, then leaves for Waigeo, an island east of the Bird's Head, in the Radja Ampats, never to be seen again.

F.J.F. van Hasselt's 1914 version covers the episode with the Star, the birth of Konori, and the dance feast. In this version as well, the angry villagers destroy all the houses on Wundi, then leave. On Wundi, Manarmakeri creates food for his family, then a canoe, so they can leave the island. The Biak version of the story ends here, van Hasselt notes, but the Numfor version continues, describing the hero's creation of islands to Biak's west, where his son gets out to play. The baptism in fire occurs on Numfor in this version, which also includes the part of the story in which a child gets sick, and a faithless mother refuse to believe the hero's promise to bring him or her back to life.

Ten Haaft (1947–48), in his description of the 1939–43 movement, briefly summarizes the myth. His version includes the hero's departure from Sopen after an argument over a pig; the meeting with the Morning Star on Wundi; the birth of the miraculous child; the conjuring of food and a boat after the hero and his wife and son are abandoned by her family; the hero's creation of islands for the child to play on; and a brief reference to Numfor people's faithlessness, which causes the hero to leave. "People don't know where he went. But in the song people ask themselves whether he might be in the distant west, perhaps in Holland, that land of wonders" (ibid.: 163).

Finally, Kamma includes among his unpublished papers a manuscript from Ottow and Geissler dated January 29, 1857, which recounts the myth. Ottow and Geissler speculate that it dates to the mid-sixteenth or seventeenth century, when the "Mefoorezen" first settled in the village of Awek on "Jobi" island (presumably Yapen). In this fairly detailed version, the people from Awek move to "Weokwoen" with the old man. The story begins with the theft of palm wine and the struggle with the Morning Star; the old man receives a magic piece of wood and a fruit to throw at a woman to make her pregnant. Next come the dance feast, then the villagers' flight from the island, then Manarmakeri's miraculous creation of everything the family needs. It is the child in this version who is not satisfied with the situation; Manarmakeri creates a boat to take his son to look for playmates. The old man creates Mefoor, where he rejuvenates himself and provides companions for his lonely wife by conjuring four houses out of four sticks stuck in the sand. The myth ends with a history of the migrations of Numfor's original inhabitants, some of whom settle in Doreh Bay and still own some of the porcelain created from the hero's skin.

See also Manusaway-van den Berg 1979 for a semiological analysis of several renditions of the myth.

Chapter Six
The Subjection of the Papuan

1. The colonial state and private industry initially discouraged the migration of married Europeans to the Indies. See Stoler 1989a: 636–639; see also Taylor 1983. The European population rose 167 percent between 1905 and 1930. Gender ratios went from 471.6 to 884.5 women per thousand men. See Drooglever 1980: 5; Nieuwenhuys 1982: 201; van der Veur 1955.

2. For a discussion of the unrest that accompanied the sudden collapse of Dutch colonial rule in many parts of the archipelago, see Cribb 1991: 38; Lucas 1991: 28–29; Reid 1979: 84–103; Frederick 1988: 75; Anderson [1983] 1990: 99, 111. On the

social upheaval sparked by the Japanese surrender across of the archipelago, see Kahin 1985b.

3. A handful of Dutch officials spent the bulk of the war in New Guinea running intelligence operations under MacArthur's command. See Derix 1987: 118–132; van Baal 1989, vol. 2: 151–152; de Jong 1985, part 2: 1,078–1,086.

4. Biak may have been the entry point in 1528. See Haga 1884, vol. 1: 5–6. In 1545, Inigo Ortiz de Retes also had a brush with Biak's "Papuans." His ship was passing between a large island, probably Biak, and many small ones—the Padaidos, Haga thinks—on June 15. "From the largest, 23 canoes, manned by Papuans, paddled up to the ship and let them (the Spaniards) know by signs that it should anchor in a bay of that island. When the boat sailed on, they shot arrows to prevent it from leaving, but were driven back by cannon fire." Five days later, Ortiz de Retes landed on the mainland, which he christened New Guinea and claimed for the Spanish Crown (ibid.: 10). See also Sollewijn Gelpke 1993.

5. By 1848, the northern end of the line had slipped eastward to Cape Bonland, at 140 degrees 47 minutes, close to what is now the city of Jayapura. See Haga 1884, vol. 2: 28, 78; see also van der Veur 1966.

6. In 1730, Corporal Wiggers accompanied the Tidoran *hongi* from Patani to Gebe, south Waigeo, Raam, Dorei, the Schouten and Padaido Islands, Jappen, Massis (probably Kurudu), and Koemamba. In all, the *hongi* killed 53 Papuans, took 178 as slaves, and destroyed three villages. See Haga 1884, vol. 1: 208; see also Kamma 1947–49, Part 4. In 1849, shortly after official endorsement of the new boundary, a Tidoran *hongi* and a Dutch naval schooner made the voyage together, this time reaching the Arimoe Islands, on the eastern edge of Geelvink Bay. See de Bruyn Kops 1850. For an account of three later expeditions, see Robide van der Aa 1879.

7. See de Bruyn Kops 1850: 203, 229 for descriptions of the erection of escutcheons on Roon and in Korrido.

8. I was told that some Biak warriors ended up in Boven Digoel during the 1930s. For a description of the camp, see Salim 1973; Mrázek 1994: 128–138; Shiraishi 1997.

9. Beekman (1989: 40) stresses the importance of the Franco-German war of 1870 in Dutch colonial policy. Fearing annexation and the loss of the Indies, the Dutch came to recognize how much they depended on the British for the protection of their colonial holdings.

10. The Utrecht Mission Society worked through its contacts in the Ministry of Colonies to gain tentative permission to open a post in New Guinea. However, the final decision rested with the resident and sultan of Ternate (Kamma 1981: 48, 51).

11. Later visitors were less impressed; see Kamma 1976: 213, 365; Wallace [1869] 1986: 498.

12. Hartweg, who settled in Korido in 1924, was equally perturbed by this trait. After his first visit to Biak's well-populated north coast, he remarked, "What a people sit there! And they sit much stiller than on the north coast of Supiori" (1925b).

13. See Swadling 1996 on New Guinea trade cycles. Between 1880 and World War I, up to 80,000 birds of paradise were killed and exported from Dutch New Guinea each year (Purcell and Gould 1992: 68, 76). In 1879, there was a drop in trade (Haga 1884, vol. 2: 373). But in 1880, commerce was "livelier than ever," thanks to damar brought onto the market from Yapen, the Schouten Islands, and Wandamen. By 1882,

the "thousands of picols of damar" produced on Biak had made Bosnik "one of the most visited ports in Geelvink Bay" (ibid.: 399). A resin procured from various trees that grow in Indonesia, New Guinea, and New Zealand, damar was used for caulking ships and as the key ingredient in resin; see Oxford English Dictionary 1991: 386; Klein 1935–38, vol. 3: 606; Levi 1984: 149. With the abolition of the bird hunt in the late 1920s, sales and production of damar surged. Apart from a brief experiment in collecting taxes in resin, until the early thirties the trade was solely in the hands of Chinese merchants. Some had shops at posts like Bosnik (which boasted ten in 1937); others did business from the decks of passenger ships (Klein 1935–38, vol. 3: 606–610). Much of the "old" porcelain used in marriages in the early 1990s presumably came from these traders. For more on New Guinea's economy, see Klein 1953–54.

14. In 1890, the Dutch founded the Korps Márechausée, which were small units of indigenous troops, each with a European commander, to fight in Aceh. The Korps served as a model for the divisions of field police used in New Guinea and other "crime-ridden" lands (van Goor 1986; Cribb 1991: 31). On the role of the KPM in promoting state formation, see à Campo 1986: 123; Beekman 1989: 52. For a brief history of sea transportation in New Guinea, see Klein 1935–38, vol. 2: 730–739.

15. A close associate of Governor General van Heutsz who later held a series of influential cabinet posts in the Dutch government, Captain H. Colijn received an order in February 1906 to conduct a investigation aimed at providing suggestions on how the colonial administration could bring its income from New Guinea more in line with its expenditures in the territory. Colijn's advice was to either cut back government spending or massively increase it, but only after a more thorough investigation of the region's potential. See Smeele 1988: 59. Military expeditions were launched in the 1910s, but the findings were inconclusive. The failure of an attempt to administer New Guinea as a separate unit resulted in the suspected suicide of Resident C. Lulofs, who died suddenly in 1922 after learning that the government was drastically cutting his budget (ibid.: 44). In 1923, a German aristocrat approached the Dutch government with a request for a concession covering most of western New Guinea. The proposal was taken quite seriously, until the press got wind of the plan and the resulting uproar forced the prospective partners to drop it (ibid.: 79–80). In the 1930s, "neglected" New Guinea once again became the topic of debate. This time, the excitement was generated by a wave of depression-era plans to settle the territory with Dutch and Indo-European colonists. For an overview of Dutch New Guinea's administrative history, see Beets [1938] 1991.

16. Not always effectively enough, according to Hartweg (1925b, c; 1926; 1927).

17. The NKK had cotton plantations at Waren and Sarmi, and damar concessions in Ransiki and, briefly, Bosnik (Klein 1935–38, vol. 3: 735, 745). Beets [1938] 1991: 92 suspected that political motives lay behind these enterprises.

18. "The labor problem will long prevent big capital from seeking its field of action on New Guinea and is very certainly one of the reasons why New Guinea is still in such a backward state" (Beets [1938] 1991: 110). Beets recommended that the Coolie Ordinance of 1931/1936 be amended in New Guinea to allow the companies to retain local workers under one-year contracts, a necessary measure given the Papuans' tendency to work for a few months and go home.

Biaks were among the most willing of recruits—so willing that the villages of South Biak and North Yapen were emptied of the able-bodied young men (Beets [1938]

1991: 109). "At great distances from the Geelvink Bay, one finds Biak coolies who hire themselves out for all kinds of labor against free food and a wage varying from f2.- to f6.- per month." With its poor soils and limited sago complexes, the infertile island could not support its dense population "so the young men must seek a livelihood and income elsewhere, now that through the exercise of our authority, fighting and raiding from secure shores no longer yields any profit" (Klein 1935–38, vol. 3: 495).

For a portrait of some of the places where young Biaks worked, see Klein 1935–38, vol. 2: 599–718; vol. 3: 900–1,235. Several hundred Papuans labored on small plantations; over a thousand were employed at the NNGPM site in Babo, a port on the western side of the Bird's Head (ibid., vol. 3: 941). The founding of the NNGPM, along with a general growth in trade in West New Guinea, made Sorong a prime destination for Biaks seeking income and adventure (ibid., vol. 2: 739). Biaks also flocked to the NKK sites at Waren and Nabire (ibid., vol. 2: 654; vol. 3: 494–495).

19. The author of conference notes submitted to the Utrecht Mission Society Board was "sad to say" that school had "killed" the art of decoration (Response to Inspection Report 1923). At the start of his tenure on Biak, Hartweg (1925a) expressed concern about the mission's goals, which should be "not to win the Papuans for our notions and ideals, but for the living God." A decade later, Klein (1935–38, vol. 3: 1,213) noted that if "custom" was "too little respected" in New Guinea, the Ambonese mission teachers—not their Dutch supervisors—were to blame. For concerns over plans to hold a meeting on Roon of the political organization Insulinde, which had recently been involved in peasant strikes on Java, see Utrechtsche Zendingsvereeniging 1920: 87–88; see also Shiraishi 1990: 117–774. Haji Misbach, a Communist and Muslim activist, was exiled to Manokwari in 1924 (Shiraishi 1990: 284; van de Graaff [1925] 1991b: 15; see also [1925] 1991a. On the Dutch reaction against native politics in the 1930s, see Mrázek 1994: 105–111; Shiraishi 1997.

20. Kamma notes that Angganeta's son brought her food and water. He also repeats a rumor regarding an Islamic trader, related to Angganeta by marriage, who sought her out to teach her "all sorts of magic." In Marcus Kaisiëpo 's version of the anecdote, as recorded in Sharp's transcript, the old man was wearing a white cloak. He called to her, "Angganeta, rise and follow me!" "As if she were dreaming, Angganeta, still with paralyzed legs and arms, heard what the man was calling, and so she stood up and followed him to the middle of the island of Insumbabi where the person disappeared. She then realized that she was standing in the middle of nowhere, in the bush. She was happy and started dancing (loud). She called out, 'Hurrah, hurrah. . . .' She was so excited (excited voice)" (Sharp with Kaisiëpo 1994: 102).

21. Movements explicitly involving the delivery of tribute or references to the sultan occurred in Numfor in about 1855 (Kamma 1972: 106), Wandamen in 1861 (ibid.: 110), Dusner and Wandamen in 1867 (ibid.: 112–113), Waropen and Numfor in 1868 (ibid.: 115), Dore in 1868 (ibid.: 116–117), Kau and Halmahera in 1875–76 (ibid.: 121), Biak on an unknown date (ibid.: 126–127), Numfor in 1910 (ibid.: 139), and Manokwari 1920 (ibid.: 139–140). The Manokwari uprising occurred when news reached the coastal communities of the appointment of a Tidorese regent for the new Residency of New Guinea. The participants believed that the taxes the Papuans had been paying were going to be used as bridewealth so that the regent could marry a Dutch girl. Manarmakeri, who was on his way to New Guinea, "was

angry because the Administration had been collecting taxes for eight years, while he had only given permission for four years." He would abolish taxation and forced labor, and repay the Papuans what they were owed.

The other uprisings roughly correspond to events listed in the table of contents of Haga's history of New Guinea: the erection of escutcheons by the Circe and the *hongi* in 1850; the shipwreck of the Possa and the Etna's punitive expeditions to Roon, Wandamen, and Numfor in 1857 and 1858; the posting of a Tidoran detachment in Dore in 1864; the missionaries' tour of lower Geelvink Bay in 1866; pressure on Tidore to suppress piracy in 1875; the freeing of slaves in Tidore and their return to New Guinea in 1879; the expansion of trade in 1880; and the missionaries' visit to the thriving port of Bosnik in 1882 (Haga 1884, vol. 2: xi–xxxix). The movement on Numfor in 1910 took place when the Corps of Topographical Engineers began an expedition up the Mamberamo River, which, as we have seen, has a role in the myth of Manarmakeri. Claiming that he had seen Manarmakeri on the Mamberamo, the prophet Mangginomi instructed the people on Numfor to prepare for his arrival. Mangginomi received a tribute of valuables and young girls in his house, which was divided by a partition. Followers told the missionary that behind this partition "now and then the kings of Ternate, Tidore, Djailolo, Batjan, Holland, and England came here to dance in honor of the prince of the Papuans whose coming was imminent" (Kamma 1972: 137–139).

22. Ottow confronted two prophets, challenging them to take him with them as a witness to the Papuan heaven. The prophets promised to come back, but never did. "Two years later, Ottow died" (Kamma 1972: 108).

23. In about 1926, in the Padaido Islands, one prophet's message "linked up with the expectations awakened by the Regent of Tidore. For the people would turn into *Amberi* (foreigners, in this case Tidorese)" (Kamma 1972: 141).

24. Such was the case with Korano Baibo, whose followers attacked a European trading vessel on July 22, 1886, killing the captain and three of his crew. A month later, HMS *Tromp* arrived to avenge the murder. It is not clear what happened. But a year later, when the resident of Ternate visited Biak, Baibo gave the official a slave girl and two strings of tortoise shells to compensate for Captain Holland's death. "The Korano was then (October 15, 1887) by permanent appointment 'attached to the Colonial Administration'" (Kamma 1972: 130).

25. Three steamships linked the damar and cotton concerns at Nabire and Momi to Tokyo (Klein 1935–38, vol. 3: 735, 745). The NNGPMs exploration site at Babo, West New Guinea, had two coastal steamers at its disposal and was occasionally served by the KPM's international Saigon-Java-Noumea line (ibid.: 735, 742). The site at Babo also featured a meteorological station and an airstrip; as of 1936, the geological troops were equipped with twenty-four radio telegraph/telephones (ibid.: 777; see also Fabricius 1949: 69–70). Outside of Babo, New Guinea had a total of thirteen radio stations available for government and private use. Through a connection in Ambon, wires could be received from Java and even The Netherlands. Mail service was available via the KPM (Klein 1935–38, vol. 3: 776).

26. That would definitely be the case for those at Babo in early 1942. Workers witnessed an orgy of destruction, ordered by Dutch managers before they fled the oil fields to prevent valued infrastructure from falling into enemy hands (Fabricius 1949: 77).

27. I assume that the situation on Biak was similar to that on Numfor, where this rule was promulgated (Kamma 1972: 181).

28. The search for these lizards (*kasip*) to cover a drum head is the most time-consuming step in crafting a Biak drum (*sireb*).

29. A small fleet of canoes traveled to Bosnik in late June to request Angganitha's release. Tilly, the assistant district officer, promised Angganeta's relatives that the Japanese would return her to Sowek. She boarded a ship, which stopped in Korido to drop off a new official, then proceeded to Manokwari. Kamma reports that the prophet remained in prison until roughly August, when both she and her successor, Stefanus Simopyaref, were beheaded. Some of my consultants insisted that Angganeta was impossible to execute and that she was still alive in *Sup Amber*.

According to Kamma, Angganeta sent a note to those who came for her. "'If the Japanese disembark me in Korido all will be well. Our country and our people will know peace. If this does not happen, a hard fate awaits us for my work will be unfinished. But after these dark times the Morning Star will rise in the east, Japan will be defeated, and we shall rise again.' The informant added 'By the Morning Star in her prophecy Angganitha meant MacArthur'" (Kamma 1972: 175; see also Mampioper 1976: 65–66).

30. Guru Tomasilla was one supporter (Kamma 1972: 201). The Chinese shop-keepers in Biak "expressed their willingness to join the A.B. (America-*Babo* = New America) movement" (ibid.:188). Mr. Senyenem of Opiaref, whom we met in the previous chapter, was a secretary to the leaders at Manswam.

31. My informants recounted the incident somewhat differently than Kamma, who placed the attack on Bosnik in January 1943 and the attack on Numfor in February and March 1943. Biromor's encounter with the Japanese officer, in Kamma's narrative, occurred right before the movement ended (1972: 201–202).

Chapter Seven
The Subject of Biak?

1. Such a limit to interpretation is not unlike what Freud ([1900] 1965: 143) called the "navel" of a dream; see also ibid.: 564: "The dream thoughts to which we are led by interpretation cannot, from the nature of things, have any definite endings; they are bound to branch out in every direction into the intricate network of our world of thought."

2. "Most astonishing . . . is the fact that all the followers of the movement later calmly attended religious services, as if nothing had happened. After such an unmistakeable demonstration of how little they had understood the Gospel, one would rather have expected them to return to the 'previous paganism.'" Kamma accounts for this phenomenon by referring to the "real and emotional background of Biak culture" and its ability to "freely accept all kinds of foreign elements which are, however, adapted and adjusted to the indigenous system, and may even wholly lose their original character . . . The associations will continue to rise from the subconscious, even if the conscious mind has chosen the Gospel. This also includes what might be called 'the historical contents of the conscious.' . . . It is impossible, therefore, for the so-

called real *Koreri* followers to have any sense of guilt about their *Koreri* expectations
. . . Their views on the essence of the *Koreri* belief are not so easily expressed. The
'shy smile' to the outsider also indicates that they realize their inability to explain the
substance of this belief to an outsider" (1972: 210–211).

3. Mambesak, the most famous of the troupes, performed at receptions for visiting
dignitaries and on the radio program Ap hosted. Osborne reports that the authories
used Mambesak's music for propaganda purposes. "The army sometimes boomed its
songs into the jungle through loudspeakers in the hope of persuading OPM members
to surrender" (Osborne 1985: 148). See also Defert 1996: 361, who notes the irony
that figures like Ap, now viewed as martyrs for the Papuan nationalist cause, could
just as well have been cited as examples of successful integration of the Papuan elite
into Indonesian society.

4. Spreading from the provincial capital to rural areas along the border, the crackdown that began with Ap's arrest and intensified following a flag raising demonstration in Jayapura on February 13, 1984, led 11,000 refugees to flee the province into
neighboring Papua New Guinea (Smith and Hewison 1986). The majority of the first
wave of refugees, which included military deserters from Jayapura, were Biak and
Serui (Osborne 1985: 100).

5. According Seth Rumkorem, then the leader of one of the OPM's feuding fac-
tions, Ap was "the home affairs minister in my government" (Osborne 1985: 150). I
also heard rumors that Ap was channeling grant funds intended for the museum to
the fighters. Friends in Biak did not mention these reports. But one recalled a banner
that flew over the road past the provincial university at the height of Ap's activities; it
read "Kebudayaan adalah identitas bangsa" ("Culture is national identity").

6. Among the other reports that appeared during December and January were *Republika* 1993d, e, f, g; Suryadi 1993; Hutomo 1993; *Jakarta Post* 1993a, c, d; *Jakarta-
Jakarta* 1993; *Femina* 1993. This list includes the majority of major national publications of the day, ranging from dailies to monthly news journals to popular women's
magazines. Some editors included abbreviated versions of seminar papers; others
printed photographs and descriptions of particular performances; many reported on
the news conference held before Lisan's opening, and the speeches given by the minister of culture and development and other luminaries during the course of the festival
and seminar. One of the most vivid images to circulate was a photograph of Joop Ave,
the minister of tourism, post, and telecommunications, striking a traditional drum to
officially open the event. See *Republika* 1993c; *Jakarta Post* 1993b.

7. I borrow this distinction between the objects of narrative longing inherent in the
souvenir and the collection from Stewart 1993: 132–170.

8. Sam thought it likely that these songs were also sung at Yuliana Workrar's "palace" in the 1970s.

9. Osborne (1985: 148) reports that in 1981 Arnold Ap "began to foster the rebirth of the Koreri legend."

10. I would like to thank Takashi Shiraishi for suggesting this comparison.

11. On the cultural production of fear, see Taussig 1987: 3–36. Tsing (1993: 72–
103) discusses how the Meratus reverse dominant discourses in their stories of government headhunters. See also George 1996: 264–266. Rumors of the sort described
by Tsing also circulated on Biak during the period of my fieldwork. It was said that

government contractors were on the prowl for sacrificial victims to use in rites to strengthen the bridges being built on the north coast.

12. The "Outer Islands," called the "Buitenbezittingen" or "Outer Holdings" by the Dutch, include the large islands of Sumatra, Kalimantan, Sulawesi, and (western) New Guinea, along with the smaller islands of Nusa Tenggara Timor, Nusa Tenggara Barat, and the Moluccas. The "Inner Islands," housing the bulk of Indonesia's vast population, include Java, Madura, and Bali (Geertz 1963).

13. A Dutch head of government on Biak also discusses how employers were considered liable for any injury incurred by their employees during the performance of official duties (van Gendt 1954: 144–145).

14. On the involvement of Irian Jayans in Pemuda Pancasila, a quasi-official protection agency recruited by the Indonesian military for various underground operations, see Ryter 1998.

15. Although the other women understood Willemina's lesson, it is not clear that they completely approved. Not long afterward, Fransina retaliated by making off with my bag at a time when Willemina was supposed to be guarding it.

16. Italics in original. Steedly draws on Feldman in her analysis of "narrative experience" among the Karo Batak, while raising the problem of exclusion, an issue Steedly (1993: 29–30) views as neglected by Feldman. "What does it mean to say that a non-narratable event is, in effect, a non-event?"

17. Isak Arwam composed the following wor on the day we left Ujung Pandang.

KADWOR

1. Wo arwanama, arwanjama.

2. Yenai ra yabindamyasi insapi yibenda.

3. Yaswaro menu kubur aniwara, iwarai.

FUAR

1. *Inai insoso Amerikae* arwanama, arwanjama.

2. Yenai ra yabindamyasi insapi yibenda.

3. Yaswaro *Jakarta* menu kubur aniwara, iwarai.

TIP

1. Oh, the morning approached, the morning approached.

2. I awoke and began to rise, but then rolled back.

3. I longed for the village we left back there, back there.

FUAR

1. *Young woman, young American maiden*, the morning approached, the morning approached.

2. I awoke and began to rise, but then rolled back.

3. I longed for *Jakarta*, the village we left back there, back there.

18. When one of the singers came down with a serious case of malaria, the others blamed a member of a nearby community who felt that he should have been part of the troupe. An album of photographs from the trip had disappeared shortly after I visited the man's community; it was implied the man had taken the pictures in order "create difficulties" for the singers.

Epilogue
On Limits

1. The Oxford English Dictionary defines "limiting" through the example of "limiting parallels": "the parallels of latitude within which occultation of the stars or planets by the moon are possible" (Oxford English Dictionary 1991: 977).

2. For an account of how "what counts as a story" can be contested, see Steedly 1993: 174–202.

Glossary

amber	B: foreign or foreigner
ararem	B: bridewealth
ben bepon, ben beba, ben in	B: types of porcelain used in bridewealth
beyuser	B: narrative wor song
bin bena wor	B: hostess at a feast
bingon	B: out-married woman
bupati	I: regent
camat	I: subdistrict chief
Doberok	B: Biak ancestor, literally, "the Noisy Thing"
dow beba	B: literally "big song;" also a term for a feast
fandadiwer	B: ceremonial meal
fan-fan	B: literally "nurture"; type of food gift
fno	B: cross-sex sibling's child
hongi	I: Moluccan war fleet
imem	B: mother's brother or father's sister's husband
inanai	B: flying fish
jaman Belanda	I: Dutch times
jef	B: dance step
keret	B: patrilineal descent group or clan
Koreri	B: utopia, literally, "We Change Our Skin"
korwar	B: small religuary
Madirai	B: Biak ancestor
mambri	B: Warrior
Manarmakeri	B: Biak ancestor, literally, "the Itchy Old Man"
mebin	B: father's sister or mother's brother's wife
more-more	B: type of porcelain used in bridewealth
munsasu	B: exchange of food for ceremonial wealth
naek	B: same-sex sibling
napirem	B: cross-cousin
New Order	authoritarian regime that ruled Indonesia from 1966 to 1998
Pancasila	Indonesia's official state ideology, which consists of five basic principles: "belief in God," "national consciousness," "humanism," "social justice," and "sovereignty of the people"
rumsom	B: clan house
rumsram	B: men's house
samfar	B: shell bracelet once used in bridewealth
Sampari	B: the Morning Star
sarak	B: silver bracelet forged from coins

sarong	I: type of textile worn around the waist
sembarang	I: random
sim	B: subgroup of keret, literally "room"
sireb	B: hourglass-shaped drum; see also *tifa*
srar	B: opposite-sex sibling
Sup Amber	B: the Land of the Foreigners
tifa	I: hourglass-shaped drum
wor	B: type of singing; also a kind of feast
wor angyon	B: breaking-the-walking stick feast
wor famarmar	B: clothing feast
wor kapnaknik	B: haircutting feast
wor ramrem	B: anointing feast
wos amber	B: foreign speech, language
wos Biak	B: Biak language
yosim pancar or *yospan*	B: type of dance

References

Abraham, Nicolas, and Maria Torok. 1986. *The Wolf Man's Magic Word: A Cryptonymy.* Translated by Nicholas T. Rand. Minneapolis: University of Minnesota Press.
————. 1994. *The Shell and the Kernel: Renewals of Psychoanalysis.* Vol. 1. Edited and translated with an introduction by Nicholas T. Rand. Chicago: University of Chicago Press.
à Campo, J. 1986. "Een Maritiem BB. De Rol van de Koniklijke Paketvaart Maatschappij in de Integratie van de Koloniale Staat." In *Imperialisme in de Marge: De Afronding van Nederlands-Indië,* edited by J. van Goor, 123–178. Utrecht: HES.
Acciaioli, Greg. 1985. "Culture as Art: From Practice to Spectacle in Indonesia." *Canberra Anthropology* 8 (1–2): 148–172.
Adam, Ahmat. 1984. "The Vernacular Press and the Emergence of Modern Indonesian Consciousness (1855–1913)." Doctoral dissertation, University of London.
Adams, Kathleen M. 1997. "Touting Touristic 'Primadonas': Tourism, Ethnicity, and National Integration in Sulawesi, Indonesia." In *Tourism, Ethnicity, and the State in Asian and Pacific Societies,* edited by Michel Picard and Robert E. Wood, 155–180. Honolulu: University of Hawai'i Press.
Adatrechtbundels. 1955a. "Onderafdeling Schouten-Eilanden a) Volksordening op Biak; b) Biakse Titels. Ontleend aan aantekeningen van de hand van Dr. F. C. Kamma, welwillend ter beschikking van de commissie gesteld." Serie S. Nieuw-Guinea. No. 44. *Adatrechtsbundels.* XLV, *Nieuw-Guinea,* 148–152. The Hague: Martinus Nijhoff.
————. 1955b. "Iets over Erfrecht op Biak. Ontleend aan aantekeningen van Dr. F. C. Kamma, vgl. No S. 44 en 84 dezer serie Serie S Nieuw-Guinea No. 94." *Adatrechtsbundels.* XLV, *Nieuw-Guinea,* 536. The Hague: Martinus Nijhoff.
Adriani, M. A., W. B. Bergsma, E. H. Van Leeuwen, and A. Voorhoeve. 1896. Response to question posed by Mr. W. B. Bergsma and Ds. A. Voorhoeve in Algemeene Vergadering of 1895. Library Copy Irian B5b/290. Oegstgeest, the Netherlands: Archives of the Hendrik Kraemer Institute.
Agter, Hendrik Jan. 1921. Letter to the Board of October 29. UZV K31, D1. Oegstgeest, the Netherlands: Archives of the Hendrik Kraemer Institute.
————. 1922a. Letter to the Board of July 21. UZV K31, D1. Oegstgeest, the Netherlands: Archives of the Hendrik Kraemer Institute.
————. 1922b. Letter to the Board of July 27. UZV K31, D1. Oegstgeest, the Netherlands: Archives of the Hendrik Kraemer Institute.
————. 1922c Letter to the Board of September 23. UZV K31, D1. Oegstgeest, the Netherlands: Archives of the Hendrik Kraemer Institute.
Althusser, Louis. 1971. "Ideology and Ideological State Apparatuses (Notes towards an Investigation)." In *Lenin and Philosophy and Other Essays.* Translated by Ben Brewster, 127–186. London: New Left Books.
American Heritage Dictionary. 1982. Second College Edition. Boston: Houghton Mifflin.
Andaya, Leonard Y. 1993. *The World of Maluku: Eastern Indonesia in the Early Modern Period.* Honolulu: University of Hawaii Press.
Anderson, Benedict R. O'G. [1966] 1990. "The Languages of Indonesian Politics." In

Language and Power: Exploring Political Cultures in Indonesia, 123–151. Ithaca: Cornell University Press.

———. [1972] 1990. "The Idea of Power in Javanese Culture." In *Language and Power: Exploring Political Cultures in Indonesia*, 17–77. Ithaca: Cornell University Press.

———. [1979] 1990. "A Time of Darkness and a Time of Light: Transposition in Early Indonesian Nationalist Thought." In *Language and Power: Exploring Political Cultures in Indonesia*, 241–270. Ithaca: Cornell University Press.

———. [1983] 1990. "Old State, New Society: Indonesia's New Order in Comparative Historical Perspective." In *Language and Power: Exploring Political Cultures in Indonesia*, 94–120. Ithaca: Cornell University Press.

———. [1983] 1991. *Imagined Communities: Reflections on the Origin and Spread of Nationalism*. London and New York: Verso.

———. [1985] 1990. "Further Adventures of Charisma." In *Language and Power: Exploring Political Cultures in Indonesia*, 78–93. Ithaca: Cornell University Press.

———. 1988. "The Point of No Return." In *Born in Fire: The Indonesian Struggle for Independence*, edited by Colin Wild and Peter Carey, 86–91. Athens: Ohio University Press.

Anonymous. 1892. *Jaarverslag van het Seminarie te Depok*. Oegstgeest, the Netherlands: Archives of the Hendrik Kraemer Institute.

———. 1960. "Lima Orang Bersaudara Srarbori." Manuscript, 7 July 1960. F. C. Kamma Papers. Oegstgeest, the Netherlands: Archives of the Hendrik Kraemer Institute.

———. 1978. "Mamberok." Unpublished songbook.

———. 1992. *Biak-Numfor dalam Angka 1991*. Biak: Kantor Statistik dan Bappeda Tk. II.

———. 1998. *Berkas Perkara Tersangka atas Nama Drs. Filep Yacob Semuel Karma alias Yoppi Melakukan Tindak Pidana Kejahatan terhadap Keamanan Negara atau Makar*. Biak: Polri Daerah Irian Jaya Resort Biak Numfor.

Appadurai, Arjun. 1996. *Modernity at Large: Cultural Dimensions of Globalization*. Minneapolis: University of Minnesota Press.

Atkinson, Jane Monnig. 1989. *The Art and Politics of Wana Shamanship*. Berkeley: University of California Press.

Austin, J. L. 1976. *How to Do Things with Words*. London: Oxford University Press.

Baker, James N. 1993. "The Presence of the Name: Reading Scripture in an Indonesian Village." In *The Ethnography of Reading*, edited by J. Boyarin, 98–138. Berkeley: University of California Press.

———. 1994. "Ancestral Traditions and State Categories in Tidorese Village Society." In *Halmahera and Beyond: Social Science Research in the Moluccas*, edited by L. Visser, 35–57. Leiden: KITLV Press.

Barnes, J. A. 1962. "African Models in the New Guinea Highlands." *Man* 62: 5–9.

Barraud, Cécile. 1994. "Introduction to a Comparative Study of Two Kinship Vocabularies in the Moluccas." In *Halmahera and Beyond: Social Science Research in the Moluccas*, edited by L. Visser, 97–114. Leiden: KITLV Press.

Basso, Keith. 1988. "'Speaking with Names': Language and Landscape among the Western Apache." *Cultural Anthropology* 3 (2): 99–130.

Bataille, Georges. [1933] 1985. "The Notion of Expenditure." In *Visions of Excess: Selected Writings, 1927–1939*, translated by Allan Stoekl, 116–129. Minneapolis: University of Minnesota Press.

———. [1957] 1987. *Eroticism*. Translated by M. Dalwood. London: Boyars.

———. [1955] 1990. "Hegel, Death and Sacrifice." In *On Bataille*, edited by Allan Stoekl. New Haven: Yale University Press, Yale French Studies 78: 9–28.

———. [1967] 1991. *The Accursed Share: An Essay on General Economy*. Vol. 1. Consumption, translated by Robert Hurley. New York: Zone Books.

Bateson, Gregory. 1972. "The Cybernetics of 'Self': A Theory of Alcoholism." In *Steps to an Ecology of Mind*, 309–337. New York: Ballantine Books.

Battaglia, Debbora. 1991. "Punishing the Yams: Leadership and Gender Ambivalence on Sabarl Island." In *Big Men and Great Men: Personifications of Power in Melanesia*, edited by Maurice Godelier and Marilyn Strathern, 83–96. Paris: Maison des Sciences de l'Homme.

Bauman, Richard, 1983. *Let Your Words Be Few: Symbolism of Speaking and Silence among Seventeenth-Century Quakers*. Cambridge: Cambridge University Press.

Bauman, Richard, and Charles L. Briggs. 1990. "Poetics and Performance as Critical Perspectives on Language and Social Life." *Annual Review of Anthropology* 19: 59–88.

Becker, Alton L. 1995. "Text Building, Epistemology, and Aesthetics in Javanese Shadow Theater." In *Beyond Translation: Essays toward a Modern Philology*, 23–70. Ann Arbor: University of Michigan Press.

Beekman, Elke. 1989. "Driekleur en Kruisbanier, De Utrechtsche Zendingsvereeniging op Nederlands Nieuw-Guinea 1859–1919." Doctoraalscriptie, Erasmus University, Rotterdam.

Beets, K. Th. [1938] 1991. "Memorie van Overgave Noord Nieuw-Guinea, Manokwari 1938 [MMK 373]." Reproduced in Irian Jaya Source Materials No. 2, Series A-NO. 1: *Memories van Overgave van de Afdeling Noord Nieuw Guinea*, edited by J. Miedema and W.A.L. Stokhof, 18–113. Leiden and Jakarta: DSALCUL/IRIS.

Bellwood, Peter, James J. Fox, and D. Tryon. 1995. "The Austronesians in History: Common Origins and Diverse Transformation." In *The Austronesians: Historical and Comparative Perspectives*, edited by P. Bellwood, J. J. Fox, and D. Tryon, 1–16. Department of Anthropology as part of the Comparative Austronesian Project. Canberra: Research School of Pacific and Asian Studies, Australian National University.

Benda, Harry J. 1958. *The Crescent and the Rising Sun: Indonesian Islam under the Japanese Occupation, 1942–1945*. The Hague and Bandung: W. van Hoeve.

Benjamin, Walter. [1920–21] 1978. "Critique of Violence." In *Reflections: Essays, Aphorisms, Autobiographical Writings*, edited by Peter Demetz, translated by Edmund Jephcott, 277–300. New York: Schocken Books.

———. [1923] 1968. "The Task of the Translator: An Introduction to the Translation of Baudelaire's Tableaux Parisiens." In *Illuminations: Essays and Reflections*, edited by Hannah Arendt, translated by Harry Zohn, 69–82. New York: Schocken Books.

———. [1936]. 1968. "The Work of Art in the Age of Mechanical Reproduction." In *Illuminations: Essays and Reflections*, edited by Hannah Arendt, translated by Harry Zohn, 217–251. New York: Schocken Books.

———. [1968]. 1984. "Some Motifs in Baudelaire." In *Charles Baudelaire: A Lyric Poet in the Era of High Capitalism*, translated by Harry Zohn, 107–154. New York and London: Verso.

Benveniste, Emile. [1958] 1971. "Subjectivity in Language." In *Problems in General Linguistics*, translated by Mary Elizabeth Meek, 223–230. Coral Gables: University of Miami Press.

Bergsma, W. B., A. A. Looijn, and A. Voorhoeve. 1889. Reports A and B. Algemeene Vergadering 1889. UZV K26–15. Oegstgeest, The Netherlands: Archives of the Hendrik Kraemer Institute.

Berigten van de Utrechtsche Zendingsvereeniging. 1904. "N. Guinea." January: 4–8.

Berlant, Lauren. 1991. *The Anatomy of National Fantasy: Hawthorne, Utopia, and Everyday Life*. Chicago: University of Chicago Press.

———. 1997. *The Queen of America Goes to Washington City: Essays on Sex and Citizenship*. Durham: Duke University Press.

Berman, Marshall. 1983. *All That Is Solid Melts into Air: The Experience of Modernity*. London and New York: Verso.

Bhabha, Homi K. 1990. "DissemiNation: Time, Narrative, and the Margins of the Modern Nation." In *Nation and Narration*, edited by Homi K. Bhabha, 291–322. London and New York: Routledge.

Bloch, Maurice. 1975. "Introduction." In *Political Language and Oratory in Traditional Society*, edited by Maurice Bloch, 1–28. New York: Academic Press.

———. 1992. *Prey into Hunter: The Politics of Religious Experience*. Cambridge: Cambridge University Press.

Bloch, Maurice, and Jonathan Parry. 1982. "Introduction: Death and the Regeneration of Life." In *Death and the Regeneration of Life*, 1–44. Cambridge: Cambridge University Press.

Blust, Robert. 1984. "Indonesia as a 'Field of Linguistic Study.'" In *Unity in Diversity: Indonesia as a Field of Anthropological Study*, edited by P. E. de Josselin de Jong, 21–37. Verhandelingen van het Koninklijk Instituut voor Taal-, Land- en Volkenkunde 103. Dordrecht/Providence: Foris.

Boddy, Janice. 1989. *Wombs and Alien Spirits: Women, Men and the Zar Cult in Northern Sudan*. Madison: University of Wisconsin Press.

Bond, George C. 1987. "Ancestors and Protestants: Religious Coexistence in the Social Field of a Zambian Community." *American Ethnologist* 14 (1): 55–72.

Boon, James. 1990. "Balinese Twins Times Two: Gender, Birth Order, and 'Household' in Indonesia/Indo-Europe." In *Power and Difference: Gender in Island Southeast Asia*, edited by Jane Monnig Atkinson and Shelly Errington, 209–234. Stanford: Stanford University Press.

———. 2000. "Showbiz as a Cross-Cultural System: Circus and Song, Garland and Geertz, Rushdie, Mordden, . . . and More." *Cultural Anthropology* 15 (3): 424–456.

Boyarin, Jonathan, ed. 1993. *The Ethnography of Reading*. Berkeley: University of California Press.

Breman, Jan. 1983. *Control of Land and Labour in Colonial Java: A Case Study of Agrarian Crisis and Reform in the Region of Cirebon during the First Decades of the Twentieth Century*. Verhandelingen van het Instituut voor Taal-, Land- en Volkenkunde 101. Dordrecht/Providence: Foris.

Brenneis, Donald, and Fred Myers, eds. 1984. *Dangerous Words: Language and Politics in the Pacific*. New York: New York University Press.

Brenner, Suzanne. 1995. "Why Women Rule the Roost: Rethinking Javanese Ideologies of Gender and Self-Control." In *Bewitching Women, Pious Men: Gender and Body Politics in Southeast Asia*, edited by Aihwa Ong and Michael Peletz, 19–50. Berkeley: University of California Press.

———. 1998. *The Domestication of Desire: Women, Wealth, and Modernity in Java*. Princeton: Princeton University Press.

Brubaker, Rogers. 1996. *Nationalism Reframed: Nationhood and the National Question in the New Europe*. Cambridge: Cambridge University Press.

Bruner, Edward M., and Barbara Kirshenblatt-Gimblett. 1995. "Maasai on the Lawn: Tourist Realism in East Africa." *Cultural Anthropology* 9 (4): 435–470.

Budiardjo, Carmel, and Liem Soei Liong. 1988. *West Papua: The Obliteration of a People*. London: Tapol.

Bull, Malcolm. 1999. *Seeing Things Hidden: Apocalypse, Vision and Totality*. London: Verso.

Burridge, Kenelm. 1960. *Mambu: A Melanesian Millennium*. London: Methuen.

————. 1969. *New Heaven, New Earth: A Study of Millenarian Activities*. Oxford: Basil Blackwell.

Cannell, Fenella. 1991. "The Power of Appearances: Beauty, Mimicry and Transformation in Bicol." In *Discrepant Histories: Translocal Essays on Filipino Cultures*, edited by Vicente L. Rafael. Manila: Anvil.

————. 1996. "Anger, Reluctance and Pity: The Construction of Women's Value in Marriage Stories from Bicol." Paper delivered to the London School of Economics Departmental Research Seminar, Michaelmas term.

————. 1999. *Power and Intimacy in the Christian Philippines*. Cambridge: Cambridge University Press.

Carsten, Janet. 1995a. "Houses in Langkawi: Stable Structures or Mobile Homes?" In *About the House: Lévi-Strauss and Beyond*, edited by Janet Carsten and Steven Hugh-Jones, 105–128. Cambridge: Cambridge University Press.

————. 1995b. "The Substance of Kinship and the Heat of the Hearth: Feeding, Personhood, and Relatedness among Malays in Pulau Langkawi." *American Ethnologist* 22 (2): 223–241.

————. 1997. *The Heat of the Hearth: The Process of Kinship in a Malay Fishing Community*. Oxford: Clarendon Press, New York: Oxford University Press.

Cendrawasih Pos (Bird of Paradise Post). 1993a. "3 Putra Irian Jadi Pahlawan Nasional." August 12: 1.

————. 1993b. "Frans Kaisiepo, Memperkenalkan Nama Irian." August 31: 1.

————. 1993c. "Frans Kaisiepo, Menjadi Gubernor Irja Terlama." September 2: 1.

————. 1993d. "Irja Akan Menjadi Tujuan Wisata Terpopuler." August 25: 2.

————. 1993e. "Giliran Sumsel Jadi Korban Tim Irja." September 13: 1

————. 1993f. "Sepakbola Irian Jayalah Juara Favorit Itu." September 13: 1.

————. 1993g. "Hotel Marauw, Iringi Laju Industri Tunjang Sektor Parawisata." September 16: 3.

————. 1993h. "Fantastis, Irja Cukur Aceh 2–0." September 16: 7.

————. 1993i. "Irja Bobol Gawang Jabar Sembilan Gol." September 18: 1.

————. 1993j. "Pattipi: Tete Manis Menolong Irja." September 18: 1.

————. 1994. "Akan Dijadikan Daerah Tujuan Transmigrasi." January 19: 3.

Chatterjee, Partha. 1986. *Nationalist Thought and the Colonial World: A Derivative Discourse?* London: Zed Books.

————. 1993. *The Nation and Its Fragments: Colonial and Postcolonial Histories*. Princeton: Princeton University Press.

Cixous, Hélène. 1993. *Three Steps on the Ladder of Writing*. Translated by Sarah Cornell and Susan Sellers. New York: Columbia University Press.

Clastres, Hélène. [1975] 1995. *The Land-Without-Evil: Tupí-Guaraní Prophetism*. Translated by Jacqueline Grenez Brovender. Urbana: University of Illinois Press.

Cohen, Benjamin. 1998. *The Geography of Money*. Ithaca: Cornell University Press.

Comaroff, Jean L., and John L. Comaroff. 1991. *Of Revelation and Revolution*. Vol. 1. *Christianity and Consciousness in South Africa*. Chicago: University of Chicago Press.

————. 1997. *Of Revelation and Revolution*. Vol. 2. *The Dialectics of Modernity on a South African Frontier*. Chicago: University of Chicago Press.

Coronil, Fernando. 1997. *The Magical State: Nature, Money, and Modernity in Venezuela*. Chicago: University of Chicago Press.

Cribb, Robert. 1991. *Gangsters and Revolutionaries: The Jakarta People's Militia and the Indonesian Revolution, 1945–1949*. Honolulu: University of Hawai'i Press.

Crossette, Barbara. 1996. "Introspection and Repression: Why Indonesia Isn't Talking." Week in Review desk, *New York Times*. June 23: 3.

Day, Tony. 1996. "Ties that (Un)Bind: Families and States in Premodern Southeast Asia." *Journal of Asian Studies* 55 (2): 348–409.

de Bruyn, Jan Victor. 1948. Jaarverslagen 1947 en 1948 van Onderafdeling Biak. Nummer Toegang 10–25, Stuk 188. Nienhuis Collectie van de Department van Bevolkingszaken Hollandia Rapportenarchief. The Hague: Algemeene Rijksarchief.

———. 1951–52. "The Mansaren Cult." *South Pacific* 5 (1): 1–10.

———. 1965. "Changing Leadership in Western New Guinea." In *Induced Political Change in the Pacific: A Symposium*, edited by Rolland Wynfield Force, Fay C. Alailima, and Cyril S. Belshaw, 75–103. Tenth Pacific Science Congress 1961. Honolulu: Bishop Museum Press.

———. 1978. *Het Verdwenen Volk*. Bussum: Van Holkema & Warendorf.

de Bruyn Kops, G. F. 1850. "Bijdrage tot de Kennis der Noord- en Oostkusten van Nieuw Guinea." *Natuurkundig Tijdschrift voor Nederlandsch Indië* 1: 163–235.

de Certeau, Michel. 1984. *The Practice of Everyday Life*. Translated by Steven Rendall. Berkeley: University of California Press.

de Clerq, F.S.A., and J.D.E. Schmeltz. 1893. *Ethnographische Beschriving van de West- en Noordkust van Nederlandsche Nieuw-Guinea*. Leiden: P.W.M. Trap.

Defert, Gabriel. 1996. *L'Indonésie et la Nouvelle-Guinée-Occidentale: Maintien des Frontières Coloniales, ou, Respect des Identités Communautaires*. Paris and Montreal: L'Harmattan.

de Jong, L. 1985. *Het Koninkrijk der Nederlanden in de Tweede Wereldoorlog*. Vol. 11b. *Nederlands-Indië* II. 2 parts. The Hague: Staatsuitgeverij.

de Josselin de Jong, J.P.B. [1935] 1977. "The Malay Archipelago as a Field of Ethnological Inquiry." In *Structural Anthropology in the Netherlands*, edited by P. E. de Josselin de Jong, 164–182. The Hague: Martinus Nijhoff.

de la Fontaine, Jean. 1973. "Descent in New Guinea: an Africanist View." In *The Character of Kinship*, edited by Jack Goody, 35–51. Cambridge: Cambridge University Press.

Delaney, Carol. 1998. *Abraham on Trial: The Social Legacy of Biblical Myth*. Princeton: Princeton University Press.

Derix, Jan. 1987. *Bapa Papoea: Jan P. K. van Eechoud, Een Biografie*. Venlo: Van Spijk.

Derrida, Jacques. 1973. *Speech and Phenomena, and Other Essays on Husserl's Theory of Signs*. Translated by David B. Allison. Northwestern Studies in Phenomenology and Existential Philosophy. Evanston: Northwestern University Press.

———. 1976. *Of Grammatology*. Translated by Gayatri Chakravorty Spivak. Baltimore: Johns Hopkins University Press.

———. 1981. *Dissemination*. Translated by Barbara Johnson. London: Athlone Press.

———. 1982. *Margins of Philosophy*. Translated with additional notes by Alan Bass. Chicago: University of Chicago Press.

———. 1985. "Des Tours de Babel." In *Difference in Translation*, edited by Joseph F. Graham, 167–185. Ithaca: Cornell University Press.

———. 1986. *Glas*. Translated by John P. Leavey, Jr., and Richard Rand. Lincoln: University of Nebraska Press.

———. 1988. *Limited Inc*. Evanston: Northwestern University Press.

———. 1992. *Given Time: I. Counterfeit Money*. Translated by Peggy Kamuf. Chicago: University of Chicago Press.

———. 1995. *The Gift of Death*. Translated by David Wills. Chicago: University of Chicago Press.

Dirks, Nicholas B. 1990. "History as a Sign of the Modern." *Public Culture* 2 (2): 25–32.

Djopari, John R. G. 1993. *Pemberontakan Organisasi Papua Merdeka*. Jakarta: Gramedia Widiasarana Indonesia.

Dove, Michael, ed. 1988. *The Real and Imagined Role of Culture in Development: Case Studies in Indonesia*. Honolulu: University of Hawai'i Press.

Drake, Christine. 1989. *National Integration in Indonesia: Patterns and Policies*. Honolulu: University of Hawai'i Press.

Drooglever, P. 1980. *De Vaderlandse Club 1929–1942: Totoks en de Indische Politiek*. Franeker: T. Wever V. C.

Du Bois, John W. 1993. "Meaning without Intention: Lessons from Divination." In *Responsibility and Evidence in Oral Discourse*, edited by Jane H. Hill and Judith T. Irvine, 48–71. Cambridge: Cambridge University Press.

Duranti, Alessandro. 1988. "Intention, Language, and Social Action in a Samoan Context." *Journal of Pragmatics* 12: 13–33.

Durkheim, Emile. [1893] 1984. *The Division of Labour in Society*. Introduction by Lewis Coser, translated by W. D. Halls. Basingstoke: Macmillan.

———. [1912] 1965. *The Elementary Forms of the Religious Life*. Translated by Joseph Ward Swain. New York: Free Press.

Echols, John M., and Hassan Shadily. 1989. *An Indonesian-English Dictionary*. 3rd ed. Ithaca: Cornell University Press.

Editor. 1994. "Sastra Lisan di Simpang Jalan." January 7: 39.

Ellen, R. F. 1986. "Conundrums about Panjandrums: On the Use of Titles in the Relations of Political Subordination in the Moluccas and along the Papuan Coast." *Indonesia* 41: 46–63.

Elmberg, J. E. 1968. *Balance and Circulation: Aspects of Tradition and Change among the Mejprat of Irian Barat*. Stockholm: Ethnographical Museum.

Engineering Consulting Association, Japan. 1990. "Biak Island: Draft Report of the Development Situation and Needs Assessment." Unpublished document dated August.

Errington, J. Joseph. 1998. *Shifting Languages: Interaction and Identity in Javanese Indonesia*. Cambridge: Cambridge University Press.

Errington, Shelly. 1989. *Meaning and Power in a Southeast Asian Realm*. Princeton: Princeton University Press.

———. 1990. "Recasting Sex, Gender and Power: A Theoretical and Regional Overview." In *Power and Difference: Gender in Island Southeast Asia*, edited by Jane Monnig Atkinson and Shelly Errington, 1–58. Stanford: Stanford University Press.

Escobar, Arturo. 1995. *Encountering Development: The Making and Unmaking of the Third World*. Princeton: Princeton University Press.

Ewald, J. 1988. "Speaking, Writing and Authority: Explorations in and from the Kingdom of Taqali." *Comparative Studies in Society and History* 30 (2): 199–224.

Fabian, Johannes. 1982. "Scratching the Surface: Observations on the Poetics of Lexical Borrowing in Shaba Swahili." *Anthropological Linguistics* 24 (1): 14–50.

Fabricius, Johan. 1949. *East Indies Episodes: An Account of the Demolitions Carried Out and of Some Experiences of the Staff in the East Indies Oil Areas of the Royal Dutch Shell Group during 1941 and 1942*. London: Shell Petroleum Company.

Fautngil, Christ, Frans Rumbrawer, and Bartolomeus Kainakaimu. 1994. *Sintaksis Bahasa Biak*. Jakarta: Pusat Pembinaan dan Pengembangan Bahasa, Departemen Pendidikan dan Kebudayaan.

Feld, Steven. 1988. "Aesthetics as Iconicity of Style, or, 'Lift-Up-Over-Sounding': Getting into the Kaluli Groove." *Yearbook for Traditional Music* 20: 74–113.

———. 1990. "Wept Thoughts: The Voicing of Kaluli Memories." *Oral Tradition* 5 (2–3): 241–266.

Feldman, Allen. 1991. *Formations of Violence: The Narrative of the Body and Political Terror in Northern Ireland*. Chicago: University of Chicago Press.

Femina. 1993. Photograph. December 9–15: 67.

Feuilletau de Bruyn, W.K.H. 1916. Militaire Memorie der Schouten-eilanden, 31 August 1916, Nummer Toegang 10–25, Stuk 183. Nienhuis Collectie van de Department van Bevolkszaken Hollandia Rapportenarchief. The Hague: Algemeene Rijksarchief.

———. 1920. *Schouten en Padaido-eilanden*. Mededeelingen Encyclopaedisch Bureau 21. Batavia: Javaasche Boekhandel.

———. 1933. "Economische Ontwikkelingsmogelijkheiden van Noord-Nieuw-Guinea in het Bijzonder door Kolonisatie van Europeanen en Indo Europeanen." *Koloniale Studiën* 17: 514–539.

———. 1936–37. "De Bevolking van Biak en het Kolonisatievraagstuk van Noord Nieuw-Guinea." *Tijdschrift Nieuw Guinea* 1 (1–6): 169–177.

———. 1940–41. "De Biaksche Tijdrekening naar de Starrenbeelden." *Tijdschrift Nieuw-Guinea* 5: 1–10.

———. 1954. "Goedenruil en Handel bij de Primitieve Stammen van Nieuw-Guinea." *Tijdschrift Nieuw-Guinea* 5: 1–11.

Forrest, Thomas. [1780] 1969. *A Voyage to New Guinea and the Moluccas, 1774–1776*. London: Oxford University Press.

Foucault, Michel. [1975] 1979. *Discipline and Punish: The Birth of the Prison*. Translated by Alan Sheridan. Harmondsworth: Penguin.

———. 1980. *The History of Sexuality*. Vol. 1. *An Introduction*. Translated by Robert Hurley. New York: Vintage.

Fox, James J. 1974. "'Our Ancestors Spoke in Pairs': Rotinese Views of Language, Dialect, and Code." In *Explorations in the Ethnography of Speaking*, edited by Richard Bauman and Joel Sherzer, 65–85. London: Cambridge University Press.

———, ed. 1980. *The Flow of Life: Essays on Eastern Indonesia*. Cambridge: Harvard University Press.

———, ed. 1988. *To Speak in Pairs: Essays on the Ritual Languages of Eastern Indonesia*. Cambridge: Cambridge University Press.

———. 1995. "Austronesian Societies and Their Transformations." In *The Austronesians: Historical and Comparative Perspectives*, edited by P. Bellwood, J. J. Fox, and D. Tryon, 214–228. Department of Anthropology as part of the Comparative Austronesian Project. Canberra: Research School of Pacific and Asian Studies, Australian National University.

Frederick, William H. 1988. "The Japanese Occupation." In *Born in Fire: The Indonesian Struggle for Independence*, edited by Colin Wild and Peter Carey, 75–80. Athens: Ohio University Press.

Freud, Sigmund. [1900] 1965. *The Interpretation of Dreams*. Edited and translated by James Strachey. New York: Avon.

———. [1918] 1963. "From the History of an Infantile Neurosis." In *Three Case Histories*, edited by Philip Rieff, 161–280. New York: Collier.

———. [1920] 1961. *Beyond the Pleasure Principle*. Translated and edited by James Strachey. New York and London: W. W. Norton.

———. [1922] 1963. "Medusa's Head." In *Sexuality and the Psychology of Love*, edited by Philip Rieff, 202–203. New York: Collier.

———. [1927] 1963. "Fetishism." In *Sexuality and the Psychology of Love*, edited by Philip Rieff, 204–209. New York: Collier.

———. [1938] 1963. "Splitting of the Ego in the Defensive Process." In *Sexuality and the Psychology of Love*, edited by Philip Rieff, 210–213. New York: Collier.

Friedman, Thomas L. 1997. "The Globalutionaries." Editorial desk, *New York Times*. July 24: A21.

Furnivall, J. S. 1944. *Netherlands India: A Study of Plural Economy*. Cambridge: Cambridge University Press.

————. [1948] 1956. *Colonial Policy and Practice: A Comparative Study of Burma and Netherlands India*. New York: New York University Press.

Galis, K. W. 1946. Dagboek over April 1946. Nummer Toegang 10–25, Stuk 179. Nienhuis Collectie van de Department van Bevolkingszaken Hollandia Rapportenarchief. The Hague: Algemeene Rijksarchief.

————. 1955. *Papua's van de Humbolt-Baai*. The Hague: Voorhoeve.

Garnaut, R., and C. Manning. 1974. *Irian Jaya: The Transformation of a Melanesian Economy*. Canberra: Australian National University Press.

Geertz, Clifford. 1963. *Agricultural Involution: The Process of Ecological Change in Indonesia*. Berkeley: University of California Press.

————. 1973. "Deep Play: Notes on the Balinese Cockfight." In *The Interpretation of Cultures*, 412–453. New York: Basic Books.

————. 1980. *Negara: The Theatre State in Nineteenth-Century Bali*. Princeton: Princeton University Press.

————. 2000. "Indonesia: Starting Over." *New York Review of Books* 47 (8) (May 11): 22–26.

Geertz, Hildred. 1961. *The Javanese Family: A Study of Kinship and Socialization*. Glencoe, Ill.: Free Press.

Geissler, J. G. 1857. Letter of January 29. UZV K41 D3. Oegstgeest, the Netherlands: Archives of the Hendrik Kraemer Institute.

Gellner, Ernest. 1983. *Nations and Nationalism*. Ithaca: Cornell University Press.

George, Kenneth M. 1990. "Felling a Song with a New Ax: Writing and the Reshaping of Ritual Song Performance in Upland Sulawesi." *Journal of American Folklore* 103 (407): 3–23.

————. 1996. *Showing Signs of Violence: The Cultural Politics of a Twentieth-Century Headhunting Ritual*. Berkeley: University of California Press.

Gewertz, Deborah, and Frederick Errington. 1991. *Twisted Histories, Altered Contexts: Representing the Chambri in a World System*. Cambridge: Cambridge University Press.

Giddens, Anthony. 1990. *The Consequences of Modernity*. Cambridge: Polity.

Gietzelt, D. 1989. "The Indonesianization of West Papua." *Oceania* 59 (3): 201–221.

Godelier, Maurice. [1982] 1986. *The Making of Great Men: Male Domination and Power among the New Guinea Baruya*. Translated by R. Swyer. Cambridge: Cambridge University Press; Paris: Maison des Sciences de l'Homme.

Goffman, Erving. [1974] 1986. *Frame Analysis: An Essay on the Organization of Experience*. Boston: Northeastern University Press.

————. 1981. "Footing." In *Forms of Talk*, 124–159. Philadelphia: University of Pennsylvania Press.

Gouda, Frances. 1993 "The Gendered Rhetoric of Colonialism and Anti-Colonialism in Twentieth-Century Indonesia." *Indonesia* 55: 1–22.

————. 1995. *Dutch Culture Overseas: Colonial Practice in the Netherlands Indies, 1900–1942*. Amsterdam: University of Amsterdam Press.

Goudswaard, A. 1863. *De Papoewa's van de Geelvinksbaai*. Schiedam: H.A.M. Roelants.

Graeber, David. 1996. "Beads and Money: Notes toward a Theory of Wealth and Power." *American Ethnologist* 23 (1): 4–24.

Gramsci, Antonio. 1971. *Selections from the Prison Notebooks*. Edited and translated by Quintin Hoare and Geoffrey Nowell Smith. New York: International Publishers.

Habermas, Jürgen. 1990. "Modernity's Consciousness of Time." In *The Philosophical Discourse of Modernity: Twelve Lectures*, 1–22. Cambridge: Polity.

Haenen, Paul. 1991. "Weefsels van Wederkerigheid: Sociale Structuur bij de Moi van Irian Jaya." Doctoral thesis, Katholieke Universiteit van Nijmegen.

Haga, A. 1884. *Nederlandsch Nieuw-Guinea en de Papoesche Eilanden: Historische Bijdrage*. 2 vols. Batavia: Bruining; The Hague. Martinus Nijhoff.

Handler, Richard. 1988. *Nationalism and the Politics of Culture in Quebec*. Madison: University of Wisconsin Press.

Hartweg, F. W. 1925a. Letter to the Board of February 27. UZV K31, D12. Oegstgeest, the Netherlands: Archives of the Hendrik Kraemer Institute.

———. 1925b. Letter to the Board of July 7. UZV K31, D12. Oegstgeest, the Netherlands: Archives of the Hendrik Kraemer Institute.

———. 1925c. Letter to the Board of October 26. UZV K31, D12. Oegstgeest, the Netherlands: Archives of the Hendrik Kraemer Institute.

———. 1926. Letter to the Board of September 23. UZV K31, D12. Oegstgeest, the Netherlands: Archives of the Hendrik Kraemer Institute.

———. 1927. Letter to the Chair of the New Guinea Conference of February 7. UZV K31, D12. Oegstgeest, the Netherlands: Archives of the Hendrik Kraemer Institute.

———. 1932–33. "Das Lied von Manseren Mangundi (Biak-Sprache)." *Zeitschrift für Eingeborenen-Sprachen* 23: 46.

Hefner, Robert W. 1993a. "World Building and the Rationality of Conversion." In *Conversion to Christianity: Historical and Anthropological Perspectives on a Great Transformation*, edited by R. Hefner, 3–46. Berkeley: University of California Press.

———. 1993b. "Of Faith and Commitment: Christian Conversion in Muslim Java." In *Conversion to Christianity: Historical and Anthropological Perspectives on a Great Transformation*, edited by R. Hefner, 99–128. Berkeley: University of California Press.

Hegel, G. W. F. [1807] 1977. *The Phenomenology of Spirit*. Translated by A. V. Miller. Oxford: Clarendon Press.

———. [1822] 1991. *Lectures on the Philosophy of History*. Translated by J. Sibree. Buffalo, N.Y.: Prometheus Books.

———. [1907] 1977. "The Spirit of Christianity and Its Fate." In *Early Theological Writings*, translated by T. M. Knox from German publication of c. 1798–99 manuscript, 182–301. Philadelphia: University of Pennsylvania Press.

Held, G. J. 1951. *De Papoea, Cultuurimprovisator*. The Hague/Bandung: Van Hoeve.

———. 1957. *The Papuas of Waropen*. KITLV Translation Series 2. The Hague: Martinus Nijhoff.

Heldring, O. G. 1847. *De Christen-Werkman den Zendeling Toegevoegd als Mede-arbeider*. Offprint from *Tijdschrift de Vereeniging Christelijke Stemmen*. Amsterdam: H. Höveker.

Helms, Mary W. 1988. *Ulysses' Sail: An Ethnographic Odyssey of Power, Knowledge, and Geographical Distance*. Princeton: Princeton University Press.

———. 1993. *Craft and the Kingly Ideal: Art, Trade, and Power*. Austin: University of Texas Press.

Henley, David. 1993. "A Superabundance of Centers: Ternate and the Contest for North Sulawesi." *Cakalele* 4: 39–60.

Heryanto, Ariel. 1988. "The Development of 'Development'." Translated Nancy Lutz. *Indonesia* 46: 1–24.

Het Seminarie te Depok. 1895. Mededeelingen vanwege het Centraal Comite voor de Oprichting en de Instandhouding van een Seminarie nabij Batavia over 1895. Oegstgeest, the Netherlands: Archives of the Hendrik Kraemer Institute.

Hobsbawm, Eric J. 1990. *Nations and Nationalism since 1780: Programme, Myth, Reality*. Cambridge: Cambridge University Press.

Hoffman, John. 1979. "A Foreign Investment: Indies Malay to 1901." *Indonesia* 27: 65–92.

Hoog, Aletta, and H. B. de la Bassecour Caan. 1917. *Van een Klein Papoea*. From the series *Leesboek voor School en Huis*, edited by J. C. Wirtz. Arnhem: H. ten Brink.

Hooker, Virginia Matheson. 1993. "New Order Language in Context." In *Culture and Society in New Order Indonesia*, edited by Virginia Matheson Hooker, 272–293. New York: Oxford University Press.

Horton, Robin. 1971. "African Conversion." *Africa* 41 (2): 85–108.

———. 1975. "On the Rationality of Conversion." *Africa* 45 (3): 219–235; (4): 373–399.

Hoskins, Janet. 1993. *The Play of Time: Kodi Perspectives on Calendars, History, and Exchange*. Berkeley: University of California Press.

Human Rights Watch. 1998. Indonesia: Human Rights and Pro-Independence Actions in Irian Jaya. Internet posting.

Hutomo, Suripan Sadi. 1993. "Transformasi Cerita Sarahwulan dalam Kentrung dan Wayang Krucil." *Suara Karya*. 12 December: 5, 8.

Ivy, Marilyn. 1995. *Discourses of the Vanishing: Modernity, Phantasm, Japan*. Chicago: University of Chicago Press.

Jacquemond, Richard. 1992. "Translation and Cultural Hegemony: The Case of French-Arabic Translation." In *Rethinking Translation: Discourse, Subjectivity, Ideology*, edited by Lawrence Venuti, 139–158. London: Routledge.

Jakarta-Jakarta. 1993. "Mulut ke Mulut: Astari Rasyid." Photograph. 18–24 December: 54.

Jakarta Post. 1993a. "Festival to Recall 'Wor' Music Genre of Biak." By Danilyn Rutherford and Sam Kapissa. 9 December: 6.

———. 1993b. "Seminar on Oral Tradition at TIM." 10 December: 6.

———. 1993c. "Betawi Storyteller Hangs on in Modern Age . . . with Traditional Tales of Kings." 18 December: 7.

———. 1993d. "Scholars Want Government to Pay More Attention to Culture." Photographs. 18 December: 7.

Jakobson, Roman. 1987. "Poetics and Linguistics." In *Language in Literature*, edited by Krystyna Pomorska and Stephen Rudy, 69–94. Cambridge: Belknap Press of Harvard University Press.

Jens, F. J. 1915. Jaarverslag. UZV127 K21, D6. Oegstgeest, the Netherlands: Archives of the Hendrik Kraemer Institute.

———. 1916. "Het Insos- en K'bor-feest op Biak en Soepiori." *Bijdragen tot de Taal-, Land- en Volkenkunde van Nederlandsch-Indië* 72: 404–411.

Jolly, Margaret. 1991. "Soaring Hawks and Grounded Persons: The Politics of Rank and Gender in North Vanuatu." In *Big Men and Great Men: Personifications of Power in Melanesia*, edited by Maurice Godelier and Marilyn Strathern, 48–80. Paris: Maison des Sciences de l'Homme.

Kahin, Audrey R. 1985a. "Introduction." In *Regional Dynamics of the Indonesian Revolution: Unity from Diversity*, edited by Audrey R. Kahin, 1–20. Honolulu: University of Hawai'i Press.

———, ed. 1985b. *Regional Dynamics of the Indonesian Revolution: Unity from Diversity*. Honolulu: University of Hawai'i Press.

Kahin, George McTurnan. 1952. *Nationalism and Revolution in Indonesia*. Ithaca: Cornell University Press.

Kahn, Joel S. 1993. *Constituting the Minangkabau: Peasants, Culture, and Modernity in Colonial Indonesia*. Providence and Oxford: Berg.

Kaisiëpo, Manuel. 1994. "Ke-irian-an dan Ke-indonesia-an: Mengkaji Nasionalisme dalam Konteks Lokal." *Bina Dharma* 12 (44): 41–54.

Kamma, Freerk C. 1939–41. "Levend Heidendom." *Tijdschrift Nieuw-Guinea* 4: 206–213, 247–258, 320–333, and 5: 22–35, 69–90, 117–135.

———. 1947–49. "De Verhouding tussen Tidore en de Papoese Eilanden in Legende en Historie." *Indonesië* 1: 361–370, 536–559; 2: 177–188, 256–275.

———. 1972. *Koreri: Messianic Movements in the Biak-Numfor Culture Area.* The Hague: Martinus Nijhoff.

———. 1976. *Dit Wonderlijk Werk.* Vol. 1. Oegstgeest: Raad voor de Zending der Ned. Hervormde Kerk.

———. 1977. *Dit Wonderlijk Werk.* Vol. 2. Oegstgeest: Raad voor de Zending der Ned. Hervormde Kerk.

———. 1981. *Ajaib di Mata Kita.* 2 vols. Jakarta: Gunung Mulia.

———. 1982. "The Incorporation of Foreign Culture Elements and Complexes by Ritual Enclosure among the Biak-Numforese." In *Symbolic Anthropology in the Netherlands,* edited by P. E. de Josselin de Jong and E. Schwimmer, 43–84. The Hague: Martinus Nijhoff.

Kamma, Freerk C., and S. Kooijman. 1973. *Romawa Forja: Child of the Fire: Iron Working and the Role of Iron in West New Guinea (West Irian).* Leiden: E. J. Brill.

Kapissa, Sam. 1980. "Dari 'Puteri Koreri' ke 'Nyora Pindah Pindah.'" Unpublished paper.

Kaplan, Martha. 1995. *Neither Cargo nor Cult: Ritual Politics and the Colonial Imagination in Fiji.* Durham: Duke University Press.

Keane, Webb. 1997a. *Signs of Recognition: Powers and Hazards of Representation in an Indonesian Society.* Berkeley: University of California Press.

———. 1997b. "From Fetishism to Sincerity: On Agency, the Speaking Subject, and their Historicity in the Context of Religious Conversion." *Comparative Studies in Society and History* 39 (4): 674–693.

———. 1997c. "Religious Language." *Annual Review of Anthropology* 26: 47–71.

———. 1997d. "Knowing One's Place: National Language and the Idea of the Local in Eastern Indonesia." *Cultural Anthropology* 12 (1): 37–63.

Keesing, Roger M. 1987. "African Models in the Malaita Highlands." *Man* (n.s.) 22 (3): 431–52.

Kepper, G., and L.H.W. van Sandick. 1937. "Het Arbeidvraagstuk voor Nieuw Guinee. English Summary." In *Nieuw-Guinee,* edited by W. C. Klein, Vol. 2: 942–943. Amsterdam: J. H. de Bussy.

Kermode, Frank. 1967. *The Sense of an Ending: Studies in the Theory of Fiction.* New York: Oxford University Press.

Kierkegaard, Soren. [1843] 1985. *Fear and Trembling.* Translated by Alastair Hannay. Harmondsworth: Penguin.

Kijne, I. S. n.d. Het Voorkomen en de Viering van Volksfeesten en Kerkelijke Feesten in het Gebied van de Evangelische Christelijke Kerk in Nieuw Guinea. F. C. Kamma Papers. Oegstgeest, the Netherlands: Archives of the Hendrik Kraemer Institute.

Kipp, Rita Smith. 1996. *Dissociated Identities: Ethnicity, Religion, and Class in an Indonesian Society.* Ann Arbor: University of Michigan Press.

Klein, W. C. 1937. "In- en Uitvoer, Handel en Nijverheid." In *Nieuw-Guinee,* edited by W. C. Klein, Vol. 2: 599–731. Amsterdam: J. H. de Bussy.

———, ed. 1935–38. *Nieuw-Guinee.* 3 vols. Amsterdam: J. H. de Bussy.

———, ed. 1953–54. *Nieuw Guinea: De Ontwikkeling op Economisch, Sociaal en Cultureel Gebied in Nederlands en Australisch Nieuw-Guinea.* 3 vols. The Hague: Staatsdrukkerij.

Knauft, Bruce M. 1978. "Cargo Cults and Relational Separation." *Behavior Science Research* 13 (3): 185–240.

———. 1996. *South Coast New Guinea Cultures: History, Comparison, Dialectic.* Cambridge: Cambridge University Press.

Kompas. 1993a. "Festival dan Seminar Tradisi Lisan." 7 December: 12.

———. 1993b. "Sastra Lisan yang Kehilangan Fungsinya Terancam Kepunahan." 10 December: 16.

———. 1993c. "Tradisi Lisan Nusantara Disisihkan oleh Modernisasi." 13 December: 16.

Kroskrity, Paul V. 2000. "Regimenting Languages: Language Ideological Perspectives." In *Regimes of Language: Ideologies, Polities, Identities*, edited by Paul V. Kroskrity, 1–34. Santa Fe: School of American Research Press.

Kuipers, Joel C. 1990. *Power in Performance: The Creation of Textual Authority in Weyewa Ritual Speech*. Philadelphia: University of Pennsylvania Press.

———. 1998. *Language, Identity and Marginality in Indonesia: The Changing Nature of Ritual Speech on the Island of Sumba*. Cambridge: Cambridge University Press.

Kulick, Don. 1992a. *Language Shift and Cultural Reproduction: Socialization, Self, and Syncretism in a Papua New Guinea Village*. Cambridge: Cambridge University Press.

———. 1992b. "'Coming up' in Gapun." In *Kam-ap or Take-off: Local Notions of Development*, edited by G. Dahl and A. Rabo, 10–34. Stockholm: Stockholm Studies in Social Anthropology.

Kulick, Don, and Chrisopher Stroud. 1993. "Conceptions and Uses of Literacy in a Papua New Guinean Village." In *Cross-Cultural Approaches to Literacy*, edited by Brian Street, 30–61. Cambridge: Cambridge University Press.

Lacan, Jacques. 1977. "The Agency of the Letter in the Unconscious or Reason since Freud." In *Écrits: A Selection*. Translated by Alan Sheridan, 146–178. London: Tavistock/Routledge.

———. 1982. "The Meaning of the Phallus." In *Feminine Sexuality: Jacques Lacan and the École Freudienne* edited by Juliette Mitchell and Jacqueline Rose, 74–85. New York and London: W. W. Norton.

———. 1988. *The Seminar of Jacques Lacan: Book II: The Ego in Freud's Theory and in the Technique of Psychoanalysis 1954–1955*. Edited by Jacques-Alain Miller, translated by Sylvana Tomaselli. Cambridge: Cambridge University Press.

Landler, Mark. 1999. "New Crisis Frames Even Tougher Test of Indonesian Unity." Foreign desk, *New York Times*. November 21: 1, 17.

Lanternari, Vittorio. 1963. *The Religions of the Oppressed: A Study of Modern Messianic Cults*. London: MacGibbon and Kee.

Lattas, Andrew. 1998. *Cultures of Secrecy: Reinventing Race in Bush Kaliai Cargo Cults*. Madison: University of Wisconsin Press.

Lawrence, Peter. [1964] 1971. *Road Belong Cargo: A Study of the Cargo Movement in the Southern Madang District, New Guinea*. Prospect Heights, Ill.: Waveland.

Leach, Edmund. 1983. "Melchisedech and the Emperor: Icons of Subversion and Orthodoxy." In *Structuralist Interpretations of Biblical Myth*, edited by E. Leach and D. A. Aycock, 67–88. Cambridge: Cambridge University Press.

Levi, Primo. 1984. *The Periodic Table*. Translated by Raymond Rosenthal. New York: Schocken.

Lévi-Strauss, Claude. [1949] 1969. *The Elementary Structures of Kinship*. Translated by James Harle Bell, John Richard von Sturmer, and Rodney Needham, Boston: Beacon.

———. [1950] 1987. *Introduction to the Works of Marcel Mauss*. Translated by Felicity Baker. London: Routledge and Kegan Paul.

Lieberman, Victor. 1995. "An Age of Commerce in Southeast Asia? Problems of Regional Coherence—A Review Article." *Journal of Asian Studies* 54 (3): 796–807.

Liep, John. 1991. "Great Man, Big Man, Chief: A Triangulation of the Massim." In *Big Men and Great Men: Personifications of Power in Melanesia*, edited by Maurice Godelier and Marilyn Strathern, 28–47. Paris: Maison des Sciences de l'Homme.

Lijphart, A. 1966. *The Trauma of Decolonization: The Dutch and West New Guinea*. New Haven: Yale University Press.

Lindstrom, Lamont. 1984. "Big Men and the Conversational Marketplace of Tanna (Vanuatu)." *Ethnos* 53 (3–4): 159–189.

———. 1990. *Knowledge and Power in a South Pacific Society*. Washington, D.C.: Smithsonian Institution Press.

———. 1993. *Cargo Cult: Strange Stories of Desire from Melanesia and Beyond*. Honolulu: University of Hawai'i Press.

Locher-Scholten, Elsbeth. 1981. *Ethiek in Fragmenten: Vijf Studies over Koloniaal Denken en Doen van Nederlanders in de Indonesische Archipel 1877–1942*. Utrecht: HES.

———. 1994. "Dutch Expansion in the Indonesian Archipelago around 1900 and the Imperialism Debate." *Journal of Southeast Asian Studies* 25 (1): 91–111.

Lontar Foundation and the Faculty of Letters of the University of Indonesia. 1993. "Lisan: A Celebration of Indonesian Oral Traditions." Unpublished funding proposal. Jakarta.

Lorentz, H. A. n.d. *Eenige Maanden onder de Papoea's*. Privately published edition dedicated to Prof. Dr. C.E.A. Wichmann, Leader of the New Guinea Expedition of 1903.

Lucas, Anton. 1991. *One Soul, One Struggle: Region and Revolution in Indonesia*. Sydney: Allen and Unwin.

MacCannell, Dean. 1976. *The Tourist: A New Theory of the Leisure Class*. New York: Schocken.

Maier, H.M.J. 1993. "From Heteroglossia to Polyglossia: The Creation of Malay and Dutch in the Indies." *Indonesia* 56: 37–65.

Malinowski, Bronislaw. [1922] 1961. *Argonauts of the Western Pacific*. New York: E. P. Dutton.

Mampioper, A. 1976. "Mitologi dan Pengharapan Masyarakat Biak-Numfor." Unpublished manuscript.

Mann, Michael. 1996. "Nation-States in Europe and Other Continents: Diversifying, Developing, Not Dying." In *Mapping the Nation*, edited by Gopal Balakrisnan, 295–316. London: Verso.

Manning, Chris, and Michael Rumbiak. 1991. "Irian Jaya: Economic Change, Migrants, and Indigenous Welfare." In *Unity and Diversity: Regional Economic Development in Indonesia since 1970*, edited by Hal Hill, 77–106. Oxford: Oxford University Press.

Manusaway-van den Berg, Paula. 1979. "Een Struktureel-Semiologiese Analyse van de Mythe van Manarmakeri." Doctoral thesis. Department of Sociocultural Anthropology, University of Nijmegen, the Netherlands.

Margadant, Ted W. 1984. "Review Article: Tradition and Modernity in Rural France during the 19th Century." *Journal of Modern History* 56 (4): 667–697.

Marin, Louis. 1984. *Utopics: Spatial Play*. Translated by Robert A. Vollrath. Atlantic Highlands, N.J.: Humanities Press.

———. 1992. "Frontiers of Utopia: Past and Present." *Critical Inquiry* 19 (3): 397–420.

Markowitz, Fran. 1996. "Israel as Africa, Africa as Israel: 'Divine Geography' in the Personal Narratives and Community Identity of the Black Hebrew Israelites." *Anthropological Quarterly* 69 (4): 193–205.

Marx, Karl. [1867] 1967. *Capital*. Vol. 1. Edited by Frederick Engels, translated by Samuel Moore and Edward Aveling, from the third German edition. New York: International Publishers.

Mauss, Marcel. [1925] 1967. *The Gift: Forms and Functions of Exchange in Archaic Societies*. Translated by Ian Cunnison. New York and London: W. W. Norton.

———. [1902–1903] 1972. *A General Theory of Magic*. Translated by R. Brain. London: Routledge and Kegan Paul.

McKenzie, D. F. 1987. "The Sociology of a Text: Oral Culture, Literacy and Print in Early New Zealand." In *The Social History of Language*, edited by Peter Burke and Roy Porter, 161–197. Cambridge: Cambridge University Press.

McKinnon, Susan. 1991. *From a Shattered Sun: Hierarchy, Gender, and Alliance in the Tanimbar Islands*. Madison: University of Wisconsin Press.

———. 1995. "Houses and Hierarchy: The View from a South Moluccan Society." In *About the House: Lévi-Strauss and Beyond*, edited by J. Carsten and S. Hugh-Jones, 170–188. Cambridge: Cambridge University Press.

———. 2000. "Domestic Exceptions: Evans-Pritchard and the Creation of Nuer Patri-lineality and Equality." *Cultural Anthropology* 15 (1): 35–83.

McVey, Ruth. 1996. "Building Behemoth: Indonesian Constructions of the Nation-State." In *Making Indonesia: Essays on Modern Indonesia in Honor of George McT. Kahin*, edited by Daniel S. Lev and Ruth McVey, 11–25. Ithaca: Cornell Southeast Asia Program Publications.

Media Indonesia. 1993. "Tradisi Masa Lalu, Pijakan Pembangunan di Masa Depan." 10 December: 10.

Mehrez, Samia. 1992. "Translation and the Postcolonial Experience: The Francophone North African Text." In *Rethinking Translation: Discourse, Subjectivity, Language*, edited by Lawrence Venuti, 120–138. London: Routledge.

Messick, Brinkley. 1989. "Just Writing: Paradox and Political Economy in Yemeni Legal Documents." *Cultural Anthropology* 4 (1): 26–50.

Miedema, Jelle. 1984. *De Kebar 1855–1980: Sociale Structuur en Religie in de Vogelkop van West-Nieuw-Guinea*. Verhandelingen van het Koninklijk Instituut voor Taal-, Land- en Volkenkunde 105. Dordrecht, Holland/Cinnaminson, N.J.: Foris.

Mordden, Ethan. 1990. "A Critic at Large: I Got a Song." *New Yorker*. October 22: 110–143.

Mrázek, Rudolf. 1994. *Sjahrir: Politics and Exile in Indonesia*. Studies in Southeast Asia 14. Ithaca: Cornell Southeast Asia Program.

Munn, Nancy. 1986. *The Fame of Gawa: A Symbolic Study of Value Transformation in a Massim (Papua New Guinea) Society*. Cambridge: Cambridge University Press.

Mydans, Seth. 1997. Restive Indonesians Find Little Hope in Vote. Foreign desk, *New York Times*. May 29: A3.

———. 1999. "The World: Indonesia's Many Faces Reflect One Nation, Divisible." Week in Review desk, *New York Times*. September 5: 5.

Myers, Fred R. 1986a. *Pintupi Country, Pintupi Self: Sentiment, Place, and Politics among Western Desert Aborigines*. Washington, D.C.: Smithsonian Institution Press; Canberra: Australian Institute of Aboriginal Studies.

———. 1986b. "Reflections on a Meeting: Structure, Language, and the Polity in a Small-Scale Society." *American Ethnologist* 13 (3): 430–447.

Nagel, Thomas. 1986. *The View from Nowhere*. New York: Oxford University Press.

Nandy, Ashis. 1987. *Traditions, Tyranny and Utopias: Essays in the Politics of Awareness*. Delhi: Oxford University Press.

New York Times. 1996a. "Stirrings in Indonesia." Editorial desk, July 20: 18.

———. 1996b. "Turmoil in Indonesia." Editorial desk, August 1: A26–29.

Nieuwenhuys, R. 1982. *The Mirror of the Indies: A History of Dutch Colonial Literature*. Amherst: University of Massachusetts Press.

Niranjana, Tejaswini. 1994. "Colonialism and the Politics of Translation." In *An Other Tongue: Nation and Ethnicity in the Linguistic Borderlands*, edited by Alfred Arteaga, 35–52. Durham: Duke University Press.

O'Hanlon, Michael. 1995. "Modernity and the 'Graphicalization' of Meaning: New Guinea Highland Shield Design in Historical Perspective." *Journal of the Royal Anthropological Institute* (n.s.) 1 (3): 469–493.

O'Leary, Brendan. 1998. "Ernest Gellner's Diagnoses of Nationalism: A Critical Overview, or, What is Living and What is Dead in Ernest Gellner's Philosophy of Nationalism?" In *The State of the Nation: Ernest Gellner and the Theory of Nationalism*, edited by John A. Hall, 40–90. Cambridge: Cambridge University Press.

Onghokham. 1978. "The Inscrutable and the Paranoid: An Investigation of the Brotodiningrat Affair." In *Southeast Asian Transitions: Approaches through Social History*, edited by Ruth T. McVey, 112–157. New Haven: Yale University Press.

Orlove, Benjamin, and Arnold J. Bauer. 1997a. "Giving Importance to Imports." In *The Allure of the Foreign: Imported Goods in Postcolonial Latin America*, edited by Benjamin Orlove, 1–30. Ann Arbor: University of Michigan Press.

———. 1997b. "Chile in the Belle Epoque: Primitive Producers, Civilized Consumers." In *The Allure of the Foreign: Imported Goods in Postcolonial Latin America*, edited by Benjamin Orlove, 113–150. Ann Arbor: University of Michigan Press.

Osborne, Peter. 1995. *The Politics of Time: Modernity and Avant-Garde*. London: Verso.

Osborne, Robin. 1985. *Indonesia's Secret War: The Guerilla Struggle in Irian Jaya*. Sydney: Allen and Unwin.

Oxford English Dictionary. 1991. *The Compact Oxford English Dictionary*. 2nd ed. Oxford: Oxford University Press.

Parker, Andrew, and Eve Kosofsky Sedgwick. 1995. "Introduction: Performativity and Performance." In *Performativity and Performance*, edited by Andrew Parker and Eve Kosofsky Sedgwick, 1–18. New York: Routledge.

Parry, Jonathan. 1986. "The Gift, the Indian Gift, and the 'Indian Gift.'" *Man* (n.s.) 21: 453–473.

Pauwels, S. 1994. "Sibling Relations and (In)temporality: Towards a Definition of the House (Eastern Indonesia)." In *Halmahera and Beyond: Social Science Research in the Moluccas*, edited by L. Visser, 79–96. Leiden: KITLV Press.

Pawley, A., and M. Ross. 1995. "Prehistory of Oceanic Languages: A Current View." In *The Austronesians: Historical and Comparative Perspectives*, edited by P. Bellwood, J. J. Fox, and D. Tryon, 39–74. Department of Anthropology as part of the Comparative Austronesian Project. Canberra: Research School of Pacific and Asian Studies, Australian National University.

Pemberton, John. 1994. *On the Subject of "Java."* Ithaca: Cornell University Press.

Picard, Michel. 1993. "'Cultural Tourism' in Bali: National Integration and Regional Differentiation." In *Tourism in Southeast Asia*, edited by Michael Hitchcock, Victor T. King, and Michael J. G. Parnwell, 71–98. London: Routledge.

———. 1997. "Cultural Tourism, Nation-Building, and Regional Culture: The Making of a Balinese Identity." In *Tourism, Ethnicity, and the State in Asian and Pacific Societies*, edited by Michel Picard and Robert E. Wood, 181–214. Honolulu: University of Hawai'i Press.

Picard, Michel, and Robert E. Wood, eds. 1997. *Tourism, Ethnicity, and the State in Asian and Pacific Societies*. Honolulu: University of Hawai'i Press.

Pietz, William. 1985. "The Problem of the Fetish, I." *Res* 9: 5–17.

———. 1987. "The Problem of the Fetish, II: The Origin of the Fetish." *Res* 13: 23–45.

———. 1988. "The Problem of the Fetish, IIIa: Bosman's Guinea and the Enlightenment Theory of Fetishism." *Res* 16: 105–123.

———. 1993. "Fetishism and Materialism: The Limits of Theory in Marx." In *Fetishism as Cultural Discourse*, edited by Emily Apter and William Pietz, 119–151. Ithaca: Cornell University Press.

Pigg, Stacy Leigh. 1992. "Inventing Social Categories through Place: Social Representations and Development in Nepal." *Comparative Studies in Society and History* 34 (3): 491–513.

Platenkamp, J.D.M. 1984. "The Tobelo of Eastern Halmahera in the Context of the Field of Anthropological Study." In *Unity in Diversity: Indonesia as a Field of Anthropological Study*, edited by P. E. de Josselin de Jong, 167–189. Verhandelingen van het Koninklijk Instituut voor Taal-, Land- en Volkenkunde 103. Dordrecht/Providence: Foris.

Poe, Edgar Allan. 1981. *Marginalia*. Edited by John Carl Miller. Charlottesville: University Press of Virginia.

Pouwer, J. 1960. "'Loosely Structured Societies' in Netherlands New Guinea." *Bijdragen tot het Land-, Taal-, en Volkenkunde* 116: 109–119.

Purcell, Rosamond Wolff, and Stephan Jay Gould. 1992. *Finders, Keepers: Eight Collectors*. New York and London: W. W. Norton.

Rafael, Vicente L. [1988] 1993. *Contracting Colonialism: Translation and Christian Conversion in Tagalog Society under Early Spanish Rule*. Durham: Duke University Press.

Raheja, Gloria G. 1988. *The Poison in the Gift: Ritual, Prestation, and the Dominant Class in a North Indian Village*. Chicago: University of Chicago Press.

Ranger, Terrence. 1993. "The Local and the Global in Southern African Religious History." In *Conversion to Christianity: Historical and Anthropological Perspectives on a Great Transformation*, edited by R. Hefner, 65–98. Berkeley: University of California Press.

Reid, Anthony. 1979. *The Blood of the People: Revolution and the End of Traditional Rule in Northern Sumatra*. Kuala Lumpur: Oxford University Press.

———. 1988. *Southeast Asia in the Age of Commerce, 1450–1680*. Vol. 1. *The Lands below the Winds*. New Haven: Yale University Press.

———. 1993. *Southeast Asia in the Age of Commerce, 1450–1680*. Vol. 2. *Expansion and Crisis*. New Haven: Yale University Press.

Renck, Günther. 1990. *Contextualization of Christianity and Christianization of Language: A Case Study from the Highlands of Papua New Guinea*. Erlängen: Verlag der Ev.-Luth. Mission.

Republika. 1993a. "Esok, Festival Tradisi Lisan Dibuka." 8 December: 12.

———. 1993b. "Mendikbud Wardiman Djojonegoro: Tradisi Lisan Sudah Saatnya Diperhatikan." 10 December: 16.

———. 1993c. Photograph, 11 December: 7.

———. 1993d. Photograph. 12 December: 1.

———. 1993e. "(Tak) Usah Ratapi Sastra Lisan." 15 December: 12.

———. 1993f. "Pertunjukan Lisan: Dulu Mengkritik Raja, Kini Memuja Pembangunan." 15 December: 12.

———. 1993g. "Tradisi Lisan dan Hegemoni Budaya." By Ridwan Effendy. 15 December: 12.

Response to Inspection Report. 1923. Response to Inspection Report of October 31, 1923 from Mansinam. UZV 13. Oegstgeest, the Netherlands: Archives of the Hendrik Kraemer Institute.

Riches, David. 1986. "The Phenomenon of Violence." In *The Anthropology of Violence*, edited by D. Riches, 1–27. Oxford: Blackwell.

———. 1991. "Aggression, War, Violence: Space/Time and Paradigm." *Man* 26 (2): 287.

Robide van der Aa, P.J.B.C. 1879. *Reizen naar Nederlandsch Nieuw-Guinea Ondernomen op Last der Regeering van Nederlandsch-Indië in de Jaren 1871, 1872, 1875–1876*. The Hague: Martinus Nijhoff.

Robinson, Geoffrey. 1998. "*Rawan* is as *Rawan* does: The Origins of Disorder in New Order Aceh." *Indonesia* 66: 127–156.

Rosaldo, Michelle Z. 1980. *Knowledge and Passion: Ilongot Notions of Self and Social Life*. Cambridge: Cambridge University Press.

Rush, James R. 1983. "Social Control and Influence in 19th Century Indonesia: Opium Farms and the Chinese of Java." *Indonesia* 35: 53–64.

Rutherford, Danilyn. 1996. "Of Birds and Gifts: Reviving Tradition on an Indonesian Frontier." *Cultural Anthropology* 11 (4): 577–616.

———. 1998. "Trekking to New Guinea: Dutch Colonial Fantasies of a Virgin Land, 1900–1940." In *Domesticating the Empire: Race, Gender, and Family Life in French and Dutch Colonialism*, edited by Frances Gouda and Julia Clancy-Smith, 255–272. Charlottesville: University Press of Virginia.

———. 2001a. "Waiting for the End in Biak: Violence, Order, and a Flag Raising." In *Violence and the State in Suharto's Indonesia*, edited by Benedict R. O'G. Anderson, 189–212. Ithaca: Cornell Southeast Asia Program Press.

———. 2001b. "Intimacy and Alienation: Money and the Foreign in Biak." *Public Culture* 13 (2): 299–324.

———. n.d. "The Bible Meets the Idol: Writing and Conversion in Biak." Unpublished manuscript, Department of Anthropology, University of Chicago.

Ryter, Loren. 1998. "Pemuda Pancasila: The Last Loyalist Free Men of Suharto's Order?" *Indonesia* 66: 45–74.

Sahlins, Marshall. 1972. *Stone Age Economics*. New York: Aldine de Gruyter.

———. 1981. *Historical Metaphors and Mythical Realities: Structure in the Early History of the Sandwich Islands Kingdom*. Ann Arbor: University of Michigan Press.

———. 1985. *Islands of History*. Chicago: University of Chicago Press.

Sakai, Naoki. 1989. "Modernity and Its Critique: The Problem of Universalism and Particularism." In *Postmodernism and Japan*, edited by Masao Miyoshi and H. D. Harootunian, 93–122. Durham: Duke University Press.

Salim, I.F.M. 1973. *Vijftien Jaar Boven-Digoel, Concentratiekamp in Nieuw Guinea: Bakermat van de Indonesische Onafhankelijkheid*. Amsterdam: Uitgeverij Contact.

Saltford, John. 2000. "United Nations' Involvement with the Act of Self-Determination in West Irian (Indonesian West New Guinea), 1968–69." *Indonesia* 71: 71–92.

Sangren, P. Steven. 1991. "Dialectics of Alienation: Individuals and Collectivities in Chinese Religion." *Man* (n.s.) 26 (1): 67–86.

———. 1993. "Power and Transcendence in the Ma Tsu Pilgrimages of Taiwan." *American Ethnologist* 20 (3): 564–582.

———. 1995. "'Power' against Ideology: A Critique of Foucaultian Usage." *Cultural Anthropology* 10 (1): 3–40.

Sassen, Saskia. 1999. *Guests and Aliens*. New York: New Press, W. W. Norton.

Scarry, Elaine. 1985. *The Body in Pain: The Making and Unmaking of the World*. Oxford: Oxford University Press.

Schieffelin, Bambi B. 1990. *The Give and Take of Everyday Life: Language Socialization of Kaluli Children*. Cambridge: Cambridge University Press.

Sharp, Nonie. 1977. *The Rule of the Sword: The Story of West Irian*. Malmsbury, Victoria: Kibble Books/Arena.

Sharp, Nonie, with Markus Wonggor Kaisiëpo. 1994. *The Morning Star in Papua Barat*. North Carlton, Australia: Arena.

Shiraishi, Saya. 1986. "Silakan Masuk. Silakan Duduk. Reflections in a Sitting Room on Java." *Indonesia* 41: 89–131.

Shiraishi, Takashi. 1990. *An Age in Motion: Popular Radicalism in Java, 1912–1926*. Ithaca: Cornell University Press.

———. 1997. "Policing the Phantom Underground." *Indonesia* 63: 1–46.

———. n.d. "Before Dawn: A Note on 19th Century Java." Unpublished manuscript.

Siegel, James T. 1978. "Curing Rites, Dreams, and Domestic Politics in a Sumatran Society." *Johns Hopkins Textual Studies (Glyph)* 3: 18–31.

———. 1986. *Solo in the New Order: Language and Hierarchy in an Indonesian City.* Princeton: Princeton University Press.

———. 1997. *Fetish, Recognition, Revolution.* Princeton: Princeton University Press.

Silverstein, Michael. 1976. "Shifters, Linguistic Categories, and Cultural Description." In *Meaning in Anthropology*, edited by K. H. Basso and H. A. Selby, 11–55. Albuquerque: University of New Mexico Press.

———. 1996. "Monoglot 'Standard' in America: Standardization and the Metaphors of Linguistic Hegemony." In *The Matrix of Language: Contemporary Linguistic Anthropology*, edited by Donald Brenneis and R. Macaulay, 284–306. Boulder: Westview.

———. 2000. "Whorfianism and the Linguistic Imagination of Nationality." In *Regimes of Language*, edited by Paul V. Kroskrity, 85–188. Santa Fe: School of American Research Press.

Silverstein, Michael, and Greg Urban, eds. 1996. *Natural Histories of Discourse.* Chicago: University of Chicago Press.

Smeele, Rogier. 1988. "De Expansie van het Nederlandse Gezag en de Intensivering van de Bestuursbemoeienis op Nederlands Nieuw-Guinea 1898–1942." Doctoral thesis, Institute of History, Utrecht University.

Smith, Alan, and Kevin Hewison. 1986. "1984: Refugees, 'Holiday Camps' and Deaths." In *Between Two Nations: The Indonesia-Papua New Guinea Border and West Papua Nationalism*, edited by R. J. May, 200–217. Bathurst, New South Wales: K. Brown.

Smith, Anthony D. 1986. *The Ethnic Origins of Nations.* Oxford, U.K. and Cambridge, Mass.: Blackwell.

Smith, Robert Ross. 1953. *The U.S. Army in World War II: The War in the Pacific.* Vol. 3. *The Approach to the Philippines.* Washington, D.C.: Office of the Chief of Military History.

Soeparno. 1977. *Kamus Bahasa Biak-Indonesia.* Jakarta: Pusat Pembinaan dan Pengembangan Bahasa, Departemen Pendidikan dan Kebudayaan.

Soja, Edward W. 1989. *Postmodern Geographies: The Reassertion of Space in Critical Social Theory.* London: Verso.

Sollewijn Gelpke, J.H.F. 1993. "On the Origins of the Name Papua." *Bijdragen tot het Land-, Taal- en Volkenkunde* 149 (2): 318–332.

Spivak, Gayatri Chakravorty. 1999. *Critique of Postcolonial Reason: Toward a History of the Vanishing Present.* Cambridge: Harvard University Press.

Spyer, Patricia. 1996. "Diversity with a Difference: Adat and the New Order in Aru (Eastern Indonesia)." *Cultural Anthropology* 11 (1): 25–50.

———. 1997. "The Eroticism of Debt: Pearl Divers, Traders, and Sea Wives in the Aru Islands, Eastern Indonesia." *American Ethnologist* 24 (3): 515–538.

———. 1998. "The Tooth of Time, or Taking a Look at the 'Look' of Clothing in Late Nineteenth-Century Aru." In *Border Fetishisms: Material Objects in Unstable Spaces*, edited by Patricia Spyer, 150–182. New York and London: Routledge.

Steedly, Mary Margaret. 1993. *Hanging without a Rope: Narrative Experience in Colonial and Postcolonial Karoland.* Princeton: Princeton University Press.

Stewart, Susan. 1993. *On Longing: Narratives of the Miniature, the Gigantic, the Souvenir, the Collection.* Durham: Duke University Press.

———. 1995. "Lyric Possession." *Critical Inquiry* 22 (1): 34–63.

Stølen, K. A. 1991. "Gender, Sexuality and Violence in Ecuador." *Ethnos* 56 (1–2): 82–100.

Stoler, Ann Laura. 1985. *Capitalism and Confrontation in Sumatra's Plantation Belt, 1870–1979.* New Haven: Yale University Press.

————. 1989a. "Making Empire Respectable: The Politics of Race and Sexual Morality in 20th Century Colonial Cultures." *American Ethnologist* 16 (4): 634–660.

————. 1989b. "Rethinking Colonial Categories: European Communities and the Boundaries of Rule." *Comparative Studies in Society and History* 31 (1): 134–61.

————. 1995. *Race and the Education of Desire: Foucault's History of Sexuality and the Colonial Order of Things*. Durham: Duke University Press.

Strathern, Marilyn. 1988. *The Gender of the Gift: Problems with Women and Problems with Society in Melanesia*. Berkeley: University of California Press.

Street, Brian. 1984. *Literacy in Theory and Practice*. Cambridge: Cambridge University Press.

————, ed. 1993. *Cross-Cultural Approaches to Literacy*. Cambridge: Cambridge University Press.

Suryadi. 1993. "Persoalan Konsep dan Objek Penelitian." *Republika*. 11 December: 6.

Swadling, Pamela. 1996. *Plumes from Paradise: Trade Cycles in Outer Southeast Asia and Their Impact on New Guinea and Nearby Islands until 1920*. Boroko, PNG: Papua New Guinea National Museum/Robert Brown.

Tapol Bulletin. 1984a. "New Arrests in West Papua: Paracommandos in Charge." *Tapol Bulletin* no. 61 (January): 1–2.

————. 1984b. "West Papua in Revolt: Many Flee from Indonesian Reprisals." *Tapol Bulletin* no. 62 (March): 1–3.

————. 1984c. "The Killing of Arnold Ap and Eddy Mofu." *Tapol Bulletin* no. 64 (July): 3.

Taussig, Michael T. 1987. *Shamanism, Colonialism, and the Wild Man: A Study in Terror and Healing*. Chicago: University of Chicago Press.

Taylor, Jean Gelman. 1983. *The Social World of Batavia: European and Eurasian in Dutch Asia*. Madison: University of Wisconsin Press.

Teljeur, D. 1994. "Life-cycle Rituals among the Gimán of South Halmahera." In *Halmahera and Beyond: Social Science Research in the Moluccas*, edited by Leontine E. Visser, 165–194. Leiden: KITLV Press.

Tempo. 1993. "Sastra Mulut Berkumpul, Menjadi Festival." 18 December: 80.

ten Haaft, D. A. 1947–48. "De Manseren-Beweging op Noord-Nieuw-Guinea 1939–1943." *Tijdschrift Nieuw-Guinea* 8 (1–6): 161–165.

Thimme, Hans-Martin. 1976. *Koreri: Tafsiran dan Evaluasi Teologica tentang Mite Manarmakeri*. Jayapura: Sekolah Tinggi Teologia Gereja Kristen Injili.

Tijdeman, E. 1912. "De Legende van Miok Woendi." *Mededeelingen van het Bureau voor de Bestuurszaken der Buitenbezittingen bewerkt door het Encyclopaedisch Bureau* 2: 253–256.

Tilly, Charles. 1979. "Did the Cake of Custom Break?" In *Consciousness and Class Experience in Nineteenth-Century Europe*, edited by John M. Merriman, 17–44. New York and London: Holmes and Meier.

————. 1990. *Coercion, Capital, and European States, AD 990–1990*. Cambridge, Mass.: Basil Blackwell.

Tooker, Deborah. 1996. "Putting the Mandala in Its Place: A Practice-Based Approach to the Spatialization of Power on the Southeast Asian 'Periphery'—the Case of Akha." *Journal of Asian Studies* 55 (2): 323–358.

Traube, Elizabeth. 1986. *Cosmology and Social Life: Ritual Exchange among the Mambai of East Timor*. Chicago: University of Chicago Press.

Travel Indonesia. 1994. "Lisan, Festival of Indonesian Oral Traditions." January: 14.

Tryon, D. 1995. "Proto-Austronesian and the Major Austronesian Subgroups." In *The Austronesians: Historical and Comparative Perspectives*, edited by P. Bellwood, J. J. Fox, and D. Tryon, 17–38. Department of Anthropology as part of the Comparative

Austronesian Project. Canberra: Research School of Pacific and Asian Studies, Australian National University.

Tsing, Anna Lowenhaupt. 1990. "Gender and Performance in a Meratus Dispute Settlement." In *Power and Difference: Gender in Island Southeast Asia*, edited by Shelly Errington and Jane Monnig Atkinson, 95–126. Stanford: Stanford University Press.

———. 1993. *In the Realm of the Diamond Queen: Marginality in an Out-of-the-Way Place*. Princeton: Princeton University Press.

Tsuchiya, Kenji. 1986. "Kartini's Image of Java's Landscape." *East Asian Cultural Studies* 25 (1–4): 59–86.

———. 1990. "Javanology and the Age of Ranggawarsita: An Introduction to Nineteenth-Century Javanese Culture." In *Reading Southeast Asia*, 75–109. Ithaca: Cornell University Southeast Asia Program.

Turner, Terrence S. 1977. "Transformation, Hierarchy, and Transcendence: A Reformulation of van Gennep's Model of the Structure of Rites de Passage." In *Secular Ritual*, edited by Sally F. Moore and Barbara G. Myerhoff, 53–70. Assen and Amsterdam: van Gorcum.

———. 1980. "The Social Skin." In *Not Work Alone: A Cross-Cultural View of Activities Superfluous to Survival*, edited by eds. Jeremy Cherfas and Roger Lewin, 112–140. Beverly Hills: Sage.

———. 1991. "'We are Parrots,' 'Twins are Birds': Play of Tropes as Operational Structure." In *Beyond Metaphor: The Theory of Tropes in Anthropology*, edited by James W. Fernandez, 121–158. Stanford: Stanford University Press.

Tuzin, Donald. 1997. *The Cassowary's Revenge: The Life and Death of Masculinity in a New Guinea Society*. Chicago: University of Chicago Press.

Utrechtsche Zendingsvereeniging. 1909. *Laatste Berichten uit Nieuw-Guinea*. Utrecht: J. van Boekhoven.

———. 1920. *Handelingen van de Utrechtsche Zendingsvereeniging*, 87–88.

———. 1926. "Het Maleis op Onze Scholen." Conference Report from Miei. Received March 30. UZV 13. Oegstgeest, the Netherlands: Archives of the Hendrik Kraemer Institute.

Vademecum voor Nederlands-Nieuw-Guinea. 1956. Rotterdam: New Guinea Institute in cooperation with the Ministry of Overseas Territories.

van Baal, Jan. 1952 Dansen en Feesten: Praeadvies ten Behoeve van de Raad van Volksopvoeding. Hollandia. April 9. F. C. Kamma Papers. Oegstgeest, the Netherlands: Archives of the Hendrik Kraemer Institute.

———. 1954. "Volken." In *Nieuw-Guinea: De Ontwikkeling op Economisch, Sociaal en Cultureel Gebied in Nederlands en Australisch Nieuw-Guinea*, edited by W. C. Klein, Vol. 2: 439–441. The Hague: Staatsdrukkerij.

———. 1989. *Ontglipt Verleden*. 2 vols. Franeker: Wever.

van Baaren, Thomas P. 1968. *Korwars and Korwar Style: Art and Ancestor Worship in North-West New Guinea*. The Hague: Mouton.

van de Graaff, W. [1925] 1991a. Memorie van Overgave van de Afdeeling Noord-Nieuw-Guinea, Manokwari 1925 [MMK 372]. Reproduced in Irian Jaya Source Materials No. 2, Series A—No. 1: *Memories van Overgave van de Afdeling Noord Nieuw-Guinea*, edited by J. Miedema and W.A.L. Stokhof, 7–12. Leiden and Jakarta: DSALCUL/IRIS.

———. [1925] 1991b. Geheim. Bestuursmemorie bij Overgave van het Bestuur over de Afdeeling Noord Nieuw-Guinea, Manokwari 1925 [Appendix MMK 372]. Reproduced in Irian Jaya Source Materials No. 2, Series A—No. 1: *Memories van Overgave van de Afdeling Noord Nieuw-Guinea*, edited by J. Miedema and W.A.L. Stokhof, 13–17. Leiden and Jakarta: DSALCUL/IRIS.

van den Berg, G.W.H. 1981. *Baalen Droefheid: Biak-Nederlands Nieuw-Guinea Sche(r)tsenderwijs*. The Hague: Moesson.

van der Leeden, A. C. 1956. *Hoofdtrekken der Sociale Struktuur in het Westelijke Binnenland van Sarmi*. Leiden: Eduard IJdo.

———. 1960. "Social Structure in New Guinea." *Bijdragen tot het Land-, Taal- en Volkenkunde* 116: 119–141.

van der Roest, J.L.D. 1921. *Van een Papoesch Slavenkind: Een Vertelling voor Kinderen*. Oegstgeest: Zendingsbureau.

van der Veur, Paul W. 1955. "Introduction to a Socio-Political Study of the Eurasians of Indonesia." Doctoral dissertation, Cornell University.

———. 1966. *The Search for New Guinea's Boundaries: from Torres Straits to the Pacific*. Canberra: ANU Press.

van Eck, R. 1881. "Schetsen uit het Volksleven in Nederl. Oost-Indië." *De Indische Gids* 3: 368–88.

van Fraassen, Christian F. 1987. "Ternate, de Molukken en de Indonesische Archipel." 2 vols. Doctoral thesis, University of Leiden.

van Gendt, G. J. 1954. Memorie van Overgave Onderafdeling Biak 1951—31 December 1954. Nummer Toegang 10–25, Stuk 197. Nienhuis Collectie van de Department van Bevolkszaken Hollandia Rapportenarchief. The Hague: Algemeene Rijksarchief.

van Goor, J., ed. 1986. *Imperialisme in de Marge: De Afronding van Nederlands-Indië*. Utrecht: HES.

van Hasselt, F.J.F. 1914. "De Legende van Manseren Mangoendi." *Bijdragen tot de Taal-, Land- en Volkenkunde van Nederlandsch-Indië* 69: 90–100.

———. 1916. Jaarverslag 1915–16: Schouten-eilanden. UZV K16, D 39. Oegstgeest, the Netherlands: Archives of the Hendrik Kraemer Institute.

———. 1921. "Iets over de Roem-Seram en over Nanggi (naar Aanleiding van Feuilletau de Bruyn's Rapport, Gepubliceerd door het Encyclopaedisch Bureau)." *Tijdschrift voor Indische Taal-, Land-, en Volkenkunde* 60: 108–114.

———. 1929. "Or, Mana, For en Verwante Begrippen bij de Papoea's, Voornamelijk van den Noemfoorschen Stam." Voordracht gehouden op de Conferentie van zendelingen op Nieuw-Guinee. April.

———. n.d. *Petrus Kafiar de Biaksche Evangelist: Een Bladzijde uit de Nieuw-Guinea Zending*. Utrecht: Utrechtsche Zendingsvereeniging.

van Hasselt, J. L. and F.J.F. van Hasselt. 1947. *Noemfoorsche Woordenboek*. Amsterdam: H. de Bussy.

van Hasselt, Johannes. 1868. *Allereerst Beginselen der Papoesch-Mefoorsche Taal*. Utrecht: Kemink and Son.

———. 1888. *Gedenkboek van een Vijf-en-Twintigjarig Zendelingsleven op Nieuw Guinea (1862–1887)*. Utrecht: Kemink and Son.

———. 1889. "Enkele Aanteekeningen aangaande de Bewoners der N.Westkust van Nieuw-Guinea, Meer Bepaaldelijk de Stam der Noefoorezen. Tweede Gedeelte." *Tijdschrift Bataviaasch Genootschap* 32: 261–272.

van Sandick, L.H.W. 1934. *Ontwikkeling van en Kolonisatie in Nieuw-Guinea*. Rapport van de Studiecommissie ingesteld door de Vaderlandsche Club in Nederland. The Hague: van Cleef.

van Wouden, F.A.E. 1968. *Types of Social Structure in Eastern Indonesia*. Translated by R. Needham. Koninklijk Instituut voor Taal-, Land-, en Volkenkunde Translation Series, vol. 11. The Hague: Martinus Nijhoff.

Venuti, Lawrence. 1992. "Introduction." In *Rethinking Translation: Discourse, Subjectivity, Ideology*, edited by Lawrence Venuti, 1–17. London: Routledge.

Verdery, Katherine. 1993. "Whither 'Nation' and 'Nationalism'?" *Daedalus* 122: 37–46.

Visser, Leontine. 1984. "Who Are the Sahu and What Do They Belong To?" In *Unity in Diversity: Indonesia as a Field of Anthropological Study*, edited by P. E. de Josselin de Jong, 198–220. Verhandelingen van het Koninklijk Instituut voor Taal-, Land- en Volkenkunde 103. Dordrecht/Providence: Foris.

von Rosenberg, C.B.H. 1875. *Reistochten naar de Geelvinkbaai op Nieuw-Guinea in de Jaren 1869 en 1870*. The Hague: Martinus Nijhoff.

Wallace, Alfred R. [1869] 1986. *The Malay Archipelago: The Land of the Orang-Utan and the Bird of Paradise*. Singapore, Oxford and New York: Oxford University Press.

Wallerstein, Immanuel. 1976. *The Modern World System: Capitalist Agriculture and the Origins of the European World-Economy in the Sixteenth Century*. New York: Academic.

Watson-Gegeo, Karen Ann, and Geoffrey M. White, eds. 1990. *Disentangling: Conflict Discourse in Pacific Societies*. Stanford: Stanford University Press.

Weber, Eugen. 1976. *Peasants into Frenchmen: The Modernization of Rural France, 1870–1914*. Stanford: Stanford University Press.

Weber, Samuel. 1991. *Return to Freud: Jacques Lacan's Dislocation of Psychoanalysis*. Translated by Michael Levine. Cambridge: Cambridge University Press.

Weiner, Annette. 1976. *Women of Value, Men of Renown: New Perspectives in Trobriand Exchange*. Austin: University of Texas Press.

———. 1985. "Inalienable Wealth." *American Ethnologist* 12 (2): 210–27.

———. 1992. *Inalienable Possessions: The Paradox of Keeping-while-Giving*. Berkeley: University of California Press.

White, Hayden. 1987. *The Content of the Form: Narrative Discourse and Historical Representation*. Baltimore: Johns Hopkins University Press.

Williams, Brackette F. 1989. "Class Act: Anthropology and the Race to Nation across Ethnic Terrain." *Annual Review of Anthropology* 18: 401–444.

Willis, Sharon. 1989. "Disputed Territories: Masculinity and Social Space." *Camera Obscura* 19: 4–23.

Wittgenstein, Ludwig. 1958. *Philosophical Investigations*. 2nd ed. Translated by G.E.M. Anscombe. Malden, Mass.: Blackwell.

Wolters, Oliver W. 1982. *History, Culture and Region in Southeast Asian Perspectives*. Singapore: Institute of Southeast Asian Studies.

———. 1994. "Southeast Asia as a Southeast Asian Field of Study." *Indonesia* 58: 1–17.

Woolard, Kathryn A., and Bambi B. Schieffelin. 1994. "Language Ideology." *Annual Review of Anthropology* 23: 55–82.

Worsley, Peter. 1968. *The Trumpet Shall Sound*. New York: Schocken.

Yamashita, Shinji. 1994. "Manipulating Ethnic Tradition: The Funeral Ceremony, Tourism, and Television among the Toraja of Sulawesi." *Indonesia* 58: 69–82.

Yampolsky, Philip, and Danilyn Rutherford, eds. 1996. *Music of Biak, Irian Jaya: Wor, Church Songs, Yospan*. Volume 10 of *The Music of Indonesia*. Washington, D.C.: Smithsonian Institute/Folkways Records.

Young, Michael W. 1971. *Fighting with Food: Leadership, Values, and Social Control in a Massim Society*. Cambridge: Cambridge University Press.

Zahn, F. L. 1870. *Faijasi rijo Refo Mansren Allah Bieda (Bijbelsche Geschiedenissen)*. Translated from Dutch to Papuan-Numforese by J. G. Geissler. *Utrecht: Kemink and Son*.

Zimmer, Benjamin G. 1998. "The New Dis-Order: Parodic *Plésétan* and the 'Slipping' of the Soeharto Regime." *Antara Kita* 54: 4–9.

———. 1999. "Unpacking the Word: The Ethnolexicological Art of Sundanese

Kirata." SALSA VI: Proceedings of the Sixth Annual Symposium about Language and Society. Austin, Texas Linguistic Forum No. 42, 275–284. Austin: Texas Department of Linguistics.

Žižek, Slavoj. 1989. *The Sublime Object of Ideology.* London: Verso.

———. 1994. "Introduction: The Spectre of Ideology." In *Mapping Ideology,* edited by Slavoj Žižek, 1–33. London: Verso.

Index

Abraham, Nicolas, 135
Acciaoli, Greg, 141–42
Act of Free Choice, xvi
Adadikam, Dominggus, 90, 137, 172
Adams, Kathleen M., 142
Africa, 231–33
agency: creative action and, 107–8 (*see also* surprise; wor; yospan); the Itchy Old Man and, 23–24; in warrior stories, 78
agriculture, 241n15
Agter, Hendrick Jan, 191, 193
airport, 6, 47, 84, 99–100
Althusser, Louis, 12, 143, 145
amber, xvii–xviii; Biak's first local foreigner, 33; children and mother's credit for, 45–46; evolution of the term, 16; global order, Biak's place in, 172; hostility to, 133, 197; multiple meanings of, xx, 22. *See also* the foreign
ancestors. *See* kinship; Manarmakeri (Itchy Old Man); potency
Andaya, Leonard Y., 18
Anderson, Benedict, 8–10, 15, 35, 134, 144, 179
Angganeta. *See* Menufandu, Angganeta
Annan, Kofi, 13
anthropology: Biak as a limiting case for, 230–31; job of, xviii–xix
Ap, Arnold, 212–13, 258n3–5, 258n9
apocalypse, 27. *See also* millenarianism; utopia
Appadurai, Arjun, 235
ararem. *See* bridewealth (*ararem*)
Arwam, Isak, 223–24, 259n17
asal usul (legends). *See* narratives
authority: of absence (*see* authority of absence); earthly and millenarianism, 134; entextualization and recontextualization, 113; food as source of, 43–49, 52; of New Order leaders, 120; of prowess and kinship, 35, 115–16; recognition of state, 207; "unnative" of Indonesian state, 135
authority of absence, 23; Angganeta Menufandu and, 194; big foreigners, making of, 115–17; language and, 117–20; marriage

negotiations and, 109–11; reading and (*see* reading); textuality and interpretation of, 111–15
Ave, Joop, 212

Baibo, Korano, 256n24
Baker, James N., 112, 248n4
Bali, tourism on, 140, 142
Bali Tourist Development Corporation, 138
barak, 17, 168. *See also* potency
Bataille, Georges, 159, 167
Bauer, Arnold J., 14–15, 239n13
Beekman, Elke, 253n9
Beets, K. Th., 187, 254–55n18
Benjamin, Walter, 78, 204, 249n16
Berlant, Lauren, 11, 210
Berlin Conference, 182
Berman, Marshall, 231
Besi, Goeroe, 172
Bhabha, Homi K., 210
Biak (island group): Christianity in, 30, 33; Dutch colonialism in (*see* Dutch colonialism); economic development, 6–7, 137–40 (*see also* modernity; tourism); fetishization of the foreign, 134–35 (*see also* fetishization of the foreign); flag raising, 1–3, 13–14, 25, 228; integration into Indonesia, 3–4; kinship and the foreign, 39; as a limiting case, 229–34; map, xiv; national identity in, 5–8; New Order cultural initiative, 39–40, 207–10, 213–16, 228; population, 238n4; wealth in, 117; World War II, 180, 200–201. *See also* New Guinea
Biak (language): *amber*, significance of term, xvii–xviii, 16; "person," term for, 241n14; written, status as, xi
Biak-Numfor (island group). *See* Biak (island group)
Biaks: *amber* and (*see amber*); authority of leaders (*see* authority of absence); Christian conversion of, 136 (*see also* Christianity); cosmopolitanism of, 5–7; elite, membership in, 9–10; fetishization of the foreign, 22–23; foreignness, perception of, 17; modernity, imagined image of, 177;